Bourdieu's Secret Admirer
in the Caucasus

Bourdieu's Secret Admirer in the Caucasus

A World-System Biography

GEORGI M. DERLUGUIAN

The University of Chicago Press
Chicago and London

The University of Chicago Press, Chicago 60637
The University of Chicago Press, Ltd., London
© 2005 by The University of Chicago
All rights reserved. Published 2005
Printed in the United States of America

14 13 12 11 10 09 08 07   2 3 4 5

ISBN: 0-226-14282-5 (cloth)
ISBN: 0-226-14283-3 (paper)

Frontispiece: Shanib in 2003.

Library of Congress Cataloging-in-Publication Data

Derluguian, Georgi M.
Bourdieu's secret admirer in the Caucasus : a world-system biog-
raphy / Georgi M. Derluguian.
   p. cm.
Includes bibliographical references and index.
ISBN 0-226-14282-5 (cloth : alk. paper) — ISBN 0-226-14283-3
(pbk. : alk. paper)
   1. Shanibov, IU. M. (IUrii Mukhamedovich) 2. Revolutionaries—
Russia (Federation)—Chechnia—Biography. 3. Chechnia (Russia)—
Ethnic relations. 4. Chechnia (Russia)—Relations—Russia (Fed-
eration) 5. Russia (Federation)—Relations—Russia (Federation)—
Chechnia. 6. National liberation movements—Russia (Federation)—
Chechnia. I. Title.
   DK511.C37D47 2005
   947.5'2—dc22

                                                    2004065903

⊗ The paper used in this publication meets the
minimum requirements of the American National Standard
for Information Sciences—Permanence of Paper
for Printed Library Materials, ANSI Z39.48-1992.

CONTENTS

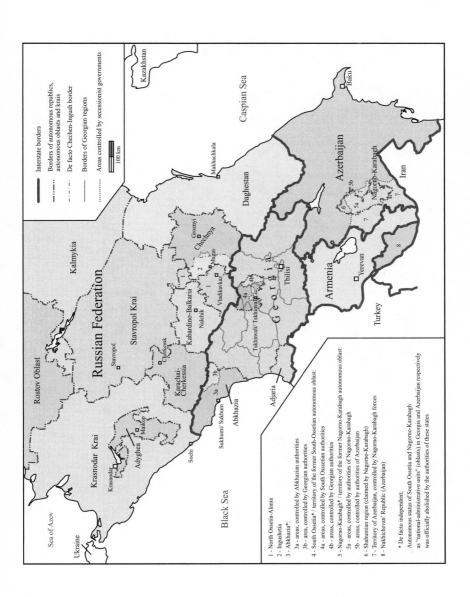

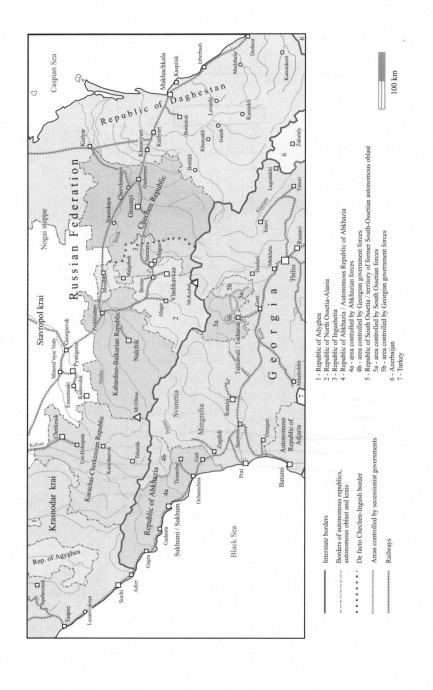

Caspian Sea

Republic of Daghestan

Derbent
Izberbash
Makhachkala
Kaspiisk
Madzhalis
Kasumkent
Zakataly

Republic of Adyghea
2 - Republic of North Ossetia-Alania
3 - Republic of Ingushetia
4 - Republic of Abkhazia / Autonomous Republic of Abkhazia
    4a - area controlled by Georgian government forces
    4b - area controlled by Abkhazian forces
5 - Republic of South Ossetia / territory of former South-Ossetian autonomous oblast
    5a - area controlled by South Ossetian forces
    5b - area controlled by Georgian government forces
6 - Azerbaijan
7 - Turkey

Interstate borders

Borders of autonomous republics,
autonomous oblast and krais

De facto Chechen-Ingush border

Areas controlled by secessionist governments

Railways

100 km

Photo 1. Participants in the regional seminar of clubs
of culture organizers, 1954. A vintage Stalin-era image,
even with the head of one participant, exposed as enemy
of the people, cut out from the picture.

Photo 2. Student self-governance meeting under the obligatory
portrait of Lenin, 1970.

Photo 3. The most damning image, perhaps. Abkhazia, 1993.
Sitting to Shanib's right, in the beret of Chechen commander,
is Shamil Basayev—the man who now claims responsibility
for the hostage takings at the Moscow theater in 2002
and at the Beslan school in 2004.

Photo 4. Shanib at home, late 1990s.

INTRODUCTION

Does Globalization Breed Ethnic Violence?

"In the Caucasus all good stories acquire the tendency to branch out."

Fazil Iskander, *Sandro of Chegem*, (New York: Vintage Books, 1983)

The empirical story to be told in this book remained buried in my files until now for a variety of reasons. The immediate issue was one of personal ethics, insofar as the story involves passionately contested events and contemporary personalities, some of whose names have become notorious in their parts of the world. Secondly, there were complex conceptual–theoretical problems posed by the underlying narrative: its empirical richness called for an extensive and varied theoretical apparatus that took some years to assemble. Thirdly, the problem was political, insofar as the material to be presented had to do with phenomena commonly described as ethnic conflict, Islamic militancy, and international terrorism. Let me begin then with the personal, and with what pertains to my title: Bourdieu's secret admirer in the Caucasus.

AN UNCOMMON MAN

The basis for my story originated in a chance encounter with one Musa Shanib, a fearsome Circassian rebel from the North Caucasus, whose lieutenants once included the even more fearsome Chechen fighters Shamil Basayev and Ruslan Gelayev.[1] In the course of our meeting, which I describe in greater detail in chapter one, I discovered that Shanib was a much more complex figure than one might have at first assumed. To my no little astonishment, at some point in our conversation (or, rather, his monologue) Shanib suddenly revealed himself to be an enthusiastic student of the sociology of Pierre Bourdieu. This proved to be just the first of many ironies that marked out Shanib's life story as being of unique interest. Shanib's biography, suffused as it is with paradoxes and bitter disillusionments, seemed to summarize the trajectory of a whole generation of Soviet citizens who were born under Stalin, came of age in the expansive and wildly optimistic atmosphere of Khrushchev's Thaw, spent the long uneventful years of Brezhnev's "stagnation" in a kind of internal exile, and finally reemerged during Gorbachev's perestroika in an ebullient surge of public activism that led, tragically, to a disastrous climax.

It turned out that in Shanib's native town of Nalchik, the small provincial capital of the Republic of Kabardino-Balkaria, the 1989–1992 protests against the Soviet regime were organized and headed by largely the same network of people who had organized the previous wave of revolutionary contention between 1968 and 1972. Musa Shanib himself – or rather, Yuri Muhammedovich Shanibov, as he was known in a Russified form for much of his life – turned out to be a local version of what the French call a *soixante-huitard*: one of the New Left rebels of 1968. Shanibov's circle of rebels consisted of educated men and a few formidable women connected through the local university, mostly via the departments of history, philosophy, and philology. They were characteristic examples of the upwardly mobile cadres, specialists, and national intellectuals produced during the tremendous expansion of Soviet higher education in the 1950s. The dazzling career prospects which opened up in the wake of Khrushchev's de-Stalinization program soon brought this group to the threshold of the Soviet bureaucratic elite: the so-called *nomenklatura*. However, in the momentous year of 1968, they were still considered too junior to be fully inducted into this elite group; and, besides, many of them nurtured different aspirations in the fields of social research and artistic creativity. Yuri Shanibov himself forfeited a promising career as a law enforcement official (already in his twenties he had served as a district attorney, or *prokuror*), and instead became a junior lecturer working towards his dissertation on the role of law in socialist self-governance – a distinctly anti-Stalinist topic.

In the meantime, *nomenklatura* positions were rapidly being filled as the old Stalinist stalwarts came to be replaced by a new cohort of bureaucrats. Towards the mid-1960s there emerged all over the Soviet provinces closed networks of bureaucratic patronage and privilege that would hold their grip on power for years to come – in a refashioned form, these bureaucratic networks still proved able to provide the basis for the post-communist oligarchic restoration of the 1990s. In the small world of Nalchik, when I first visited there in 1997 and met Musa Shanib, this phenomenon was particularly transparent – the local rulers were still the same communist bureaucrats of the late 1950s and early 1960s, or else their personally selected successors. On the other side of the barricades, the local opposition was also still made up of mostly the same sixties intellectuals, or their former students. Back in 1968, the suppression of the democratic movement in Czechoslovakia had signaled to the Soviet *nomenklatura* the urgency of aborting any movement that might have developed similar demands for "socialism with a human face." It was in this climate that the energetic young lecturer Yuri Shanibov was selected for a show of punishment, and subsequently became regarded locally as kind of a dissident, or at least as a troublemaker possessing unusual ideas.

After a hiatus of nearly two decades, Gorbachev's program of reform from above offered people like Shanibov a second chance to engage in public debate and to organize reform movements from below. But in a few years, as Gorbachev's half-hearted liberalization fell further and further behind the exploding expectations of Soviet citizenry, Shanibov's circle of friends, colleagues, and former students radicalized their political demands to include the wholesale removal of the old *nomenklatura* from power. They first sought to achieve this goal through the competitive elections of 1989 and 1990 – elections that soon turned into street protests as it became clear that the electoral process had been brazenly manipulated by local officials. Street politics, however, were a quite different matter from debating in intellectual clubs. It now proved necessary to mobilize people from other classes of society against the intractable *nomenklatura*. In the process, a totally new kind of protestor, with totally new demands, emerged from the poor and disorderly semi-rural suburbs. These were much cruder, less disciplined people, who soon showed themselves prone to direct action which was characteristically violent in nature. Their idea of democratization may have boiled down to punishing the "fat bureaucrats and official thieves," but these masses were a real force – so, like many revolutionaries before them, Shanibov and his companions decided to ride the tiger of popular wrath.

The protagonists during the stormy events of 1989 to 1992 were still the same network of local bureaucrats who had ruled in Nalchik for decades, versus the same oppositional network of alienated intellectuals and junior specialists whose careers had been blocked by the corrupt *nomenklatura*. But the character of contention and its ideology had changed radically. All talk of a better form of socialism disappeared after 1989. Instead, the talk was now of free markets, parliamentary democracy, and joining the "civilized Western world." Once the socialist-era taboo on private property was gone, another crucial taboo fell with it – that prohibiting the use of nationalism in political mobilizing. The masses who were now supporting the insurgent movement organized by Shanibov and his allies proved more responsive to the localized demands of nationalism than to the rhetoric of capitalist transition that to them sounded too abstract and devoid of passion. It was in this context that Yuri Shanibov decided to change his name to the more native form, Musa Shanib, and donned the traditional tall sheepskin hat (*papaha*) of a Circassian prince.

Our story becomes still more complex and evocative because Shanib was not a member of the Moscovite intelligentsia – which typically serves as the main source for examples of Soviet reformism. Rather, he belonged to one of the Muslim highlander nationalities of the Caucasus, the Kabardins (who are in turn one of several closely-related Circassian peoples). In 1989, his *annus mirabilis*, Shanibov strove to become the latter-day Garibaldi of the Caucasus, organizing revolutionary mobilizations both in his native Kabardino-Balkaria and in the neighboring province of Checheno-Ingushetia. In the early 1990s, during the Soviet disintegration, he became President of the Confederation of Mountain Peoples of the Caucasus, an insurgent political movement seeking to transform itself into an independent state. While the independence of the North Caucasus remained an elusive goal, the Confederation was nonetheless able to acquire its own volunteer army – which Shanib led into battle in Abkhazia's war of independence from Georgia. Elements of this army later formed the backbone of the Chechen resistance to the Russian military effort to roll back the wave of highlander separatism. In the course of the Chechen wars, some of Shanib's former volunteers embraced the ideology of Islamic jihad and apparently joined forces with militant Islamic movements operating in the Middle East. By that time, however, Shanib had been forced out of politics and had reverted to a life of internal exile. In the late 1990s he quietly returned to academia, while some of his erstwhile disciples switched their tactics to bombing and hostage taking, all justified by a *fatwa* issued by a semi-literate radical preacher from Chechnya.

In February 1997 I returned from my trip to the Caucasus to write – mainly for the private consumption of friends and colleagues – a field report that included an

Author of
Utopistics

account of my first encounter with Shanibov. (It now serves as the basis for chapter one.) On its completion, I sent a copy of my report, along with several photographs, to Immanuel Wallerstein. Since he was in Paris at the time, I jokingly suggested that he might startle Bourdieu with the picture of a Circassian rebel chieftain wearing the *papaha* and holding a worn Russian-language edition of one of Bourdieu's books. Once the letter was sent, I realized with some apprehension that my complete ignorance of the Parisian intellectual scene might potentially render my joke in very poor taste.[2] References to Bourdieu do not occur anywhere in Wallerstein's notoriously extensive footnotes, and a similar discreet silence was reciprocated on the part of Bourdieu. Fortunately for me, Wallerstein is endowed with a seemingly inexhaustible reserve of gracious tolerance, manifest particularly during my many attempts to argue with him.

My fears were soon dispelled by a postcard from Pierre Bourdieu himself. As it turned out, Wallerstein did pass on my field report and the photo of Shanibov. Bourdieu's reaction was perhaps perfectly natural: he was surprised and curious to learn more. But how could I hope to explain the complexity of Shanibov's life story, even if my interlocutor was a sympathetic Pierre Bourdieu? Inevitably, I responded with a very long letter detailing the local context and Shanibov's background as a kind of Soviet *soixante-huitard* who had turned to nationalist causes during the disintegration of communist rule, but ultimately suffered defeat on every front. Bourdieu's evaluation of this informal essay was, frankly, very flattering. For someone like myself (at the time I was looking for a job as a sociologist but felt desperately unqualified to meet any of the job descriptions then on the academic market), reading in Bourdieu's letter that my essay was "a marvelous text," and even that its author was endowed with "*beaucoup de talent*," was more astounding than meeting Shanibov in the first place. Besides that, Bourdieu confided that he would have loved to publish my essay in his journal *Liber* if only he were not himself *un peu le "héros" de cette histoire* – a bit of a "hero" in the story. His letter imposed on me the double obligation of eventually making the story public – for it clearly had merit and Bourdieu would not in principle object to its publication – yet doing so without superficial sensationalism, and in a fashion as dignified towards Bourdieu as it would be towards Shanibov. As it now stands, this book is my way of honoring the memory of the great French sociologist. On many occasions Bourdieu urged us to think beyond his own formulations, to resist that closure of thought that paves the way for intellectual orthodoxy. Rather than eulogizing Bourdieu, which he would have no doubt detested, my tribute is to take up his principle in earnest.

SOCIAL SCIENCE

We come then to the second issue that had to be confronted when setting out on the present study: the insufficiency of the available theories and conceptual languages to provide the robust shape, analytical depth, and narrative fluency adequate to the empirical story. While the latter originated in a chance encounter, the sources of my theoretical concerns might best be approached by way of a ground-breaking essay by the three founders of world-systems analysis: Giovanni Arrighi, Terence Hopkins, and Immanuel Wallerstein. Written over a decade ago, but published only recently, the essay goes under the blunt title: "1989: The Continuation of 1968."[3] Let me first recapitulate its key propositions.

The authors directly relate the eventual undoing of socialist as well as nationalist developmental states to their own past success in creating new kinds of educated industrial labor, including, in particular, an intellectual stratum of professional technicians, mid-level administrators, scientists, and educators more or less directly involved in production processes. In 1968, the first surge of political activity intended to update the institutions of bureaucratic control took the form of a democratic movement mainly because the iron grip of the Communist Party over the whole of production and social life was preventing the new intelligentsia from effectively deploying its technical capabilities and from gaining a status and power commensurate with its growing significance. In the face of the demands for democratization, however, the power of the ruling communist bureaucracy proved stronger and more resilient than that of the revolutionaries. For this reason, when the unfinished business of 1968 was vigorously resumed in 1989, it was driven by a "wind of madness" that was perceptible in the revolutionaries' adherence to that least plausible of all ideologies – the monetarist dogma that only a ruthless "economizing" can lead to the degree of wealth and power currently to be found in the West. This deployment of neoliberalism by the East European rebels against the old Soviet régime might appear paradoxical, but it is explicable once we recognize that these Soviet-produced intellectuals nurtured a deep distrust of any bureaucracy, that in the polarized climate of the Cold War they regarded the West as their ideal, that they thus sought to convert the existing ideological paradigm of state socialism into its complete opposite, and that as a consequence they saw Reagan, Thatcher, and even Pinochet, as inspiring heroes who had successfully dragged their countries out of the economic morass of the 1970s and early 1980s.[4]

But what these revolutionary agents of change did not realize at the time was that the road of neoliberal reform – or what was then called economic shock therapy – was to lead them (or at least most of them) not to the promised land of North America, but to the harsher realities of Latin America (or worse). Instead of channeling industrial conflict into the democratization of political institutions and restructuring the economy towards a more stable social-democratic regime (as happened in Spain after the death of Franco), the majority of East Europeans faced a severe decline in, if not a complete destruction of, state powers, and thereby a weakening of the state's contradictory founding counterpart, civil society. Arrighi, Hopkins, and Wallerstein predicted that popular reactions to this harsh situation would range between frustration and cynicism on the one hand, and, on the other hand, the promise of alternative moral communities offered, at least in the short run, either by a nationalist replication of stateness or a religious fundamentalist negation of stateness. Between these two possibilities, however, lay various inter-mediate alternatives wherein people would be integrated "outside the law" (and thereby outside civil society) and become centers for all manner of illegal relational activities whose spheres of circulation spread throughout society as a whole, and often beyond national boundaries. Such are the phenomena known today by names like "the mafia," "shanty-towns," "inner cities," "drug-lord domains," or "warlord fiefdoms," etc.

The analysis conducted by Arrighi, Hopkins, and Wallerstein certainly presented an evocative picture, but does it hold any truth? Can it be substantiated and defended in a rigorous analytical fashion? Furthermore, how might their sweeping and para-doxical propositions translate into an analysis of specific historical patterns in the Caucasus or elsewhere? These are the kind of questions that were nagging me for several years. Clearly many different factors would be involved in formulating adequate answers. But the problem was how to identify those factors and combine them into a coherent causal account. To be sure, there was always the temptation of easy escape through one of the conceptual frameworks that had dominated the analyses of post-communism and ethnic conflict during the previous decade: demo-cratic and market transitions; identity construction; globalization; or the new security challenges. But a number of personal dispositions militated against taking this route, some the result of my own background – not least, my direct experi-ence of several wars, first in Africa and later in the Caucasus; and perhaps also the wide-ranging curiosity imbued in me by the undisciplined Russian intellectual tradi-tion and the years spent working with Arrighi, Hopkins, and Wallerstein. Immanuel in particular jokingly insisted that "we do not believe in small things"; but if that were the case, how could one go about writing a biography from a world-systems perspective?

My attempt to do precisely that required the labor of building and fitting together whole batteries of theoretical supports. The project in view is not that of testing a particular theory by bringing to it new data. Rather, a variety of intermeshing theories will be utilized to interpret the data (much of it indeed new) in many different but, I hope, mutually reinforcing ways. It is no doubt too soon to formulate a definitive, overarching theory. This remains our large and necessarily collective task for the future. With regard to scope of the present work, an appropriate analogy might be that of the archeological survey, where the exploration of a new site begins with the digging of a cross-cutting trench to expose the stratigraphy of historical layers, thereby to identify the most promising leads for a more detailed excavation.

Narrowly put, my main goal here is to provide a plausible explanation as to why in some regions, mainly in the Caucasus, the catastrophic end of Soviet rule resulted in ethnic conflicts and the emergence of weak states that are thoroughly corrupt, not to say criminalized. The argument can then be extended to explain why in some places, predominantly but not exclusively in Chechnya, state structures withered away almost completely to be replaced by phenomena variously described as mafia, religious fundamentalism, warlord armies, and international terrorism.

While current social science theories tend to place their focus elsewhere than on patterns of national character, for the majority of people – whether politicians, journalists, or the people directly affected by ethnic wars – ethnic culture clearly plays a major role in explaining the patterns of different societies. Indeed, there seems to be an enduring coherence in, for instance, how the English and Americans do business, or how the Germans and Northern Italians approach the state and corporatist institutions. Perhaps then we should not be surprised if there is also a certain coherence in how the Russians relate to their rulers – intermittently with hope and cynical distrust – or in how the Chechens fight their wars. But how do we identify and rationally explain these sources of "national character"?

Perhaps ethnic cultures bear the imprint of often long-gone geopolitical and socioeconomic configurations. The imprint itself is, in fact, a complex process of transmission through mechanisms of collective memory and actualization in regular rituals (and likewise de-actualization, through forgetting). Of course, one could simply take for granted the established ethnic reputations of the different Caucasian peoples, as many travelers and observers have done routinely. Alternatively, and following the contemporary intellectual fashion, one could adamantly refuse even to mention popular ethnic stereotypes. My own part-native intuition, however, insists that ethnic cultures, though they may be tricky to analyze, must nonetheless play an essential role in explaining how a particular people construes both itself and its expectations regarding others – sometimes fatefully. To illustrate the essential point here, let me relate a personal anecdote that may also serve as an introduction to the region. It also serves to clarify my own background, which seems warranted since in this book I do much the same in relation to many others.

My childhood was spent in Krasnodar, a typically multiethnic provincial town in the North Caucasus situated halfway between Chechnya and Abkhazia. Until about the age of ten or so we remained largely oblivious of our nationalities. Relationships in the schoolyard were organized according to time-honored distinctions between friends and bullies, boys and girls, younger and older. One day my friend Aslan (his real name is different) came up with the proposition that if anyone "messed with" me, I should leave to him to do the fighting. This seemed eminently sensible, given that Aslan was the school champion in freestyle wrestling, his father used to be a boxer, and besides he had three brothers (which was considered a lot), who would all readily jump in to fight for each other, including the little first-grader, Murat. But it was Aslan's explanation of his proposal that sounded exotic: *Look, you are an Armenian, the smart nationality. When you grow up, you gonna be a doctor, or maybe a composer like Aram Khachaturian, or the world chess champion like Tigran Petrossian. And I am a Cherkess* [i.e. Circassian] *of the Shapsug tribe, the warrior people. When I grow up, I gonna be a professional wrestler and then a coach. Because you are my kunak* [sworn brother] *it is my honor to fight for you!* [5]

Years later, in 1992, Aslan missed the war in Abkhazia as he was serving a long prison sentence after a spectacular spree of armed robberies of jewelry and hard currency stores across the province. But his youngest brother Murat did join the Circassian volunteer brigade, and went to fight in Abkhazia. Murat returned as a local hero but soon vanished from sight. Some say he became a drunk, unable to cope with his wartime traumas; others loudly object, claiming that Murat got married, opened a gas station, and built a splendid house somewhere up in the ancestral mountains; and still others whisper, shaking their heads, that he went off to fight again in Chechnya, maybe even in Afghanistan.

The last I heard of my former friend Aslan was from an old schoolmate, an ethnic Russian called Alexei who had turned prematurely into a balding, beer-bellied adult. After graduating from school and serving in the army, Alexei first became a policeman and then later, in the nineties, chief of private security at the local, now (since the nineties) American-owned, tobacco factory. According to him, Aslan was on the run after a botched attempt to kidnap the daughter of one of the town's *nouveaux-riches* merchants – one of Aslan's fellow Muslim Circassians, who had made a fortune trading with the Arab Emirates. Alexei, who had helped Aslan get parole after his first conviction, angrily promised that next time he would finish him off as a wild beast.

Such is the story of three childhood friends from the latter years of the Soviet Union – a Russian, a Circassian, and an Armenian – and three divergent life trajectories that took us far apart. As a sociologist, I couldn't help asking what the cause of it all might be: historical legacies, ethnic identities, different local networks, the varying social capital of our families, the disorderly political economy of post-communism, the sweeping effects of global flows, or, perhaps, all of the above – but then, in what layers of causation and in what configuration?

Seeking the answers to such questions required widening the focus of inquiry in many directions. Micro-processes and ground-level situations are but fine grains caught up in the larger flows of historical trends and social configurations. But close empirical analysis of such micro-processes can help us to cut the building blocks useful for constructing explanations on a larger scale. To put it another way: a comprehensive interpretation of specific micro-interactions necessarily requires articulating their relational position within macro-contexts; but by the same token, an account of global trends will have no force or substance unless its observations and analyses are rooted in empirical situations.

Of course, this is much easier said than done. A detailed account of a handful of situations intended to illustrate the operations of much larger processes may be dismissed as mere anecdotalism; while bringing big theories to bear on ground-level processes inevitably risks incurring accusations of *ad hoc* postulation and mechanistic structuralism. The academic variety of common sense suggests that we play it safe and "get focused." In practice, this means either limiting the inquiry to the detailed description of specific empirical cases that are defined at most by the usual two-by-two table of variables (the familiar idiographic preference of area studies experts as well as the majority of historians and anthropologists) or, conversely, engaging in an abstract and highly technical generalization (the long-standing nomothetic ambition of modern economics, as of those sectors of political science and sociology that aspire to emulate the mathematical standards of neoclassical economists).

The idiographic/nomothetic opposition, or, as it is known in current terminology, the dilemma of agency/structure, has been at the center of many a methodological dispute since the late nineteenth century. The confrontations were as passionate and inconclusive as one might expect from debates involving clashing ideas regarding virtue. The real problem is to avoid taking sides in such academic controversies, moving beyond both extremes by way of an elusive *via media*. The founders of social analysis were certainly aware of this, for what else was at stake in Marx's call to bring dialectics to bear on the practice of historical materialism, or in Durkheim's principled rejection of the antinomy of structural goals and subjective choice of means, or in the famous (and famously obscure) concept of "substantive rationality" in the late writings of Max Weber? It is not by chance revealing that in recent decades the same search for a *via media* has emerged, in different forms, in the writings of such figures of the new social science as Pierre Bourdieu, Charles Tilly, and Immanuel Wallerstein. Their formulations must be acknowledged as the principal sources of theoretical inspiration that made this book possible.

A particular concern here is the loss of historical horizon. Abstract theorizing tends to blur that horizon, while an empiricist focus on specific cases inevitably limits our perspective. The leitmotif of the present book is that of a particular individual's life story developing in conjuncture with the society to which our hero belongs. The personal focus seems justified because our exemplary character is broadly indicative of the changing fortunes of an entire generation. But along the way we shall have regular recourse to our theoretical navigation-gear to keep the historical horizon in view.

This strategy serves two principal purposes. First, we may be able to grasp the complex and dynamic interplay between the movement of historical structures and the actions of a particular man as he struggles to stay on course in relation to shifting political opportunities and constraints. Second, it allows us to reexamine some common assumptions regarding different structural forces that might otherwise remain hidden under over-familiar labels ("historical tradition," "state socialism," "modernization," "democratization," "global flows," "ethnic cultures," etc.).

As usual in a learning process, particularly that of scholarly inquiry, the slow maturation of ideas comes interspersed with bursts of rapid crystallization – those proverbial moments when the apple falls on one's head at the opportune time. To me, the gracious knock was delivered by America's celebrated writer on natural history, Stephen Jay Gould, through his book *Full House*.[6] In this collection of unabashedly diverse and intellectually teasing essays, Gould expressed his own mature understanding of three fundamental principles, each of which is relevant to the analyses that follow.[7]

First, the evolution of complex systems does not proceed in a uniformly ascendant and pre-ordained progressive development. Rather, it takes twisted routes spreading through many sectors of possibility and results in a "copious bush of life." The process is not driven by an invariant law striving towards the higher excellence of some ideal form. The causation is multiple, often contingent, and therefore always complex. It might be a question of the presence or absence of a factor in a given environment (for instance dangerous predators, whether animal or human); or of what is inscribed in one's morphology and genes (perhaps an archaic imprint of past adaptations that suddenly finds a new use); but not infrequently the determinant is sheer chance: whether an asteroid hitting the Earth, an epidemic, or the invasion of previously unknown conquerors from another continent, like the ancient Huns or modern Westerners.

Second, and more directly relevant for the arguments of this book, Gould urged us to grasp whole *systems of relations* (the emphasis is his, but I would put it in still bolder form). He eloquently demanded the abandonment of abstract measures of self-propelling reified essences implicit in the assumption of a progressive development among orders of animal species. In the human case, such measures might be the ideologically construed essences of feudalism, capitalism, socialism, or globalization as presumed stages of historical evolution. Rather, the objects of study should be situated in their extended environments and analyzed by locating them within pulsating and slowly evolving webs of relations. For us, this suggests that instead of measuring, for instance, the "actually existing socialism" of the former Soviet bloc against the yardstick of some socialist ideal or some grotesque caricature of totalitarianism, it might be more fruitful to relate the Soviet situation to the contemporary capitalist experience of the West, or to the various histories of Third World development in the twentieth century.

Gould's third principle, still more relevant for us, postulates that reframing problems within a systemic historical perspective may produce totally unexpected solutions to longstanding controversies. Gould mischievously used the example of declining scores in American baseball to show that statistical evidence is more or less what we make of it. The appearance of the game's gradual decline is produced by the conventionally agreed ways of coding and aggregating the data, such as the batting averages. The results provoke passionate debate among players, commentators, and fans alike. Competing explanations are formulated in terms of either moral turpitude, as soulless technology displaces "character" (a familiar conservative trope), or of the hype and growing commercialization of sports and media (typically a liberal complaint).

Gould was hardly an enemy of statistics. In fact, he possessed an extraordinary ability to explain statistical methods in a lucid and accessible way that many university instructors in quantitative analysis might envy and emulate, no doubt to the considerable gratitude of their students. The lesson rather is that statistical data, like other kinds of evidence, can be properly interpreted only when taken as the expression of an evolving system of relations. What looks like a decline in baseball's glories suddenly emerges, when placed in the systemic historical perspective of the game, as the measure of its improvement. Over the last century, processes of professionalization and rationalization in sport have been driving standards of athletic performance closer to the limit of what is humanly possible, a process which has, in effect, made it ever harder to achieve the legendary high scores of earlier periods.

But the same principle can run equally well in the opposite direction. What is praised as universal improvement could instead turn out to be the result of aberrant statistical perception and narrowed vision, bounded by deep-seated and thus mostly unnoticed ideological assumptions. Globalization is a case in point. Here we approach our main substantive question: does globalization breed ethnic violence and terrorism? Bluntly stated, the answer is no. Not because the worldwide spread of ethnic violence has nothing to do with changes in the world environment, but rather because the rhetoric of globalization does not provide a framework within which we can discover the causes of, and possibly some solutions to, problems that are characteristically political.

CONTEMPORARY POLITICS

Our third issue then, concerns contemporary world politics. Tragic events such as the attacks on the World Trade Center in September 2001, or the taking of hostages in a Moscow theater in October 2002, forced wide-ranging public debates on the darker aspects of globalization. A direct causal link between globalization and ethnic or religious violence was unquestioningly assumed on all sides, often in a highly polemical fashion. The more radical critics, decrying capitalist greed and Western arrogance, equate globalization with the rise of an American global empire. But these critics often seem at a loss when attempting to situate heterogeneous and anti-systemic forces such as the Taliban, African warlords, Andean political drug-traffickers, Balkan paramilitaries, Chechen guerrillas, or al-Qaeda. On the other side, the much more numerous and powerfully positioned intellectuals of the Western ideological mainstream tend to discuss the "crisis of globalization" mostly in terms of policy failures and the unwillingness of non-Western societies to face the challenges of liberal modernity and market discipline. By their own lights, these public intellectuals face far fewer problems when situating exotic terrorists, ethnic warlords, drug-trafficking rebels, and violent crowds in far-off places. Their prevalent characterizations invoke the familiar essentializing tropes representing all that is opposed to the self-identity of the liberal West: irrational ("hateful, raging, instinctively base"); unmodern ("medieval, obscurantist, atavistic"); intolerant ("misogynist, sectarian, zealous, fanatical"); incompetent ("backward, corrupt"); deviant ("criminal, murderous, sadistic"), patently unsuccessful (thus "envious of Western comforts"); or simply the enemy of bourgeois cosmopolitanism and urbanity.[8]

Against this backdrop of normative–juridical judgments proffered from across the political and intellectual spectrum, my particular inspiration was provided by Randall Collins's sober analysis of the Durkheimian ritualism and accompanying irrationalities in the aftermath of what the Americans call simply 9/11. True to the best traditions of American micro-sociology, Collins went out into the streets to register the distribution of US flags on houses, cars, and clothes (a distribution which turned out to be surprisingly uneven and generally much lower than impressions at the time might have suggested), and then drew correlations between the varying display of flags and the differences in social status inscribed in the places people live and work, in the cars they drive, in the clothes they wear. Collins went on to analyze the phases of public reaction, from the stunned and disoriented atmosphere of the first couple of days, to the emotional explosion of the following weeks, during which a momentary competition among alternative descriptions of events and ways of commemoration eventually passed away, to be replaced by a consecrated official version that gelled nicely with the contemporary policies of the American government.[9]

The power of Collins's expert micro-sociological analyses within a ground-level situation contrasts sharply with what generally passes for explanation within the rhetoric of globalization. Globalization stands for many real (as well as arguably less real) phenomena. In fact, it stands for too many. This all-encompassing concept refers primarily to the revived teleology of market-driven economic progress. This immediately betrays a major reification: the latest technological embodiment of Hegelian universal spirit pursuing its self-realizing plan. In this respect the word globalization is as tendentious and fuzzy as its predecessor, modernization.[10] Their genetic and semantic connections seem straightforward enough: both expressions hail the progressive worldwide diffusion of Western political and economic patterns. Albeit that multiculturalist trends now incorporate non-Western elements into the panoply of consumer products (from "world music" and techniques of meditation to fashion and "fusion food") that appeal primarily to the globally-connected, urban and cosmopolitan middle classes.

In particular, the rhetoric of globalization optimistically misrepresented as a new beginning the debacle suffered by the erstwhile socialist and nationalist states during the 1980s and 1990s. After only a decade, the widespread hopes associated with democratic and market transitions had to be scaled down, with accompanying confused excuses and dissembling talk of "growth pains." Today, the optimism seems well on its way out, amidst sobering recognitions of market volatility, political corruption, extreme nationalist and fundamentalist backlash, and new geopolitical insecurities. Rather than engage in moral condemnation, I will stick to the example set by Randall Collins and attempt to analyze, in a succession of empirical situations, what went wrong and how in the recent reintegration of former Soviet lands into the global networks of capitalism.

In a condensed form, my argument runs as follows. Among the key conditions affecting the contemporary world are the lasting effects of the erosion or outright collapse of the former developmental states. The Soviet Union was the largest and, for several decades by its own measure, the most successful example of a state-directed effort to industrialize in order to catch up with the West. Since the late 1980s, the waning of developmentalist ideologies, the delegitimation and dramatic weakening of central governance, the introduction of competitive elections, and rapid marketization have unleashed in the new periphery two main reactive strategies. Their combinations and divergent effects, the causes of which are embedded in local historical contexts, account by and large for all the various outcomes registered across the reemerging peripheries.

The first reactive strategy, pursued by bureaucratic elites and ascendant political interlopers, consists in a practice of corrupt patronage that relies on the privatization of state offices. In the Weberian theoretical tradition this practice is conceptualized as "neopatrimonialism," or the familial appropriation of the state and the state-engendered economy. It comprises the following familiar, and mutually related, traits:

- comprador oligarchies that monopolize the nexus between global economic flows and the local extraction of resources;

- state degeneration as "corrupt" neopatrimonial principles override formal bureaucratic governance;

- decay of economies previously integrated and protected by national developmental states (not helped by the emergence of globally-connected but locally-isolated market enclaves);

✳ defeat and demoralization of the self-conscious social groups we usually call 'civil societies', which are dissolving apace with the dissolution of their conditions (namely, stable patterns of employment, social benefits and calculable expectations, with associated social statuses and class cultures);

✳ more or less competitive elections, held in superficial conformity to the expectations of powerful external forces, but that nonetheless disguise the actual conduct of domestic politics through convoluted internecine intrigues;

✳ finally, occasional bouts of political violence that occur mainly in the form of mafia-style assassinations and rebellions by subordinate or threatened neo-patrimonial "clans" and communities of patronage, rather than constituting transformative revolutions.

resistance The second reactive strategy seeks to mobilize ethnic and religious solidarities (the latter seems a more accurate term than "identities"). This strategy is pursued as a form of resistance by some of the most downgraded locales and threatened social groups of the world's population. Objectively, their resistance is directed against what Karl Polanyi called, in his seminal dissection of the previous wave of globalization, the market destruction of the substance of local societies.[11] But subjectively, the revived evocation of traditional moral communities tends to scapegoat competing ethnic groups, weak and corrupt local governments, and, increasingly, the common enemy that is American "global plutocracy."

This kind of resistance emerges after the collapse of an old order. In this sense, ethnic and religiously-construed violence reflects processes going back some time – though not primarily to a distant past of ancient civilizations (which is a common self-description of such movements), but rather to the more recent past of (trans)formative industrialization and national state-building experience. Nevertheless, retrograde identity-invoking activism is now becoming a process that potentially threatens to structure the world's future. The immediate effect is critical, because these cycles of violent contention and repression, like the Russian–Chechen conflict or the American "war on terror," could indeed make the world a more dangerous and oppressive place. At this historical juncture social science can only hope to make a difference by providing analytical clarification of the actual processes involved, and by delineating alternative possibilities for the future.

COMPOSITION

The book is organized along the following lines. Chapter one describes the contemporary situation in the empirical field of the North Caucasus. The second chapter outlines what appears to be an evolving epistemic alternative to nineteenth-century ideas of sociohistorical progress.

After these two different and equally necessary kinds of introduction, we retrace the life trajectory of Musa Shanib as it developed through changing structural circumstances. Chapter three provides an overview of Soviet history from the peak of Stalinist military-industrialization in 1945 to the subsequent de-Stalinization of 1956–1968. Chapter four analyzes the dilemmas of the Soviet state and the conflicts around the symbolic date of 1968 that served as a prelude to what happened during Gorbachev's perestroika and its chaotic aftermath. If this statement seems a truism, consider that the new economistic orthodoxy presents the breakdown of the communist state as a completely new beginning. My intention here is rather to stress the continuities, and to treat the 1990s as indeed being the tail phase of Soviet developmentalism, the trajectory taken after disintegration, or what Michael Burawoy has aptly called the post-Soviet industrial involution.[12]

Chapter five then gives a more analytical outline of the social structure that emerged from Soviet industrialization and which largely endures to this day. Here the analysis focuses on three principal classes: the executive bureaucracy, called the *nomenklatura* in Soviet-bloc countries; the proletarians who in Soviet times included the majority of university-educated specialists; and the awkward "non-class" of sub-proletarians which plays an important role in the subsequent theory of the causes of violence, including those of ethnic form, during the revolutionary upheaval of 1989–1992.

Chapter six expands this theory to show, in substantive detail, how the different social compositions and institutional settings in the Soviet republics from the Baltic to the Caucasus and Central Asia conditioned the divergent outcomes of revolutionary contention. The key question here is why nationalism ultimately prevailed over all other political programs and why in some republics, mainly in the Caucasus, the shift to nationalism also invited the sub-proletarians into politics and led to violent confrontations. Chapter seven, "The Scramble for Soviet Spoils," focuses on the processes of local revolutions, separatism, and civil war in the Caucasus republics where Musa Shanib was actively involved: Checheno-Ingushetia, Kabardino-Balkaria, and Abkhazia.

Along the way we turn our gaze towards other movements and political mobilizations across the Soviet bloc, particularly during the perestroika years. This will help us to situate the struggles of Shanibov and his networks of friends, followers, and circumstantial allies in their chaotically changing context. Here we will find an explanation as to why, during the disintegration of communist rule, Shanibov becomes a nationalist leader rather than something else, such as a market neoliberal, a social democrat, or an environmentalist, as he might have become in a less peripheral locale such as, for instance, Poland.

In the end, three different sets of questions are to be dealt with. First, we consider the kind of social organization that emerged from the collapse of Soviet order, and try to determine where the fault lines inherent in its contradictions – some new, some old – might appear. Second, we address a set of larger historical-theoretical questions relating to the nature of the Soviet experience, including its actual achievements and ultimate failures. Third, the book concludes with some farther-reaching suggestions regarding the emerging relationship between the macro-processes subsumed under the rubric of globalization and the local processes occurring on the darker side of global transformation. The concluding chapter avoids taking a deterministic stance on the future. It is rather, everywhere, a question of *possibility*.

DATA

A note on the sources of information is in order here. This presents more than the usual scholarly dilemmas in accounting for obscure materials or dealing with what the academic bureaucracy designates as "human subjects" of research.

From the sidelines, I observed many group discussions, rallies, protests, and public ceremonies, as well as the area experts and journalists themselves who were reporting on these events. Chapter one provides a sense of how this methodology worked. Over the years, I have been closely reading the obscure local newspapers, pamphlets, leaflets, and other documents generated by various political movements from the region. After some hesitation, caused mostly by my conservative training in historiography, I decided not to clutter the text with long footnotes detailing these ephemeral publications and odd pieces of documentation unless absolutely necessary. A more detailed explanation could be provided in personal communication.

There are only a few tables and charts in this book, and I hope they serve what the tabulation of data was supposed to be – a compressed and mostly impressionistic form of presentation, pictures really. In general, much effort went into making this book more accessible to a wider public, because I believe the material is publicly relevant, while preserving a necessary degree of theoretical sophistication and scholarly accountability. There is still a lot of sociology in this book which is, after all, about a peripheral provincial sociologist who had admired a famous sociologist from the world-system's core written by a sociologist whose own life has spanned both core and periphery. But there are also empirical descriptions, impressionistic sketches, and anecdotes that are intended to facilitate the understanding of social realities that to a majority of readers might seem unfamiliar, perhaps counter-intuitive, or downright exotic.[13] For example, many readers have probably never heard about the existence of Adjaria, which might be lucky for the Adjarians because their small corner of the earth seems, frankly, so insignificant today that it would never make it into the world headlines unless there were a massacre sizable enough to warrant sending a CNN crew. But there was no massacre in Adjaria, although, analytically, the place looked like a smaller replica of Bosnia. The factor that quite possibly changed the historical structural determination has a name, in fact a locally famous aristocratic name, real flesh and bones, and evidently possesses wits and quite some guts. The full story follows in chapter seven – a story of how one lucky bullet changed the course of history cannot help being rather dramatic. And I did not want to leave this book dwelling only on depressing examples.

My chance encounter with Shanibov established a level of trust that facilitated a rare opportunity to interview at length the members of the Kabardin opposi-tional network, meet Chechen politicians and intellectuals, and seek out Shanibov's former fighters in Abkhazia. My field data had to serve as the principal source of information because the area experts focus mostly on the politics of Islam and oil in the Caspian–Caucasus region. Since there exist precious few competent accounts of contemporary society in the North Caucasus, I was forced to rely heavily on obser-vations and interviews. The interviews often contained a political bias. However, information was cross-referenced in other interviews with politically unengaged intel-lectuals, members of the official patronage network, and simply the people among whom I lived and traveled. Moreover, talking to Shanibov offered an unusual advan-tage in that he often felt torn between his politics and Bourdieu's call to reflexive sociology. In the end, Musa Shanibov remained loyal to his sociological vocation.

Given the present political circumstances, in most instances I decided to provide only generic references to my interviewees or else none at all. Sometimes I really did not know their names. Over the years I have conducted several hundred inter-views. I never used tape recordings and those familiar with the region might understand why. Normally, I would write down a few key points during the conver-sation and then, at night, add more detail while the memory remained fresh. Many conversations could not be transcribed at all due to various ethical and political concerns, or just the circumstances in which the exchanges took place. As a matter of principle, I always maintained a safe distance from the details of financing or planning combat operations. Let me declare bluntly that I learned enough about recent events to offer a sociological explanation – which is mostly the extent of what journalists know – but never sought to know more than that.

THE DILEMMA OF VIOLENCE

Besides these legal and political considerations, there remains an ethical issue to which I found no resolution, but which cannot be avoided – the issue of war atrocities, which emerged in many interviews relating to the conflicts in Abkhazia, Karabagh, and Chechnya. In a few instances I sensed that my interlocutors might have been complicit in such atrocities, and some were prepared to admit it themselves – whether because they were oblivious to the world's definition of what constitutes a war crime, or because they enjoyed bragging about their toughness, or because they thought their actions justified given analogous acts on the opposing side. Usually I stopped the conversation at this point, in order not to fall foul of a potential set-up, or simply out of disgust.

Two troubling thoughts, however, linger on. First, the war atrocities themselves present us with difficult sociological questions. In chapter seven of this book, where I describe the ending of the war in Abkhazia, I offer some considerations regarding the organizational and socio-psychological causes of brutalization, and the consequent military strategy that, in the 1990s, came to be called ethnic cleansing. Second, it is possible that some of the perpetrators of the atrocities were suffering from manic psychosis, the effects of drugs, or other such conditions. But I have never talked to or observed these types directly – indeed, the individuals I did meet all appeared to be quite normal people capable of recognizing the horrible nature of their own stories. On at least two occasions it seemed to me that the man sitting opposite felt the urge to confess his sins before a stranger. Here social science reaches its limit. Nonetheless, I cannot help recalling a comment once made to me by Brendan O'Leary, to the effect that many of the men who joined the clandestine Irish Republican Army would, in a different life, have made good policemen. There may be something important in this observation.

A NOTE ON TRANSLITERATION

Throughout the book I have violated (in full consciousness and good faith, and I hope in a consistent manner) the scholarly conventions of the English transliteration of foreign names in order to make them sound more phonetic. North Caucasian names are usually rendered in English from their Russian versions, but this can create unnecessary difficulties. For example, the name of Chechnya's first president, usually transliterated from the Russian as Dzhokhar Dudaev, should rather be spelled Djohar Dudayev. This seems not only more straightforward and elegant, but is actually more correct. The name Djohar (or even simpler, Johar) finds its root in the Arabic word for jewel or gem, which in turn probably descended from an ancient Greek root, and thus the English words gem and jewel may well be related to the name Djohar. (It finds a further reflection in the Indian name, Jawaharlal.) Likewise, I used Daghestan instead of Dagestan, because the former stands closer to the Turko-Persian Dagh-e-stan, literally the "Mountain Land." However, names that already possess an established English transliteration, such as Khrushchev (rather than Hruschyov) or Abkhazia (rather than Abhazia), were left in their standard forms.

Furthermore, not all names could be transliterated phonetically, simply because the shortage of letters in the English alphabet often prohibits the transliteration of the wonderful phonetic complexities to be found abundantly in the Caucasian languages. Not least of all, I was ultimately defeated in spelling my own name. *Derlu*, according to family lore, was the name of the mountain somewhere in Eastern Anatolia where my Armenian ancestors once lived; the "g," I guess, appeared in our family name for purely phonetic purposes; the Latin letter "u" serves simply to separate it from the letters that follow it and is not pronounced; while "-*ian*" or "-*yan*" is the possessive suffix typically used in the Armenian language to create surnames. The stress in all Armenian surnames falls on the last syllable – but if you cannot pronounce it, it is all right. Beginning with my teachers and platoon commanders, many people had trouble with this proud ancient appellation.

ACKNOWLEDGEMENTS

At Moscow State University we were trained in the classical historiographical trick of starting to read a scholarly monograph from the back, with the footnotes and bibliography first. The idea was to situate the monograph's author in a particular intellectual tradition and scholarly network. The Anglo-American academic ritual of opening books with acknowledgements serves the same purpose, perhaps in a more explicit and personal fashion.

Many different people and institutions offered me support and inspiration during the long process of writing this book, and acknowledging these many debts seems not only honorable but also intellectually useful. Intellectually useful, because it amounts to describing how the book has emerged. (This relates to a basic epistemological conviction that meaningful social science is engaged in tracing the complex and contingent historical trajectories – or, as Perry Anderson might say, the lineages – of all social phenomena, from world-economies and nation states to individual human acts and artifacts, including cultural products such as books.) Honorable, because it seemed morally imperative to clarify, in a relational and reflexive way, my own stance and sociological position, since the book not only describes the acts of really existing individuals but also seeks to reframe several contemporary theories not by direct confrontation but by offering an alternative account.

My first debt then, perhaps unusually, belongs to an impersonal institution: the American university libraries and especially the marvel of open access to the stacks. Many days over the years have been spent lurking amidst the bookshelves in these Aladdin's caves – and those familiar with the Soviet-era institution of *spetskhran* (special sections for banned books) will appreciate the sensation. Here I might come across elaborate devices of unknown use, or treasures which at a closer inspection proved to be false, or just a lot of old trash (though some of it manufactured very recently). But the rewards were great, in the discovery of many unexpected conceptual gems to be added to the growing assemblage.

Scores of more personal debts were incurred as I labored on this book. The book itself would not have been possible without the unflagging support of Perry Anderson, Tariq Ali, Tim Clark, and the reviewers at Verso who continued to trust over the years that if I could learn how to build houses in the middle of America, and describe the experience in fluent and sociologically informed prose, then I should be able to manage a monograph, too.

Giovanni Arrighi, Terence Hopkins, and Immanuel Wallerstein opened up for me the perspective of the world. But it does not stop there. Twice in my life, Wallerstein appeared *Deus ex machina* (though he denies any sense of drama), on the second occasion miraculously extricating me from the imbroglio caused by the Central Committee's ban on my first dissertation – which they considered to be "maliciously exaggerating the difficulties of socialist orientation" in Africa. Regarding this episode, I must thank without naming the KGB officers of the Foreign

Directorate (this institutional detail matters), whose calmly professional attitude to my case provided a surprising glimpse into the internal fissures affecting the Soviet regime during its last days. The Soros Foundation of New York made my personal transition to the West technically possible. For the five years of a totally unexpected new life at Binghamton, I could feel almost at home thanks to the staff and fellow researchers at the Fernand Braudel Center for the Study of Economies, Historical Systems, and Civilizations.

I owe a great debt to Randall Collins for his synthesizing efforts to identify and connect up the different currents of social theory which may prove to be the most useful for understanding the contemporary world. Collins suggests that over the last three decades we have witnessed the "Golden Age" of historical macrosociology.[14] Nearly a century and a half ago, the pioneering cohort of mostly "dead Germans and some French" (i.e. Marx, Engels, Weber, Simmel, or Durkheim and Mauss) began the intellectual enterprise of explaining the key processes of the modern age. These, according to Collins, may be listed as capitalism; bureaucratization; the growth of state penetration and revolutionary resistances to the state; and the secularization of culture and knowledge. The intellectual project of macro-historical sociology reached maturation after a series of theoretical breakthroughs made during the late 1960s and the 1970s. Today it continues on a truly world scale.[15] I shall discuss in the second chapter of this book where the key breakthroughs appear to be situated and how they might relate to each other. Though my account on this score does not completely overlap with that of Collins, it is nonetheless his writings which have played the breakthrough role in my own understanding of the processes involved in the construction, ossification, and undoing of state socialism, all the way to the neopatrimonial patterns of rule and ethnic-based resistances emerging in the wake of the Soviet collapse.

Over the years the ideas in this book were presented at numerous conferences and lectures. I am deeply grateful to all those people and institutions who invited me to speak, and especially grateful for the reactions of my listeners who taught me a great deal, even if sometimes inadvertently. To mention just one example, at the fellows' conference of the SSRC-MacArthur program on peace and security, held, of all places, in Istanbul, my discussant was a young, formally dressed and very serious woman who was a political scientist from a leading American university. (She is now a good colleague.) Evidently puzzled by what I had hoped was a nuanced description of prevalent social types among post-communist warlords in the Caucasus, she asked bluntly: *Now, where are your testable hypotheses, what are your dependent variables, and how can you falsify your claims?* For a moment I was terrified, scarcely ever having heard such language before. Luckily, another young woman who was dressed rather exotically, an anthropologist from the same elite university, immediately lept to my aid, objecting passionately to the question before going on to extol the virtues of thick description, shifting meanings, multivocal narrative, and deconstruction. Despite my sincerest gratitude to this anthropologist, her discourse sounded to me no less odd. As the polemic grew to engulf virtually all those present in the room, I sat there quietly, feeling much as I had during a memorable night in central Mozambique a decade earlier. On that occasion, together with a group of Soviet geologists, I was caught in the cross-fire between Matsanga rebels and the government's *Milícias Populares*. As the sparkling tracer bullets criss-crossed above our heads in the resplendent African night sky, it remained only to lay low and try to enjoy the fireworks.

As I was adjusting to a different intellectual world, tremendously helpful practical academic advice was generously offered by Bob Huber, first in his role at the Social Science Research Council (SSRC) and later at the National Council for Eurasia and Eastern Europe Research (NCEEER). At Cornell, Valerie Bunce, Matthew Evangelista, Peter Katzenstein, Judith Reppy, and Sidney Tarrow taught me a great deal about political science and how to construct an argument, while personal encounters with Benedict Anderson taught me much about how to understand nationalism. Barbara Anderson, Nancy Tuma, Mikk Titma, and Mayer Zald gave me many valuable lessons in American sociology, and Julia Adams was a cheerful guide. Michael Burawoy, Grzegorz Ekiert, Gay Seidman, Michael Urban, Jeff Goodwin, and Richard Lachmann provided much appreciated encouragement. Aníbal Quijano and Mahmood Mamdani shared their wise and sad observations regarding the current situation of the Third World. Alexander Motyl challenged me to write, in fifty pages, accounts of socialism, capitalism, and nationalism. But it took Michael Kennedy to convince me that this could be done seriously.

My debt to William H. McNeill is of monumental proportions. I have learned from this wise doyen of world historians so many things that I simply despair of being able to enumerate them. I hope that he will forgive me, as he forgave my less sanguine view of many world historical processes and events. It was his personal example that was so inspiring. Corresponding with McNeill was a joy and a major source of intellectual stimulation, sometimes totally unexpected – as, for instance, when William Ivanovich (as I insisted on politely calling McNeill, since his father's name was John) responded to my description of Shanib's small army with the following: *What you describe is strikingly reminiscent of the ways in which the Biblical prophets sometimes raised armies of disaffected young men. Have you read the Book of Saul lately?*

The economic analyses of Vladimir Popov and David Woodruff helped to fill an important gap in the architecture of the book. Popov once commented that the Soviet planned economy disappeared just at the moment when we were beginning to make sense of it. It might be rather that we began making sense of the planned economy, and generally of the Soviet Union, only when and because they were about to disappear. Part of the reason may be that the USSR's collapse was preceded by the erosion of Soviet ideology and its enforcement mechanisms, an erosion that opened the regime to empirical study and analysis.

The opening up of the Soviet Union during perestroika gave rise to a new generation of scholars, both in the USSR and in the West, whose work significantly improved on the old Soviet studies. In the 1990s this generation suffered many losses as Western interests shifted elsewhere, and as the academic infrastructure of the former USSR fell victim to the post-collapse depression. Nonetheless the work goes on, and in crucial ways it has shaped my own understanding of the Soviet era and post-communism. The Russian-American Program on New Approaches to Russia's Security (PONARS) provided a regular opportunity to meet experts on the former USSR from across several disciplines and from both sides of the Atlantic. I say *spasibo* to all Ponarsians for their companionship, intellectual stimulation, and the incredible collective expertise so generously shared in electronic exchanges. My email correspondence with Oleksandr Fisun – an erudite theorist from the Ukraine and a fellow aficionado of big ideas – played such an important role that it must be acknowledged separately.

Because our north-eastern corner of the Greater Mediterranean world is so rich in people with whom one can talk all day long, over coffee or tea, exchanging ideas and observations, the list of names that follows is necessarily long. It gives me great pleasure to mention everyone here with thanks: the Turkish sociologists Faruk Birtek, Çaglar Keyder, Fatma Müge-Göçek; the Americans adopted into the region, Charles King, Chip Gagnon, Robert Hislope, and Ned Walker; the Armenian intellectuals Kevork Bardakjian, Ronald Grigor Suny, Levon Abrahamian, and Stepan Astourian; my Azeri friends Mais Nazarli, Lana Shihzamanova, and Radjab Mamedov; the Georgian scholars Ghia Nodia and Gia Tarkhan-Mouravi; the fellow Slavs and intellectual companions Piotr Dutkiewicz, Leonid Chekin, Andrei Korotaev, Vladimir Solonari, Mikhail Molchanov, Maria Todorova, Alexander Knysh, and the Chicagoan Michael Khodarkovsky; the North Caucasians Barasbi Bgazhnokov, Vahit Akayev and Lyoma Usmanov, Manolis Chahkiyev, Galina Khizriyeva, Vladimir Degoyev, Ruslan Khestanov, Artur Tsutsiyev, Nikolai Kirei, and the late B.M. Djimov; the anthropologists from Moscow Yura Anchabadze,

Ian Chesnov, Grigory P. Lezhava, Givi V. Tsulaya, and Sergei A. Arutyunov; the legendary nomadologist Anatoly M. Khazanov; my old teachers of Middle Eastern studies, Mikhail S. Meier and Feride M. Atsamba. Dmitry Furman set a high standard by his personal example. And to Igor Kuznetsov and his wife Rita Mamasahlisi-Kuznetsova I owe more than intellectual debts. These people all helped me to find a way through the historical complexities of our native corner of the world. Several new hypotheses emerged and received early substantiation in discussions with esteemed members of the Academic Council on Historical Sciences and Anthropology at Kabardino-Balkarian State University.

Many debts were also incurred to my colleagues at Northwestern University: John Bushnell, Bruce Cumings, Timothy Earle, Frank Safford, and Andrew Wachtel. Will Reno became a friend and a regular partner in discussing the nasty wars in the Caucasus. The graduate students Scott Greer, Christina Nyström, Elif Kale-Lostuvali, Han Sun, Gabriel Abend, and Alan Czaplicki all played their part in shaping this book. Last but not least, Northwestern's Department of Sociology became truly my home community and a site of what Arthur Stinchcombe aptly called the "communism of knowledge." Among social scientists Stinchcombe enjoys the reputation of being quite a difficult person, and I suspect that he relishes it. He is indeed difficult in that his scribblings on one's manuscripts can cause no small amount of bewilderment and frustration, and moreover because he abides by exceedingly high intellectual standards. But in large part this book is different from its original version, and I believe more solid, precisely because of Stinchcombe's being so difficult. Of course, the responsibility for what I have written (and, in some instances, drawn) remains entirely mine, though to *mnogouvazhaemyi* Academician Arthur Gomerovich Stinchcombe I owe a lot, including his sufferance of my early drafts. Charles Ragin was not difficult in the same sense, but in his presence one could not afford to be sloppy. Carol Heimer, Jeff Manza, Ann Shola Orloff, and many other colleagues provided great intellectual stimulation. And Bruce Carruthers graciously pretends that he suggested only a few finishing touches.

The central parts of this book's argument were presented at the 2002 convention of the American Sociological Association, and benefited from a thorough discussion with my fellow members of the panel on the political economy of world-systems (PEWS). At another panel dedicated to the memory of Bourdieu, the responses of Craig Calhoun and Viviana Zelizer helped to clarify several key points in what became the second chapter of my book.

Over the years, my research and my visits to the Caucasus have been supported by fellowships and grants from the SSRC-MacArthur Program on Peace and

Security, IREX, NCEEER, and the Center of International and Comparative Studies of Northwestern University. In particular, the trip to Chechnya during which I first met Shanibov was sponsored by the Jennings Randolph Program at the US Institute of Peace (USIP).

I am extremely grateful to Vartan Gregorian, President of the Carnegie Corporation of New York, for honoring my lectures with his presence and comments. The book was in fact written during the tenure of a Carnegie Scholar of Vision award. (Admittedly, I originally promised to write something completely different – a study of organized crime and corruption in the former Soviet republics – and I still intend to keep the promise.) The events of September 2001 changed many things, which in one small instance included my writing plan pledged to the Carnegie Corporation. I sincerely hope that they accept this book as a valid and timely substitution.

In preparing the book and during research trips I met and came to respect many journalists, some of whom also became friends. They include Pilar Bonet (*El Pais*), Bruce Clark (*The Economist*), Anatol Lieven (formerly of *The Times*), Andrew Meyer (*Time*), Anne Nivat (*Libération*), Charlie Madigan (*Chicago Tribune*), Lyudmila Telen (*Moskovskie novosti*), Alexander Ivanter and Pavel Bykov (*Ekspert* magazine), and the filmmaker Vardan Hovhannisian (*BARS Media*). The "rogue reporter" and now trans-Caucasus biker Thomas Goltz shared with me his videotape footage of what few outsiders could have ever observed: the bitterly contentious micro-politics involved in the formation of a village detachment in Samashki, Chechnya.

I owe a special debt to the memory of my friend Andrei Fadin. In the 1990s he wrote some of the most penetrating analyses of the Caucasus wars for *Obschaia gazeta* – when that forum for Moscow's democratic intelligentsia still existed. Three days before his death in a car crash in the slippery winter streets of Moscow, Andrei gave a lecture at Northwestern University and was guest of honor at my home. Even before he was laid to rest, the Russian tabloids splashed the sensational story that Andrei had been murdered, allegedly over a secret tape detailing a plot to assassinate the shining light of Russian privatization, Anatoly Chubais. I can attest that this story was pure fabrication because, contrary to what these provacateurs claimed, I could not have passed on such a tape to Andrei because I neither enjoy, nor have ever wished for, access to the CIA's listening services, and least of all take an interest in the intrigues of the likes of Boris Berezovsky. The sad irony is that the people who disseminated the story knew this just as well. One of them was a former student of mine, whose name need not be mentioned here, but whose boss, the notorious political operator Gleb Pavlovsky, was a close collaborator with Andrei Fadin back in the revolutionary days of 1989–1991. Since our ways parted, these two individuals gained considerable influence in Russian ruling circles and no small personal fortunes. Both occupied offices in Mr. Putin's administration where they were put in charge of (what else?) the management of mass media. This book, at a deeply personal level, is also my revenge for Andrei Fadin. But instead of playing an avenger, how much more do I wish that Andrei could read my arguments that in so many ways are responses to the questions he posed.

The project that led to this book took not only several years, but also a lot of moral support from my family. This, however, as all sociologists know, is a shifting category. In America, the many Bogdasarians of all generations extended their family to include us in its caring embrace. The Rejebians, the Dukes, the Petrovs, and the Naumovs became such close friends that they now amount to an extended family. Mark Kulikowski was not only a family friend but also a heroic bibliographer. Tom Mellers and his wife Carmen have been virtual in-laws since our children went to pre-school together, and who knows what the future holds?

My wise elder sister always suspected that I was unlikely to keep my promise of not going to Chechnya or Karabagh, just as earlier I had gone to Mozambique rather than some safer place. But all these years she kept caring about our parents, looked after my children during the summers while their father was away doing serious research, and provided me with the highest example of kindness. My wife Liuba not only cared for the children and me during the rest of year; she also wrote a dissertation on the history of slave trading in the Caucasus that caused much curiosity among the specialists, earned praises from high authorities like Arthur Stinchcombe, and critically informed my own understanding of the region's past. Soon I hope to see Liuba's published acknowledgement to our sons and me for enabling her to write her own monograph. We promise to try hard.

1

The Field

"One of the most extraordinary rewards of the craft of sociology is the possibility it affords to enter the life of others, to experience all human experiences."

Pierre Bourdieu and Loïc Wacquant, *An Invitation to Reflexive Sociology*
(Chicago: University of Chicago Press, 1992, p. 205)

Before engaging in the historical-theoretical reconstruction of the lineages leading from past to present, which is the main method of this book, we first of all need to gain some practical sense of the complex and perhaps exotic environments we shall be investigating.[1] This practical sense may serve as a variety of what Schumpeter called "vision," defined as "a preanalytic cognitive act that supplies the raw material for analytic effort."[2] In this chapter I shall try to convey something of what one may experience and observe today when visiting places like Chechnya and Kabardino-Balkaria. To some extent then, I try to emulate what comes naturally to good journalists or "foreign correspondents," especially when they enjoy sufficient space and editorial freedom, as they do when writing journalistic books or longer articles for magazines like the *New Yorker*. Journalists rely on a practical knowledge born of their experience in reporting from particular regions for extended periods of time, a knowledge they attempt to translate into images and metaphors

understandable to a domestic readership. Being a sociologist rather than a journalist, I shall rely on theoretical concepts drawn from contemporary social science
and a professional knowledge of research methodologies. I shall also indicate here
– albeit only in passing – various hypotheses linking my empirical observations to
deeper structural processes that can be construed only theoretically.

Inevitably, the foreign visitor to the Caucasus – a category which applies to the
majority of Russians almost as much as to any other outsider – faces an inchoate
and chaotic stream of impressions which may at first seem overwhelming. The
various impressions I record in this chapter are presented here as a series of "snapshots" of the region, which I shall endeavor to contextualize in the later chapters.
Our immediate task, though, is simply to observe and take note; though this in
itself may not be as straightforward as it sounds. In particular, attention needs to
be paid to things that otherwise might seem too mundane to be worth considering.
For example, a traveler who comes from a country where rice is the main source
of food is likely to neglect to mention in his report home that the locals eat rice
too. Only if their staple diet seems unusual – if it is, say, maize or buckwheat, or
the American wonder of pre-sliced bread – might this fact attract the visitor's attention sufficiently to be thought worth mentioning. Historians and anthropologists
may be professionally prepared to detect such simple bias, but this is not, of course,
the only potential pitfall we may face.

Sometimes the phenomena observed may be distorted by our own expectations
or research agenda. For example, the visiting scholar who intends to study, say, the
contemporary role of Islam in Caucasian politics, or the nature of the Chechen
guerrilla resistance, may be so focused on his chosen subject matter that he fails to
notice important variations and connections in the broader social environment and
context. Of course, those "natural" scientists whose subject matter affords them
the luxury of working in a laboratory do indeed seek to isolate their object of study
from its broader environment in order to treat it in its purest and most concentrated form. Adopting a similar approach, the scholar interested in the Islamic
revival may visit only the newly built mosques, while the one focused on guerrilla
warfare may talk only to military and political leaders. Now of course, these are
indeed concentrated expressions of the chosen objects of study, and some may
claim that, insofar as they are typical and culturally authentic, they are the only
relevant such objects. But can such social phenomena ever exist in isolation? If
one implicitly assumes they can, one can all too easily become trapped in an

ideological image, thereby missing the attendant complexities, ironies, and hidden tensions. A case in point might be the following description of my first encounter with Musa Shanib. Were it not for my accidental slip of the tongue, Shanib would have been recorded in my field notes as merely a fiery nationalist ideologue proudly wearing his traditional *papaha* hat. But then the previous life of this exotically dressed man would have escaped our attention – the life in which he had languished in provincial obscurity, unpromoted for twenty years, while reading critical sociology, listening to jazz, and dreaming of social reforms.

Admittedly, I am not just a social scientist; I am also a native – as are we all, somewhere. I grew up in the North Caucasus and was thus inculcated with a practical sense of local realities. But this socialization was never completed to the point of becoming unreflected habitus, since I left home at the age of sixteen – first to study in Moscow and then to work in Africa and later in America. In what follows, therefore, I should be able to offer the fresh insight of a "learned foreigner" (noticing, for instance, what the locals serve at the table) combined with the intimate knowledge of a native (enabling me, usually, to tell why what they serve is being served). Pierre Bourdieu considered this a special observational advantage, similar to that involved in his own study of village life in south-western France, from where he himself originated.[3]

But such local social knowledge also imposes its own limitations. To take one instance, the fact that I was a man in a strongly patriarchal setting often prevented me from interviewing women. Imagine how it feels to be seated at a banquet table together with the head of the household (himself perhaps a professor) while the elder son, in a ceremonious display of ethnic tradition, silently stands to attention, as befits a young squire. His job is to pour drinks; while the women emerge only briefly from the kitchen to bring new dishes: meat with herbs, pickled vegetables, millet bread, pies with feta cheese, traditional dumplings in garlic sauce. They smile but hardly utter a word. Now, as an American sociologist, I strongly suspected that these women could provide a different perspective on the new Islam or guerrilla warfare. But in order to talk to them one has to wait for a less ritually scripted occasion which may or may not arrive. The guest in the Caucasus, as a local proverb goes, is the captive of his hosts. One way around this impasse was to pay particular attention to the accounts of the region published by women journalists such as Galina Kovalskaya, Sanobar Shermatova, Anna Politkovskaya, or Anne Nivat, whose acumen and courage deserve the greatest respect.[4] I also acted by proxy, relying on researchers like the incredibly energetic Daghestani Galina Khizriyeva to ask the questions that I could not.

The importance of gender considerations may be illustrated by a seemingly simple question: in the more traditional households, which are dominated by parental authority, how does the family behave towards a son who joins a guerrilla unit? Here is an account that claims to describe the general pattern of behavior: *Ostensibly, the mothers cannot interfere directly, but in fact they have the final say. A mother can emerge from the kitchen with her son's belongings neatly packed for a long journey, or she can loudly refuse to let him go, especially if he is the only son – and then he can leave only over her dead body.*[5] This may of course be a romanticized version of what happens. Yet some sketchy quantitative data I managed to gather regarding the families of guerrillas – not only in Chechnya but also in the wars of Nagorny Karabagh and Abkhazia – indicates that a disproportionate number of fighters did indeed come from families with three or more sons. Such a large number of children became relatively rare in the Soviet republics, following the industrialization which was for the most part completed in the 1950s–1960s. Only among specific social and ethnic groups (such as rural Chechens) did high fertility rates still persist. Of course it was possible to find only sons among the fighters too; but these were mostly idealistic students hailing from large towns.

It seems apparent that adult women in the war zones are quietly engaged in complex, almost subliminal negotiations with their own families and communities (neighbors, extended clan networks, religious circles) where perceptions of family status are at stake. Would it appear shameful and treasonous if a family with several sons failed to produce a single volunteer? Might it be acceptable for an only son to be spared? Importantly, in a patriarchal setting, such as we are confronting here, a mother with many sons possesses the highest status attainable by a woman. The self-abnegating mother of a patriotic hero attains perhaps the highest status of all, thereby making a significant contribution to the status of both her family and her clan. But this hypothesis, which might apply to Palestinians and Afghans as well, would require women scholars to conduct the minute field research. This is perhaps one way in which the recent ethnic wars have served to accentuate the patriarchal distribution of gender roles. On other fronts, however, gender is a very ambiguous factor, as I shall seek to demonstrate in my observations on contemporary Chechen women. In part, this is because Caucasian nationalities have been profoundly influenced by Soviet patterns of social mobility and formal education, but it is also, perhaps, because Caucasian women have devised a variety of gendered strategies to cope with extreme hardships and multiple threats to survival.

*

While the immediate goal of this chapter is to provide an introductory ethnographic description of a relatively obscure region, my intention is also to render it a little less exotic. This is particularly necessary because Caucasian realities are too often presented in very romantic terms, both by foreigners and by many natives, especially when the latter are trying to impress the former.[6] The literary tradition of romanticizing the Caucasus goes back to the gentleman travelers of the Victorian era. Such gentlemen came mainly from Britain or other Western countries; they included geographers, military officers and spies, diplomats, private adventurers, and no less a celebrity than Alexandre Dumas *père*, who toured the Russian empire during the late 1850s. Almost invariably, they depicted all the various peoples of the region, whether the native highlanders or my mother's Cossack ancestors, as noble savages.[7] For its part, the Russian literary tradition created an impressive Caucasian mythology of its own, from Alexander Pushkin and Leo Tolstoy to Solzhenitsyn and Fazil Iskander.[8] During the last decade these traditions have re-emerged with a vengeance in Caucasian nationalist discourses, in artistic works sympathetic to the Chechens and other Caucasians (for example, the Oscar-nominated film *Prisoner of the Mountains* [1996]), and particularly in the Western media's coverage of the Chechen wars.[9] In the "journalistic" record that follows, then, I shall try at least to reverse this romanticizing trend by bringing a range of sociological concepts to bear on my own first-hand impressions of contemporary Caucasian reality.

CHECHNYA, THE FREEDOM SQUARE

In January 1997, the Russian anthropologist Igor Kuznetsov and I spent the best part of a long day in Freedom Square, Grozny – the ruined capital of Chechnya. My primary purpose that day was to observe the social interactions occurring at the various election-campaign rallies that were then underway. The public space of the huge square was clearly divided between the Chechen political speakers, small groups of their active supporters standing close to the tribunes improvised on flatbed trucks, a much larger group consisting of several thousand people who might be avid listeners one moment, casual onlookers the next, and last but not least the scores of foreign correspondents who camped at the outer perimeter of the rally.

It was the period of what turned out to be only a temporary cessation of hostilities. A few weeks earlier the last Russian troops had withdrawn from Chechnya after their military defeat in August 1996. An armistice followed, and an agreement was reached to hold internationally supervised elections of Chechnya's new president and parliament. For a short while it looked like the promising beginning of a new, peaceful era and of Chechnya's de facto national independence, a promise which attracted to the region nearly two hundred journalists from around the world.

In mundane reality, it was cold, damp, and very dirty in downtown Grozny on the day of my visit. Despite the valiant efforts of the new mayor and his teams of volunteers to clean up the main streets, one still had to walk over the sticky, crunching mixture of broken glass, plaster, brick, and bullet casings left after the recent battles. For hours on end, the parade of secondary activist speakers went on rehearsing the standard patriotic rhetoric of the period. The majority of people at the rally looked bored. Some were leisurely conversing in small circles or arguing heatedly among themselves; others just wandered around or smoked cigarettes. Still the square was obviously the main show in town, the physical location of what Randall Collins would call the focus of emotional attention.[10] The people wouldn't leave the square even in bad weather and despite the unimpressive speakers. One could feel the universal urge to stay together, discuss the public issues, and witness history.

Perhaps the best confirmation of this feeling was the presence of the tight-knit groups of giggling teenage girls, dressed up almost identically in fashionable leather coats from Turkey, and carrying colorful shopping bags from the duty-free shops of Abu Dhabi or Cyprus. They looked as if they were going shopping or to a discotheque rather than attending a political rally. These urbane girls actually outnumbered the people in unusual kinds of dress such as military uniform, Islamic headcovers or Chechen folkloric costumes; but of course nobody noticed their ordinary presence.

In sharp contrast, the assembled journalists could not fail to notice a small boy, no more than five or six years old, kitted out with a tiny brand-new replica of a guerrilla's camouflage uniform and carrying a toy gun, being paraded around the square by his proud parents. The journalists readily took his picture. The spectacle had an air of carnival, perhaps due to the child's cherubic face and the earnest pride of his parents. Later, on many different occasions, I saw pictures of this same child with quite different captions: *We Shall Never Give In! The Nation Lives!* or else *Bandits From the Youngest Age*, or *Preparing for the Jihad*.

Otherwise the journalists looked very bored, discussing among themselves the prospects for moving on to find somewhere with more action. For my companion Igor and me, it remained to wander around (keeping clear of the surrounding ruins, which were littered with unexploded ordnance) and register the details.

*

The first things to capture our attention were the street signs. A poster on a battered lamp post read: *The headquarters of the Islamic battalion are now located at Rosa Luxemburg Street, 12.* There was an ironic combination of the rising political force and a name from the socialist past. Other place names came as the totally unexpected expressions of more recent politics: *Mikhail Gorbachev Avenue* and *Nikita Khrushchev Square.* Where on earth might there exist another place named after Khrushchev? He was, of course, the Soviet leader who in 1957 rescinded Stalin's 1944 order to deport the Chechens and restored their autonomous republic. The street names were the statements of hopeful gratitude to the better Russian rulers, both of them democratic reformers.[11] Importantly, this did not seem to be a purely official effort to see something positive in Soviet rule. From many ordinary families we heard the standard stories told with considerable passion, of a Russian soldier or railwayman dropping a loaf of bread to the starving people in the cattle cars in which they were transported to exile; of an old Cossack, himself long since exiled to Kazakhstan, sharing his fur coat in the first desperate winter; or of a Volga German woman sharing her cow's milk with the Chechen children. Such stories, perhaps embellished, served to underscore that the Chechens would never forget good deeds, as they would never forgive evil. Moreover, they made possible the prospect of living as peaceful neighbours of the Russians in the future.

By the time of my visit Chechnya's capital was no longer called Grozny, at least not in the official pronouncements. A few days earlier, by the decree of the outgoing interim president, Zelimkhan Yandarbiyev, Grozny had been officially renamed Djohar-kala – the town of Djohar – named after the first president, General Djohar Dudayev, who had been slain a year earlier by a Russian guided missile. Grozny was, of course, not only a Russian name but an explicitly colonial one given to the town by its infamous founder, Viceroy Yermolov, in 1818. Grozny means Fearsome or Terrifying, as in the name of the Russian Tsar Ivan Grozny, traditionally rendered in English as Ivan the Terrible.

Changing the town's name, however, was a politically self-serving act on the part of Yandarbiyev. Since the revolution of 1991 this former Soviet poet had been the ideologist lurking behind President Dudayev. The majority of Chechens did not seem to take Yandarbiyev too seriously – nobody is much interested in the right-hand man when to his left stands a charismatic authoritarian. But Yandarbiyev, evidently a man of large ego, as is fairly common of mediocre provincial poets, emblazoned the walls and lamp posts of Grozny/Djohar-kala with his electoral posters, and nothing in his appearance was left without some uncanny symbolism: his large, recently grown beard symbolized Islamic piety and maturity; his tall sheepskin hat linked him to Caucasus traditions; the camouflage jacket marked him for a warrior; while underneath the military fatigues one could see a white shirt and necktie, which were tokens of Yandarbiyev's urbanity and intellectualism. The poster's caption summed him up: "Politician, Poet, Patriot."[12]

President Dudayev himself was not always taken very seriously during his lifetime, possibly because of his endless bombastic pronouncements, which were in sharp contrast with the stark reality of Chechen life after the country proclaimed itself independent. That disparity had only become greater during the recent war, in which General Dudayev had not distinguished himself as a commander. Instead, the armed resistance to the Russian invasion of 1994 was jointly organized by Aslan Maskhadov – an artillery colonel who in his past life had been named best officer in the Soviet Army Group stationed in Hungary – and Shamil Basayev, a former drop-out student of Moscow University who had proven a brilliant autodidact in guerrilla warfare, if in little else. In the presidential elections of 1997 the two war heroes, Maskhadov and Basayev, were clearly the frontrunners. But Djohar Dudayev remained an enduring symbol of the project of Chechen national independence. And now Vice-President Yandarbiyev, the successor to Dudayev, desperately sought to inscribe the symbolism of independence in the name of Chechnya's capital. Perhaps this is why almost nobody except the die-hard nationalists, and the printers of official letterheads, used the name Djohar-kala.

Moreover Chechnya itself was no longer called Chechnya but rather, in a sort of compromise, the "Chechen Republic Ichkeria." This was a typical nationalist invention of tradition. Ichkeria is neither Chechen in origin nor a single word, but in fact two words that translate from Kumyk, one of Daghestan's major languages, as something like "that place over there" – *ich keri*. For close to a thousand years Kumyk and Tatar, the Turkic tongues of the dominant steppe dwellers, served as the lingua franca throughout the multi-ethnic North Caucasus (much like Swahili in East Africa). When the geopolitics shifted and the Great Steppe of Eurasia ceased to be an open frontier, Russian replaced the Turkic languages as the new medium of inter-ethnic speech. But in the late eighteenth century Kumyk was still commonly used in the North Caucasus, when Russian military cartographers borrowed the expression *ich keria* from their native guides. Between the 1810s and 1830s "Ichkeria" denoted the mountainous south-eastern corner of greater Chechnya, and then the word gradually fell into disuse. The word that has eventually prevailed – Chechnya – was itself derived, in a manner typical of colonial cartography, from the name of a border village, Chechen-aul, beyond which lived the linguistically distinct group of natives who would cause so much trouble to the expanding Russian empire. Thereafter they were called the Chechens.

As is the common fate of semi-forgotten words, Ichkeria acquired a poetic flavor. It sounded mellifluous to an ear attuned to Indo-European languages such as Russian. Ichkeria had survived mainly in the romantic verses of Mikhail Lermontov, Russia's answer to the defiant and brooding genius of Byron. It is indicative of the differences between the countries that produced these two poets that, instead of seeking heroic peril like Lord Byron, Lieutenant Lermontov was demoted from the Guards Regiment in St. Petersburg to the Caucasus Army Corps for his widely circulated 1837 poem on Pushkin's tragic death – the usual punishment for unruly and politically suspect officers during the disciplinarian reign of Nicholas I.

Epochs passed. In November 1990, as the Soviet perestroika was entering its last somber winter, the Second Congress of the Chechen People convened to resume the quest for nationhood. (The First Chechen Congress, incidentally, had taken place in 1918 during the upheaval of the Civil War.) During the preparation for the Second Congress it was realized that Chechnya had no native name of her own. The Chechen people's only inheritance from the past was their self-appellation: *Nokhchi*. There had never been a sovereign political unit congruent with this people, hence no native name for their whole country. But it was now 1990, and the old Russified Soviet names were being rejected across the board, along with the discredited political institutions of Soviet federalism: Belorussia was becoming Belarus; Moldavia – Moldova; Tataria – Tatarstan; Yakutia – Sakha; Kalmykia – Halm Tang'ch; while referring to the Ukrainian capital in the old-fashioned manner as Kiev rather than Kyïv left one open to the charge of Russian imperial chauvinism.

In their rush to find an appropriate name for their country, the heralds of Chechen nationalism raced off in different directions. The proposed names – *Nokhchi-Mokhk* (literally "Chechen-Land") or *Nokhchi-cho'* ("Chechen-ia") – might have conformed to the grammar and the richly consonant phonetics of North Caucasian languages, but the newly invented names seemed too new, too idiosyncratic, and thereby artificial. In the fairly provincial Autonomous Soviet Socialist Republic (ASSR) of Checheno-Ingushetia, as it was then called, no academic or national writer possessed enough institutional and moral stature to impose his version.

The Gordian knot was cut by General Dudayev, an ethnic Chechen who had spent most of his life in garrisons all around the former Soviet Union. Dudayev's command of his native tongue may have become rusty over the years, but he was a great admirer of Lermontov and could recite by heart his poems about the dashing lads of Ichkeria galloping into battle. Any objection to the fact that Lermontov was a European romantic who regarded the Chechen warriors as magnificent untamed beasts was dismissed as pedantry by Dudayev. "Ichkeria" sounded glorious, historical, unifying, and, moreover, it was much easier to pronounce than Nokhchi-Mokhk – which was indeed a sound consideration when attempting to put a new nation on the map.

THE ARCH-TERRORIST

The rusty iron stele, pockmarked by bullets, must have stood since Soviet times in the middle of the roundabout. As a bitterly ironic reminder of recent prosperous, if hypocritical, times, large faded letters carried a typical Soviet slogan: *Peoples of the Planet, Do Not Allow the Destruction of Peace!* Plastered all over the stele were electoral portraits with the bearded face of Shamil Basayev, accompanied by slogans and even whole manifestos that, to my astonishment, were addressed to the Russians. Basayev, leader of the resistance to the Russian invasion of 1994, was begging forgiveness for his past acts and calling for reconciliation!

Basayev's biography is very revealing of a certain type of Islamist fighter. He was born in 1965 in the highland village of Vedeno, the same Vedeno that a century earlier served as headquarters to the legendary Shamil, the imam of the Chechen and Daghestani holy war – called *ghazawat* in the Caucasus.[13] Of course, Basayev's first name, Shamil, echoed the name of this legendary imam, and his birthplace Vedeno is one of those places where nearly every rock is associated with some epic tale, usually involving a valiant warrior who made his last stand there. But Basayev also grew up in the Soviet era, when Vedeno became the home of a large state farm. His first and only conventional job was as a "cattle-breeding technician." Basayev quickly aspired to greater things and so, after military service, the young Chechen headed for Moscow to study to become a land surveyor. Though he dropped out after a year because of bad grades, while at the university he met students from Cuba who gave him a picture of Ernesto Che Guevara.[14] Reportedly, he always carried Che's portrait in the breast pocket of his uniform. During the attempted reactionary coup in August 1991, Basayev was among the defenders of President Yeltsin and democratic Russia. Two months later, he hijacked an airplane to protest against Yeltsin's refusal to recognize Chechnya's independence. That episode ended peacefully in a matter of hours, but it instantly provided Basayev with a militant reputation. He fought briefly on the Azeri side in Nagorny Karabagh, and later in

1992 led the Chechen volunteer battalion to Abkhazia. According to the counter-terrorism experts in Washington, Basayev spent several months in Afghanistan in 1994 where he established contact with al-Qaeda training groups – though, given his skills, one might wonder who was training whom.

In June 1995 a detachment led by Basayev seized around two thousand hostages in the town hospital of Budyonnovsk in southern Russia and demanded an end to the Russian offensive in Chechnya. Basayev declared that since the Chechen resistance had no airplanes or missiles to retaliate against the Russian attacks on Chechen civilians, he and his fighters had decided to become "human missiles" in order to take the war into Russia's heartland.

The Russian special forces sent to the scene suffered considerable loss of life and failed to take back the hospital. Basayev had ordered women in white gowns to stand in the windows and beg the soldiers not to shoot. There were indications that the Russian generals had been preparing to flatten the hospital from a distance with artillery fire, but in Moscow they realized that the televised siege was being watched by the whole world. In the middle of the crisis, Yeltsin left the country for a summit with the G7 leaders. This looked like an alibi prepared in advance and, as political insiders and journalists speculated, it forced the Russian officials to begin thinking about who would be scapegoated following the expected slaughter. In the event, in a bid to avoid both the slaughter and the scapegoating, Prime Minister Chernomyrdin allowed Basayev and his detachment to return triumphantly to their bases in Chechnya with the promise of peace talks. The talks dragged on half-heartedly for five months until, in the absence of a political solution, the violence escalated further as a result of the actions of radical militarists on both sides.[15]

But by the winter of 1997, the presidential hopeful Shamil Basayev was promising to travel to Budyonnovsk to beg forgiveness.

A MARKETPLACE OF SYMBOLS

At the edge of Freedom Square, in front of the ruins of what looked like a Soviet-era department store, local vendors had established an improvised market. At stalls made mostly of bricks and pieces of board, one could find an instructive variety of popular merchandise. The enterprising owner of a satellite dish was doing a brisk trade in long-distance phone calls (the old land-line telephone system had been badly damaged along with the rest of the urban infrastructure). A couple of vendors specialized in patriotica: Chechen flags of different sizes; the green velvet berets of the armed resistance; calendars and posters featuring medieval fortresses and similar historic monuments; and the portraits of national heroes such as sheik Mansur (a legendary rebel of the eighteenth century), imam Shamil, and Chechnya's first president, Djohar Dudayev. One could also buy a photo of a wolf, the new national symbol, accompanied by the boastful inscription *Think Twice Before Messing With Me*; there were even homemade rugs decorated with the figure of a she-wolf and slogans like *God, Freedom, Ichkeria!* Most Chechens did not seem to notice that the wolf smacked of paganism, or that in the Chechen slogans "God" was usually rendered by the word *Dela* – rather than Allah – which was a survival from historically recent paganism.[16] Vahit Akayev, Director of Chechnya's Institute of History before the war, admitted to me that the origin of the she-wolf as a national symbol was a mystery. During the perestroika era, when there was a deluge of publications about the national past, an elderly amateur historian, affectionately known as the "people's academician," popularized the she-wolf as the mythological guardian of ancient Chechens. After the popular historian's death, Akayev dispatched his own graduate students to organize the personal archives of the deceased, but nowhere could they find any document regarding the wolf. The symbol, however, had caught the popular imagination and made it on to the new national flag.[17]

The flag itself, insists Lyoma Usmanov, who helped design it, was supposed to employ a purely nationalist and secular symbolism: the narrow red stripe stands for the blood spilled in many wars; the broader white band stands for the hope of the Chechen nation, and the deep green field for the fertility of native soil.[18] It may sound improbable that Usmanov didn't think at the time that the green color might also be interpreted as an Islamic symbol. But then Lyoma seems a true Soviet-era dissident: earnest, passionately committed, and perhaps seeming a bit naïve when set against the backdrop of ruthless post-communist politics.

Shortly after the Chechen revolution in November 1991, Usmanov was poised to win the election for mayor of Grozny, but in the final count victory eluded him, probably because General Dudayev needed to reward a more powerful supporter, Beslan Gantamirov. The latter was an erstwhile Soviet policeman who in the late eighties had turned to business after failing at Moscow's law school. In 1990 Gantamirov returned to Chechnya a wealthy man and surrounded himself with a group of armed retainers whom he called the Party of the Islamic Path. They became the stormtroopers of the 1991 revolution and, after its victory, joined the new "municipal police" of the city of Grozny.

Two years later, in 1993, mayor Gantamirov violently split with President Dudayev. According to local opinion, their quarrel was over the control of oil exports that Gantamirov had effectively privatized and which Dudayev wanted to renationalize to help build his army and state. In 1994, with the not-very-covert support of the Russian intelligence services, Gantamirov established in Chechnya a private army of "contras" and tried to oust Dudayev by force; he failed miserably. Deeply embarrassed, his backers in Moscow then convinced Yeltsin to invade with the regular Russian army.

Gantamirov's own militia was one of the first groups to attach Islamic symbolism to the green of the Chechen flag. Given the mercenary cynicism of Gantamirov, the appeal to religion here was a thin ideological disguise. But the move was likely approved by his Russian handlers, who relied on their own previous experience in Afghanistan. Clearly, religion in Chechnya was being politicized from several different sides. Yet we should not be distracted by the conscious political manipulation of religion, whether it is as cynical and superficial as Gantamirov's or as well-funded and zealous as the new Wahhabi puritanism that began to arrive in Chechnya from the Middle East during the war. Just as the CIA in the eighties helped to create in Afghanistan and across the Middle East new fundamentalist movements and clandestine networks that soon acquired an autonomous dynamic, the inchoate and violent political struggles in Chechnya of the nineties gave rise to a public religious discourse which often had unexpected ramifications. In the language of sociology, this added a new layer of causality to contemporary processes. But religion did not become a potent force in itself – to claim that would be a reification, as if religion were indeed a self-propellant phenomenon. Rather, Islam became a means of political and moral legitimation, a channel to the resources of Middle Eastern political circles, and the source of a discourse that gradually replaced a discredited nationalism. If religion became a hotly contested field, it was because different personalities and the armed formations behind them now claimed Islam for their own purposes.

VIDEOS

Leaving the patriotica behind, I spent some time examining the video tapes displayed at another stand. The assortment of pirated and poorly reproduced copies, sold at about a dollar each, represented the lower end of the video market such as can be found anywhere in post-Soviet countries: the simplest American cartoons like *Tom & Jerry*; Indian musical melodramas; a few nostalgic Soviet-era favorites; martial arts films from Hong Kong; and a lot of Hollywood action movies with Schwarzenegger, Stallone, and Van Damme. Little wonder then that many Chechen fighters looked more like Rambo than their legendary ancestors. Topping the bestseller list in Chechnya at the time was *Braveheart*. The Scottish researcher Fiona Hill tells a revealing story about Basayev, who considers the Scots as fellow high-landers, and the film *Braveheart* as capturing like nothing else the spirit of the Chechen's centuries-long resistance to the treacherous and cruel Russian domination.[19] Basayev, as it turns out, dreams of dying with a cry of *Freedom!* on his lips – like the hero of *Braveheart* played by Mel Gibson.[20]

It took some asking to find any Chechen-made videos. A boy, dispatched to check with another merchant, came running back and brought with him eight tapes. Watched later, this small archive turned out to contain mostly amateur video recordings of political rallies, pronouncements by guerrilla commanders made clan-destinely during the war, raw footage of battles with Russian troops, and news broadcasts from Chechnya (mainly by ITN, BBC, CNN, and Russian NTV) that were recorded via a satellite dish. During the war the Chechens learned about events in their own country from foreign sources, and, besides this often being their only source of information, they were anxious to know that their struggle and suffering were being seen by the outside world.

One tape contained the Islamist propaganda of jihad. In the first lengthy segment it recorded the ambush of April 1996 that destroyed a Russian armored column. The detachment that attacked the column was led by Khattab, the Jordanian Islamic internationalist who had previously fought in Afghanistan.[21] The commentary on the video was provided in Arabic by Khattab himself. Translated later by one of my Arab-American students, it proved to be a repetitive account of events occurring immediately after the battle: *Look how many tanks are destroyed. Allah gave us this victory. Allah is Great!* Curiously, Khattab was also filmed commu-nicating with the Chechens in rudimentary Russian. In the last segment the tape carried a medley of combat scenes: a Chechen machine-gunner firing at Russian helicopters; guerrillas marching along a mountain trail; burnt-out tanks and burning houses. The images were accompanied by Middle Eastern marching music that sounded markedly at variance with Chechen tastes. Together with the fact that Khattab's commentary was in Arabic, this made one suspect that the tape was probably part of the Islamists' fundraising propaganda intended for distribution abroad.

As I was preparing to pay for the whole video collection, a man from among the vendors tried to withhold one tape. He was cleanly shaven, which had now become a sign of modern sophistication, and was thus opposed to the rising tide of Islamic ideology. I bought the tape despite his claims that it didn't belong to him and he would never allow it to be watched in his house. The episodes filmed were extremely gruesome indeed: they included the trial and execution by firing squad of a Chechen teacher accused of collaborating with the Russian administration and the killing of captured Russian soldiers by slitting their throats with a dagger. It was claimed that the soldiers had committed atrocities. When this tape was first circulated in Chechnya during the war, it left many Chechens shocked, perplexed, and indignant. It was also cited in Russian war propaganda as proof of the enemy's savagery. However, among the less educated villagers, and especially among the unemployed rural youths who hardly attended school after 1991 and who bore the main brunt of the fighting, these gruesome scenes were apparently hailed as an appropriate act of retribution.

ELECTIONS

In the Chechnya of January 1997, the prevalent attitude towards Russia appeared conciliatory. It was expressed in the Chechen newspapers and campaign leaflets that I picked up at the improvised bazaars. Some of the most conciliatory remarks came from Shamil Basayev, who seemed understandably anxious to shed his reputation as a terrorist now that the elections gave him a chance of high state office. Two months later the newly elected president, Aslan Maskhadov, would appoint Basayev to head his cabinet in the hope of avoiding "the Afghanistan scenario." In doing so, Maskhadov hoped to placate his leading rival, who had gathered more than a quarter of the votes in the presidential race. But ultimately the barely educated Basayev showed himself embarrassingly inadequate as a statesman. He resigned in utter frustration and went over to the radical opposition. Until then the Chechen nationalist hardliners and the Islamic revivalists had only been a conspicuous presence on the fringe of the political sphere. In the Chechen elections of 1997, their candidates (Yandarbiyev and the likes) amassed barely 10 per cent of the vote in total. This figure seems an accurate expression of the contemporaneous Chechen attitudes. In contrast to elections in most post-Soviet countries, which are routinely marred by manipulation, apathy, and fraud, the Chechen elections were competently organized and enthusiastically attended by the voters.

The celebrity of the moment was the Swiss diplomat Tim Guldimann. Fluent in Russian, he was appointed as the OSCE mediator during the war and spent most of his time inside Chechnya.[22] Guldimann evidently belonged to the new generation of Swiss public servants who were inspired by the European ideology of international legal protection for human rights. Unexpectedly for a diplomat from a neutral country who is placed in the thick of a ferocious war, he proved a very stubborn negotiator. After the war's end it was Guldimann who raised the European funds and organized the electoral equipment and the teams of observers necessary to assure the legitimacy of the new president and parliament of Chechnya. His activism earned him many threats, and he became *persona non grata* on three different occasions: first, during the war, when the puppet Chechen regime installed by Russia was aggrieved at not being treated as an independent player; second, when he fell out with the Russian parliament dominated by the parties of Great Power nostalgia, like the neo-communists of Zyuganov or the fascists of Zhirinovsky; and lastly when the interim president of Chechnya, Zelimkhan Yandarbiyev, sensing the looming defeat at the ballot box, resorted in desperation to the radical Islamist argument that the Chechen elections would be better off without Western sponsorship and supervision. Yet clearly a majority of Chechens appreciated and admired the role of Guldimann. This was not so much for his assistance in helping them to choose their post-war leaders (59 per cent readily voted for the reserved and politically moderate chief commander Aslan Maskhadov, and had the refugees outside Chechnya been able to participate in the elections, the percentage surely would have been greater) but mainly because the active presence of the Swiss diplomat was regarded as confirmation of Europe's involvement in the future of Chechnya.

GENDER AND ISLAM

Chechen newspapers and TV broadcasts of winter 1997 reveal another political problem, one arising from a deep-seated tension in the field of gender relations. Scores of commentaries were devoted to the issues of polygamy and the abduction of young women for marriage. Both practices were often presented as the revival of age-old traditions. Yet from the conflict of opinions it became evident that these practices did not at all derive from the deep recesses of ancestral customs that had been repressed by the communist modernizers. They were clearly a manifestation of acute social instability.

The advocates of polygamy, among whom there were surprisingly many articulate middle-aged women, argued that in a society with so little social protection and so many widows the revival of the polygamous marriage offered women a more stable and dignified way to survive than they would enjoy through cohabiting illicitly – a practice common during the war. An additional argument was explicitly nationalist: women must bear more children after the devastation of a war which had taken the nation to the brink. Indeed there are many reports (but no reliable statistics) indicating that despite the extreme hardship, fertility had risen in recent years, at least among the rural Chechens. With so many men killed or missing, went the argument, the best way to ensure the legitimacy of new births was polygamy. Predictably, the religious authorities were supportive of such views; and besides, there existed strong precedents from only a generation earlier. During the Stalinist collectivization, and especially after the 1944 deportation of Chechens and Ingushes to Central Asia, Islamic practices were reconfigured to cater specifically for the numerous widows. In the early 1930s there appeared whole mosques attended solely by women and, after all the mosques were closed by the Soviet authorities, religious women switched to the secretive Sufi circles.

Nonetheless the opponents of polygamy – among whom there were also many articulate middle-aged women – loudly objected to the onset of "barbarism." They claimed that polygamy had never been a Chechen custom but rather belonged to the "Persian shahs and Turkish sultans." Polygamy was not entirely unknown in the past, but certainly it was very rare – mainly for economic reasons. The North Caucasian peasants were always poor and, besides, they had no social use for the harems. (For them, weapons were usually the most expensive possession and the hallmark of social status.)

As for marriages by abduction, a woman teacher appearing on Ingushetian TV formulated a plausible if depressing hypothesis. She claimed that while some abductions were probably conducted with the secret consent of the bride (as they had been for ages by those who wanted to avoid the huge expense of bridal gifts and weddings), still the majority of current abductions were pure lawlessness and rape. The problem was the growing cultural gap between the sexes. Many girls did better at school and tended to continue their education for longer, while many boys were encouraged neither by their social environment nor by their peers to be equally assiduous pupils. As a result, the young males knew nothing of the restraints and rituals of traditional courtship, lacked any modern manners, and possessed no notion of legality. She concluded with a stark question: *What should we all do about a generation containing so many uneducated and socially maladjusted brutes?* Being herself a product of the secular Soviet-era education system, she stopped there. But the next speaker on the program, a bearded man introduced as a teacher at the newly established Islamic University, outlined how the norms of *sharia* law might address such issues. His speech was calmly confident, competent and detailed in regard to the Islamic legal tradition, and therefore came across as fairly convincing.

In reality, except for a few male-dominated areas, like operating wildcat oil wells, maintaining satellite phones, selling videos, driving cars, or slaughtering animals at the butcher's stand, women seemed to be in charge of whatever economic activity remained in Chechnya. This was mostly a matter of subsistence and street trade. In Grozny the majority of market vendors were women bundled up in woolen kerchiefs selling ordinary goods: chewing gum, aspirin, pencils, roasted sunflower seeds, homemade snacks, cigarettes, imported bananas, and soft drinks.

No alcohol was on display, though a few vendors kept a case of beer or vodka hidden under the stall. Large, hastily painted signs warned in the still-official Russian: *Do Not Anger Allah, Stop Drinking!* The prohibition was an expression of a more popular Islamic revival that had arisen during the war out of the need for a greater internal solidarity and a measure of wartime discipline (the latter being also an act of cultural resistance meant to contrast with the behavior of the Russian invaders). But this development was far from uncontentious.

On the day prior to our visit to Freedom Square, we had lunched in a small, impeccably clean café adorned with ornate, crisply starched curtains and garlands of gaudy plastic flowers. A bearded old man had walked in and started to scold the woman who ran the café. She replied with an emotional diatribe, while making gestures at us. My local driver translated with a faint smile: *That was a mullah who demanded she close the café because the faithful must observe the fast during the holy month of Ramadan. But the woman is a tough cookie! A widow, you see. She told him to go away because her customers are not only Muslims and besides she has two kids and a disabled brother to feed.*

THE USES OF CLAN PROTECTION

Finding an acceptable driver with a car proved challenging after the train of global media had passed through town and hugely impressed the locals by paying them from fat bundles of hundred-dollar bills. The locals adapted to the suddenly booming market in a variety of ways: the educated ones offered themselves as inter-preters, consultants, or stringer reporters; the owners of good cars became chauffeurs, demanding fares far in excess of the cost of a limo ride in Manhattan, and similarly they charged extortionate fees to the guests in their homes. Soon it transpired that the Kalashnikov rifle was the trump card in this market, and now squads of bodyguards competed with robbers and hostage-takers for the purses of foreign journalists. My own adaptation was to dress inconspicuously and generally ride on buses like everyone else, hoping that the crowd's unpromising look and the loud cries of women might deter would-be assailants.

All the same, cars were more convenient and local drivers could double as interpreters.

Our driver was hired for a modest fee in neighboring Ingushetia. (Before 1991 Ingushetia was part of the joint Checheno-Ingushetia Autonomous Republic, and the languages of the Ingushes and the Chechens are close enough for them to understand each other.) The ride was arranged by a new-found Ingush friend of ours. Before 1991 our friend had obtained a diploma in history from the Checheno-Ingushetian University and freely admitted that he had hoped to become a communist party official. As it turned out, he had had to move in to a relative's rural house with twenty other people, half of them refugees from another conflict – the Ingush territorial dispute with North Ossetia. This urbanite was suffering acutely from the tedium and traditional regimentation of village life. For my sociological purposes, however, this fact made him a valuable informant capable of understanding matters on both sides of the urban–rural cultural divide. Early one morning we met at the taxi-rank in the marketplace. After a series of negotiations, our Ingush friend introduced us to a shy elderly man called uncle Muharbek and whispered in Russian: *I've never met him before but we talked a little and established that we belong to the same clan. So if … God forbid … well, you know … he bears responsibility for you as the guests of the clan. Our traditions are perhaps not much of a guarantee these days, but still better than nothing.*

The traditional clans, or perhaps more accurately patri-lineages, called by the Arabic term *taip* in Chechnya and Ingushetia, have been the subject of much speculation during the recent revolutions and wars. The romantic nationalists revived the old idea of a special "third way" towards modern democracy that would be pursued under the traditional clan governance. The Orientalist-minded elements in the Russian intelligence services and some journalists charted elaborate schemata outlining the clan influences that supposedly revealed the hidden springs of politics in the North Caucasus. Let me suggest instead a practical interpretation based on the two sociological concepts that in my opinion best describe the key functions of these clans.[23] First, they are repositories of collective reputations that are used as *social capital* within their ethnic communities. Second, the clans are *networks of trust* that are regularly invoked and activated in interactions beyond the immediate family circle of reciprocity.

But networks of trust can break down for many reasons, especially when times are hard. And besides, social capital is difficult to gauge, as it is surely not denominated in monetary units. North Caucasians commonly carry on lengthy conversations about the affairs of distant relatives, make teasing jokes regarding the worthiness of one's clan, or indulge in what seems to outsiders to be just brazen boasting. In fact, these rituals serve to establish the relative value of social capital inscribed in the clan names. The alumni of Harvard, Yale, or Northwestern

University routinely do much the same, and largely for the same purposes. The alumni networks, like the networks of highlander clans, offer the hope of finding one's way towards practical goals like securing a job, a business partner, or an acceptable bride. By the same token, clan networks can help in recruiting and evaluating young men of unknown quality into a guerrilla band.

Where no functioning police exist to enforce contracts, and no bureaucratically compiled files help in the assessment of applicants, clan reputation remains to guide judgment and build trust. It actually works – most of the time – because people are anxious not to damage their clan's reputation with some disreputable act for which they would have to face their own relatives in the first instance. But it works only imperfectly, because there exist competing forms of social capital and different types of trust network. In Soviet times they were provided by the bureaucracy; more recently, by Islamic fraternities and armed bands of fighters. Importantly, clans differ from tribes in lacking any formal authority or chieftain – they are really just extended families that can be directly observed, if at all, only at the most important weddings and funerals.

Our clan-issued security guarantee looked even flimsier after we learned that uncle Muharbek drove a wreck because his previous car had been taken away by armed Chechens. They had stopped him on the road to Daghestan: *Just like that! My car was commandeered for the national struggle, and I had to hitchhike back home.* Uncle Muharbek had bought his car with savings accumulated in the seventies and eighties, when he worked on the oilfields in Siberia. He had learned to be a driller and to speak fluent Russian in Kazakhstan, during the Stalin-era exile of the Chechen and Ingush peoples. His wife was an ethnic Ukrainian whose kulak family had been deported earlier in the thirties. She learned the Ingush language, but when I asked uncle Muharbek whether she also converted to Islam, he replied casually: *Who cares in a village where all the people know each other? My wife is with other women when help is needed, like at funerals or weddings, but she doesn't pray. It's the young folks who are into the faith now. Back in Soviet times, this was not a big issue.*

THE PROPAGANDIST

Over the wide avenue leading to Freedom Square hung a professionally executed and undoubtedly very expensive billboard that proclaimed in Russian: *Islamic Order, Vote for Movladi Udugov!* This formerly obscure local journalist and Minister of Information in Dudayev's separatist regime became the grandmaster of Chechen foreign propaganda during the recent war. His effectiveness was grudgingly recognized even by a top Russian general, who thought Udugov worth a tank regiment. The slogan of *Islamic Order* was a good example of his propagandistic effectiveness. These two very evocative words tied the Chechen's yearning for a safer, more normal life after the war together with that collective identity made salient by the resistance to the infidel Russians. Only Islamic government, insisted Udugov, could bring order, because the Chechens were too anarchistic to obey anyone but God. This was by far the most astute and articulate expression of the Islamic project in interwar Chechnya. Few outsiders, however, seemed to notice how surprisingly many Chechens held Udugov in unconcealed contempt.[24] In educated circles he was called a neo-fascist, or "baby Goebbels," and among the masses one commonly heard that Udugov was simply "not a good man."

Part of the explanation for this must lie in a social trauma he experienced at a young age. Udugov's birth is shrouded in an awkward mystery that hints at illegitimacy. The young Udugov was denied a share of his family's social capital and had to rely on himself alone. But in real life, unlike in some fiction, being orphaned does not necessarily produce humility and virtue. The people who knew Udugov during his student years say that he was a loner who never drank or dated a girl. Instead, his passion was for arguing all night long about topics ranging from philosophy to films and dissident politics. Prominent on his bookshelf were biographies of Julius Caesar, Napoleon, and Winston Churchill. During Gorbachev's perestroika he wrote, in Russian, for the emergent "informal" press where he played on the standard radical themes of the time: anti-bureaucratism, democratization, genuine socialism, ecology, the preservation of ethnic cultures.

Later, in the nineties, when Udugov became a well-funded Islamic ideologist and ran the famous website www.kavkaz.org, he still continued to write in a distinctly coarse and provincial Russian that bore the imprint of Soviet-era propaganda in grandiose titles like *The Fateful Struggle* or *Geopolitical Conflagration*. The different influences on this autodidact sometimes produced ironic effects, such as his quoting in the same paragraph from Gramsci on hegemony, Huntington's *Clash of Civilizations*, and *al-Quran*.

Restoring order in war-ravaged Chechnya was everybody's dream, but increasingly many people in the devastated land believed it would take something stronger than a state – a recovered traditional faith, perhaps – to bring back the social order. And yet, Ugdov's name masterfully attached to the slogan of *Islamic Order* was met with equally widespread skepticism. During the political campaign of 1997, Shamil Basayev joked publicly about Udugov's two wives and the champagne they drank on New Year's Eve. Basayev did not have to impersonate a religious man or a warrior – he was raised in a mountain village with strong traditions and had distinguished himself in the recent war. His strategy at the time was rather to project a more peaceful and Europeanized image, in the hope of becoming accepted as a worldly politician. But Udugov, who had spent the war talking to foreign journalists and visitors, clearly understood what it was that outsiders expected from the Chechens. Unpopular locally, his only hope in politics depended on foreign support, mainly from the Middle East. Later in 1997 Basayev himself would abandon in utter frustration the politics of national reconstruction and return to the guerrilla lifestyle. All this was justified in terms of radical Islamic ideology and supported by Middle Eastern advisors and sponsors. And in this Udugov's propagandist skills would prove indispensable once again.

THE TWISTED CAREERIST

Every now and then, waves of enthusiasm would ripple across the square. These were usually caused either by someone distributing campaign leaflets (which rapidly ran out), a group of activists beginning to chant slogans, or rumors that a celebrity guerrilla commander had arrived to address the crowd: perhaps one of the presidential favorites, Aslan Maskhadov or Shamil Basayev, or maybe the eloquent and handsome Ahmed Zakayev, who had once been an actor in Grozny's Drama Theater. In their place, however, there came the scandalous ultra-nationalist Salman Raduyev.

The *enfant terrible* of Chechen resistance arrived dressed in a bizarre uniform (decorated with what he claimed were the insignia of Gengis Khan), a black military beret reminiscent of Saddam, the checkered Arab *qufiya* kerchief around his neck, and with his face mostly obscured by a huge pair of sunglasses. Raduyev had a good reason to hide his face; it had been badly scarred by a bullet. Rumor had it that after suffering his head wound, Raduyev went mad, or at least developed an addiction to painkillers; but to many people his actions before being shot in the face did not look entirely rational either. The past of this emblematic figure warrants a little digging up, to reveal the twisted structures buried under the contemporary image of an implacable nationalist and self-avowed terrorist.

In earlier years Raduyev, who was born in 1967, had been an ascendant functionary in the Young Communist League (Komsomol).[25] He spent a year in Bulgaria studying the internal price incentives that were supposed to stimulate worker productivity in the Bulgarian agro-industrial combines. This personal trajectory pointed to a technocratic career in Soviet planning management (had such a structure continued to exist), or as an executive in the new private sector or possibly in multinational business. But things took a very different turn when, after 1991, Chechnya became a rebel enclave.

When in December 1994 President Yeltsin dispatched the regular army to "restore constitutional order" in Chechnya, Raduyev took advantage of his status as an educated man with family connections to become a second-tier commander in the Chechen guerrilla resistance. A year into the war, he led a risky foray across Chechnya's border into neighboring Daghestan where, under cover of night, they hoped to burn on the ground a squadron of Russian helicopters. The raid failed and, caught at dawn on the outskirts of a Daghestani town, Raduyev's detachment barricaded themselves inside the local hospital taking its patients and medical personnel hostage. This was clearly in emulation of Basayev's raid six months earlier. This time the Kremlin adamantly insisted on destroying the terrorists but was let down once again by the glaring inefficiency of its military machine. By some strange miracle, Raduyev's men eluded the Russian snipers and minefields and escaped into the mountains of Chechnya.[26] Dozens of Daghestani hostages perished.

Amidst the resulting scandal, recriminations, and the sacking of Russian generals, what escaped the attention of most commentators was the seminal change of attitude towards the Chechens among their Daghestani neighbors. Where they had expressed sympathy for the suffering of their fellow Caucasians, they now felt intense rage at the treacherous cruelty of Raduyev. This anger united the different ethnic groups of Daghestan in a rejection of the "Chechen way" that, by default, translated into an unlikely growth of loyalty towards the inefficient and generally aloof Russian state. This helps to explain the stiff, and totally unexpected, resistance offered by the Daghestanis in August 1999 against the self-styled "Islamic liberation expedition" launched by Shamil Basayev's private army together with religious internationalists from the Middle East.[27]

These feelings of rejection evidently activated the hidden tensions inherent in the several structural fault-lines running between the Chechens and their Daghestani neighbors: among them, the demographic expansion of the Chechens, who for several decades have had the highest birth rates in the region; the precarious distribution of power at the top of Daghestan's multi-ethnic polity and the corresponding distribution of livelihoods (land plots, trading privileges, lesser government sinecures) at the lower levels; and the tendency of Chechen warlords who emerged during the recent wars to forcefully monopolize the lucrative flow of contraband.[28] The emotions caused by Raduyev's fateful raid focused in local opinion these structural factors which changed the prevalent attitudes in Daghestan. But this remained unnoticed by many experts who discussed at great length the shades of Islamic identity or the merits of consociational democracy that supposedly saved multi-ethnic Daghestan from the fate of Chechnya.

The personal transformation of Salman Raduyev from rising technocrat into daredevil guerrilla and terrorist is perhaps not too surprising after all. Here in extreme conditions we observe the workings of the social mechanism that Bourdieu called "habitus": a set of durable dispositions normally shared within particular social classes and groups.[29] As the proverb goes, once a priest always a priest. Habitus pre-rationally structures our attitudes and behavior: you need not think twice, the reaction emerges naturally. In his Soviet life, Raduyev was a beginner careerist, and so he remained during the war. Like many such beginners, he was ambitious, insecure, and impatient. Hence the propensity to gamble on high-stakes projects, like a young stockbroker. "Winner takes all" is inscribed in this kind of careerist habitus. Recklessness in this case is the manifestation of inexperience in evaluating risks and the beginner's temptation to believe that there is little to lose while a lot might be gained. Raduyev was neither suicidal nor fanatical. Once his military operation failed, he changed tactics to follow the successful example of Basayev's hostage-taking. Indeed, he managed to survive and gain a considerable notoriety.[30] But Raduyev sacrificed human lives and inflicted long-term damage to the project of Chechen independence just as thoughtlessly as Stalin's ruthless young commissars mistreated the Ukrainian peasants during collectivization.

AN ISLAMIC PERFORMANCE

At the Grozny square where I saw Raduyev for the first and only time, the majority of people voted with their feet by moving away from the flatbed truck from which he was shouting through a loudhailer his trademark rambling and incendiary discourse of permanent war. Soon another group started an alternative rally at the opposite end of the square.

A boisterous crowd of villagers arrived in a battered bus, the village's name and patriotic slogans in Russian and Chechen proudly inscribed on its mud-covered sides. The group was led by elders dressed in the traditional *papaha* hats, sheepskin overcoats, and high riding boots. A few of them wore the traditional silver-clad daggers, the Caucasian *kinzhals*. Waving their canes in the air, the elders invited everybody to shout with them *Allahu Akbar!* – meaning in Arabic *God is Great* – an assertion that currently functions as the Chechen counterpart to the Russian battle-cry *Ura!* (*Hurray!*) After this warm-up, two separate circles of men and women dressed in identical folkloric costumes (probably borrowed from the stage wardrobes of the Soviet-era village Palaces of Culture) engaged the crowd in the spectacle.

Their dance, however, was not the sparkling *lezginka* made famous worldwide by the touring Caucasian and Cossack folklore ensembles. It was *zikr*, the vigorous stomping and clapping in circles traditionally performed by members of the mystical Sufi order of Qadiriya as a central element in their group rituals. The villagers were perfectly aware of their telegenic potential and chose to dance right in front of the TV cameras. Indeed the journalists became animated and began to film the zikrists, which produced an enthusiastic response: more patriotic slogans (in Russian, so that the visitors could understand) and louder stomping, which was directed at fellow Chechens, some of whom joined in the prayer.

Standing next to me was an ordinarily dressed middle-aged Chechen who, recognizing me as a visitor, commented with bitterness: *This was a cultured modern town, but the countryside overran us, and now foreigners come here as if they were coming to a zoo. Dudayev started all this. Before him, even in the villages* zikr *was never held in public squares.* In interviews, several leading participants in the 1991 Chechen revolution confirmed that *zikr* appeared at political rallies only after the return to Chechnya of General Dudayev, who had previously served as the commander of the Soviet air force base in Estonia. In all likelihood, Dudayev witnessed Estonian nationalist rallies where the participants roused themselves by singing folksongs in mighty choruses. In revolutionary Chechnya *zikr* was consciously reinvented for a similar function.

FINDING THE UNIVERSITY

My observations were ended by a group of Chechen fighters, all well armed, stern-looking, and dressed in dissimilar but impeccably pressed uniforms. Their leader demanded to know whether I was a journalist. I said that I was a sociologist, that is, a scholar. Sensing trouble, I forestalled further questions by asking, mostly to distract the guerrilla officer, if there was a university in Grozny. He spoke briskly to his men in Chechen, then turned to me and suggested that we drive there together. Later I guessed that these fighters must be the rally wardens or the new Chechen police. At that moment, however, their courtesy sounded ominous – as the epidemic of abductions had already started in Chechnya – but the offer could not be refused. The presence of two armed guides inside the car filled it with the smell of fresh gun grease and good cologne. They were certainly doing their best to project an image of disciplined soldiers.

We drove in tense silence. At one point we saw amidst the ruins a tasteless brand-new mansion of red brick, with kitsch columns and a big Chechen national flag hanging from the balcony. Nervously, I joked to our guides that this could be their equivalent of the party district committee headquarters. Unmoved, the Chechen officer replied: *No, it's the home of a rich businessman who now tries to show that he also took part in our struggle.* He paused and added unexpectedly: *You have rich people in Russia, and we have them too. It is your rich and our rich who arranged this war to launder their money.* The guerrilla fell silent again, refusing to elaborate on his version of class analysis.

After an hour of unavoidably slow driving on bombed streets, we found the gutted building that was once the university. Before the disintegration of the USSR Grozny was a town of more than half a million people and one of the region's major centers of higher education. Despite the Stalinist purges and the wholesale deportation of Chechens and Ingushes, which began in 1944 and lasted until 1957, a sizable national intelligentsia took root. Before the Soviet collapse and the war, Grozny boasted the Oil Polytechnic, a teachers' college, and the university. The ethnic Russian professors, implanted while the Chechens and Ingushes had been in exile, fought a pitched battle for their academic positions and privileges, to the considerable anguish of the aspiring native intellectuals. This protracted struggle generated a major current of local nationalism, albeit mostly in the liberal forms favored by the national professoriate. This elite strain of nationalism was mostly undone by radical and more popular currents of nationalism after the revolution of 1991. The Russian and Western press carried no indication that university life existed at all in Chechnya during and after the war of 1994–1996. But it did.

We found the university in a small building that looked like (and indeed once was) a typical Soviet-style kindergarten. Our silent guerrilla guide stared at me and asked unexpectedly: *Did you come to help the Republic?* I could only shrug uneasily and reply: *At least, I'll make sure that people abroad know that you have a university here and that it needs help.* The Chechen fighter saluted and said: *We thank you for doing this.* They turned around and walked back to their post in Freedom Square. As I write this, I cannot help recalling the opening line from the book by the Russian journalist Anna Politkovskaya: *Many of the people described and interviewed in this book have already been killed.*[31]

KABARDINO-BALKARIA

Nalchik, the capital of the Kabardino-Balkarian Republic, despite being a mere hundred kilometers away, was a world apart from Grozny, with its politicized main square, bombed-out streets, and the university lingering in a former kindergarten. By contrast, Nalchik remains a cozy, slow-paced provincial town where on the surface nothing betrays the fact that back in 1991–1992 Kabardino-Balkaria experienced a revolutionary situation closely approximating that of Chechnya. Both revolutions belonged to the same wave of contentious politics that arose in the wake of the Soviet collapse. The Chechen and the Kabardin national movements had overlapping programs, ideologies, and circles of leadership. They developed in parallel up to a critical point. And then their histories diverged.

In Chechnya the revolution had succeeded by October 1991 and continued to radicalize through the succession of post-revolutionary power struggles and coup attempts between 1992 and 1993, culminating in the incipient civil war of summer and autumn 1994. These events triggered the large-scale emigration that deprived Chechnya of the majority of what had once been a substantial educated urban population. It thus undermined the basis of the liberal and moderate nationalist oppositions to the regime of General Dudayev. The first Russian invasion of 1994–1996 caused tremendous destruction and nearly extinguished the remnants of urban culture. The Chechen reaction to the invasion generated an armed patriotic resistance that recruited primarily among young males from the marginal spaces of sprawling suburbs and from socially conservative mountainous villages. Their hero and chief example was Shamil Basayev.

The likes of Basayev exist in Kabardino-Balkaria too, and I met some of them. But they remain largely unknown elsewhere because in their small country the revolution subsided and there was no war. Kabardino-Balkaria continues to be a loyal part of the Russian Federation as one of its autonomous ethnic republics. One indicator of the state's capacity in Kabardino-Balkaria is the ability to compile statistics regarding the number of people and the extent of the territory in their jurisdiction. These data may look very basic, but notoriously no Chechen government during the last decade has been able to supply anything comparable. Nonetheless, as the University of Texas sociologist Cynthia Buckley warns us, current statistical data from Russia must be regarded as the product of contentious political processes, especially with regard to ethnic composition.[32]

Bearing this in mind, let us assume that it is not too far off the mark to say that Kabardino-Balkaria's total population of 786,000 people consists of an ethnic Kabardin majority (488,000), an important Balkar minority (90,000), and a remainder made up of mostly generic "Russian-speakers." This population is very unevenly distributed over a territory of 12,500 square kilometers that comprises gorgeous but virtually uninhabited snow-capped mountains, fertile valleys and foothills, and the capital city of Nalchik. Officially, the capital has 252,000 registered inhabitants, but we must allow for the existence of a substantial number of illegal migrants and add the populations of several big villages that have merged to become the city's outer suburbs. Like anywhere in the former USSR, nearly the entire adult population is literate in Russian and, as regards the Kabardin and Balkar nationalities, also in their native languages. Despite the post-Soviet depression the principal economic activities remain concentrated in the mining, chemical, and metal-working industries. Large-scale state farms continue to exist. Last but not least, tourism is an important economic sector, with the resorts specializing in mountaineering and skiing, as well as the famous mineral spas.[33]

STATE ORDER

One indicator of the stability in Kabardino-Balkaria is found in the ubiquitous presence of uniformed and often heavily armed police. On the highway approaching Nalchik our driver, a native Adyghei, was stopped for speeding. He jumped out of the car and engaged the policeman in a cordial conversation conducted in the native language. (The closely related Adyghei and Kabardin languages belong to the Adyghe–Abkhazian lingusitic group, or what is commonly called the Circassian peoples.) But our driver's expression soon turned sour. He had to pay a fine and, in a rarely observed formality, even got a receipt. Returning to the car, the driver muttered: *Damned disciplinarian! He isn't one of ours. Must be one of those Balkars.*

Indeed, the Balkarian language belongs to the Qypchak group of the Turkic family. It is a mystery how the native tongue of medieval steppe nomads spread into the highest mountains, where it is spoken by modern people who do not at all resemble the Mongoloid Huns but actually look like their Kabardin or Chechen neighbors. Yet the fact is that a Balkar would not understand a Circassian language. What we witnessed was bureaucratic formality overriding an ethnic solidarity that our driver had mistakenly assumed would take precedence. And in the same episode we also saw a tiny grain of group hostility. It may have been swept away as our driver left behind his little mishap. Or the grain could have been caught up in the winds of political confrontation and added to the storm of ethnic conflict.

Another indicator of Nalchik's stability is the cleanliness of its central boulevards and squares, which are lined with neatly groomed shrubs and trees. The downtown area is dominated by typically Stalinist buildings in pseudo-classical style; but since most such buildings are quite small they do not look as graceless or imposing as they do elsewhere in the capitals of the former Soviet bloc. Ubiquitous prefabricated highrises clutter the modern residential areas; while on the outskirts the town becomes barely distinguishable from a village, consisting of haphazard stretches of privately built one- or two-story homes made of prestigious brick or else of the much cheaper cinderblocks, and even the traditional adobe. Typically such homes stand hidden behind iron gates, tall fences, and fruit trees. The tripartite pattern of the town's architecture closely corresponds to the distribution of its social groups: the ruling bureaucracy is entrenched in the grand Stalinist buildings; specialists and proletarians live in the highrises mass-produced during the 1960s and 1970s; while the semi-rural suburbs are occupied by sub-proletarian dwellers who arrived from the villages but never quite made it into the town.

Finally, perhaps the most telling indicator of what kind of regime holds power in the country was that there seemed to be no alternative whatsoever to the official local press. Following the election of January 1997, the newspapers of Kabardino-Balkaria were, in the best Soviet tradition, filled solely with a stream of loyal congratulations from working collectives, students, prominent national intellectuals (some based as far away as New York), whole police stations, or else signed simply from "mothers." These ritual messages were directed to Kabardino-Balkaria's President (and formerly the Chairman of the Supreme Soviet) Mr. Valeri Kokov on the occasion of his re-election, achieved with nearly 98 per cent of the vote. In the new post-Soviet epoch this figure looked like a dubious overachievement. Even his opponents, however, grudgingly acknowledged that the incumbent's victory was mostly genuine. After the tumult, the high hopes, and the fears of the revolutionary situation experienced by Kabardino-Balkaria in 1991–1992, the people had grown bitterly disillusioned and weary of anticipating catastrophe – the disastrous examples of Chechnya and Abkhazia being only next door.

Like many other Russian governors of the 1990s, Kokov forged extended networks of paternalistic dependency that all hinged on his maintaining office. This proved enough to re-establish his power and maintain a superficial order, though barely enough to keep the country's aging industries running, let alone to restructure them. In fact, the majority of the people were struggling to survive. Chickens were kept on the balconies of highrises, and in a far corner of a public park we spotted grazing cows. Kokov's return to normalcy, after all, did not mean a normal life, just a reduced semblance of the Brezhnev era.

The political opposition in Kabardino-Balkaria was clearly defeated. Its frustration at Kokov's continued domination was vented mostly through private conversations among intellectuals and through isolated acts ascribed to "young hot-heads." The night before our arrival in Nalchik a hand-grenade was thrown through the basement window of an official building. We also heard of a bomb planted in the town's central square at the feet of the statue of the medieval Kabardin princess Goshanei, a major local landmark. Back in 1561 she was baptized Maria and given in dynastic marriage to the Russian Tsar Ivan the Terrible. In 1961, four centuries later, the Soviet propagandists retrospectively proclaimed this event the "birth of the eternal bond between Russia and the North Caucasus" and the Circassian-Russian Tsarina Maria became the "mother of friendship among the peoples."[34] So it was that her statue became the target of regular desecration by the local nationalists – and no less regularly Nalchik's city authorities cleaned or, it is rumored, secretly replaced, the damaged monument. After the fearsome outbreak in 1991–1992, nationalist politics in Kabardino-Balkaria had been reduced to brouhaha.

ENNOBLING RITUALS

Colleagues at Kabardino-Balkarian University cordially inquired if we would like to be introduced to the local celebrity from the political opposition: Musa Shanibov, President of the Confederation of Mountain Peoples of the Caucasus. This was the pan-nationalist movement that in the early nineties produced a great stir across the region. While we awaited Shanibov's arrival, a table in the faculty lounge was set for an improvised banquet in accordance with the lofty traditions of highlander hospitality.

Kabardin ethnic culture bears a strong imprint of its aristocratic past. (Between the end of the Tataro-Mongol Golden Horde in the 1390s and the Russian conquest in the 1800s, the Kabardins were the knightly elite tribe providing protection and collecting rents from other peoples of the North Caucasus such as Balkars, Ossetins, Ingushes, and Chechens.) Generally in the Caucasus, amidst all the signs of profound Sovietization, guests are treated like royalty, with charming and embarrassingly exaggerated deference, and one cannot help noticing that the hosts behave with a nobility of manners rarely displayed among ordinary Russians. Not that many Kabardin people are the scions of noble dynasties (though a few may indeed be such survivors). Rather, after the annihilation of the historical aristocracy during the Bolshevik revolution and the Soviet transformation of society, elements of aristocratic etiquette were appropriated and perpetuated by the descendants of commoners. They used them to familiarize and structure their new urban existence, to reconstruct networks of extended friendship, and to add a socially elevating native cultural twist to their newly acquired roles in a modern industrial environment. It was one way in which the Caucasians could adapt to and resist the harsh conditions of Soviet proletarianization.

In the Caucasus, banquets are a ubiquitous social ritual. Caucasians observe elaborate rules regarding seating arrangements and colorful toasting, serve special food and drink, and elect a person, called *tamada*, to preside over the event. (Shanibov's exact title in the Mountain Confederation was not president but rather *tamada,* implying a virtual fraternal feast of the indigenous peoples.) Conducting fieldwork in the Caucasus, at least if the researcher happens to be male, requires the ability to hold one's alcohol. In Muslim areas of the Caucasus local opinion allows for the consumption of vodka, ostensibly because distillation, unlike the brewing of wine, was not yet known back in the time of the Prophet and so it could not have been prohibited. For the emergent minority of Islamic purists, of course, this excuse is an abomination, and they place the blame squarely on the corrupting Russian influence. This tension pointedly illustrates how fundamentalism is the opposite of traditionalism. It is in fact a criticism of existing traditional adaptations and social hierarchies for the sake of an idealized normative purity and egalitarianism found in the literalist interpretation of holy writ. Although fundamentalism is often presented as ultra-orthodoxy, in the field of religion its oppositional stance is rather heretical.[35]

The faculty lounge, however, was an unlikely place to encounter Islamic purists, who belonged mostly to the younger generation and socially marginal groups. Only one junior professor, while politely serving vodka to the guests and senior colleagues, markedly abstained from drinking or eating. Turning to me, a senior professor whispered with a tinge of sarcasm: *Please, never mind this poor soul, he has recently discovered God and started fasting during the month of Ramadan.* Later I learned that the same junior professor was formerly the university's Komsomol secretary.

Given the improvised nature of the banquet and the pervasive economic hardship, our treat consisted of the homemade cheese and meat pies that were sold at the university's entrance by elderly women trying to supplement their pensions. The drinks were poured from a large bottle of locally made vodka. It came from a case donated to the history department by a former student who had now become a prosperous bootlegger. Such little gifts from alumni and the parents of students stand somewhere between charity and bribe. They meet the needs of professors while, surely, they might help a not too studious younger relative to get a minimal passing grade.

The exchange of favors plays a prominent role everywhere in the provincial towns of Russia.[36] In the Caucasus this type of social relationship is especially pronounced due to the traditional solidarities of ethnicity, extended kinship, peer group, and neighborhood. An individual in a Caucasian town like Nalchik seems to know and regularly interact with many more people than an individual living in a big and socially atomized town like Moscow. The sentiments and rituals of shared living in a small town serve to maintain extensive networks running very far in many directions. This is an important observation for our purposes, as we come to examine how the networks of daily life can help but also hinder political mobilization. These networks are indeed channels, rather than causes in themselves. They can extend over ethnic and religious divides in a period of economic expansion – as the decades from the fifties to the seventies were for the USSR – and then break down, becoming barriers between communities based on ethnicity and social class.

SHANIBOV, FIRST ENCOUNTER

At last, enter Musa Shanibov, a stocky and very quick-moving man in his early sixties who immediately filled the room with his charismatic presence. Following him came a large somber man, evidently his bodyguard. The latter did not look like an intellectual (in fact, he turned out to be a construction foreman), but wore a long beard as a sign of Muslim piety. By contrast, Shanibov sported a stylish leather trench-coat and an expensive silvery-gray *papaha*. In the faculty lounge this costume looked a bit eccentric. When a senior professor jokingly asked why he dressed like a mountain shepherd, Shanibov merrily retorted that he was inventing the national tradition. At the time it seemed to me a purely coincidental echo of the famous book title.[37]

With a hearty laugh, Shanibov proceeded to regale us with one of his favorite anecdotes: *In Ankara, at the entrance to their Ministry of Defense, the young lieutenant on duty demanded that I take off my* papaha *because Turkey is a secular republic where Muslim head-dress is banned by law. Of course, I refused, saying that I am not a Turk and this is a* papaha*, not a fez. We, the Kabardin Circassians, did not take off our hats even for the Russian tsars! It took a Turkish general to come downstairs and restrain the angry lieutenant. Thus I became the first man ever since the times of Atatürk to enter Turkey's Ministry of Defense wearing a* papaha, *this very one.* The faculty laughed and nodded in approval of the story. Of course, it also served to underline Shanibov's exceptional status and unusual connections.

On Shanibov's arrival the banquet acquired the tone of a political rally. With a glass of vodka in hand, he spoke endlessly and grandiloquently about national pride, the base imperial mentality, self-determination, the pan-ethnic solidarity of the Caucasian highlanders, past sacrifices, and future challenges. Time and again I was defeated in my attempts to shift his discourse to something more specific, such as local politics, the attempted revolution of 1991–1992, or Abkhazia's war against

Georgia. We were already five hours and two dozen toasts into the feast when, trying to ask another question, I blurted out the words "cultural field." Shanibov's reaction was astonishing. He reached across the table to hug me: *Our dear guest! My Armenian brother! Now I see that you are not a spy – forgive our confusion, but you seemed to know too much about local affairs, and my security could not figure out whether you worked for the CIA because you came from America, or for the Russian FSB because you and your companion are from Russia. But now I clearly recognize in you a genuine sociologist, for you are knowledgeable about the work of Pierre Bourdieu!* (So, the long drinking session was a charade intended to sound me out for possible hidden intentions.)

I fell into my seat: *And YOU?*

Me?! – exclaimed Shanibov: *But of course! Bourdieu's* Nachala [the 1994 Russian translation of *Choses Dites*] *became the second most important book in my life after the* Holy Quran. *I studied it in my hospital bed when I was recovering from a wound received in Abkhazia.*

Shanibov dragged us one flight downstairs to his tiny office behind a steel-reinforced door. Sure enough, in his more peaceful capacity our exotically dressed host was professor of social studies at the same Kabardino-Balkarian University. He unlocked his safe and produced the proof: a worn-out copy of Bourdieu's book with Shanibov's underlining and scribbling all over it. In the safe I spotted a different kind of document: a photograph of Shanibov in the company of bearded guerrillas, one of them clearly the Chechen, Shamil Basayev. Noticing my gaze, Shanibov said: *Ah, yes, that's him, Shamil, during the Abkhazian war.* And then he added after a pause: *In those days when Shamil still took my orders.*

When I asked if I could take my own photo of him, Shanibov agreed, but suddenly suggested: *When you return to the West, please, show this picture to Bourdieu and tell him how greatly we appreciate his work here.* I had to admit that I was returning to America rather than France, and that I was not acquainted with Bourdieu. Shanibov insisted nonetheless.

THE CONVERSION OF SOCIAL CAPITAL

However unlikely it may seem, the discovery of Shanibov's other life and identity was not really so surprising. All over the Caucasus, as in Central Asia and the former Yugoslavia, we can find many intellectuals among the recent generation of revolutionary leaders and ethnic warlords.

In Georgia, the Shakespearean scholar Zviad Gamsakhurdia became President in 1990, and was soon overthrown by the modernist sculptor Tenghiz Kitovani and the film critic Djaba Ioseliani; the leaders of the 1992–1993 revolutionary regime in Azerbaijan came entirely from the national Academy of Sciences; Armenia's President Levon Ter-Petrosian was previously a keeper of medieval manuscripts, and his dreaded police chief Vano Siradeghian used to write children's stories; Abkhazia was led to war by an erstwhile student of proto-Hittite mythology, Dr. Vladislav Ardzinba.

Intellectualism *per se* is not the explanation. The tendency to bring to post-communist politics different forms of social capital accumulated during a previous career is also evident in the examples of five military generals who stormed into the leadership of the North Caucasus nationalist mobilizations: the Chechen Dudayev; the Ingush Aushev; the Balkar Beppayev; the Karachai Semionov; and the Daghestani Tolboyev, who was previously a Soviet cosmonaut and eventually returned to his original vocation to manage the Russian space industry. (And if you believe that the tendency is found solely in post-Soviet lands, think of Arnold Schwarzenegger.)

The same principle holds for the charismatic businessmen of the post-Soviet era who fought and bought their way into high office: the underground millionaire and scion of a local princely dynasty, Aslan Abashidze in Adjaria (a Georgian Muslim autonomy that has important structural parallels to Bosnia that will be briefly discussed in Chapter Seven); Süret Husseinov, the son of a black-market carpet dealer and himself a major drugs and weapons smuggler before briefly becoming the counter-revolutionary Premier of Azerbaijan in 1993; the accused money-launderer Kirsan Ilyumzhinov of Khalm Tangchi (otherwise called Kalmykia), who is the first ruler in Europe to proclaim Buddhism the state religion; the Cherkess vodka capitalist, Stanislav Derev; and the Siberian gold moghul, Hazret Sovmen, now ruling in his native Adygheia.

Shanibov's biography clearly follows a trajectory that, in recent decades, has been traced by many intellectuals in Eastern Europe and many countries of the Third World. Elsewhere in the places where post-communist democratization was sustained, we also find in the political leadership filmmakers, musicians, and scholars. Why then wouldn't a critical sociologist like Shanibov rather become a dissident intellectual and champion of democratization, like the Czech playwright Havel or the Russian scientist Sakharov?

In fact, since 1968, Shanibov has actually been the closest approximation to a dissident intellectual in his small homeland. In the 1980s, during Gorbachev's pere-stroika, he earnestly emulated Sakharov. Shanibov turned to radical nationalism only *after* the breakdown of the Soviet state – that is, not before all hope of democrati-zation and the USSR's honorable incorporation into Europe was lost and there ensued a myriad of local conflicts over the spoils of the defunct empire. This connects the story of Musa Shanibov to our main question, why and how did the end of Soviet developmentalism produce ethnic violence?

FIRST SUMMARY

Let us then attempt to draw together the various observations and situations covered thus far. In Kabardino-Balkaria, a subsidiary unit of the Russian Federation, the people have to figure out how to live with the thinly disguised authoritarian regime of restoration. A new but very familiar regime draws its resources mainly from Moscow and its legitimacy rests on maintaining a semblance of old Soviet-style order. But in the nineties the Kabardino-Balkarian bi-national state patently failed to restore the Soviet-era levels of consumption and socioeconomic stability. Furthermore this regime cannot and probably does not wish to move towards some degree of capitalist efficiency and economic dynamism. With every year it seems increasingly less plausible to consider this sort of "neo-sultanistic" regime merely transitional – an unfortunate but unavoidable and hopefully temporary way-station on the ascending historic road towards something better and more Western. It is apparently a fully formed species that has carved its own niche, and it looks there to stay. Indeed, Putin's Moscow is content, as was Yeltsin's, with the state of affairs in Kabardino-Balkaria, hoping that a similar regime can be built in Chechnya in the aftermath of Russia's brutal counter-terrorist operation.

In contrast to Kabardino-Balkaria then, in rebellious Chechnya, the people are trying to figure out how to live after the old state and its Soviet-style order have collapsed altogether. The Chechens suddenly found themselves literally amidst the ruins, which forced them to decide where to place their hopes of survival: in the traditional micro-solidarities of extended family and clan; in the nationalist project of seeking an independent state; in the forceful and eschatological promises of religious fundamentalism that would putatively bring Chechnya into the transnational Islamic community; or in some uncertain combination of all three strategies.

Two other pathways are notably absent from this list, despite the fact that they might in other circumstances be the first choices for sizable sectors of the Chechen population, especially the urban educated classes and those now middle-aged people who in Soviet times enjoyed a stable income and lifestyle. First, Chechnya cannot go back to a refashioned version of the old Soviet order, now that this has been horribly discredited by the Russian invaders. The last communist First Secretary of Checheno-Ingushetia, Doku Zavgayev, who was overthrown in the 1991 revolution, was led back into Grozny in 1995–1996 by Russian troops. Together with Beslan Gantamirov, the rogue Soviet policeman, erstwhile revolutionary, turned warlord and Russian mercenary, Zavgayev produced a grotesquely corrupt and quarrelsome regime of restoration. Moscow eventually had to put Gantamirov behind bars for embezzlement (released in 1999 he became once again a key mercenary in the second invasion of Chechnya). The hapless Zavgayev was sent for his own safety to Tanzania as the Russian ambassador.

The second historical prospect, and likely the most attractive to a great many Chechens, would be some form of beneficial integration into the world economy and the European order, as personified by the relentless Tim Guldimann. Yet this prospect seemed to grow ever more distant during the nineties as the country came to be dominated by the thousands of unemployed and scarcely educated young Chechen males who had acquired guns, the skills and dispositions of professional warriors, and an elevated perception of themselves as the heroic defenders of the nation and the Islamic faith. And besides, as a Russian journalist friend observed bitterly: *What sort of foreign capitalist would like to invest in a country where the presidential staff must run into the ruins behind their offices to answer the call of nature?*

We have so far looked at snapshots of current realities in the sites of our investigation, and formulated a few preliminary questions. In later chapters, we shall trace the main lines of Soviet transformations through the prism of Shanibov's biography as it developed in the changing macro-context from the apex of Soviet experience in the 1950s and 1960s to the breakdown of 1989–1992, which unexpectedly turned Shanibov into a nationalist guerrilla fighter. But before we engage in this retrospective enterprise, let us look at a different snapshot of contemporary reality. The following chapter attempts to describe what is happening now in the field of social science and how current intellectual developments may help us form an understanding of social developments in regions such as the North Caucasus.

2

Complex Triangulations

"The history of any entity (a group, an institution, an evolutionary lineage) must be tracked by changes in the variation of all its components – the full house of their entirety – and not falsely epitomized as a single item (either an abstraction like a mean value, or a supposedly typical example) moving in a linear pathway."

Stephen Jay Gould, *Full House: The Spread of Excellence from Plato to Darwin*
(New York: Three Rivers Press, 1996, pp. 72–73)

Our next task is to select the appropriate analytical tools to help us to make sense of the empirical ground-level phenomena introduced in the previous chapter. Of course, in the preceding ethnographic descriptions and interpretative digressions I have already inevitably alluded to a number of theoretical concepts. This is not surprising, since, as Randall Collins observes, we cannot describe particulars without using abstract categories that already presuppose a considerable degree of generalization.[1] My aim here is to explain where these concepts come from and to introduce a range of theoretical ideas that may be of use as we attempt to untangle the story of Shanibov in relation to its historical horizons.

A SKETCH OF A THEORETICAL STRATEGY

Firstly, in our analysis of states, revolutions, and counter-revolutions, we shall draw on the work of Charles Tilly, Theda Skocpol, and their numerous collaborators and fellow theorists. Secondly, in order to explain how different categories of people construe their cultural understandings and act on them in changing historical circumstances, we shall be using Pierre Bourdieu's notions of field, social capital, trajectory, and habitus. Thirdly – since it is clear that neither Chechnya nor Kabardino-Balkaria can be understood in isolation from the rest of the former Soviet bloc, from the insurgent Islamic trends of the Middle East, or from the Western capitalist core – we will need to situate the objects of our discussion on the broad plane of world-systems analysis as outlined by Immanuel Wallerstein and Giovanni Arrighi.

Names like Bourdieu, Tilly, and Wallerstein are emblematic of whole schools of social analysis that have developed in splendid isolation from each other, and which are the focus of distinct intellectual sectors.[2] Their differences of approach and empirical focus are indeed significant. Yet these differences between the three projects, I will argue here, disguise their common origins in the big debates of the sixties and early seventies and their shared epistemological thrust towards the pursuit of variation and interrelatedness within whole systems of social relations, whatever each school might consider a system to be.[3] In their shared epistemological foundations we find the theoretical possibility of meshing in mutually reinforcing ways the insights of these otherwise different analyses.

Social science of any kind can only discuss, indeed may only notice, what it is theoretically equipped to observe. The phenomena and connections that fall outside of this focus may escape detection altogether or be relegated to the margins, to categories where they are either taken for granted or considered redundant. It is somewhat like observing the physical universe with devices attuned to different wavelengths: one device captures the visible parts of the spectrum, another the X-rays. This metaphor, however, is very incomplete, because the diversity of theoretical positions in social science is not merely instrumental. It is, rather, a highly contentious and competitive diversity. Different theoretical positions correspond to fundamental epistemological choices regarding how we gain and verify our knowledge about the world. In the end (or perhaps rather in the beginning), such choices are related to the political and social dispositions of scholars. That is why some of the most emotional polemics among social scientists arise over matters of epistemology and scholarly style.

The competitive diversity here is closely related to the guild-like organization of modern social science, which is conducted by large numbers of professional scholars who are based mainly in Western research universities. This historically unprecedented situation predictably engenders what Randall Collins (here in his capacity as a sociologist of academic production) has called the "trade-union ideology" of modern scholarly enterprise, which concentrates on protecting highly specialized academic "manual labor" activities such as the collection and quantification of large data-sets, and the analysis of primary sources gathered in archives, surveys, or oral interviews. It is a situation analogous to the Hollywood union rules that prohibit anyone but a carpenter from picking up a hammer on a movie set.[4] In this context, attempts at synthesis may then be suspected of "intellectual imperialism," or else charged with superficiality. Let me be clear – I am not against the labors of data gathering and rigorous standards of analysis. I do make an attempt to engage in field research wherever possible, as the previous chapter indicates, and I also spend a lot of time in libraries and archives. But the self-encapsulation of social sciences into a seemingly infinite number of niches is no less a concern than was the tendency of Soviet nomenklatura to build closed bailiwicks, and in the long run it may prove to be as disastrous.

When they first arrived on the scene, the far-reaching and ambitious formulations of Bourdieu and Wallerstein sparked widespread controversies. There were accusations of insufficient scholarly rigor, and their ideas were dismissed as "fads" precisely because they overtly violated established professional divides and conventions. Thus they also endangered, if indirectly, many scholarly niches and livelihoods. The pioneering work of Tilly was regarded as less controversial, mainly because it developed as a sub-discipline within sociology – where it displaced a rapidly receding academic Marxism that had previously held a near monopoly in the analysis of the state – and also because Tilly deliberately used "state-building" and "contention" as his key words instead of simply speaking of "politics." This smart camouflage averted a counter-attack from the ramparts of political science. It seems doubtful, however, that this mutual avoidance can last for much longer, as the research agenda inspired by Tilly continues to develop into an alternative to mainstream political science.

However abstruse and theological the epistemic polemics among scholars might sound to the layperson, the subject matter is indeed vital to defining and legitimating one's professional and intellectual identity. Any professionalized academia, whether an art guild or the tightly interwoven and formidably institutionalized American disciplines of social science, expects its members to define themselves and compete within the currently recognized specializations. Against this deter-mining principle, the multiplicity of scholarly languages and concepts appears almost dangerous. A fairly common defense is to hide behind the label of eclecti-cism. As a strategy, this seemed to me neither very effective nor satisfactory, as I could not help recalling the bitterly ironic anecdote recorded in 1930 by the great Soviet satirist Iliya Ilf. Confronted by the Stalinist purge committee, an intellectual is forced to confess that he is an eclectic rather than a "rock-solid Marxist." A compassionate purger – the year still being 1930 – jumps in: *Wait, do you really think that eclecticism is good?* The victim agrees that evidently it is no good, and the purge committee writes down its merciful conclusion: *An eclectic, but regards eclecticism negatively.*[5]

THE GOLDEN AGE OF HISTORICAL SOCIOLOGY

Today it might be possible to move beyond a superficial eclecticism and strive for a genuine synthesis. It is too early to attempt such a synthesis in any abstract theoretical form – this goal must be achieved in an open dialogue between researchers steeped in different schools of analysis. Perhaps this process may lead to what Bourdieu intended by the "construction of the collective intellec-tual," or what Wallerstein calls, in his more structural-institutionalist fashion, a "publicly relevant historical social science" (notably in the singular: not sciences but the trans- or even uni-disciplinary science concerned with the historical evolu-tion of social environments).[6] Such a grandiosely optimistic statement may seem counterintuitive at the present time. The generally conservative atmosphere of the late eighties and nineties significantly narrowed the range of admissible "mainstream" positions in all fields of intellectual production, from cinema to social sciences. Such "end of history" situations usually favored formalistic tech-nical scholasticism and other lesser concerns.[7] Yet in the long run Randall Collins may be proved correct in considering our times the "golden age of macrohistor-ical sociology."[8]

Collins describes a series of intellectual breakthroughs occurring in parallel and whose sum may amount to a scientific revolution. The intellectual shift he identi-fies originated in the iconoclastic atmosphere of the late sixties,[9] when the contemporary Zeitgeist of "questioning Authority" suddenly opened up new or long-repressed political and intellectual issues and produced multiple reactions. It is a common analytical pitfall to reduce the chaotic complexity of the sixties to the confrontation between a stolid establishment and an insurgent New Left, for it was much more than that. The dikes burst and waters flowed in multiple streams, turbulent and often very muddy. The simultaneous crises of the bureaucratic and paternalistic establishments of the West, the communist East, and the "developing" South, no less served to unleash irrationalist movements such as the California-style new spiritualism or the militant fundamentalism that register in all historical religions. But the crises of bureaucratic regulationism also freed a neoliberal agenda based on a previously dormant nineteenth-century utilitarianist faith in the rationality of self-regulating markets and the calculating capitalist entrepreneur. It is worth remembering – and not for the sake of historical irony alone – that around 1968 Pierre Bourdieu was widely suspected of elitist conservatism, while Immanuel Wallerstein was considered something of a traitor by many radicals – at the same time as being accused of being too academic, insufficiently Marxist, negligent of gender and race identities, or, from the other side, too Marxist and anti-systemic. It takes time to appreciate the relative weights of innovation in the realm of ideas.

In problematizing the fixed ideological duality of the Cold War, the confrontations of the sixties provided the enabling condition for a multitude of innovations. Contrary to common opinion, the Cold War confrontation between the defenders of capitalism and those of a putatively socialist alternative dated back not merely to 1945, or even 1917, but as far back as the European revolutions of 1848. Two principal structures of knowledge crystallized during the mid-nineteenth century.[10] First, secular science attained ascendancy over religious transcendental "belief systems" as the dominant mode of human understanding. Second, out of the revolutionary struggles of the time, there emerged the binary opposition of "bourgeois" liberal ideology and its "proletarian" Marxist nemesis. Both ideologies were informed by the scientific optimism of their epoch and the quest to discover the deterministic laws of a "social physics" in order to advance human progress. Both camps were explicit and proud in declaring this commitment. While they thus shared the same fundamental premises, they were of course loath to recognize it.

For our purposes we need to consider only one, albeit major, underlying element of the liberal–Marxist consensus: the identification of a unilinear historical progression moving through objectively existing stages of development.[11] Specifics like the exact number of stages and their most appropriate labels could vary greatly – which produced many notoriously protracted and convoluted debates on "modes of production" or "stages of development" (the current debates on globalization being, of course, their latest incarnation). But the underlying assumption nonetheless remained the same: all countries were moving, albeit at different speeds, along the same evolutionary ladder leading towards the final stage of perfection, which would be the end of history, whether in liberal society or in communism.

This organizing and generating structure imposed a choice between two and only two powerful camps. Their visible and loudly affirmed differences of politics and analysis concentrated on debates over how the final stage of perfection might be achieved, what it should look like, and how contemporary political struggles should be reflected upon in light of it. The contentious duality of ideologies was conducive to the production of all-encompassing orthodox formulations. On both sides, such formulations appeared and became institutionalized for the most part between the 1890s and the 1930s, reaching their peak of prestige and coherence in the aftermath of 1945. As Bourdieu observed, the strongest orthodoxy does not come in one but usually in two varieties, in the presumed antinomy of mutually exclusive positions.[12] This dual ideological structure exercised a powerfully disciplinary effect on social scientific thinking about the world, not least because abandoning one camp almost automatically meant defecting to the other, with all the attendant accusations, personal dramas, and rituals of apostasy and conversion. While not inhibiting intellectual innovation entirely, this situation nonetheless channeled creativity towards canonical forms and topics. The ideological blockage remained in place until the moment that both sides of the nineteenth-century paradigm experienced a crisis simultaneously, which is what had happened in the sixties. At this point, the momentous turmoil in the dominant fields of power and ideology entailed manifold changes in dominated fields such as academia and cultural production.

The initial response in the existing social sciences took the form of a variety of efforts to recover original pre-orthodox formulations from canonical texts. Hence the popularity of various versions of neo-Marxism, neo-Weberianism, and neo-evolutionism, as well as the rise of neo-conservatism in economics and political philosophy – eventually mislabeled as neo-liberalism when it moved from the fringes to dominate the mainstream. Since many of the new trails quickly went cold or turned back on themselves, towards the early eighties the prefix *neo-* was abandoned and replaced by *post-*, as in post-structuralism and post-modernism. By no means all of the previously existing orthodox formulations became extinct. Many of them continued, albeit often in a refashioned form. For instance, the structural functionalism of the forties and fifties re-emerged in contemporary neo-institutionalism, while the traditional ideas of *Realpolitik* were recast as neo-realism in the sub-field of international relations (and in the process of academic formalization many of the subtleties of the old Great Power thinking were lost).

Nonetheless, several splinter movements that dated back to the debates of the sixties subsequently developed to produce theoretical breakthroughs. From here originates Collins's optimistic "Golden Age," which has the potential to revolutionize our understanding of the social world. But to realize that potential requires an effort to identify the routes towards a new synthesis and to work consciously and collectively to bridge the gaps – which are sometimes quite imaginary – between the different schools of thought.

Many if not the majority of sustained theoretical breakthroughs occurred in sociology. This was no doubt in part due to what Andrew Abbott calls the "interstitial" nature of sociology, which helped the discipline maintain an internal diversity while preventing it from acquiring a rigidly defined niche among the other social sciences.[13] Sociology has always found itself to be more peripheral in relation to the field of power than has political science or, more especially, economics. By the same token, sociology remains more open to patronage and influence by various social movements, from socialist currents to feminism and ecology (some branches of the discipline obviously more susceptible to this than others). This positional ambiguity is apparent in sociology's canon of classics, which absorbed a variety of pioneers in the analysis of capitalism, beginning with the founding trinity of Marx–Weber–Durkheim, and followed by lesser saints such as Pareto, Simmel, Veblen, Schumpeter, Polanyi, Mannheim, or Gramsci. Tellingly, many of these names were gradually rejected by economics as the neoclassical canon took hold of the discipline and preserved at best a ritual standing in political science.[14]

A relatively diverse intellectual tradition, reinforced by the active engagement of many sociologists in the social movements and epic debates of the late 1960s and early 1970s, helped to maintain an active interest in historical transformations. This interest continued in sociology after the extinction of the grand schemes of historical stages in both their liberal modernization and orthodox Marxist variations. Later in the eighties, in the confusing aftermath of this demise, sociology avoided being entirely swept away by postmodernist solipsism or, conversely, by the normative abstractions of rational choice theory.

But let me quickly conclude this paean to sociology before I am accused of a Caucasian penchant to boast of one's clan. My intent is only to explain why sociology seems a potentially rich source of rational substantive explanations. This directly pertains to the dilemmas bedeviling public consciousness after 11 September 2001 and the launching of the global "war on terrorism," which this book seeks to clarify by providing a study of changes in the historical social context. Compared to thirty years ago, sociologists now have a robust theoretical understanding of such diverse processes as state-building, revolutions, and democratization; the social embeddedness of markets; the emergence of nations and nationalism; the historical formation and undoing of status groups and classes; and the geopolitics and geoculture of the modern world-system. We can bring our theoretical insights to bear on contemporary issues and empirical materials in a manner that takes account of Collins's warning that no global trend has validity unless observed in empirical examples.[15] This warning should be taken seriously not only because of its methodological rationale but also because in dealing with such issues sociologists encounter audiences beyond their professional circle. We can and should strive to expand the range of analytical and political alternatives.

NASTY OLD QUESTIONS

The current debate on globalization and ethnic violence suggests that, after a hiatus of nearly a quarter of a century, the problems of world underdevelopment and its discontents are once again becoming central to the agenda. Violence in particular had no place in the original progressivist vision of globalization. This has now changed. And once again we are confronted essentially with the old nasty question: does modernization breed revolutions and the danger of totalitarianism? Today it is phrased like this: does globalization breed violent anti-Enlightenment reactions? Can democracy survive in non-Western societies? The manner in which these questions are posed makes them rhetorical, designed as they are to elicit only one answer; therefore they must be reformulated.

In a remarkable instance of intellectual continuity, it is the same Samuel Huntington whose darkly prophetic *Clash of Civilizations* established the defensive conservative stance on the jeopardy of globalization who, in his influential monograph *Political Order in Changing Societies* published at the height of the Vietnam war, posed a question regarding the connection between modernization, the dangers of revolution, and the pragmatic uses of military authoritarianism.[16] One common way of deconstructing Huntington's claims and agenda is to invoke the devastating analysis of Albert Hirschman in his *Rhetoric of Reaction* – which, with regard to the *Clash of Civilizations,* has been done by many authors.[17] In this book I take a different approach, by seeking instead to offer a substantive alternative.

Back in the early seventies, as we should be reminded today, it was Charles Tilly who vigorously responded to Huntington's challenge and demonstrated that revolutions tended to arise from a far more complex and specific historical causality than the nebulous notion of modernization can account for.[18] In a similar vein, though less directly aimed at Huntington's propositions, Theda Skocpol stressed the centrality of state breakdown in unleashing the social revolutions in France, Russia, and China. Importantly, Skocpol also demonstrated, in a theorized and relational fashion, how these respective social revolutions, when developed fully within their international contexts, culminated in the reconstitution of stronger dictatorial states.[19] This opened up a promising route for the meaningful analysis of power configurations that had been branded "totalitarian."

The breakthrough formulations of Tilly and Skocpol made possible a whole new field of study that has today achieved maturation.[20] An important offshoot of this field was the comparative historical sociology of democratization and of the institutionalization of welfare regimes in Western countries.[21] The key intellectual merit of the new approach was its ability to overcome the teleology of progress and the normative–juridical judgment that had pervaded previous theorizing on revolutions, political democratization, and the establishment of welfare regimes. In adopting the approach of Tilly and Skocpol, in combination with the work of scholars coming from related perspectives (such as Michael Mann, Dietrich Rueschemeyer, Evelyn Huber Stephens, or John D. Stephens) we may obtain a sound understanding of the complex and contingent historical processes leading to modern-era democratization.[22] The extension of these historical sociological theories outside of their traditional application to Western societies is now the order of the day.

THE SOURCES OF CURRENT TURMOIL: AN ALTERNATIVE THEORY

The main proposition of this book mirrors Tilly's critique of Huntington's thesis linking revolutions to modernization. I will argue that the violent ethnic politics of recent years did not arise as a direct result of globalization. They were, rather, desperate and particularist attempts to cope with the dismantlement of erstwhile developmental regimes,[23] a process which was taking place worldwide and which in extreme instances led to the outright collapse of states. The developmental states became impossible to sustain because they could no longer deliver on the main legitimating promise of progress and national development, that is, the promise of the fairly rapid equalization of socioeconomic conditions in their countries with those of core capitalist states.

To put it another way, the Serbs and Albanians in Kosovo, the Chechens in the Caucasus, the warlord factions in the Congo, and the Islamist radicals in Algeria, did not begin fighting because something deeply wicked lurked in their ethnic traditions, nor was it merely a perverse defense of their historical, cultural identities against the challenges presented by "McWorld."[24] Rather, they all fought and will continue to fight, in different ways, over what to do about their suddenly delegitimated states and the drastically devalued modern economies that these states once nurtured and sheltered. More specifically, these conflicts are fought over the gravely serious issues of who will profit, who will bear the costs, and who will support whom in the new system of capitalist property rights.[25]

My further claim here is that ethnic violence is neither an automatic reaction nor is it the first choice of the people who might end up being involved in such violence. It is more likely they would rather choose democracy – albeit not the "shallow" democratization limited to a formal electoral procedure and a competition among elite groups, but rather the "deep" (a hard-nosed realist would say "utopian") social democratization that seeks to open a broadly equitable access to the flow of power and goods, give equal voice to all, and ensure the self-management rights of work, residential, and cultural communities. Historically, this has been a predominantly proletarian agenda of democratization in modern Western states.[26] In the past, it expressed itself in situations where the classes dependent on wage incomes (taken broadly to include the proletarian categories from manual workers to educated wage-earning specialists like us professors) found themselves in a position to effectively lay claims on modern states. Such structural opportunities first emerged in the late nineteenth century and became more widespread after the depression of the 1930s and the world wars, when proletarians came to prevail among the core states' military recruits, voting citizens, and the employees of state bureaucracies and industries.[27]

Even more so than in the core capitalist states, structural conditions for proletarian democratization were created in the Soviet Union, and later in many other revolutionary industrializing states that were not necessarily inspired by a Marxist ideology. Such states were prolific proletarianizers as they sought to reproduce rapidly the industries and attendant educational, managerial, and social institutions to be found in the core capitalist countries, albeit without a bourgeoisie and instead under the control of a state bureaucratic executive. Arguably democratization was not their actual intent, even though it was a loudly asserted ideological claim. For the extent of their duration, these states remained post-revolutionary dictatorships that practiced the propagandistic dissimulation of a people's democracy. Nevertheless the rapid industrialization of socialist and quasi-socialist states also created a constant need for worker enthusiasm and micro-group autonomy to overcome anarchy in production (or, for that matter, in fighting serious wars), while the party–state apparatus at the point of production rendered transparent the actual exercise of power and class inequalities.[28]

It was once a standing Trotskyist expectation that socialist proletarians would eventually rebel against state bureaucracy (wherein the notion of the proletariat remained restricted to the orthodox socialist – and predominantly male – imagery of industrial manual labor, which failed to represent the university-educated special-ists, many of whom were women). This prediction, though not entirely wrong, failed to take account of two other historical possibilities. First, that the less ideo-logically committed among the technocratic managers of industry might dump the defunct ideology, turn the state assets they had administered into privately owned or corporate capital, and seek profitable alliances with global capitalist partners. Second, that the revolutionary industrializing state might simply collapse, thereby removing the main object of proletarian claim-making and the key condition of democratization. It was these possibilities, of course, that increasingly became realities with the break-up of the Soviet bloc.

The resulting erosion of industrial structures that had been created and main-tained by developmental states threatened the various proletarian categories with extinction. The breakdown of central governance also made democratization next to impossible, while increasing the likelihood of lateral struggles among locally embedded contenders. Such struggles are commonly viewed as ethnic conflicts in part because enterprising patrons, emerging from all ranks of society, adver-tise their intention to protect a particular community – as was the case with the Serbian communist apparatchik Milošević at the famous 1987 rally in Kosovo; the rogue Soviet general Dudayev in 1991 in Chechnya, and various rag-tag warlords in Africa. It is also a central message in al-Qaeda's propaganda of global jihad.

Still, we can continue to ask why it is that these conflicts are specifically ethnic. The Serbs, Chechens, Algerians or, for that matter, the presumably quiescent Chinese, do not have much in common except that they all live in locales that are incompletely industrialized and only partially and recently urbanized, with the consequence that their modern formal institutions are often superficial or simply superfluous. In such locales people know from daily experience how much their life chances depend on access to various patrons and informal networks. And when such people become convinced that they face the prospect of marginalization in a new, competitive, yet restrictive set of arrangements, they sometimes fight back – if they can find a mobilizing platform. Ethnic solidarities provide one such plat-form – to which there are few alternatives in a situation where the possibilities for democratization are being massively eroded as state institutions collapse, state-created industrial assets and bureaucracies, which embedded the existence of proletarian groups, turned into a liability in the face of global markets; and because structural unemployment now verges on permanent lumpenization.

Contemporary ethnic conflicts defy the common imagery of revolutions because they fall short of revolutionary outcomes and their proclaimed goals rarely envision the reconstitution of more progressive and universalistic states. Instead, the goals are usually to split up states and drive out unwanted "aliens," these aims being couched in vague promises to restore the traditional moral order vested in ethnic or religious communities. Nevertheless, because such struggles center on state power, are produced by state breakdown, and regularly involve mass mobilizations, they fall into what Charles Tilly and his collaborators call the extended continuum of transgressive contention, or simply "rebellions."[29]

State-centered theories of revolution and democratization help us to understand why the Soviet regime twice tried to move away from dictatorship towards democratization (first during the de-Stalinization of the 1956–1968 period and again during Gorbachev's perestroika of the late 1980s), and why instead the reforms ended in state disintegration, numerous ethnic conflicts, and the emergence of scandalously corrupt regimes of neo-*nomenklatura* oligarchic capitalism. Here we can rely on the fast-growing and increasingly sophisticated body of literature that analyzes the relatively peaceful transitions in Central Europe or Russia proper. The more disastrous case of the Caucasus region, however, comes closer to the patterns seen in Bosnia or Afghanistan than those in Hungary or Poland. These markedly different experiences map out divergent pathways of post-communism that, in turn, can be viewed as specific sectors within the wider range of historical possibilities.

The Soviet experience, which is the main empirical source for my argument, still matters a great deal, for reasons that nowadays tend to be overlooked. Historically, the Russian Bolshevik project served the modular example of anti-systemic development, or, more precisely, industrialization achieved by revolutionary state coercion. The example was followed, with various local adaptations, by many other movements of national development. The Soviet state, through its proselytizing policies, and perhaps simply by the fact of its presence in the world, served as a major resource for many revolutionary movements of its time. The prominence of the USSR enabled the anti-systemic reconstruction of the enormous state that is China, the successful survival for nearly four decades of federations as diverse as Yugoslavia once was, and socialist experiments in countries as peripheral as Mongolia, Cuba, Mozambique, or Yemen.

The Soviet Union represented the original and longest-lasting example of anti-systemic developmentalism – the strongest by virtue of its military and economic power, and also the most complete sequence of its kind. In sum, the Soviet experience provides the best source of evidence for determining precisely what historical state socialism was and was not able to accomplish in its attempt to establish an alternative to actually-existing capitalism.

Furthermore, the aftermath of the Soviet collapse offers plenty of empirical substance for discussing phenomena ranging from organized crime, corruption, and neo-sultanistic regimes, to warlordism and global terrorism, all of which appear to be part and parcel of processes now structuring the emergent peripheries. If we are to take seriously the current discussions of globalization, we cannot focus exclusively on the policies of core capitalist actors, let alone rely in our analyses on those actors' rationalizations. We should strive to grasp in our theoretical vision the whole system of globalized relations, including its worldwide variations as well as its historical antecedents and potential future trajectories. Consideration of the latter offers a promising way of overcoming the perennial tension between "academic elitism" and "populism" in the craft of social science.[30] If in the new epoch we are to maintain the stance of critical intellectuals, then our utopian alternatives had better be reflexive and "reasoned" rather than just an expression of the typical positional frustrations of intellectuals.[31]

THE WORLD-SYSTEMS PERSPECTIVE

The arguments outlined in the previous section may lead to further and broader formulations when placed in the world-systems perspective. Generally, there is a growing recognition of the potential for intellectual cooperation between the respective schools of comparative-historical sociology and world-systems analysis, especially in the context of globalization (here taken both as the current hegemonic discourse and as shorthand for a broad set of transformative global processes).[32]

The latest achievements of the world-systems school, particularly those which have come from a group of collaborators working with Giovanni Arrighi,[33] provide a robust framework in which it is possible to situate the diverse patterns of post-developmentalism. For example, what Eyal, Szelényi, and Townsley call the "second *Bildungsbürgertum*" in Central Europe may, when placed in the Arrighian framework, be viewed as a privileged pattern of semi-peripheral reintegration into the capitalist world-economy that should be related to more destructive patterns such as those observed in the former Yugoslavia.[34]

The world-systemic analysis of the Soviet state gives us the key to exploring the whole class of twentieth-century revolutionary states that attempted to emulate and transplant the adaptations of social power developed originally in the Western capitalist core. It allows us to bridge in a theorized fashion the normative gap that separated the Third World from the semi-peripheral Second World of communist states.[35] In the context of the modern world-system, the Soviet example belongs in a larger set of typically twentieth-century political programs designed to overcome underdevelopment by the revolutionary takeover of states – where, once again, the term revolution should be treated in Tilly's broad sense.

The first thing to consider, then, is the distance between these countries and those occupying the core positions in the space of capitalist world-economy. This distance was universally construed – in the then prevalent progressive-evolutionary terms – as an historical lag, i.e. in terms of the relative backwardness of peripheral and semi-peripheral states. In other words, the dynamic mutual relationship between core and periphery within the same historical system was presented and measured in terms of developmental time rather than in terms of positioning in the world social space. This had crucial implications for developmentalist ideology and political strategy, which was to deem it both possible and necessary to build ever-stronger states moving ever closer to the "stage" achieved by the core.

It is evident in retrospect that the indigenous revolutions of the twentieth century that were to lead to anti-systemic developmentalism occurred primarily in former agrarian empires with long histories of patrimonial bureaucratization: Russia, China, Turkey, India, Ethiopia, and, belatedly, Iran. These beleaguered empires traditionally harbored an elevated self-esteem – translated in modern times into a strongly unifying nationalism – and possessed sizable cultural elites capable of superimposing their frustrations onto the grievances of mainly peasant populations, through mechanisms ranging from religious sermonizing to nationalist education and communist propaganda.[36] It was the common aspiration of modern, educated specialists in such countries – the intellectuals, progressive military officers, modernizing bureaucrats, and even radicalized clerics – to acquire state power through collective action, oftentimes pursued outside the oppressive legal frameworks of the existing regimes.

In the world geopolitical and geocultural conjuncture after 1914, and especially after 1945, elite groups of radical developmentalists enjoyed extraordinarily high rates of success in taking over states. State power was then used to implement programs of rapid industrialization that would dramatically extend literacy, town development, military resources, ideological apparatuses, and what Michael Mann calls the "infrastructural reach" of the state.[37] This was effected under the banner of either communism or national liberation, which were in effect different facets of the same larger developmentalist project. In practice, the communists had to incorporate nationalist aspirations to a much greater degree than they had expected, as they found themselves ruling over national states in lieu of the projected "world revolution."[38] Similarly, Third World nationalists found it necessary to embrace a range of socialist polices in order to build popular bases of support in poor countries. Undoubtedly, the radical developmentalists also emulated and often directly aided each other. Thus the similarities between developmentalist states were both structural-positional and dynamically acquired – a fact which helps to account for the broad similarity of the ways in which the majority of these state regimes were to come to an end in the 1980s.

When reframed in the world-systems perspective, many of the phenomena currently subsumed under the rubric of globalization appear to be the interrelated consequences of the collapse of former developmentalist states.[39] Where the hegemonic imagery of globalization presents the worldwide liberalization of economic and political controls as an historical new beginning, we might rather discover that these trends represent the breakdown of a previous world order and its attendant "regime of accumulation."[40] These breakdowns were the result of internally accumulated rigidities, compounded with the shifts in political and economic strategy effected by the United States after its crises of the 1969–1982 period. The bankruptcies of state-engendered command economies opened them up to global flows of capital, while the moral and political bankruptcies of post-revolutionary dictatorships opened the way to democratization. But only in some instances did the historical opportunities of the 1980s and 1990s result in sustained democratization and capitalist growth. Even then it happened mostly thanks to the resumption of dependent development, as can be observed in Central Europe where the patterns of post-communism oddly came to resemble the semi-peripheral dilemmas of the pre-communist period.[41]

Elsewhere, the post-developmental transition failed to result in the reconstitution of state power and full integration into the capitalist world-economy. Instead, the emergent peripheries experienced lasting economic decay and a shift from dictatorial centralized governance to decentralized corruption, political patronage, and "organized crime in disorganized states."[42] The former USSR, of course, offers one of the most poignant examples of such structural criminalization and social collapse.[43] In many instances, state breakdown resulted in civil war and attempted secessions, most of which have been held in a "frozen" condition due to the political constraints imposed on the belligerents by Western mediators and the sheer weakness of the successor states with little prospect of engaging in successful conquests.

Most of the economies in the new periphery seem incapable of generating substantial profits except through the mechanisms of international debt or smuggling – whose commodities range from narcotics and diamonds to human beings. In general, the new periphery presents a burden, and potentially also a security threat, to the core capitalist states. Hence the vacillation within Western policy between "humanitarian intervention" (which due to staggering costs invariably falls far short of a comprehensive stabilization) and what Michael Mann characterizes as the strategy of "ostracizing imperialism."[44] The recent American interventions in the Middle East have only served to bring this dilemma to a head.

TOWARDS A SYNTHESIS

If the combination of the historical sociology of states and a world-systems perspective seems a relatively unproblematic way to extend our analyses to contemporary states and social movements across the peripheral zone, our proposed third major source of theoretical concepts may appear to be a non-sequitur. Nonetheless, it is to the sociology of Pierre Bourdieu that we will have to turn in order to make our provisional synthesis possible.

In his lifetime Bourdieu was considered neither a historical sociologist nor a proponent of large structural explanations.[45] This judgment was unfounded. Bourdieu did indeed attempt to go beyond excessively mechanistic forms of structuralism (in France associated mainly with Althusser's school), but so, in their own ways and contexts, did Tilly and Wallerstein. But Bourdieu's conceptualization of social fields is explicitly structural, if not structuralist in the sense attributed to the dominant schools of the sixties. His notion of habitus serves to break the structuralist cage and effectively overcomes the false antinomy of structure and agency. In this respect, by offering a positive operational concept, Bourdieu evidently moved beyond the comparable critical arguments of Tilly and Wallerstein. The latter, notoriously, neglected to elaborate the rules of his method, preferring instead to move ahead relentlessly in charting and further expanding the horizons of the world-systems perspective. Wallerstein's historical summaries and generalizations are always dazzling and enlightening but they also seem as intuitively inspired, and thus as unreproducible, as the masterpieces of the artworld. This aspect of early world-systems analysis frustrated many followers and infuriated its critics.[46] But perhaps Wallerstein was right in choosing the lightning advance over the methodical digging of trenches and the marshalling of armies of disciplined concepts. Such methodical systemization may come later; and this is indeed how scientific revolutions have come about. In the classical example: it took the inter-national efforts of Galileo and Kepler to systematize the astronomical observations of Copernicus and then, decades later, Newton to formulate in elegantly mathe-matical form the regularities of celestial motion which ultimately secured the Copernican revolution as the basis for our modern perspective on the Solar system. Let us hope it will not take as long to complete the Wallersteinian breakthrough.

In the further development of the world-systems school, the recent examples of its formalization in the work of Giovanni Arrighi indicate one possible way of supporting Wallerstein's breakthrough formulations. The body of literature produced by Charles Tilly and his international collaborators provides another rich source of sociological concepts. Yet, for all the merits of this literature, it remains critically limited on two counts. First, it has been, at least until recently, consciously centered on European history alone. Second, the panoply of social mechanisms and processes identified by Tilly and his colleagues appears on closer scrutiny to be hampered by problems similar to those bedeviling Wallerstein's analysis. The social mechanisms Tilly identifies certainly make sense at the level of his analysis; but difficult questions remain concerning what it is that drives these mechanisms from the "inside" as it were. What, for instance, drives political polarization in moments of heightening conflict; or the creation of revolutionary and counter-revolutionary alliances across different classes; or ideological shifts in the objectives of contention?[47] What, in short, are the mechanisms within the mechanisms? It is precisely at this level that concepts derived from Randall Collins (who has performed much of the necessary formalization regarding the rich intuitions of Erving Goffman) or from Pierre Bourdieu (whose tremendous contribution marked a culmination of the intellectual lineages running back to Durkheim) may be deployed to great advantage within the theoretical synthesis I am proposing here.[48]

In taking this approach we may circumvent a familiar charge against state-centered historical sociology and the world-systems school – namely that they fail to take account of cultural identities and micro-processes at the level of the indi-vidual, where the conflicting emotions and dilemmas of practical action are experienced. Admittedly, the charge is not unjustified, even if its expressions are often vague; but the problem does not seem irreparable. The conceptual apparatus that Bourdieu developed to analyze ideologies, modern culture, and intellectuals will be particularly useful in our context because alienated intellectuals have played a central role in the revolutionary developmentalist experiences of the twentieth century. In effect, Bourdieu has shown us how to apply, in research practice, the intuitions of earlier thinkers such as Karl Mannheim and Antonio Gramsci.

What makes possible and promising the combination of the apparently different approaches of Wallerstein, Tilly, and Bourdieu is their shared epistemological goal of constructing a relational and reflexive social science. Each of the three thinkers, in their own ways, began by trying to overcome the nineteenth-century teleological orthodoxies hitherto expressed in structural-functionalist theories of modernization and in traditional Marxism. From critiques of normative invariant abstractions, Bourdieu, Tilly, and Wallerstein moved on to chart the complex topologies of variation over social space and time or, to extend Dorothy Smith's consequential metaphor, towards "mapping the social landscapes" with a view to their practical navigation.[49] Their common analytical procedure is to trace the dynamic, continuously reconstituted and contentious relations of field and network.

In summarizing Tilly's method, Arthur Stinchcombe stresses that it is fundamentally "a network analysis but not of the usual kind" because Tilly "cares what it is that flows over the links between people" and sees "networks not as causes themselves, but instead as channels that deliver causes to particular places in the social system whose description is embedded in a deep analysis of the historical context."[50] For his part, Bourdieu, who was clearly in accord with much of Tilly's agenda, insisted on pursuing "a structural history, which finds in each successive state of the structure under examination both the product of previous struggles to maintain or to transform this structure, and the principle, via the contradictions, the tensions, and the relations of force which constitute it, of subsequent transformations."[51] And what is Wallenstein's world-system, after all, if not a relational time/space of intertwined networks – which may be commodity chains or the fields of geoculture and geopolitics – that have been continuously evolving through multiple contradictions and ongoing efforts to institutionalize systemic tensions? It is within the overall field of a world-system, among its various geopolitical positions and economic niches, that we can situate states, classes, and status-groups (including their formation and eventual dissolution) as well as group struggles and the making of collective cultures – which Bourdieu would have recognized as forms of capital and habitus.[52]

TOWARDS A WORLD-SYSTEMIC SOCIOLOGICAL BIOGRAPHY

To summarize then, the three different theoretical approaches, operating with epistemologically analogous premises, address distinct yet related sets of processes all of which are directly relevant to our investigation. One might say that the three approaches operate on different but intersecting planes. But rather than rely on a static spatial division into macro-, meso-, and micro-levels, I prefer to invoke Fernand Braudel's three temporalities: *longue durée*, which corresponds to Wallerstein's privileged time-scale of secular trends, long waves, and hegemonic cycles; the intermediate time of *conjoncture*, where scholars influenced by Stinchcombe, Skocpol, and Tilly situate most of their concerns with institutionalization and structural change; and the shorter time-frame of actual human action that Bourdieu connected up – in elegantly simple, yet robust and flexible ways – with the structural embeddedness of all social life.

Meshing these theoretical perspectives, we shall trace the exceptionally rich yet at the same time archetypical life-trajectory of Musa Shanibov, Bourdieu's secret admirer and the latter-day Garibaldi of the Caucasus.

The time-honored genre of biography seemed appropriate in this case, since even a master of historical analysis like Charles Tilly recognizes that the narrative form has the major advantage of being more accessible to a wider audience. Many people – or at least those socialized in modern Western modes of thinking – learn about the world by mapping it in terms of a motivated historical narrative: learning why characters do what they do in a succession of real-life situations. Our narrative here will be grounded in empirical details while addressing big analytical questions, such as why the putative democratization of the late Soviet period failed; why in many instances the process led to ethnic violence; and why the political structures now seen across the post-communist periphery have emerged in their current forms.[53]

The notions of class habitus and social capital in its various sub-forms (occupational, administrative, intellectual) will help us to define the stakes, stances, rhetorical moves, and changing strategies in the various Soviet- and post-Soviet-era power struggles. Concepts drawn from the domains of contention, state-building, and democratization will play a crucial role in explaining the dynamics of the numerous struggles in which Shanibov has participated, from the de-Stalinization of the 1950s up to the collapse of Gorbachev's perestroika, ending with the ethno-territorial conflicts of the 1990s. Finally, the world-system perspective will enable us to situate these processes on the plane of global transformation. By such a combination of means, I hope, in the end, to illuminate the current situation on the darker side of globalization.

3

The Dynamics of De-Stalinization

"The present generation of Soviet people shall live under the conditions of plenty and cultural fulfillment. The dawn of Communist society is on the horizon, dear comrades!"

from the Program of the Communist Party of the Soviet Union adopted
at the Twenty-second Congress in 1961 (cited in William Taubman,
Khrushchev: The Man and his Era, New York: W. W. Norton, 2003)

Musa Shanib was born in 1936 or 1935 (the registry is flawed) in a Kabardin village situated in the foothills of the central Caucasus. He belongs to that generation of orphans whose fathers perished in the violence of the 1930s and on the battlefields of the Second World War. Some of Shanib's ancestors had belonged to the Kabardin petty nobility, but his family's way of life was virtually indistinguishable from that of peasants. They kept some livestock and tended a patch of garden. Shanib's mother had to serve in a workers' canteen or do laundry to earn a living for the family, which consisted of herself and four children. Shanib's father had joined the Communist Party in the 1920s, once it had become clear that the regime was there to stay and that party membership offered the best way to obtain an education and get a better job. But during the purges of the 1930s he was denounced as a "socially hostile element" and expelled from the party. He was drafted into the army during the desperate summer of 1942, and a few months later the family were notified of his death.

Life for families such as Shanib's was exceedingly hard. The monthly ration of *Peasant* sugar was the children's only treat, a new pair of boots was an occasion for family *life* celebration, and a bicycle was an unattainable dream. The boys had to wear the *difficult* oversized clothes of their fathers and from an early age took on the labors and responsibilities of adult males in a peasant household. While such difficulties were profound, they were not at all unprecedented. Peasant existence in the region had been precarious throughout the epochs. It is hard for us to imagine what life must have been like after the Hun or Mongol conquests, or in the wake of Viceroy Yermolov's punitive campaigns in the 1810s–1820s, or after the exodus of the defeated highlanders to the Ottoman empire following the final Russian victory in the 1860s. On a more localized scale, plagues, failed crops, slave-raiding, blood feuds, and land disputes between communities were ongoing threats over the centuries, causing equally devastating disasters. Faced with the recurrent threat of extinction, peasants had to be stubborn survivors. After each disaster those who were left alive would recuperate – to whatever degree was geopolitically and environmentally possible – and reproduce the old patterns of peasant existence. The men and women of Musa Shanib's generation seemed destined to follow this rough cycle of raw survival and to continue the traditional peasant existence. And yet they didn't.

The developmental dynamism of Stalinist dictatorship reached the young generation mainly through the rapidly expanding institutions of mass education. It promised modern careers as mechanics, teachers, pilots, or national artists and performers, and this certainly gave credence to the official ideology. Urban life seemed incomparably better than the traditional predicament of the peasants who, in a common saying, *Never saw electric light and starved every other winter.*

The earliest political belief overwhelmingly shared by Shanib's generation was a sincere Stalinism. Among the newly proletarian masses Stalin embodied the idea of progress and symbolized the great patriotic victory of the war. Psychologically, he became a surrogate father to the generation that was coming of age in a situation where all previous social ties and norms had been broken and where state institutions had been substituted for lost fathers. The harshness of Stalin's image itself carried a promise. Long ago Barrington Moore identified perhaps the key mechanism of Stalin's cult in the egalitarian mythology that also made possible an "open season on bureaucrats" whenever Stalin felt it necessary.[1] Stalinism was full of such ambiguities. Notwithstanding its atheist ideology, popular Stalinism became a propagated quasi-religion providing what Marx and Engels famously dubbed the "heart of a heartless world, the opium of the people."[2] But Stalinism's normative frame could also provide a political weapon to the proletarian class *in statu nascendi*.

Soon after Stalin's death this would change, as the younger and better-educated Soviet proletarians and specialists gained more confidence in the collective achievement which had improved their social status and lifestyle.

Undoubtedly these young men and women knew they still had to watch what they said; but this social skill was relegated to the unreflected area of doxa, to use Bourdieu's term. The post-war normalization of life proceeded and the economic recovery facilitated an impressive degree of social mobility, such that compliance with official ideology did not require excessive hypocrisy. Grand propaganda and life were meshing before their eyes, or so the youth wanted to believe. They were in a position to hold a genuine faith in the future. Even the older generation saw the war as a historical watershed that had left all horrors behind them – to the survivors, life after the costly victory looked bright and promising.

THE NORMALIZATION OF THE SOVIET STATE

Shortly after Stalin's death in 1953 his most notorious henchmen, starting with the monstrous Lavrenty Beria, were removed in a palace coup and executed, imprisoned, or (in the lower echelons) sacked. At the Twentieth Party Congress in 1956 the new Soviet leader Nikita Khrushchev repudiated Stalin's dictatorship. The consequent program of de-Stalinization was, in effect, the purge to end all purges.

The secret police apparatus was reorganized in order to rein in its arbitrary powers; the new KGB was consciously shaped to become perhaps the most rational bureaucratic institution of the Soviet state; while the Ministry of the Interior was abolished altogether, with policing responsibilities moved to local levels. After 1953, those who had been promoted under Stalin were prone to feel like hiding away, and when their time came they did not resist the demotion, rustication (many were banished to villages), or early retirement that was imposed upon them. The weakness of the pre-war bureaucratic cohort lay in their lack of education – these men normally had no more than a basic schooling followed by two years of *Sovpartshkola* (the regional school of the party and Soviet administration, which trained mostly the native cadres). After 1945, higher education diplomas became the norm and – as all education credentials are prone to inflation – towards the early 1960s many apparatchiks were already aiming for doctorates.[3] De-Stalinization thus secured the political conditions for the maturation of the Soviet state, economy, and society.

But first, they were to enjoy a decade of tremendous material and intellectual growth, ensuring what was in many respects the most successful period in Soviet history.

The decommissioning of the Stalinist apparatus of terror was followed by the expansion of the civilian bureaucracy. This political shift produced a great number of inductions into the junior ranks, followed by many sudden promotions into the formal executive ranks of what in the USSR was called the *nomenklatura*. The new executive cadres were recruited on the merit of technical competence rather than ideological zeal, and as a result higher education credentials became major weapons of the post-Stalin cohort in their struggles for bureaucratic ascendancy. Statistics published in the reports of Kabardino-Balkaria's regional party conferences show that younger party cadres with college diplomas predominated shortly after 1960.[4] Undoubtedly, this conformed to a general trend observed across the whole Soviet bloc. Seen in a broader perspective, the rise of these young, formally educated executives was a variation on the then worldwide theme of meritocracy that had begun to emerge in the Western discourse of "managerial revolution" during the 1930s, and reached its peak in the decades following the Second World War.

The end of terroristic centralization marked the collective victory of Soviet bureaucracy over the arbitrary terror of the previous regime. The post-Stalinist *nomenklatura* was not only significantly larger and better educated, it was also more durable. While in the first thirty years of its existence the Soviet Kabardino-Balkaria had experienced four governors (half of whom ended badly), in the following thirty years – from de-Stalinization until perestroika – it had just one. (And that one's personally groomed successor, as of 2004, still occupies the same office – only the title has changed, from First Secretary to President.)

WHY DID STATE SOCIALISM OUTLIVE STALINISM?

The stabilization of bureaucratic careers became the main condition for the self-transformation of the *nomenklatura* into a new dominant class. Today's market economists, armed with hindsight and envious of China's success, bemoan the lost historical opportunity of the 1950s and 1960s when the Soviet economy might have been set on the road towards a market economy. We must then ask the counterfactual question as to why the Soviet elite failed to reinvent themselves as capitalist managers or, we must also add, as the rulers of sovereign national states. The question seems serious enough because, in essence, it asks why the events of 1989 did not happen much earlier than they actually did.[5] Building on the concept of the developmental state, let us devote a section to discussing the factors that might account for the historical divergence in the trajectories of communist states in Eastern Europe and in East Asia.

The immediate answer is simply that powerful states at the peak of their success do not change easily. To safeguard our counterfactual questions against accusations of soft-headedness, we should be reminded that the candidate most likely to turn to capitalism at the time – Lavrenty Beria – certainly was exceptional in many respects, beginning with his overt cynicism. Even if we admit that in 1953 (a point in the Soviet trajectory comparable to the twilight of Maoism in China) Beria was entertaining the prospects of personal dictatorship, of shedding the comatose Marxist-Leninist ideology, and of ending the Cold War for the sake of a rapprochement with the West, we would still face further difficult questions. Wouldn't such a post-Stalinist dictator inevitably have been toppled? After all, when in fact it came to Beria's arrest, both the party bosses and the top military seemed unanimous in their desire to rid themselves of this would-be reformer.[6] Moreover, it is very doubtful that Beria could have known in advance how far he could go in the long run. He might eventually have stumbled across the possibility of converting the military-industrial developmental state into an export-oriented developmental state, but the obstacles to such a program at the time were incomparably greater than those faced by China's Deng three decades later.

Consider three different types of obstacle. The reigning ideological orthodoxy of the 1950s prescribed import-substitution on all sides. The Western economies had just recovered their own industrial bases and ensured high levels of employment after the years of depression and war; their search for cheaper labor and new industrial bases overseas would not begin until the onset of the world economic downturn between 1969 and 1973. Furthermore, in the 1950s and 1960s it was only in exceptional instances that Soviet managers were able to engage in joint ventures with foreign counterparts – in sharp contrast not only to the Chinese transformation after Maoism but also to the experiences of Hungary and Poland in the 1970s. Last but not least, the American rapprochement with post-Maoist China cannot be divorced from the context of the American defeat in Vietnam and, in the early 1980s, the renewed Cold War against the Soviet bloc. In the early 1950s – given the then crucial importance of Cold War polarization in the American construction of international alliances and domestic political order – it is difficult to imagine why Washington would have jumped at any proposed gift from Beria of a unified and neutral Germany.

The hard historical facts are that after Stalin's death the Marxist-Leninist ideology was effectively reinvented and the state socialist form continued for another generation. Back in the early 1960s, becoming capitalist could not have been further from the minds of the post-Stalinist bureaucratic cohort. First of all, the new cadres were young and thoroughly Soviet-produced. The majority were too young to remember the bourgeois life before 1917, nor had they ever experienced it abroad. Besides, they remained very closely related to the rest of the Soviet population – there are plenty of examples where in the same family (including Shanibov's) immediate relatives, brothers, sisters, and cousins, became *nomenklatura*, intellectuals, workers, even sub-proletarians. The borderlines of rank were "soft" and permeable, and, after the post-Stalin shake-up, the ruling elite had not yet developed into a closed caste. The egalitarian communist ideology retained its hegemony in the purest Gramscian sense. Or, rather, the hegemony of communist ideas was mightily bolstered by the processes of de-Stalinization, both from above as Khrushchev struggled to restore the "Leninist norms," and from below by the masses who enthusiastically embraced the promise of unending progress and a much better life on the horizon. It probably matters no less than in the analogous case of the Chinese communist leadership during the Tiananmen rebellion in 1989 that the senior Soviet leaders at the time were not career bureaucrats but the last remaining Bolshevik veterans of the revolution. During the Civil War Nikita Khrushchev had been a frontline regimental commissar, while his closest ally, Anastas Mikoyan, veteran of the Transcaucasus underground, back in 1918 was a Baku communard who narrowly escaped execution during the British occupation. For these old cadres, moving ahead meant overcoming the legacies of Stalinism and reaching back to the rational utopianism of Lenin, which might also explain their odd mixture of romanticism and ruthless pragmatism – traits which they shared with Lenin and the early Bolsheviks.

The move to overcome Stalin's cult and recover the utopia of revolutionary progress was hailed enthusiastically in many sectors of Soviet society: among the surviving veterans of the revolution and the victory over the Nazis; among creative artists and intellectuals who suddenly felt liberated from stifling orthodoxy; among younger technical specialists; and, not least, among the new cohort of party cadres (which included people like Mikhail Gorbachev) who saw themselves in control of a bright future. The space-flight triumphs of the time added the distinctive flavor of science fiction to the ideological imagination of the "sixties" (*shestidesyatniki* – as this generation came to be called and to which our Musa Shanibov belongs). A favorite song of the epoch even romantically asserted that apple trees would blossom on Mars.

On the diplomatic front, Khrushchev successfully broke out of the international isolation into which Moscow had fallen during the last years of Stalin's rule.

Khrushchev both extended Soviet alliances to include the ascendant national liberation movements in the Third World, and achieved a form of peaceful coexistence with the West. All this reinforced the Soviets' ideological perception of themselves as a progressive force of world transformation.[7] In preparation for Khrushchev's groundbreaking visit to the United States in 1959, the extraordinary Twenty-First Congress of the CPSU officially proclaimed the creation of a "world socialist system" that in the near future would overtake the West on capitalism's native ground – in technological innovation and industrial productivity. It was a promise conveyed in Khrushchev's triumphalist threat, "We shall bury you." The launch of the orbital Sputnik in 1957 seemed to give substance to such assertions.

Between 1950 and 1965 the Soviet economy grew at the impressive rate of 5 to 7 per cent annually (the exact figures are subject to dispute among economists, but everybody agrees that the rate of growth was high). The economic gains finally began to make themselves felt in rapidly improving standards of living and higher levels of popular consumption.[8] The symbols of Khrushchev's social program were the five-story apartment blocks built right across the vast territory between the Baltic and the Pacific. Their drab architecture may have been the result of pure budget-driven functionalism, and these *khrushchevki* apartments were certainly crammed. But what a leap they signified in comparison to the peasant huts and workers' barracks of the industrialization period! The apartments created, for the first time ever, private spaces for the majority of Soviet citizens. To move into such an apartment from a communal barracks or a peasant dwelling was an experience of progress incarnate that had far-reaching effects on the material and mental structures of everyday life.

Last but not least, the Soviet military-industrial complex remained a major domestic constituency. Its elite enjoyed a formidable organizational base, control over the leading technological sectors (the space flights, of course, were their achievement), an unparalleled ability to lobby for their policies, and a major stake in the ideology of Soviet internationalist patriotism. Playing on the recent memories of German invasion and the geopolitical context of the Cold War – which did not require much effort to make it look threatening – the Soviet generals and top managers of the armaments industry became a powerful conservative force. In a very real sense, the Soviet state was built for them and by them. It should not look too ironic that the maintenance of state socialism was supported by the elites of the military-industrial complex – they were supporting the status quo.

THE CONTENTIOUS SIDE OF KHRUSHCHEV'S THAW

The de-Stalinization of 1956–1964, or what came to be called Khrushchev's Thaw, was a very optimistic and dynamic period. Khrushchev's socialist romanticism (and attending dismantling of the mechanisms of state terror) bred many hopes and opened avenues for self-organization among ordinary Soviet citizens. Accounts of Soviet politics traditionally focus on the elites and to some extent this is justifiable given the kind of sources generally available. Recently, however, the availability of archives and collections of reminiscences has allowed us to begin to appreciate the diversity and extent of what was going on in the USSR during the Khrushchev years. First of all, the old caricature of a passive society oppressed by a totalitarian regime has been entirely invalidated. It would not be an exaggeration to say that the Soviet citizens were overcome with fervent desire to forge various horizontal solidarities and to constitute themselves as autonomous actors vis-à-vis the state. In some instances (which were far more numerous than was previously thought) this resulted in transgressive violent contention by forces described in classified Soviet reports as "anti-social elements," "crowds," "provocateurs," and "hooligans."

In 1956, protestors in the Georgian capital of Tbilisi clashed with troops dispatched to remove the statue of Stalin, resulting in bloodshed and many arrests. The protest was clearly not a defense of Stalinism but rather an act of Georgian nationalism. Among the rioters was the young Zviad Gamsakhurdia, a future dissident who became the first anti-communist President of Georgia in 1991.[9]

The Chechens and Balkars returning from exile in 1957 clashed on many occasions with the local police and in particular with the settlers who had been placed in the region during the 1944 deportation. On several occasions, quelling the riots required the dispatch of regular army troops.

In August 1959 in Temirtau, Kazakhstan, construction workers (who included a significant number of recently released convicts) rioted against food shortages and terrible living conditions. There were bloody clashes between workers of different nationalities. The disturbance was put down by soldiers with much bloodshed and caused a major reconsideration of policies in Moscow.[10]

In 1961 in Kirovobad, a town in the interior of Azerbaijan, women who had spent several nights waiting in vain to buy bread rioted and pelted the police with rubbish and stones. The bread shortage was the result of Azerbaijani leaders being too eager to report to Moscow that their republic had achieved self-sufficiency in grain production, leading the central planners to cut the deliveries of grain to Azerbaijan.

In February 1961 in Krasnodar, a major town in the North Caucasus, the arrest of a soldier in the marketplace by a military patrol provoked a "crowd of market vendors and idle onlookers" to march on the town's military headquarters where the detained soldier was held. The sentries at the entrances were ordered to shoot into the air, but a bullet ricocheted, killing a young protester (a student who also happened to be the son of an army colonel). The crowd then marched along the main street of Krasnodar, swelling along the way, and seized the regional party headquarters where the "provocateurs" organized a meeting to draft a petition to Moscow. The Krasnodar party officials locked themselves up in the nuclear shelter in the basement and were freed the next day by army cadets.[11]

In June 1962, workers at a locomotive factory in Novocherkassk declared a strike in protest against an announced increase in food prices. Under red flags and carrying portraits of Lenin, they marched on the town government building where they were met with gunfire. Twenty-two workers were killed, and in the aftermath several dozen people were condemned to death or long prison sentences. Very importantly, according to the glasnost-era investigations of journalists, the army general who was first put in charge of suppressing the strikers refused to open fire, reporting back that he saw not a single German soldier, just Soviet workers, and therefore no possible targets. The locally legendary "general who didn't shoot" was hastily replaced by a KGB officer and received a dishonorable discharge. In retrospect this event, and especially the brave general's disobedience, appears highly symbolic and poignant. It showed that the Soviet leadership could not rely on the military for domestic repression, insofar as the soldiers were liable to recognize the protestors as fellow citizens and to sympathize with their grievances. This was a major condition for the emergence of democratization. The Soviet elite could, of course, still call on the secret police, but allowing the latter to kill again would only have brought back the specter of Stalin.

A year later, in 1963, food shortages once again provoked strikes, rioting, and street marches in Krasnodar, Grozny, Krivoi Rog, Donetsk, Murom, Yaroslavl, and at Moscow's automobile factory. The problems were only resolved when the first steps were taken towards the creation of a Soviet consumer society: in November 1963 Khrushchev for the first time sanctioned the importation of Canadian and American grain, ostensibly as a temporary measure. But the import of food and consumer goods was to become a permanent feature of the late Soviet state.[12]

These are just a few examples from the transgressive end of the spectrum of contention in the Khrushchev era, where we find all kinds of mobilizations: ethnic, civic, neighborhood, environmental, and economic. But the scope was much wider than has been shown here, and extended to the perfectly peaceful and non-political organizing that was occurring on a truly massive scale. Somewhere in the middle of this continuum we can locate a mode of organizing that sought to mesh official ideology with an enthusiasm for change that was perhaps not entirely placid. It is here that we find our hero, Musa Shanib.

CIVILIZING THE NEW SOCIETY

Back then he was no longer called Musa, having changed his name to the more Russian-sounding Yuri Shanibov. This was not, however, a sign of deliberate Russification. In fact, if Shanibov had not been an ethnic Kabardin, and thus a beneficiary of affirmative action in his native autonomous republic, a coveted place on the university graduate program might not have been available. And yet, like many of his contemporaries, Shanibov deemed his ethnic appellation too parochial and backward. Musa was clearly a Muslim name, so changing it to Yuri should also be regarded as a sign of secularization. (Yuri of course is the eastern Slavic form of George, the Greek name of a Christian saint, but this origin was long forgotten.) The contemporary Soviet idea of cosmopolitanism and progress was firmly associated with the Russian language and with names like Yuri Gagarin, the first cosmonaut. The ethnic form "Musa Shanib" would be readopted by Shanibov only during the Soviet disintegration.

Shanibov attended primary school in his village and went on to study in the district's middle school located in a bigger village several kilometers away. In the absence of school buses, the district party committee instructed truck drivers to give rides to pupils – a policy which is remembered fondly. He then moved to Nalchik, the capital of Kabardino-Balkaria, where he was admitted to a boarding school for the best students from the autonomous republic. After graduation, he returned to his district and rose rapidly through the ranks. His first job was as director of the local Palace of Culture, where he was in charge of organizing concerts, weekly dances, and various "creativity circles" in subjects such as drama, music, and amateur poetry. (Today he bemoans the destruction of the Palace of Culture, which was demolished to make way for a private restaurant.) He was also invited to write for the local newspaper, which soon resulted in a scandal when he exposed a group of collective farm bosses who were in the habit of writing off as "natural losses" the livestock that was actually being turned into sheesh-kebabs. The exposé earned Shanibov the enmity of village officials, but much praise from the common people, and as a result – this being the heyday of Khrushchev's Thaw –

he was offered a position on the newspaper. A few years later he was elected Secretary for Propaganda at the Kabardino-Balkarian regional committee of the Young Communist League (Komsomol).

By the sixties, Yuri Shanibov, a promising educated cadre of native nationality and a Komsomol activist, seemed well on his way to joining the ruling *nomenklatura*. He obtained a law diploma by correspondence course and became district attorney. But here his career ran into trouble, caused by what Shanibov himself calls his "fighting habitus." In 1964 Khrushchev was toppled and replaced by Brezhnev. Shanibov failed to appreciate the change in political atmosphere. He was severely reprimanded for defending a collective farmer accused of misappropriating roofing materials, which he used to build, without authorization, an addition to a cowshed for newly born calves. At the same time, as District Attorney, he was engaged in a populist crusade against local bureaucratic corruption. All this was now considered troublesome, and eventually he was forced to resign from the position of district attorney. So far this did not look too ominous. Shanibov was barely thirty years old, and still very energetic and ambitious. He had supporters in the upper echelons as well as enemies, and his resignation was presented as a promotion into a new career – university lecturership. Shanibov thus became an intellectual – another unlikely turn in the fortunes of the village orphan.

During the sixties the Kabardino-Balkarian teachers' college had been upgraded and expanded to become a university. On taking up his place there, Shanibov began working on a doctoral dissertation, in the course of which he read C. Wright Mills's *The Power Elite*, translated into Russian in 1958 purportedly as a critique of American capitalism (the book was later removed from libraries in at least some provincial universities, apparently at the initiative of local professorial censors). *The Power Elite* shaped Shanibov's lifelong interest in critical sociology and social reform. From the outset, his brand of sociology was inseparable from active intervention.

Long before Shanibov knew about Bourdieu, his sociology was a martial art indeed. His "fighting habitus" was forged in physical confrontations with street toughs that occurred when Shanibov was running the Palace of Culture in the late fifties. This experience later provided the topic of his dissertation. Young workers and students, finding themselves removed from the traditional discipline of village life, sought to adopt new cultural practices in accordance with their new social status, and struggled to establish new kinds of interaction rituals among themselves. Their search included innocuous things like learning how to perform in sports, dances, and various games, or in emulating the speech and fashions of movie stars. But conflicts were also common among the groups of young machos, especially in spaces of casual socializing such as cafés, cinemas and dance halls, and particularly over sexual partners. The conflicts often turned violent because the fast-growing towns were lacking in effective supervision, while the village mechanisms of mediation and interaction rituals failed to function in the new social environment. These were arguably familiar phenomena in many industrializing towns around the world.

In the Caucasus, the frequency and intensity of adolescent conflicts were increased by the traditional codes prescribing male warrior display, by ethnic and clan solidarities, and by the traditions of vendetta. In search of physical and emotional security, students and workers spontaneously gathered together on the basis of ethnicity and common origin, which only made matters worse by creating the conditions for bigger, nastier fights between groups of young Kabardins, Balkars, and Russians. At first acting spontaneously, Shanibov organized a self-defense group of fellow students, who established peace in the cafés and cinemas through a combination of mediation, communist moralizing, and force. After some initial, and locally famous, victories, Shanibov was invited to have a word with the secretary of the district's party committee. The party official saw an opportunity to monitor and manage the ongoing violent clashes in his jurisdiction, which is probably why he offered his support and encouragement. Shanibov admits with a chuckle, *I started my career as a Komsomol gangster.*

But the reality was no laughing matter. Some vigilante groups, especially in the tough factory neighborhoods, frequently engaged in savage acts of violence. Rapists in particular were subject to brutal executions, and there were numerous instances when those engaged in petty corruption, like shop managers or sneaky cooks at the workers' canteens, were badly beaten and had their personal property destroyed. It wasn't unusual for a private car (a luxury that had just started to become more common) belonging to an unpopular local personality to be vandalized or burnt. Interviews collected in different parts of the Caucasus and in the central provinces of the Ukraine and Russia consistently state that during the 1950s various vigilante groups became commonplace.

Faced with a wave of street violence and no longer able to utilize the draconian Stalinist measures of the previous period for the purposes of policing, Soviet officials tried to make alliances with the more disciplined among the spontaneously emerging self-defense groups. These were normally the students who could be controlled by the threat of expulsion from university and who were generally perceived as being more "cultured." The officially sanctioned groups of volunteer enforcers that sprang up all over the Khrushchev-era USSR came to be called student patrols.[13]

The students were understandably anxious to avoid being seen as police stooges, and for good reason. The reputation and effectiveness of these volunteers were based on the altruistic provision of protection and peer adjudication among the town youth. Shanibov clearly realized that his group equally had to distinguish itself from the hooligans to gain the high moral ground. As the group evolved, its methods shifted from dramatic adolescent confrontations to center on complex negotiations in dorms and neighborhoods. In several instances Shanibov was able to save the local toughs from going to jail. A typical situation might involve someone's watch being snatched in a fight (at the time a watch was likely to be a person's most valuable possession). The watches were essentially a symbolic prize – not unlike in archaic warfare – and were certainly not stolen to be resold. But from the standpoint of law, the incident was treated as armed robbery or theft. Explaining this took some effort and arguments such as *What will you look like when you return home after they throw you out of the university? What if they send you to prison instead?* The negotiations were usually successful and Shanibov specialized in returning the watches to their rightful owners on the condition that one side would never attempt such a stupid action again and the other side would not go to the police. The local police were content, too: their crime prevention statistics improved. This early experience helps to explain the attitudes that Shanibov later displayed while district attorney.

We should not underestimate Shanibov's success. The fact is that by the early 1960s the level of street crime in the USSR was lower than ever – a statistic which looks all the more impressive considering the lawlessness and mayhem present only a few years earlier. Under Khrushchev the movement for secure streets enjoyed a loosely expressed official sanction because it followed the general thrust towards the pacification of Soviet life. Following the reduction and reform of the Gulag in the fifties, the Soviet prison population reached its lowest level historically, while the contemporary regime of incarceration became almost humane.[14]

This achievement cannot be attributed to the police alone, or to the temporary abandonment of the policy of indiscriminate imprisonment. Alongside the police there operated a genuinely autonomous and widespread social movement fed by the desire of young urbanites to civilize – in the sense of Norbert Elias, perhaps – their newly established social environment.[15] This movement, of course, capitalized on the expansive and optimistic atmosphere of its time. Khrushchev, in one of his trademark pronouncements, said that he was looking forward to shaking hands with the last reformed criminal leaving the last prison.[16]

Shanibov's experience of organizing student patrols informed his dissertation on volunteer crime prevention as a function of socialist self-governance. It was very much in the spirit of the sixties – a Khrushchevite topic that embraced Shanibov's intellectual and political preferences. A few years later such preferences would cost him dearly. But here, let us take note of those skills of Shanibov's that are rarely to be found in intellectuals. He knew how to form alliances with sympathetic officials without falling into client dependency and, at the other extreme, how to persuade young toughs to do his bidding. Much later, during the mobilization for the Abkhazian war in 1992, such skills would help Shanibov in his various efforts to organize the volunteer brigades.

NATIONAL CULTURAL AWAKENINGS

Nationalism enters the Khrushchevian scene almost as an afterthought. Who would seriously contemplate secession from such a strong and dynamic state that had finally begun to deliver on its promises of a better life? Indeed, probably only a few old reactionaries miraculously still surviving from the pre-communist times, and especially daring Bohemians whose dissidence was more an aesthetic stance than politics in any real sense. The early 1960s marked the peak of the Soviet Union's cohesiveness and prestige. And yet the Khrushchev period saw the birth of national cultural movements in the non-Russian republics that prepared the scene for the emergence of national separatism in 1989. In the sixties Shanibov did not take part in this process, mainly because he did not belong to the artistic intelligentsia and was acting on the threshold of the field of power as a social reformer. He was, however, to be counted among the avid consumers of contemporaneous Soviet literature and film, as the de-Stalinization experiment allowed an emerging generation of writers, artists, and filmmakers to engage in the increasingly bold exploration of big moral issues and novel artistic forms. The vibrancy of this new artistic creativity soon extended into the historical past and national cultures of the peoples of the USSR. In effect, Khrushchev's Thaw also marked the rebirth of national cultures outside the stolid canon imposed by Soviet ideology. To understand this social dynamic, we will draw on a combination of Miroslav Hroch's historical study of national movements, modified by Bourdieu's conceptualization of the field of culture and Randall Collins's theory relating creativity to the competition for social attention space.[17]

Hroch's work sensitized us to the importance of the social background of national awakeners (artists, clerics, secular intellectuals, liberal professionals, etc.) and to the professional sub-cultures of the activists who led national movements in nineteenth-century Europe. Hroch distinguishes between several phases that he commonly found in the sequences leading to nationalist mobilizations, and it is the first of these initial phases – that of a national movement that is not yet political or nationalist – that will concern us here. In this initial phase then, the national movement seeks to identify, classify, and collect ethnographic cultural traits such as rural folklore, and then to validate and propagate the newly gathered national heritage, mainly through reprocessing it into the forms of modern high culture. National scholars create dictionaries, standardize the vernacular language and enrich it with modern vocabulary, compose music based on folk tunes, and transcribe and "ennoble" folk tales and epic songs. In short, this phase constitutes what is usually called national enlightenment. In the process, the successful national movement fosters its own audience, who are "awakened from slumber" to realize their national belonging and to learn to value their ethnic history and culture. It should be stressed that while this is not yet nationalism, it is certainly a major precondition for it, because here we find the origins of the cognitive frames, activist networks, and organizational resources that may eventually be deployed for the goals of nationalist mobilization.

The national awakeners who appeared in the non-Russian republics between 1956 and 1968 were themselves products of Soviet affirmative action; specifically, products of those official institutions dedicated to recasting ethnic cultures in modern forms: dance and theater companies, writers' unions, film studios, research centers, and teaching universities. They sought to resume the enterprise begun during the 1920s and earlier by those generations of the national intelligentsia who had been killed or silenced in the Stalinist period. In many instances the national awakening had to begin from scratch, though the tremendous educational expansion of the Soviet period created a large potential audience. The momentum of the national movements was sustained by the atmosphere of relaxed censorship and enthusiastic experimentation during Khrushchev's Thaw and by the increased availability of material resources that were poured into cultural production, civil architecture, and scientific research.

Bourdieu identified the source of the social dynamic in the field of culture in two related mechanisms. The first lies in the collective tendency of artists, writers, and intellectuals to defend the autonomy of their field against political and economic powers. The second lies in internal competition among participants in the field, where increases in symbolic capital are achieved by inventing and occupying positions in the creative avant-garde (or as Randall Collins would say, in the focus of emotional attention). In the Soviet situation of the sixties, many artists, writers, and humanistic scholars were national cultural producers, located in the national republics and operating in the national languages. Their plots, sources of inspiration, and forms of expression were found, adapted, or invented in relation to the history and folklore of their nations. Their audiences were predominantly co-national, although the higher achievements in the genres better suited for traveling across cultural boundaries – such as architecture, music, and especially film – gained prominence across the Soviet cultural scene and throughout the world.

Success invites emulation, emulation breeds competition, and competition drives the innovation that opens new positions in the field. The process eventually results in the transgression of boundaries delineated (though not always specified) by the dominant field of power. Such was the mechanism producing cultural dissidence throughout the late Soviet period; and it applies equally to the national cultural elites and to the Russian "democratizers." Competition for public attention, which inevitably offers only a limited space, develops along two often intertwined routes: carving a niche audience, where the attainment of attention is easier or even automatic; and the invention of plots, forms, and subject matters that have an emotional resonance. The exploration of past tragedies by artistic or scholarly means is one way to provoke such a resonance, especially in an audience able to identify with the events and victims. There are several examples of this process at work in the Khrushchev era; among them the wave of historical studies and artistic commemoration of the genocide of Armenians in the Ottoman Empire; the Azeri verses and scholarly monographs about the people divided by the river Arax (a direct allusion to the millions of Azeri brethren in Iran); the Georgian nostalgia for its glorious medieval kingdom and the exploration of Georgia's rural traditions infused with an astutely ironic self-glorification expressed in many wonderful films; and the North Caucasians' revival of imam Shamil's epic and the extremely popular novels about the tragic fate of *muhajeer* exiles who had been forced to leave their beloved motherland in the wake of Russian imperial conquest in the 1860s.

Of course, not all cultural production of the 1960s national revival focused on tragedies. The charmingly witty short stories of Fazil Iskander, though also nostalgic for the rapidly passing world of small mountain villages, put Abkhazia on not only the Soviet but also the larger world's map of modern literature.[18] But for the heartless purposes of social scientists like ourselves, two things stand out in this stream of national cultural creativity. First, that the choice of subject matter was in all instances cautiously removed from Soviet realities – though this was not enough to prevent the wrath of Soviet censors. Second, that the censors were absolutely right to be suspicious. This was an assertion of nationhood and, potentially at least, offered an alternative to official ideology.

Cultural producers who seek to expand the field of creativity will eventually end up testing the boundaries of the reigning orthodoxy. Iconoclasts tend to hold less symbolic capital: as amateurs, beginners, and/or intellectuals situated in more peripheral locations, they evidently have a lesser stake in the status quo and may have much to gain from challenging the orthodoxies of the epoch. The up-and-coming must often also be daring.

The same observation helps to explain the mechanism of repression that after 1968 scattered and drove underground the national cultural movements in the non-Russian republics. The locally positioned holders of powerful positions and officially consecrated symbolic capital clearly possessed a stake in preserving the status quo. Normally, there was surprisingly little need for intervention from Moscow (although in one famous instance the First Secretary of the Ukraine, Shelest, was sacked for sheltering purported cultural nationalists). In the Soviet national republics, the repression was mainly co-national and conducted by officials who willingly assumed the functions of censorship, and mobilized the state authorities for their reactionary cause. In order to grasp the complex interplay of democratization, the intractable dilemmas of Soviet ideology, and the revival of national cultures, let us take the celebrity case at the summit of Soviet power, where the key traits become very pronounced.

CULTURAL-POLITICAL POLARIZATION AND THE BIRTH OF COMMUNIST CONSERVATISM

The case is that of Alexander Solzhenitsyn, a former prisoner of the Gulag relegated to the job of village teacher, who wrote the moving story *One Day in the Life of Ivan Denisovich*, about inmates in a Stalin-era labor camp. It was published in 1961 in the leading literary magazine *Novyi Mir*, which throughout the Thaw period served as the focal point for the reform communists and the creative intelligentsia who were combating the crudest forms of censorship. This daring publication required the personal consent of Khrushchev who, judging its merits from a political standpoint, agreed that Solzhenitsyn's story carried a timely and strongly formulated denunciation of the recent excesses of Stalinism. The publication had an enormous resonance both within and outside the Soviet Union, which evidently made Khrushchev regret his miscalculation. Solzhenitsyn's prose, which was intended for domestic battles, was easily used by Western propagandists to discredit the USSR. Its worldwide acclaim gave Solzhenitsyn the confidence to select plots and approaches that went further beyond the admissible boundaries – a dynamic that shifted his work from the field of Soviet literature into that of Cold War inter-state politics, and eventually turned him into a vociferous anti-communist and Russian nationalist. (There are few indications that at the outset of his personal trajectory Solzhenitsyn was either of these.) This sequence culminated in the following decade with Solzhenitsyn being awarded the Nobel prize for literature, and with the Politburo's decision to strip him of Soviet citizenship.

In the course of his literary–political evolution, Solzhenitsyn's staunchest critics were the high-status intellectuals whose symbolic capital was embedded in the domi-nant discourse of socialist realism, which dated back to the 1930s and 1940s. This artistic mode had been officially consecrated by the Stalin Prizes in literature and arts (called the State Prizes after 1956), the receipt of which led to high positions in the USSR's "creative unions" of writers, artists, cinematographers, etc. Importantly, at the beginning of the 1960s, the attacks on Solzhenitsyn by the Stalin laureate writers did not represent an officially sanctioned campaign of ideological censorship. It was rather a watchdog activism by cultural officials who rightly saw a danger to their own power and prestige in the publication of stories like Solzhenitsyn's and the public reaction they were provoking.

This kind of reactionary response should be called the Stalinism of position rather than conviction. The public campaign against Solzhenitsyn and other icon-oclasts of the epoch served no less to identify, embolden, and organize potential conservatives who felt frightened at Khrushchev's policies. Here the audience was chiefly composed of the elite members located at the upper or middle levels of the ideological, administrative, and security apparatuses of the Soviet state, both in Moscow and in the provincial capitals, who began to coalesce into a self-conscious band of like-minded functionaries.

Ironically, these officially empowered individuals may have gained more from the de-Stalinization reforms than the rest of Soviet society – winning nothing less than personal security from the previously ever-present threat of arbitrary arrest and execution. It was only because Stalin was gone and the regime had changed that they could now in effect challenge the top ruler, Khrushchev himself, and launch their factionalist movement – for theirs was precisely a reactionary social movement developing inside the state and the Party and entirely reliant on the state's resources. Their strategic goal was to prevent the further radicalization of Khrushchev's offi-cial program.[19] But it stopped far short of a full restoration of Stalinism because obviously this elite group could hardly desire the surrender of their newly gained security of life and livelihood. The result was a political innovation for which we must use the oxymoronic designation *communist conservatism*. In Stalin's lifetime conservatism was inconceivable because the Soviet state and ideology remained in flux. Internecine struggles were waged over the selection of a route forward and the suppression of elite factions that had lost out and were proclaimed deviant. By contrast, de-Stalinization, despite its rambunctiousness, stabilized the field of power and thereby made conservatism possible.

The Soviet conservatives contributed to the polarizing tension that, in a consequential irony, helped to make the 1960s and 1970s such an inventive and boisterous period in the cultural history of the Soviet bloc. Before the conservative *nomenklatura* could topple Khrushchev and change the political regime to their liking, they pursued lesser targets – the iconoclast intellectuals who were trying to expand the limits of artistic and scholarly creativity. This is the immediate reason why the effervescent artistic fields of literary, film, and musical (jazz and rock) production in this epoch became the primary sites of power struggle.

The cultural and ideological *nomenklatura* remained in control of the distribution of formal artistic titles, appointments in the state-sponsored institutions, and material resources such as publishing and professional benefits. But this formally consecrated elite entirely lost its moral justification. They could no longer claim to represent progress or the great patriotic effort, which is why so many among them were nostalgic for Stalin, the legitimating demigod. At the same time, those creative artists and intellectuals who were driven to various sorts of oppositional and underground existence came to enjoy the undisputed possession of symbolic capital. Such capital was derived from two sources: the exercise of virtually any kind of creativity stood in sharp contrast to the hypocrisy and sterility of cultural officialdom; while the defiant transgression of imposed rules and conventions added a heroic status to almost any sort of underground movement. Of course, this was possible mainly because there now existed large groups of educated modern specialists who avidly consumed high-status cultural goods, from the films of Tarkovsky, the novels of Solzhenitsyn, and the poetry of Brodsky, to the guitar ballads of famous (and officially ignored) bards like Okudzhava and Vysotsky, and the sophisticated rock compositions that began to appear in the seventies. To various extents (depending primarily on the local depth and structure of the communities responsive to modern cultural forms) the same tension was present in the cultural fields of all national republics where, inevitably, a polarization in cultural fields was conducive to the validation of the nation's past and the newly created national cultures. Cultural censorship, enforced by crude bureaucratic measures and devoid of any vestige of moral justification, thus served as a catalyst for the construction of broad cultural coalitions in favor of democratization and nationalism. The former was widely understood as the abolition of all forms of censorship, while the latter was construed similarly as the abolition of censorship imposed on the republics by the Russian *nomenklatura* and their local puppets.

To summarize, during de-Stalinization the ruling Soviet elites developed four imperatives: there should be no more killings; there should be a ritual adherence to Marxist-Leninist ideology; striving for a better material life should be deemed a goal in itself (which included the toleration of relative inefficiency and corruption); and, given the institutional nature of the Soviet Union, the manipulation of nationalist sentiment to create local power bases should be deemed taboo. It was a cozy set of compromises, and all that remained was to maintain it until it became entrenched. A veteran functionary from the North Caucasus region recalls it this way: *A lot could be understood and absolved in the comradely circle. I mean, things like personal comforts and slacking off — of course, to a reasonable degree — or even a bit of drinking and womanizing. In a nutshell, nothing human is alien to us, as Marx said. But as for those nationalist ideas ... ah, your own comrades would bury you before Moscow could know. One must not rock the boat.*

4

From 1968 to 1989

"Major reform was as necessary as it was politically impossible."

Valerie Bunce, *Subversive Institutions: The Design and Destruction of Socialism and the State* (Cambridge: Cambridge University Press, 1998, p. 37)

Long before the spectacular confrontations that ended the Soviet Union, the stage had been set and the actors had assumed their roles. The script, however, remained a contested matter that would later in the drama create many unpleasant surprises and difficult choices for both actors and audience. The violent struggles of the nineties directly originated in the stalled revolutionary situation of 1989–1991. In their turn, the events of 1989 were shaped by the social structure that emerged from Soviet industrialization under Stalin, that expanded and matured during the dynamism of Khrushchev's era, and that generated the conflicts which were to shake the entire Soviet bloc around the symbolic date of 1968. To invoke one of Lenin's famous metaphors, while the Russian revolution of 1917 had its dress rehearsal in the revolution of 1905, the revolutionary situation of 1989 had its dress rehearsal in the revolutionary situation of 1968. In the USSR, the effective suppression of the 1968 movements prevented the formation of key resources for the movements of 1989.

THE COMFORTABLE DEATH OF SOVIET DEVELOPMENTALISM

Through de-Stalinization the Soviet executives had rid themselves of the terror and inhuman work pace that marked the epoch of dictatorial industrialization – but that was as far as they wanted to go. The ruling bureaucrats had first betrayed the world revolution during Stalinism; now their successors "betrayed" their perceived historical role as bureaucratic modernizers. The word "betrayal" must be put in cautionary quotation marks because although the Soviet *nomenklatura* proved unfaithful to the utopian project of permanent revolutionary transformation and overtaking the capitalist West, they still remained faithful to their emerging class interest. Khrushchev's futuristic vision of a communist utopia being realized in just another twenty years – as boldly promised in the 1961 edition of the Party Program – contrasted with the *psycho*-logical state of most of the *nomenklatura,* who least of all wanted a utopian campaign. In fact, such "betrayals" by the dominant classes seem recurrent in modern history. The bourgeoisie have time and again sought to acquire titles, rents, and generally transform themselves into a closed and privileged caste. This tendency perhaps subverts the ideal types of the capitalist or rational bureaucratic work ethic, in which success is supposedly the delayed gratification for self-denial and hard work. But why, the successful bourgeois invariably asks, delay the gratification? Such is the thinking that Wallerstein called the *psycho*-logical tendency to enjoy the fruits of success.[1]

By 1964 the top echelon of the post-Stalinist bureaucracy had acquired enough autonomy and confidence to topple Khrushchev and replace him with the convenient figurehead of Brezhnev. This palace coup marked a major power shift that determined the subsequent pattern of post-communist transition. Biographers of Khrushchev and Gorbachev, another toppled reformer, tend to focus on the dramatic details of intrigues, ignoring the structural problem common to the socialist and probably to every developmental state of modern times. That is, the surprising weakness of central governments, a weakness which, despite their dictatorial prerogatives, renders the rulers vulnerable to palace coups and provincial separatism. Valerie Bunce conceptualizes this aspect of socialist states as "the yawning gap between their reach and their grasp, between the institutional density and institutionalization."[2]

The immediate cause of the problem, long stressed by neoclassical economists, was information scarcity.[3] Because the socialist state established its monopoly in every social arena, from the command economy to fictitious electoral politics and a strictly censored press, it could not objectively evaluate the performance of its own bureaucracies and instead had to buy into the pervasive propagandistic hypocrisy of the bureaucrats own making, or else relied on hearsay and secret police reports. Economists critical of socialism, however, did not explain that it was out of weakness, not strength, that certain varieties of the socialist state tried to suppress or internalize social mechanisms outside their direct control. In order to enforce their policies state rulers multiplied the controlling agencies, launched propagandistic campaigns, experimented with reforms, or lashed out against self-serving bureaucrats in purges and cultural revolutions. Alternatively, especially during the glasnost and perestroika period, they sought out public criticism and introduced competitive elections. In short, the communist rulers who actually sought to govern had to be rambunctious, as Valerie Bunce has put it.[4]

Between 1956 and 1968 Khrushchev and other *nomenklatura* reformers – such as Premier Kosygin – experimented with various ways of improving state and economic governance within the new framework of "socialist legality," i.e. by refusing to resort to state terror while preserving Leninist ideology and the existing political framework. All such experiments in post-Stalinist governance boiled down to two ideas: economically, they allowed limited self-management at the level of economic sectors, territorial units, and enterprise, but did not permit bankruptcies; politically and culturally, they prescribed tolerance for the "socialist pluralism of ideas" and allowed for limited competitive elections that nonetheless had to stop short of challenging the basics of official ideology or changing the party in power. Both ideas promised increased popular participation and threatened to put the mid-ranking economic and administrative executives under pressure. This condition structured the key conflicts of both 1968 and 1989, in which the middle echelons of the *nomenklatura* had to fight threats from the routine-breaking reforms from above and their enthusiastic supporters pressing from below. The Soviet proletariat, especially its younger and better educated members, enthusiastically took Khrushchev's experimentation as an invitation to become an active force in the contemporary expansion of political and cultural fields. Shanibov and his volunteer patrol represented just one instance in the much wider wave of popular activity that developed in support of the official reform line.

We cannot know for sure where Khrushchev's experimentation was heading in the long run. Nonetheless, given the analogous and more pronounced trends in the socialist countries of Central Europe, we can confidently surmise that in a few years, as the factional contradictions within the ruling elites grew more apparent, popular activity could have escalated into a revolutionary mobilization similar to Czechoslovakia's Prague Spring of 1968. It would have most likely failed.

Nonetheless, the legacy of a significant popular mobilization for democracy would have proved a major structuring condition in the long run.

In hindsight it seems evident that the divergent outcomes of post-communist transitions after 1989 have been largely pre-structured by the patterns of contention emerging around 1968.[5] Put differently, the relative strengths of the 1956, 1968, and early 1980s popular mobilizations in Soviet bloc countries such as Hungary, Czechoslovakia and Poland may serve as a robust predictor of their successful democratizations after 1989.[6]

In Yugoslavia, the strong pressure of 1968 anti-authoritarian movements led to the adoption in 1974 of a new constitution suffused with the spirit of self-administration. Among other things, the new Yugoslav constitution granted an extensive autonomy to the ethnic Albanian majority in Kosovo and recognized the legal existence of a Muslim Slavic nationality in Bosnia-Herzegovina.[7] But instead of the intended economic and political democratization that attracted a lot of sympathetic attention at the time, Yugoslavia had in reality become a complex confederation of ethno-territorial units and self-managing enterprises. Due to its multiple internal contradictions and geopolitical exposure, the Yugoslav confederation proved particularly ill-suited to deal with adverse changes in the global economic climate during the late seventies and the eighties. In common with the recent theorizing on revolutions inspired by the groundbreaking works of Theda Skocpol and Charles Tilly, a materialist theory of ethnic conflict would identify the key causal factors involved in the wars of Yugoslavian succession within the institutional distribution of resources and the differentiated access to those resources enjoyed by the emerging contenders. In a bitter historical irony, it was the muddled outcome of Yugoslavia's 1968 student and worker protests, and the ongoing strife inside the ruling bureaucracy (rather than the wickedness of ethnic imagination), that set the scene for the later violent struggles over the spoils of a defunct communist developmentalism.

The Soviet Union combined the elements of the patterns observed in Yugoslavia and the socialist countries of Central Europe, though they were developed in a suppressed fashion evidently because the USSR remained a much stronger state and its rulers enjoyed very substantial economic and coercive resources. Nevertheless, under Brezhnev, Moscow's control over the national republics and provinces weakened considerably as the locally-based *nomenklatura* successfully entrenched and normalized their positions.[8] Additionally, the period of Thaw permitted artistic intellectuals of national republics to gain various degrees of creative autonomy and to forge the networks that sustained the new fields of national culture despite reactionary attempts to re-impose official ideological controls. Alongside these developments in the vertical hierarchy of Soviet power, the coalescing social classes of educated specialists and workers put strong pressure on the ruling bureaucracy to deliver on the ideological promises of improving life and social mobility. While the KGB effectively suppressed the nascent democratic dissidence that attempted to articulate the shifts in Soviet social structure in a new political program, nonetheless, the 1968 movement for "socialism with a human face" delegitimated the *nomenklatura*, and presented conservative bureaucrats with moral and ideological arguments they could not answer. Instead, officialdom resorted to censorship, propagandistic hypocrisy, and consumer subsidies. These were embarrassingly transparent and costly strategies intended to tame industrialized society, which called for more subsidies and the toleration of inefficiencies. The 1973 windfall of petrodollars facilitated this policy, ensuring that the death of Soviet developmentalism and the erosion of centralized governance could be made quite comfortable.

But pre-socialist history also mattered. Dissident democratic mobilizations in the socialist states of Central Europe drew strength from the survival of latent oppositional traditions within the networks of middle-class families that dated back to the petty nobility, bourgeoisie, and intelligentsia of pre-socialist formation.[9] Inside the USSR, similar conditions were found only in several smaller national republics, mainly Estonia, Latvia, and Lithuania, that had been independent states during 1918–1940, but also in Armenia and Georgia and, to a still lesser degree, in Moldavia and the western parts of Ukraine. The fact that the national intelligentsias in these regions traced their lineages to the states that at some point had been outside Soviet control determined the fusion of nationalism and the intelligentsia's opposition to the rule of communist officals.

In the post-Stalinist USSR the revamped *nomenklatura* matured in advance of a nascent opposition of intellectuals and industrial proletarians, who in trying to form a coherent movement after the decades of Stalinism had to begin from scratch. In the mid-sixties the *nomenklatura* sought to incorporate themselves into a privileged caste, to protect themselves both from the popular pressures below and from the central government above. But since the looming revolutionary crisis made this passive approach seem insufficient, for a short while conservative activism gained precedence. Correctly sensing the danger to its power and privileges, in August 1968 the top echelon of the Soviet bureaucracy sent tanks into Prague and stepped up internal censorship and policing across the USSR and its satellite states.

These moves helped to prevent the reform movement escalating into revolution, but in the long run the Soviet state paid a heavy price as it degenerated. In the late 1960s the successful corporatization of the Soviet *nomenklatura* created at the level

of provinces and economic sectors concentrations of vested interests that effectively resisted unwanted interference and the pressure to reform. The enforcement
of censorship by the KGB and watchful officials at various levels prevented all but
the most ritualistic discussion of problems and possible solutions. A small dissident underground and the forced emigration of political activists provided the
principal base for alternative formulations, but the pariah status of dissidents ruled
out the possibility of the elite making use of their suggestions. The Soviet apparatus became inertial, fractured into insulated bureaucratic turfs, and overall willfully
ignorant of its own problems. Put differently, the blindness and sclerosis of Soviet
bureaucracy was actually the achievement of the *nomenklatura*, and a major condition of Brezhnev-era comfort and security. As Arthur Stinchcombe points out, all
organizations regularly commit mistakes, but the smart ones correct them faster
and better.[10] We need not therefore blame Brezhnev's senility or the notorious
intransigence of Gromyko, who was called in the West *Mr. Niet*. Rather, the accen-
tuated irrationalities of the Soviet state – manifested in its ever clumsier propaganda
machinery, puzzlingly inept decisions in foreign policy, and the way petrodollars
were wasted in the seventies – should rather be regarded as the consequences of a
repressive conservative restoration that took hold after 1968.

INTELLECTUAL POLITICS AND CONTENTION

The fate of Yuri Shanibov once again reflects the bigger processes underway in the
Soviet Union. Before 1968 Shanibov would have seemed a very unlikely dissident.
At this early stage his combination of an ethnic background subject to affirmative
action, university credentials, and officially sanctioned activism in student patrols
presented the right kind of social capital for an executive career. He had already
served as the secretary of Kabardino-Balkaria's branch of Komsomol and as district
attorney; from here the way was open to *nomenklatura* positions such as faculty dean,
judge at his republic's Supreme Court, ideological supervisor in the party apparatus,
or perhaps KGB general. Instead, Shanibov became something completely
different. From the analytical standpoint, his fall from grace was not unlike the
more spectacular examples of celebrity writers such as Solzhenitsyn, whose early
work had received the approval of Khrushchev himself, or of top scientists such
as Andrei Sakharov, who already in his thirties was an academician and a Hero of
Socialist Labor (the highest civilian medal). In order to explain the reversal in
Shanibov's career, we will need to gain some understanding of the contemporaneous academic field. This task, however, requires some additional explanation,

insofar as the social sciences were organized differently in the USSR than in the West.

When Shanibov became a junior lecturer at university, he eagerly accepted the inauspicious position of faculty supervisor at the student residences, which suited his personal disposition and fitted well with his earlier experience in organising student patrols. In the capacity of faculty supervisor he had to deal largely with the same issues of drinking and adolescent violence, and to organize more civilized recreational alternatives. Shanibov's solution was born out of his previous experience and followed the officially sanctioned policy: the creation of student self-governance. But in the spirit of the times Shanibov took the assignment too earnestly. The student elections rapidly acquired the enthusiastic tone of genuine debate regarding the student candidates and the policies governing the residences. The young energetic instructor in social studies soon became a popular personality on campus and gathered around himself a circle of student activists and like-minded junior lecturers.

A few years later, in the early seventies, Shanibov submitted his overdue first-degree dissertation entitled "On student self-governance as a learning process of socialist democracy." Here the key word is "self-governance" or "self-management" (*samoupravlenie*), which indicates his role as a communist reformer. My field notes contain biographical data on nearly two hundred political intellectuals from the Caucasus and Russia that show a surprisingly robust correlation between the topics of their diploma theses and dissertations and their subsequent political stance. Amongst this data, however, one has to interpret the contemporary academic conditions, symbolic markers, and euphemisms. For instance, dissertations on what were called the "politically current" (*aktualnye*) topics, and which were playing along with the wooden discourse of official ideology, indicated an aspiration to an administrative career and a conservative communist stance. Conversely, during perestroika, interests in native history, philology, and folkloric arts were strongly correlated to a variety of nationalist stances.

In the USSR the main breeding ground for liberal dissidents was the "hard" sciences, especially the advanced fields of nuclear research and space exploration. During the 1950s–1970s, these scholarly communities enjoyed privileged funding, exceptionally high public acclaim, and relatively unrestricted intellectual exchanges with their Western colleagues. After the atomic scientists came linguists (some of them directly inspired by the writings of Noam Chomsky), archeologists, anthropologists, and psychologists, whose obscure interests lay beyond the focus of official Marxist-Leninist ideology. At the same time such scholarly interests helped to foster cohesive communities with a sense of professional dignity and kinship with the intellectual community outside the USSR. It is no small matter that such disciplines normally required a familiarity with esoteric concepts and at least a basic knowledge of foreign languages, which tended to deter administrative careerists. Since the atomic scientists were rarely found in the provincial universities, there the majority of future democratic publicists and mobilizers tended to be social and humanistic scholars.

The ranking of universities, which generally reflected the administrative ranking of territories, played a very significant role in enabling the emergence of a liberal intelligentsia. The topmost Soviet universities were located in Moscow, Leningrad, and Novosibirsk (the brand-new campus in Siberia specializing in advanced technological research). Then came the capitals of union republics, followed at a distance by the provinces, while all the way down at the bottom of the hierarchy were the local technical colleges. Within individual institutions academic seniority also tended to reflect and determine political leanings. For instance, despite the conservative professorial establishment at the faculties of economics and law in the largest and most prestigious universities of Moscow and Leningrad, the junior faculty and graduate students were in the best position to learn about Western neoliberal ideas. After Gorbachev's perestroika, the young iconoclasts successfully wielded this counter-official discourse against the senior professoriate. Likewise the young natural scientists and engineers were able to utilize their mathematical skills in the study of the new economics. The majority of post-Soviet liberal technocrats came from these two groups of junior specialists, but it must be stressed that the opportunity of converting scholarly credentials and knowledge in this interdisciplinary fashion was present in the elite universities alone.

Judged by Western conventions, Shanibov's dissertation would belong in sociology. But such a discipline had been absent from Soviet universities ever since the legendary deportation of Pitirim Sorokin in 1922. Instead, social studies were organized into four peculiarly Soviet areas. Already in the 1920s there were the disciplines of dialectical philosophy and political economy. Their corpus of classics, in accordance with old Marxist tradition, included not only the works of Marx and Engels, but also their sacred precursors, like Adam Smith, Ricardo, Spinoza, and Hegel. Moreover the Second International giants such as Kautsky and Plekhanov remained in the libraries, probably because Stalin cared to acknowledge the lineage of Marxist thought. Courses in philosophy and political economy had to follow the exceedingly narrow and dogmatic textbooks approved by the most senior party members. Teaching stressed the memorization of maxims and quotes, but within this theological style of learning some quasi-heretical disputation was still possible.

In 1938 Stalin himself instituted the new discipline of the political history of the Bolshevik Party and underwrote its infamous textbook, *A Brief Course in the History of the VKP(b)*. It dogmatically repudiated as misguided, opportunistic or "turncoat" all other socialist currents, from the nineteenth-century Narodniki to the Trotskyists, and presented Stalin as the defender and inheritor of the one true Marxist-Leninist doctrine. In 1962 Stalin's name was removed from the text to be replaced by the generic expressions "true Leninists" or "Our Communist Party," and the rhetoric was toned down. But, after some debate in the Politburo, essentially the same course was left in place because conservative elements were fearful of opening the Pandora's box of Soviet political history. This fear was in fact well founded, as was later proved by glasnost. The latter unleashed among historians and publicists a competition to deliver ever more stunning revelations regarding the dark spots in the Soviet past, a process which within just a couple years utterly wrecked the legitimizing discourse of the Soviet state.

With de-Stalinization ordained by Khrushchev in 1956, however, the Soviet ideological leaders felt an acute need for a progressive and scientifically argued legitimation. Besides, in the minds of Soviet leaders before 1968, the accelerating development of the communist reform movements in Poland, Hungary, and Czechoslovakia called for a substantive response. Thus in the mid-1960s the latest discipline of Soviet social studies was instituted, under the name of *scientific communism*.

Like many Soviet intellectuals interested in modern social science, Shanibov eagerly set out to institutionalize the new discipline, using the resources and academic positions that were generously offered to support the new field – each and every institution of higher education was to acquire a new department. The enthusiasts for the new discipline were indisputably loyal to socialist ideology, yet their attempts to foster a scientifically informed transformation of Soviet society (computers and research surveys were all the rage) inevitably clashed with established bureaucratic interests. In the early days of scientific communism its younger progressive wing recurrently ended up recapitulating the arguments of the Czech reform movement, despite the fact that Soviet censorship had made the direct diffusion of Czech arguments unlikely (although their echoes were heard with great curiosity). It was the contemporary structure of the Soviet ideological field itself that continuously suggested moves bordering on "loyal dissent."

Let us see what people like Shanibov were reading in the 1960s. Besides the Marxist-Leninist classics (which now included the recently published *Gründrisse* and other manuscripts of Marx, as well as excerpts from Gramsci – grudgingly acknowledged by Soviet officials as a communist martyr), the young social scientists had access only to the Soviet economic debates of Khrushchev's period and a very patchy selection of up-to-date Western translations. These included, however, the Russian translation of *The Power Elite* by C. Wright Mills, as already mentioned; the works of John K. Galbraith on the convergence between the planned and the market economy, which flattered the technocratic faction in Moscow; and selections from progressive French sociologists like Alain Touraine, who were presented as expressive of the Western proletarian struggle for industrial democracy. Translations of the sophisticated, advanced, or world-class works of Polish and Hungarian sociologists provided a very important example of, and transmission mechanism for, Western theoretical ideas and research methods. A major channel of world intellectual diffusion lay in Soviet renditions of scholarly books from abroad that for the sake of censorship were disguised as Marxist-Leninist critiques and therefore were oftentimes written in very opaque language. These ostensibly critical works were published in restricted numbers and circulated under the rubric "for scientific libraries only," which made them even more sought-after. This also explains the mechanism of the short-lived publishing boom during perestroika, when the books of any hitherto unavailable but famed author – be it Solzhenitsyn, Kafka, Nietzsche, Freud, or Von Hayek – sold in the hundreds of thousands, and even millions, throughout the wide expanses of the Soviet Union. Curiously enough, Max Weber was rather neglected, perhaps because from afar his sociology of capitalism seemed to Soviet intellectuals merely a version of Marxism. Likewise Louis Althusser, by virtue of looking a little too Marxist-Leninist, did not provoke nearly as much interest as Albert Camus or Raymond Aron. Selections from Durkheim were actually included in the officially approved courses on anthropology and in another Soviet discipline called scientific atheism.

In summary, there was little coherence to the list of books commonly read in the social sciences. Nonetheless, almost everything was eagerly consumed because of acute informational shortage and the presence of a large educated audience. The intellectual value of a text was judged to be in reverse proportion to that given it by official Soviet ideology. Fernand Braudel became a celebrity because the editor of the Russian translation of his work (himself no other than Yuri Afanasiyev, who in 1989–1990 stood next to Sakharov and Yeltsin in the leadership of the democratic movement) tricked the Central Committee's censors and astutely put on the dust-jacket of *Material Civilization and Capitalism* the catch-phrase "the acclaimed masterpiece of non-Marxist historiography." (The queue at the shop door eagerly awaiting the book's release had begun before dawn.)

Now we can appreciate why the keyword "self-governance" – reminiscent of Yugoslavia's heterodox variety of socialism – in the title of Shanibov's dissertation might look daring, especially for a provincial university. After 1968, the crackdown on the youthful boom in social science research was severe. Following the suppression of the Prague Spring the departments of scientific communism were "reinforced" with stalwart professors transferred from the older orthodox disciplines, mainly from Party history. The majority of instructors in scientific communism rapidly developed distinctly conformist attitudes when faced with the choice between comfortable careers and outright expulsion from academia.

By the contemporary standards of the more cosmopolitan Moscow or Novosibirsk, Shanibov's dissertation did not look too provocative. But Nalchik was a small provincial capital. In addition, Shanibov's prospects were undercut by two distinct developments of the late sixties. The first was the saturation and closure of *nomenklatura* positions. The vacancies created in the 1956–1968 period were mostly filled by people only slightly older than Shanibov. They had already negotiated privileged spaces for themselves and forged their patronage networks. Subsequently career mobility slowed and almost came to an entire halt. Shanibov was no longer perceived as a young promising careerist but rather as a dangerously disruptive claimant.

Secondly, the change in crime-fighting policies made the arguments of Shanibov's dissertation appear questionable. Shortly after Brezhnev's coming to power the USSR's Ministry of the Interior was restored. The volunteer patrols were now closely supervised by the local police and party organs and thus the former youth movement became the usual hypocritical dissimulation of volunteerism. The police were instructed to remove all sorts of disruptive individuals from the streets of big cities, and the courts issued the longest possible prison sentences. Consequently, the Soviet prison population probably exceeded in total number the figure reached during the Stalinist purges. In the comparably uneventful and prosperous years of Brezhnevism, perhaps as many as one in six adult Soviet males spent time behind bars.[11] Among the ethnic minorities who have historically been alienated from the Soviet state, especially Muslims like the Balkars and Chechens, the rate of incarceration was significantly higher. On average, prison sentences of three to five years were issued for acts categorized as "hooliganism," "anti-social idleness," or "crimes against socialist property," i.e. workplace theft and shadow entrepreneurship. But these extremely troubling social indicators remained secret, and the general public ignored them because the prison industry was not part of mainstream Soviet experience. Under Brezhnev the prison population consisted predominantly of young workers and sub-proletarians from smaller towns. But for the socially invisible underclass of those precariously employed – youths from tough neighborhoods in industrial towns, alcoholics, black marketeers, rural sub-proletarians, poorly educated single mothers – the Soviet prison system became the central socializing institution. Later in the 1980s this would provide the breeding ground of the new post-Soviet mafia.[12]

The long preparation for the public defense of his dissertation (a highly ritualistic and bureaucratic convention of the Soviet university system) placed Shanibov's work at the center of a growing controversy. The repressions initiated by the senior professoriate and the university administration were pre-emptive, which made them look like an overreaction. The young lecturer stood accused simultaneously of "Czech pseudo-liberalism" and "Maoist ultra-leftism" in his mobilizing of the student youth against the "mature generation of seasoned cadres" – though the activists of student self-governance only mildly disagreed with the dean's opinion at a meeting. This was enough for the local branch of the KGB to open an investigation. The charges were eventually dismissed but not before Shanibov underwent the moral torture of public confessions and was forced to renounce his research or give up on any prospect of academic employment. In the end, Shanibov was left to teach at the university. But he never received a promotion and for years had to live on the miserable salary of a junior lecturer.

Many colleagues and student activists felt embarrassed by the witch-hunt and personally sorry for Shanibov. This sympathy and the covert friendship constituted Shanibov's personal and thus counter-official concentration of symbolic and social capital that endured over the years. It must be stressed that Shanibov's circle was not a dissident cell. These young intellectuals simply continued to live in the same town and remained friends. During Brezhnevism they were politically disengaged, though many took an interest in the fashions of the contemporary intellectual counter-culture, like yoga, jazz, the songs of Soviet underground bards, or the existentialist novels of Albert Camus (see Table 4, page 328, First Period). Nalchik, however, was too small and provincial a town to support a genuine underground. At best, Shanibov's friends were an embryonic counter-elite.

The ordeals of Shanibov followed a familiar pattern observed after 1968 across the USSR and its East European bloc. Yet the ubiquity of similar examples does not mean that it was a centrally waged campaign. Dramatic events such as the removal of Khrushchev and the dispatch of armies to Prague, together with Moscow's ideological instructions (which were transmitted openly through the propaganda editorials or through the "closed directives" sent for discussion to party cells) combined to create a flow of signals that were interpreted, correctly enough, as an authorization to fight potential dissenters locally. It was clearly stipulated that the victims were neither to be killed nor, in most cases, arrested. On this issue de-Stalinization endured. Harassment was considered a sufficient warning. The majority of victims were intellectuals because, as we saw earlier, the fields of academia and cultural production became the key points of symbolic confrontation between the conservative and reformist factions of the *nomenklatura*. Locally, the selection of victims seemed to follow mostly the lines of career succession among the intellectuals. The senior professoriate in the official ideological disciplines and academic administrators essentially used the bogey of the KGB to keep junior scholars in their place and in particular to prevent the formation of an alternative symbolic capital that would make reference to the world outside, i.e. to Western intellectual arenas.

Close in time and space to Shanibov, we find a similar victim in similar trouble. In the mid-1970s the party committee of the Checheno-Ingushetian University "signaled" to the local branch of the KGB their concern over the dubious sentiments brewing in the self-organized student poetry club Prometheus, whose amateurish poetry vaguely and rather innocuously praised the glories of the native mountains. The source of indignation lay in the fact that the young Chechen poets failed to submit their compositions for assessment by the local Union of Soviet Writers. Years later, this provincial micro-conflict would re-emerge in the Chechen national revolution, where the formerly aspiring poets led the radical fringe against the moderate national intellectuals, some of whom had once been their censors. In the suppressed poetic circle we find Zelimkhan Yandarbiyev, future co-founder, together with Shanibov, of the Mountain Confederation, the leading ideologist of Chechnya's independence, its interim president in 1996–1997, and later a religious fundamentalist exiled in the Middle East.

In retrospect Yandarbiyev's biography, as he likes to relate it in his books, appears to trace a clear line of increasing radicalization. It was Yandarbiyev who in 1990 founded in Checheno-Ingushetia the Vainakh Democratic Party and in 1991 became the chief ideologist of Chechnya's unilateral independence. It is the same "Politician, Poet, Patriot" who in 1997 ran for the presidency of Chechnya and renamed Grozny as Djohar-kala, after the first president Djohar Dudayev, and was assassinated in Qatar in February 2004 (recall chapter one). But the fact is that in the mid-1980s Yandarbiyev succeeded in joining the official Writers Union and was on his way towards becoming its secretary, in charge of distributing publication quotas, vacation packages, apartments, and other tangible benefits of Soviet *nomenklatura* existence. One really wonders what Yandarbiyev would be today if 1989 had never happened.

Back in the seventies the local branches of the KGB took on these almost ridiculous cases for two reasons. First, in the new era of enforced stability and consensus the local secret police wanted to maintain good relations with the local elite and party organs who requested their help. Secondly, being bureaucratically accountable, these branches of the KGB had to report to Moscow that work was being done. But, given the climate of Brezhnevism, the activity they were suppressing could not look too extreme because otherwise it would cause alarm. The harassment of sincere communist reformers like Shanibov and aspiring poets like Yandarbiyev provided the secret police with convenient cases for the dissimulation of work. The former KGB officers whom I interviewed admit that it was standard practice occasionally to call colleagues in other provinces and, to quote directly from one, in a "friendly, collegial fashion decide collectively" what kind of operations and of what intensity the chief directorate in Moscow would find satisfying. Informally and collectively negotiated dissimulation became the quintessential strategy of bureaucratic power in Brezhnev's USSR.

Following the upheaval of 1968, the last thing Brezhnev's conservative Politburo wanted to do was unleash another purge that, as they knew from experience, could easily get out of hand. Shanibov's internal exile was a typical example of the "softer" and mostly muffling repression of the time. Instead Brezhnevism derived its legitimation from a ritualistic struggle against the rival that was America, which was fought mainly by gathering clients in the Third World and became another ongoing ideological dissimulation of world revolutionary transformation. Domestically, the Brezhnev regime of stabilization relied on the pervasive toleration of slacking and on paternalistic consumer subsidies that dramatically improved the material situation of socialist proletarians over this period without giving them a voice. But the strains accompanying these strategies only tended to accumulate over the years.

THE DISCONTENTS OF BUREAUCRATIC CONSERVATISM

The next fifteen years of Shanibov's public life were wasted in internal exile, so let us look beyond his biography to the contemporary uneventful context where we find the structural causation of the Soviet state breakdown. Today the Brezhnev period tends to fall into limbo, lost somewhere between the interests of historians and the more contemporary-oriented social scientists. Yet the implosion of the Soviet bloc and the trajectories of its successor states cannot be explained without accounting for the failure of the Soviet ruling bureaucracy to act on the early signs of economic decline and social crisis. But why should they have felt very concerned? The reform movements of 1968, which were swiftly and quite easily suppressed, were willfully presumed to be an aberration. In the 1970s the Soviet state continued to enjoy the advantages of a very big and relatively vigorous economy; an educated and still expanding population; an increased prestige as a superpower now that the US was running into trouble; and, after 1973, a hefty oil bonus. The problems, however, were deeply structural and therefore mostly hidden from sight at the time. These problems can be analyzed as arising from three sources of strain: superpower geopolitics, advanced proletarianization, and the entrenchment of bureaucracies.

Geopolitical Strain

Geopolitically, the Soviet state carried an enormous burden of superpower obligations in the form of the arms race against a much wealthier United States and subsidies to a widening circle of foreign clients. This produced the first major source of fiscal strain.[13] Aside from its sheer wealth, the US enjoyed the capitalist advantage of commercialized warfare, which mitigated its fiscal burden through a mechanism sometimes called "military Keynesianism" (the maintenance of productivity through government orders justified in terms of national security); technological feedback from defense research and development in the civilian sectors; and the wielding of diplomatic power to aid the international interests of American business.[14] The organizational morphology of the USSR – in the absence of a price-setting market and real money (which the sector-specific, non-convertible "cashless rubles" were not) – did not allow the Soviet economy to emulate the Western commercialization of warfare. And so its fate was very different: investment resources were buried in the production of armaments to the detriment of civilian sectors; there were administrative curbs on the diffusion of new technologies due to the paranoidal pursuit of military secrecy; and the ironic situation arose where the dominant imperial state had to buy the allegiance of client states with grants and subsidized exchange without much prospect of exploiting them in return.

The intensity of geopolitical and ideological confrontation could be reduced by the mutual agreement of the two superpowers when they faced other crises, like the American defeat in Vietnam and the frightening Soviet border clashes with China. In the early seventies the combination of respective geopolitical failures and domestic pressures prompted Brezhnev and Nixon to initiate the policy of superpower détente. It is doubtful whether the policy of détente could have really lasted for long. The conservative ideologists and military-industrial complexes on both sides were certainly the most visible and serious barriers. But perhaps a bigger factor was the overall configuration of international and domestic political fields structured by the Cold War regime of interstate relations. The USSR was caged in its superpower status. The structural forces expressed themselves, as they usually do, in what appear to be the vagaries of history – such as Moscow's apparent failure to restrain its military planners and the developers of medium-range missiles, or its temptation to use a small portion of the idle army to score a victory in Afghanistan.

The strictly geopolitical explanation of Soviet collapse proposed by Randall Collins is certainly correct in stressing the long-running military overextension.[15] Yet this theory remains insufficient insofar as it does not explain how, for instance, in earlier periods and at a much lower level of industrial development the USSR survived the direct attacks of Japan in 1938 and then of Nazi Germany. To expand our explanation we therefore need to turn to internal dynamics.

The Strain of Advanced Proletarianization

Socially, the Soviet population had been largely recast as modern, educated and fully wage-dependent proletarians. The birth rate dropped correspondingly within the lifespan of one generation, and the reserve pool of peasantry, at least in the core Slavic republics of the USSR, was soon drained of manpower. For the first time ever in history, the rulers of Russia had to face relative shortages of labor force and military recruits. From their side, all proletarians sooner or later learn how to organize and wield as bargaining tools their concentrated numbers, their acquired skills, and the crucial threat of withdrawing their labor from the production process. When industrial managers, whether capitalist or socialist, can no longer rely on bringing new and less demanding workers – either recent peasants, women, or immigrants from poorer countries – the workers acquire the historical possibility of becoming a class for itself in the Marxist sense, and thus a real force to be reckoned with.

In a socialist state that was daily pronouncing itself to be at the service of workers, the ideological vision of class was a given fact. Yet for the same reason translating it into genuine proletarian politics was an extremely difficult task. The political reality of socialist dictatorships did not allow for genuine labor organizing. Hence the social power of workers translated primarily into shopfloor bargaining through the diffuse, mostly tacit, and continuous withdrawal of labor instead of the concentrated, explicit, and concerted withdrawal that happens during a strike. Surely strikes were less exceptional events than the official propaganda ever admitted. Still open strikes were very dangerous. The workers had to choose a very different strategy on a daily basis and, cumulatively, it proved to be a great success.

The notoriously shoddy quality of Soviet-made goods was in fact the perverted triumph of class struggle under state socialism. Denied the institutionalized means to increase their wages through collective bargaining, the workers tacitly sought ways to decrease their labor inputs.[16] Such is the political economy behind one of the most famous Soviet-period jokes: *"They pretend to pay and we pretend to work."* In the face of falling labor inputs and slackening industrial discipline, the Soviet state chose inaction because it was trapped by its own official ideology of Marxism-Leninism, its commitment to full employment, and the unwillingness of civilian *nomenklatura* to allow the revival of Stalinist terroristic methods of worker intimidation. This victory of the Soviet workers had lasting, pernicious effects on the work ethic, helping to bring about the toleration of workplace theft and to encourage drinking, a generalized cynicism, and an apathy regarding civic engagement, including labor organizing. Wary of the political consequences of acting otherwise, the Soviet leadership had to tolerate the lowered productivity of labor while further extending a convoluted system of indirect benefits through the workplace. This policy tremendously boosted the trend for civilian consumption between the late 1950s and the mid-1980s, a trend which ran in the opposite direction to the decreasing productivity growth rates of Soviet labor, thereby creating further contradictions.

The generously subsidized popular consumption, especially in the largest cities, now relied on the rapidly growing number of consumer imports, which could be paid for with petrodollars. In the short run this policy had a socially taming effect and provided some incentives in the strategically important industries, especially the military-industrial complex, where the availability of imported goods through "consumer ordering" in the workplace became a major perk. This is the main reason why the Brezhnev period is fondly remembered by many people in the former USSR. The consumer imports introduced Soviet proletarians to the consumption patterns of Western societies. Escalating consumer expectations put yet another potential political pressure on the Soviet state, whose stringent border controls, non-convertible currency, and inept bureaucracy seemed the only impediments to the enjoyment of Western goods. Needless to say, Western propaganda eagerly advertised the lifestyle differences between the two societies.

In order to counter the decreasing effectiveness of its economy, the Soviet government relied extensively on new capital investments to build more enterprises. This policy provided an appearance of industrial growth and thus seemed to validate the Soviet developmentalist ideology long after the real developmentalist spurt had ended. But in reality it caused chronic labor shortages, which added to the bargaining power of skilled and semi-skilled workers and the pervasive waste of resources. The consequences of the completion of Soviet proletarianization thus constituted the second major source of fiscal strain and political problems.

The Self-Encapsulation of the Nomenklatura

The third major structural contradiction of the Soviet state lay in the structure of the ruling bureaucracy itself. The Soviet bureaucracy had begun to normalize on its own terms as early as the twilight years of Stalin. Once the dreadful despot was gone and his henchmen purged, the process of bureaucratic self-normalization took off, despite the meddling attempts of Khrushchev, who desperately sought a remedy against the resulting encapsulation of bureaucratic realms.

The inherent bureaucratic parochialism of the Soviet and post-Soviet fields of power has often prompted parallels with feudalism, but this comparison is over-drawn. David Woodruff, whose breakthrough study of money in the Soviet Union and Russia builds on the theories of Simmel and Polanyi, perhaps comes closer to the truth.[17] Woodruff argues that the creation of national currencies was a key premise and achievement of modern state-making. In this (and perhaps only this) regard the USSR and Russia in the 1990s do resemble early absolutist states on the eve of monetary consolidation, although the resemblance is not genetic but rather homological. The ruble served as the national currency in the modern sense when it was tied to the gold standard between 1893 and 1914, and again during the NEP from 1922 to 1928. But the gold standard could not be kept under the imposed rate of industrialization. To deal with the many shortages and repress inflation, Soviet industrialization had to be conducted with a multiplicity of sector-specific quasi-monies, regional rationing coupons, and horizontal barter exchanges. This developmental strategy, at first construed as a policy of crisis management which would last only for the duration of the industrial leap, became embedded in the institutions, ideology, habituses and dispositions of Soviet industrial management. In the absence of the commensurability provided by a single currency – how otherwise could one compare butter with timber or with fighter-bombers? – the central planning bureaucracy had to rely on crude material indicators and inter-agency bargaining with subordinate echelons to determine the needs and plan the targets of the different branches of the economy, the regions, and the republics. It was therefore in the vested interest of mid-level bureaucracies inside the economic sectors and territorial administrative units to pursue such familiar practices of Soviet industrial management as the creation of vertically extended patronage networks, horizontal barter schemes, the hoarding of resources, and under-estimating productive capacities while overestimating the demands for the centrally distributed resources. Moreover the managers resisted interference in their affairs, including the organizational and technological innovations imposed on them from above.

Neoclassical economists blame these problems on the inherent inefficiency of a command economy. There were indeed structural contradictions, but the accusation of general failure, which is accepted today as unarguable, is empirically false. In its earlier periods the Soviet command economy performed incredible feats, vastly outperforming the Third Reich in the production of tanks and airplanes, restoring the devastated country after the war, and later in the 1950s and 1960s keeping up with American advances in strategic nuclear weapons and aerospace delivery systems. In the light of its previous achievements, Moscow's failure to keep up with the advances made in computers and micro-electronics – where Soviet backwardness had already become manifest in the late 1960s – is puzzling. Manuel Castells and Emma Kiselyova provide an excellent description of this failure, but their interpretation through the lens of the "information society" seems foggy.[18] The root cause of the failure in computer technology was not the sophistication of the new machines, although computers to a certain degree do bring about the decentralization of decision-making; at the root was the organizational evolution of the Soviet state.

The ferocious Stalinist campaigns to catch up in arms production with the enemies of the USSR kept the industrial executives liable to pay with their heads, yet promised to these same managers extraordinary powers and prestige in the event of success. The despotic powers of Stalinist central authority could override all lesser concerns and concentrate the scarce resources on the achievement of strategic goals. For instance, in the late 1940s the chief nuclear scientist Academician Kurchatov (himself familiar with the Gulag) was disposing of as much as one-tenth of Soviet GDP and overseeing legions of researchers, workers, soldiers, labor-camp prisoners, and foreign spies – it was perhaps the command economy at its pinnacle.[19] The Soviet problem with electronics lay not with the relative complexity of computers, since the task of developing the atom bomb and ballistic rockets was probably no less daunting. The problem was fundamentally political.

The command economy could only work – forgive the unavoidable tautology – as long as there existed a supreme commander. The dictatorial transformation of all revolutionary regimes in the twentieth century, whether of the communist or national-liberation variety, cannot be attributed solely to the personal dispositions of, for example, Stalin, Mao, Tito, Castro, Atatürk, or Nasser. Such leaders arose out of the stringent logic that concentrated scarce resources in the hands of a centralized state for the purpose of speeding up development. Furthermore, such actively transformational dictatorships had to inspire no less than terrorize. The utopian ideology must be recognized as a necessary component of revolutionary developmentalism, alongside the periodic recourse to terror. In the late 1960s the USSR no longer met either of these two conditions. The Soviet ideology had been gutted, embalmed, and mummified. Moscow was transformed from the commanding center into the principal nexus of corporativist lobbying and intra-bureaucratic bargaining.[20] Caught in the middle, the Politburo and the government ministries now allocated resources in the worst possible way, doing it blindly and according to bargaining weights of sectors and provinces that were continuously negotiated in Byzantine bureaucratic intrigues. The stolid sovereign managers of the industrial sectors and territories turned every campaign into a bureaucratic ritual of endless meetings – a pretext for demanding more resources and an occasion for the distribution of more medals.

The Russian economist Vladimir Popov suggested an elegant theoretical formulation that relates the strengths and weaknesses of a command economy to the different phases in its material life cycle. Command economies, if supported by the necessary state institutions, should normally be more successful than capitalist markets in achieving short- and medium-term targets in the massive production of material output – such as is needed for rapid industrialization or winning wars. However, the effectiveness of a command economy rapidly declines after approximately thirty years when, in Popov's estimate, the amortization of over half of the industrial assets reaches the point of replacement. For this task, command economies of the Soviet variety possessed neither the appropriate legal and organizational mechanisms nor ideological justification.[21] It might prove impossible to restructure or shut down the obsolete factory that was once the pride of the first Five Year Plan or that provides the livelihood for a whole town. In short, a command economy can produce miracles but has a limited lifespan.

Additionally, because the Soviet economy was very heavily biased towards weapons production and prestigious industrial and infrastructural projects, its accumulated resources could not be effectively redirected to meet the rising consumer demand of the wage-earning population after industrialization had been successful. The Soviet economy, caught in its obsolete organizational form, continued along the path of early industrialization, albeit with managers now virtually untouchable and workers comfortably incorporated in relaxed regimes of production and consumer subsidies. From the economic standpoint, so Popov concludes, the best opportunity to restructure the Soviet economy was missed in the 1960s, i.e. three decades after Stalinist industrialization. In this respect the Central European countries and China, whose industrialization dated back to the 1950s, were in a better position when launching their market transitions in the 1980s.

Here Popov's theory meets the arguments of Peter Evans regarding the unavoidable accumulation of various political interests and economic rigidities that together contributed to the dismantling of developmental states.[22] At the point of social maturation and the onset of industrial obsolescence, the future political course would seem to depend largely on external pressures (military, economic, ideological) and the outcome of internal struggles. In the mid-1960s the emergent conservative wing of the Soviet bureaucracy gained a control of the state that was sufficiently powerful to continue with the paternalistic socioeconomic compact and to insulate itself from external pressures, at least for another couple of decades.[23] Already in the late 1960s many members of the Soviet elite thought that conservative inertia would undermine the state's viability in the long run. But the majority of Soviet executives, especially those leaders at the political controls, could not resist the temptation to enjoy the newly gained relaxation and transform their administrative positions into sources of rent. Indeed rent is a more precise term than corruption.

Rent from administrative positions is a key factor in the economic, cultural and political choices of Brezhnevite conservatism. Analytically, the rentier faction in the late Soviet bureaucracy might be compared to the conservative agrarian aristocracy of older periods. This points to the potential for extending Theda Skocpol's theory of revolution and using it to explain the intra-elite cleavages and the sociopolitical dynamics of the Soviet implosion.[24] Skocpol's theory can furthermore help us understand the state breakdown and revolutionary situation that ended the Soviet experience. The three conservative strategies of Brezhnev's period – the prestigious race against America, the taming of domestic unrest through subsidized consumption, and the toleration of bureaucratic inefficiencies – accumulated huge fiscal strains that the Soviet government could barely contain even with the unexpected help of petrodollars. The knockdown effect was delivered in the early 1980s not by military defeat but by the decline in oil prices and the vigorous activism of the Reagan administration which undertook the re-channeling of world financial flows to revitalize US domestic consumption.[25] Then the accumulated fiscal strains of the USSR, as well as of many other ossifying developmentalist states, suddenly turned into escalating foreign debt that, in turn, became a big source of the recent financial globalization. It is then possible to extend Skocpol's classical outline of revolutionary sequence in which defeat on the foreign front robs the ruling regime of its legitimacy, and creates the untenable fiscal strain that leads to the fracturation of the elite, to popular rebellions, and to state breakdown. All this seems to apply to the collapse of the Soviet bloc.

GORBACHEV'S CONVERSIONS

Behind the stolid façade of the superpower, the ruling Soviet elite felt a deep-seated anxiety. The recently available *nomenklatura* memoirs and documents from the previously secret archives provide ample evidence of such sentiments. But the long-standing practices of censorship and the public dissimulation of politics deprived the Soviet bureaucratic apparatus of alternative policy formulations and forced it to proceed by inertia, interrupted with occasional improvisation. The reformers still emerged. They belonged to the younger generation of the *nomenklatura*, the top management of the leading economic sectors, and the elite corps of KGB officers, especially those who operated abroad. They all shared the pragmatic desire for a more rational, vigorous, centralized state. Democratization was not their goal. It was rather the means that emerged later in the intra-elite factional struggle between the reformers and the conservatives.

The first attempt to overcome bureaucratic rigidities and economic stagnation was neo-Stalinist. During his brief reign in 1982–1983 Yuri Andropov launched an anti-corruption purge combined with a campaign of communist moralizing.[26] Andropov's efforts, however, immediately ran into problems which had long before been predicted by Isaac Deutscher and Barrington Moore.[27] The bureaucracy was now securely embedded in the industrial base and could resist the purge collectively, even if unable to prevent the show punishment of particularly corrupt officials. Meanwhile the majority of the Soviet population became accustomed to a normalized proletarian existence based on steady work, lengthy formal education, and incrementally rising consumption. Many among them certainly felt disgusted with the bureaucrats but overall the proletarian class became too self-conscious to hail the punitive arbitrariness of another despotic cult.

Gorbachev emerged from a reform current in the Soviet leadership whose origins dated back to the early 1960s. In opposition to the conservative bureaucratic rentiers, the reformers embodied the activist administrative and intellectual habitus developed by the younger upwardly mobile cadres in the expansive period of Khrushchevism. Yegor Ligachev – during perestroika the number two in the Politburo and Gorbachev's main rival – describes in his memoirs how in the 1970s the differential of habitus operated in pre-political divisions among the top administrators of Soviet industries and territories, who regularly met at the plenary sessions of the Central Committee: "Separation emerged as if by itself. We just knew each other's worth, who meant real business and who achieved promotions through connections, ritual sloganeering, and flattery."[28]

The activist administrative habitus was concentrated in the managerial elite of the large capital-intensive enterprises which were predominantly situated in the Urals and Siberia (e.g. the Politburo members Ligachev, Premier Ryzhkov and Yeltsin) and in the elite foreign directorates of the KGB (e.g. Andropov and, in another generation, Putin). In the face of mounting Soviet problems, these self-assured executives, accustomed to a very demanding work schedule, to great responsibility, and to solving major problems on a daily basis, felt the urge to do something. Yet they could not have an articulated program. Gorbachev has often been called naïve, misguided, or duplicitous; but if an admittedly shrewd bureaucratic manipulator appears not to know what he is doing, the problem must lie not merely in his personal faults but in the structural conditions.

A major institutional weakness of the Soviet *nomenklatura* was a consequence of its apparent strength. The fused monolithic hierarchy suppressed factionalism and thereby severely constrained the intra-elite circulation of relevant information and put a choke hold on the debate of policy.[29] A dictatorial figure like Stalin or, for that matter, Khrushchev or, in another epoch, Yeltsin and Putin, could steer by the ancient Machiavellian rulebook, which meant surrounding themselves with secret advisors, playing one bureaucratic clique against another, lashing out and periodically demonstrating other kinds of despotic rambunctiousness. But by the end of the Brezhnev period the mid-level *nomenklatura* had accumulated such a formidable staying power that even the fearsome Andropov within months of his accession appeared almost ridiculous in his attempts to lash out.

A gradual democratization from above appeared to be, in view of Andropov's failure, the only viable strategy. Its major advantage was the profound legitimacy of the socialist democratic rhetoric that Gorbachev borrowed directly from the dissident discourse of 1968. (Andropov, who had served as the Soviet ambassador to Hungary during the suppression of the 1956 revolution, could hardly have adopted such a discourse.) Like Andropov, Gorbachev felt that the bureaucratic apparatus must be purged and brought to heel before it could be recast in more rational and responsive organizational forms. His perestroika was essentially a "velvet" purge. By promoting public discussion, glasnost served the dual purpose of providing propagandistic support in the struggle against the party conservatives and generating a range of policy advice through open competition among bureaucratically connected intellectuals – much in the way that Western politicians rely on think-tanks, universities, and elite periodicals. Later there appeared the idea of institutionalizing an ongoing rotation of mid-level *nomenklatura* by allowing journalistic criticism and competitive elections. This strategy strongly appealed to the educated specialists – the group that according to the 1989 census comprised as much as 28 per cent of the employed population in Russia.[30] The educated specialists, especially those situated immediately below the threshold of *nomen-klatura* appointments, got a chance to jump over the heads of their stolid bosses. Given their powers, the elite reformers confidently expected to stay in control while extending their patronage to the politically ascendant technocrats and intellectuals. Moreover, a partial democratization served to meet the perceived need to conform to the norms of the "civilized world." Gorbachev's perestroika is inseparable from the activist appeasement on the Western front. The renewed détente was not merely a diplomatic tactic but indeed a major strategic objective. The Soviet rulers, having exhausted the economic and ideological potential of anti-systemic developmentalism, in effect embarked on a reintegration into the capitalist world-economy.

In all likelihood, at the time they imagined the goal to be the production of an extended version of the 1970s détente. In effect, it was conceived of as a kind of *Ostpolitik* running in the reverse direction, where Moscow would now take the initiative and engage in commercial and cultural rapprochement with Germany and other capitalist states of Western Europe that seemed better partners than hostile America. In Moscow they expected that ending the Cold War would help them to resume and expand economic cooperation with major French, West German, and Italian businesses. The immediate precedent was offered by the government-negotiated mega-contracts of the kind that in the 1960s and 1970s had secured Fiat's participation in Soviet automobile production or the exchange of Soviet natural gas for West German technology and consumer goods.

The puzzle as to why Gorbachev attempted his reforms in the first place, and why he refused to use state repression against revolutionary challenges, largely dissolves if we accept that the ultimate goal of perestroika was to allow Russia to join the capitalist core on honorable terms. The historical sociologist Jeff Goodwin nicely summarized the four political conditions that so unexpectedly made possible the peaceful capitulation of communist rulers: the permissive "Gorbachev factor"; the prevalent view among the "enlightened" *nomenklatura* that their defeat in competitive elections would be a temporary loss; the absence of a physical threat from the opponents; and the "embourgeoisement" of the *nomenklatura* in the late 1980s.[31] Goodwin's four factors add up to the strategy of negotiating for the elite the least disruptive and collectively profitable transition from one developmentalist project to another, from a state-bound and isolationist economy to market-driven and externally conjugated economic growth.

Objectively, Gorbachev's strategic goals could be summarized as three conversions. First, the conversion of the defunct communist ideology into the vaguely liberal non-confrontational discourse of "common human values." Second, the conversion of communist bureaucrats into technocratic administrators and corporate owners of economic capital. And ultimately, the conversion of Soviet geopolitical weight into the negotiated advantages of Western investment, which would mean access to markets, and thus a profitable reintegration into the capitalist world-economy.

Yet at the level of human subjectivity, every indication is that, even in private, Gorbachev could not admit that his goal was the reintegration of the Soviet state into world capitalism. Like most of his generation, his parents were peasants and he was brought up in an atmosphere of extraordinary social mobility and material improvement after the Second World War. To the people of this generation the idea of socialism had a direct experiential validation in their collective and personal trajectories. Rebelling against Brezhnev's "epoch of stagnation" and the renewed Cold War of the early eighties, they sought a resumption of the expansive conditions of their youth, not a capitalist future. Moreover they intuitively acknowledged the value and power of Soviet egalitarianism. It is perhaps for this reason that Gorbachev failed to create the control mechanisms that in a time of crisis would have allowed him to steer between the dismantling of old command structures and the projected institutionalization of a representative democracy and capitalist market. And the problem is not merely that Gorbachev acted without a detailed plan, relying instead on intuitive improvisations. The habitus of reform communists did not allow the Gorbachevites to think through rationally the further implications of their own political program. It was a tragic contradiction.

Whatever the limitations inside the heads of Gorbachev and his associates, they were learning fast. But time runs very fast during a revolution. Gorbachev's strategic concessions to the West were not so much naïve as frantically hasty. The same desperate desire to secure an invitation to the liberal West must explain the puzzling restraint in the use of state repression against the revolutionary movements of 1989 in Eastern Europe. The Soviet rulers expected the reintegration into the capitalist world-economy to take place on honorable terms, an expectation expressed in Gorbachev's typically fuzzy appeals for integration in a "common European home." The status of the rulers of the superpower allowed for nothing less.

In reality, reintegration proved to be immensely more expensive, more disruptive and contentious than anyone could have foreseen. It included numerous attempts to replace the government in stormy elections, coups, and revolutions, and to create new states through secession and civil war.

5

Social Structure

"Capitalism is the society where man exploits man. Socialism is its complete opposite."

East European folk saying of the late twentieth century

At this point we have to take a detour in our chronological exposition of Soviet history. This intervening chapter will be of a more analytical nature. Before we confront the empirical chaos of the revolutionary situations that brought about the unintended collapse of the USSR, we need to gain at least an impressionistic understanding of the social structure that emerged from Soviet industrialization. This should provide us with a relational taxonomy of Soviet society and allow us to see how the key groups came to (or failed to) engage in contention. We should then be able to trace the emergence of collective interests, political agendas, alliances and cleavages, and the prevalent forms of expression before and after the revolutionary events of 1989–1991.

In considering state socialism, one major obstacle lies in the familiar clichés generated by the propaganda machineries on both sides of the Cold War divide, and especially the various dissident critiques of "really existing socialism" that sometimes verged on caricature. Moreover the task becomes tricky because, in the domain of social sciences, the traditional approaches to conceptualizing modern societies in recent years have become subject to devastating criticism from many different corners.[1] In particular, theoretical doubts and controversies have focused on the ways in which the structural positions of social classes and status groups translate into identities and concerted political action.[2] In other words, the question is how classes and nations can emerge as collective human agencies. We are in the midst of an intellectual and political transition whose outcome is not yet evident.

How do we proceed? We still need an analytical map to make sense of what was going on in the previous chapters and, just as importantly, to find our way through the chapters that follow. Provisionally then, I propose mapping devices which are perhaps no more sophisticated than the portolan charts used by the Iberian navigators during their voyages of oceanic discovery. The old portolans relied on crude yet fairly robust measurements and moreover on the practical acumen that, most of the time, succeeded in getting the navigators to their destination. And so we shall pray that our charts will not drive us on to the reef.

BASIC PRINCIPLES

The social structure of Soviet-type societies was powerfully mystified by the reigning ideologies of the Cold War era and the strict censorship exercised by communist bureaucracy. If we can now see it better, perhaps this is because at least one of the walls that blocked the view of our predecessors has been reduced to rubble. For the people who had directly experienced the realities of state socialism and dared to ask which class comrade Stalin and his acolytes belonged to, such questioning posed not merely an intractable intellectual problem; it was dangerous to one's career and even one's life. And yet the questions were asked time and again.

Some of the most important early advances were made by sociologists from Poland, Hungary, and Yugoslavia. (The latter must be acknowledged in particular because the destruction of Yugoslavia has overshadowed the legacy of buoyant intellectual life in what used to be the most idiosyncratic of socialist states.) Hungary preserved an especially strong tradition of social inquiry dating back to the intellectual glories of pre-1914 Vienna and Budapest. If much of the best sociological analysis of state socialism and the post-socialist transformation focused on the Hungarian experience, it cannot be said that Hungary didn't deserve it. This chapter draws inspiration from the work of Central European sociologists and especially from Iván Szelényi and his various collaborators. Following in Szelényi's footsteps is not easy because over the years they have been of varied shape and have seemed to go in different directions.[3] This might be expected in a groundbreaking movement. The more recent work of Szelényi served as the prototype model for the following outline of Soviet social structure. My sketch might seem different in that it downplays the importance and autonomy of intellectuals (who had always been central to Szelényi's analysis of Hungarian society) while adding a whole class of sub-proletarians. This is not, however, due to any fundamental theoretical disagreement regarding the principles of social stratification or the configuration of classes under state socialism. These modifications seemed necessary to the particular task of describing Soviet society, and especially its variant in the Caucasus. Besides, I am not going to attach any precise numerical values to the descriptions of social groups in this chapter, because precious little statistical data exists in this regard. Our stony field has never been as thoroughly ploughed as has Hungary's.

Szelényi's combination of the category of class, inherited from the Marxist tradition, with the notion of differentiated social capital associated with the work of Pierre Bourdieu seems particularly important.[4] Unlike Eyal, Szelényi and Townsley, we shall bypass the long-standing debate between Marxists and Weberians regarding the distinction between elites, status groups, and classes. In part, this omission is for the sake of provisional simplicity. However, it can be justified by the powerful theoretical arguments of Arrighi, Hopkins, and Wallerstein regarding precisely this controversial topic.[5]

Certainly, classes are very broad categories and should be regarded heuristically. Yet, I believe, in modern societies classes possess sufficient coherence, and they can be distinguished from each other by the composition of household incomes. In turn, the prevalent types of household income reflect structural positions regarding the flow of power and goods, which translate into sets of social strategies and dispositions typical to each class. Bourdieu conceptualized them as class habitus and social capital. Like all theoretical innovations, the concept of social capital generated its own panoply of debates and controversies.[6] In our sketch it offers an important corrective to the economic criteria of stratification and helps to clarify the dynamics of positioning and strategy pursued by the members of different classes and class fractions – which prevents us from making automatic assumptions about class interests in any historical situation. In particular, social capital gives us a good tool to differentiate the intellectuals from other educated specialists without falling into the usual normative judgment regarding intellectualism. To the best of my knowledge, Bourdieu never provided a concise and straightforward explanation of what exactly constitutes the various kinds of social capital, although his own use of the term makes its meaning sufficiently explicit. Therefore in keeping with the principle of provisional simplicity, let us revert to the pragmatic definition suggested by Immanuel Wallerstein: capital describes the ways in which people store accumulated successes. These could be a matter of economic gains, which are the "capitalist capital" proper; political positions and support bases; administrative capital vested in office promotions and special kinds of bureaucratic insider knowledge; symbolic intellectual prestige, diplomas, access to high culture practices, and professional positions; the traditional symbolic notions of family honor, kinship and patronage connections; the workers' occupational capital, expressed through their work skills, shopfloor rights, and solidarity; or the social capital of marginal populations vested in their resilience, resourcefulness, the possession of valuable friends, and the skills they use to avoid brushes with law.[7]

ANTISYSTEMIC DEVELOPMENTALISM

What sort of modern society was created in the USSR? Here is not the place to review the accumulated social theories that have tried to answer this question. Rather, I am going to proceed by way of a number of concise statements that, I hope, have the potential to become the seeds of future theories. In general, the typical pitfalls besetting many attempts to analyze Soviet-type societies were a consequence of these societies being considered separately from the rest of the world, and then measured against normative ideological standards of one kind or another. Thus, Western leftist intellectuals found that Soviet society fell far short of their expectations of socialist emancipation; while at the opposite extreme its Cold War critics dismissed the Soviet Union as "totalitarian" and aberrant. It is impossible to understand the Soviet experience in isolation from the twentieth-century world that created and constrained it.

After 1914 the mutual near-extermination of the European powers left many different forces to pick up the pieces. This implosion at the core of the world-system provided the initial condition for the waves of revolutions, rebellions, and decolonizations that spread eventually to the most distant peripheries throughout the century. In October 1917, the Bolsheviks, who were in fact a tightly organized party of radical intelligentsia, showed the rest of the world how to seize state power at a moment of military defeat and disarray. Once in power, the Bolsheviks proceeded resolutely to devise practical measures intended to avoid the fate of the Parisian communards, and soon they also showed how to survive a ferocious civil war and foreign intervention. Victory was achieved by building an extensive, adaptable, and ideologically inspiring revolutionary dictatorship. The Bolsheviks managed to become something that Max Weber himself could not have imagined – a charismatic bureaucracy that negated dichotomies between "Utopia" and "development."[8] The dictatorial apparatus of the Bolshevik party-state was then applied to perform a third historical feat: the lightning transformation of a predominantly agrarian country into a military-industrial superpower. The USSR's industrialization acquired a distinctly military character because in order to stay in power and become an important actor in the world arena the Soviet government had to develop a formidable coercive capacity.

Coercion was integral to the Soviet pattern of industrial revolution. The country had endured immense violence between 1905 and the early 1950s, starting with the Russian civil war, continuing through the collectivization of the peasantry from 1929 to 1932, the purges of 1936–1938, the ethnic deportations of the 1940s and, of course, the Second World War. These continuous upheavals had erased the Old Regime's multiplicity of social statuses, ranks, classes, and religious communities. As a result of all this violence, no landowners or aristocrats, no capitalists or petty bourgeoisie, no autonomous intelligentsia or liberal professionals were left; only a small remnant of the clergy remained, and there were not very many peasants. The social hierarchy was drastically reduced to a semi-closed caste of cadre bureaucrats and a newly created mass who could be defined as proletarians in the most fundamental sense: a social class whose livelihood was rigidly tied to wage employment. Within a generation the Soviet Union became a gigantic industrial enterprise that had self-consciously developed in emulation of Ford's factories – the symbol of the technological and organizational progress of the age.[9] This extremely rapid and near universal proletarianization conducted by despotic methods was indeed the biggest tragedy and the biggest achievement of Soviet developmentalism.

Yet coercion alone cannot explain the profoundly transformative effect of Stalinist rule. Instead, it was its success in building new industries, towns, the army, state bureaucracies, and an educational system that generated on a massive scale modern occupations and lifestyles.[10] The communist state was a prolific proletarianizer, which is why it also had to be paternalistic and protective towards its proletarians. This was not merely the effect of Marxist ideology. It was largely due to the same structural concerns that had led Bismarck systematically to extend welfare provision in Germany: there was a scarcity of skilled labor in a rapidly industrializing country that could not rely on foreign immigrants, and therefore technical education became a state priority; workers had to be isolated from radical political influences by a combination of pervasive spying and the state provision of basic social protection; in a mercantilist command economy virtually devoid of unemployment, the political and economic managers needed to devise an alternative set of incentives, sanctions and interaction rituals to foster a sense of paternalistic community and encourage worker discipline; and moreover it was important to nurture good health and patriotic allegiance in a working class whose males and many females doubled as military recruits.[11]

Victory in the Second World War was a major validation of the Soviet experience. Contrary to a common misconception, the Soviet command could not have defeated a fighting machine as formidable as the German Wehrmacht simply by sacrificing millions of Russian soldiers. Such a victory was inconceivable without the vast scientific-industrial capacity applied to the design and production of modern armaments. The statistical indicators of Soviet industrial output during 1941–1945 directly correlated with victories on the battlefields. For example, the Soviet production of steel recovered after huge losses in the early period of the war, and matched the German level of production at about the middle of the battle of Stalingrad; after that, Soviet industry entered a period of sustained and rapid growth, exceeding the productive capacity of the whole Nazi Reich.[12] Growth continued into the 1960s, when the Soviet success served as an attractive example to the Third World liberation movements that came to control many new sovereign states on the world's periphery.

At the time this industrial transformation went by the generic names of modernization and national development. Essentially this meant a rationally planned push to rapidly create a modern industrial base, infrastructure, institutions of predominantly technical education, and the corresponding social structures in backward and poor non-Western countries.[13] In the end, they were intended to match and, hopefully, outpace the earlier achievements of advanced capitalist countries. The modern bureaucratic state was considered the key means to the goal of national development. This idea was encapsulated in the concept of the "developmental state." However, mainly owing to the power of the Cold War binary opposition between capitalism and socialism, in scholarly usage this label was applied too narrowly. It was used to describe non-socialist national mercantilism in countries like Brazil and India, which did not fit into the strictures of market-versus-plan dichotomy, and in particular to explain the extraordinary success of bureaucratic authoritarian industrialization in Japan and South Korea.[14] Today, now that we have a clearer retrospective view of the twentieth century, it no longer seems useful to speak of the developmental state in the ideal-typical singular. We might instead set out to explore the actual variety of developmental states: very diverse in their ideologies and politics but united essentially by the common vision of catching up with the core countries through the concerted application of state power in building industrial enterprise.

The outcome of the Bolshevik effort was proclaimed "socialism" by virtue of the official anti-capitalist ideology and the state expropriation of economic assets taken from the annihilated property-owning classes, which had ranged from landowners and bourgeoisie down to the dispossessed peasantry.[15] But the model of antisystemic developmentalism found a much wider appeal and inspired numerous attempts at emulation. Wallerstein aptly called it the "Leninist strategy, with or without Marxism."[16] The native intelligentsia and modernizing bureaucrats in the colonial countries, who led the movements of national liberation, attempted much the same course of action as the Bolsheviks, albeit pursued only up to a certain point and justified in predominantly nationalist terms. Both the socialist and national liberation strategies of accelerated industrial development were trying to catch up with the core capitalist countries. The means towards this goal, however, differed radically from the hegemonic Anglo-American imagery of modernity achieved through a free market with a minimal state. Starting with Soviet Russia, all developmental states in effect copied the coercion-intensive practices of a mercantilist economy, the best example of which, prior to 1914, had been Wilhelmine Germany.[17] When Mussolini, a developmental dictator of the fascist variety, issued the promise to make the Italian trains run on time, he clearly implied that Italy should aspire to become the Germany of the Mediterranean.[18]

Though it is a brutal simplification, let me suggest this seed of a theory. The difference between the twentieth-century socialist and national liberation revolutions (in Tilly's broad definition of revolution) lay fundamentally in the degree of the state's expropriation of resources, which was conditioned by the class composition, outlook, and administrative capacities of the revolutionary elite. The revolutions that were called socialist brought to power an intelligentsia without property who would then expropriate ("socialize" or "collectivize") all economic assets down to peasant households. Such conditions were found usually in large semi-peripheral states, like Russia or China, that possessed long traditions of imperial bureaucratic rule and spiritual remonstration against the "vices" of rulers. The predominantly peripheral revolutions in formerly colonial or quasi-colonial states that empowered more diverse alliances of patriotic intelligentsia, mid-level functionaries and military officers, and, possibly, some national capitalists, were called movements of national liberation. Once in power, such alliances sought to expropriate ("nationalize") the assets of select groups whom the national revolutionaries considered alien or reactionary: foreign capitalists, unwanted ethnic minorities, the clergy, landowners, etc.[19]

The Soviet example approximated the ultimate outcome of state-bound indus-trial development which, if running long enough, might be expected to sort out the population into just two large classes (although within the classes there still existed important divisions along the lines of ethnicity, locality, gender, and the rela-tive possession of social capital dependent mostly on education). The ruling class comprised the centrally appointed bureaucratic executives who had enjoyed the exclusive prerogative to make all political and managerial decisions, including those regarding their own well-being. The majority of the state's citizenry consisted of proletarianized (wage-dependent) workers, specialists, and intellectuals who had been incorporated in the state hierarchies of broadly defined production and redis-tribution. There remained, however, the inchoate residual category of those who, for many different reasons, had not been fully incorporated in state industrial hier-archies. These people remained reliant on subsistence production in the household, seasonal migrant employment (*shabashka*), and participation in various networks of the "popular," "informal," or "smuggling" economy. This awkward underclass or side-class has often been overlooked in the analyses of state socialism. However, it could be very numerous and occasionally played a significant role in post-communist politics and, as we are going to see, in ethnic conflicts in particular.

The impression that in the USSR officialdom and the rest of society existed at polar extremes might seem empirically unfounded by the measure of material inequality. Even at Stalinism's imperial height in the late 1940s, which marked the highest degree of rank differentiation in Soviet history, the disparities of personal wealth remained less pronounced than in contemporary America and certainly did not surpass the enormous disparities observed in tsarist Russia.[20] Of course, there persisted the thorny question of who owned the vast assets accumulated by the Soviet state.[21] For the duration of the Soviet Union, the question remained purely theoretical and probably unanswerable in principle. But if we overcome the current political prejudice that relegates the socialist past to complete irrelevance and instead view the post-socialist nineties as the continuation of many structural trends that originated in the last decades of Soviet rule, then the recent oligarchic privatization of the Soviet state's assets appears to be the fruition of the disparities in political power between the bureaucratic executive class and the rest of society. After 1991 the disparity became brutally material. It is the result of the catastrophic failure of Soviet workers and specialists to collectively lay claim to state assets. It is in order to understand how this happened that we must look at the social structure that emerged from Soviet industrialization. Despite the collapse of communist ideological and political structures, largely the same social structure endures today, and it still remains centered on the state.

The historically specific forms of incorporation and the configuration and proportions of class structure remain a major task for empirical research, one which might be expected to have a direct import in explaining cultural and political outcomes. In broad strokes, Table 1 on page 325 illustrates the situation in the less industrialized areas of the former Soviet Union, such as the Caucasus and Central Asia, and in the more provincial locales such as Kabardino-Balkaria, Chechnya, Karabagh, or Abkhazia where the high-status and thus relatively autonomous intelligentsia was poorly represented and where the main peculiarity was the relative number of sub-proletarians.

BUREAUCRATIC EXECUTIVES, THE DOMINANT CLASS

The class of Soviet bosses took its semi-official name, *"nomenklatura,"* from the 1919 decision of the Bolshevik Central Committee to reserve for itself the right of appointment to the list, or "nomenclature," of key positions in all institutions from military units to banks, factories, universities, newspapers, and trade unions.[22] The mechanism of *nomenklatura* appointments was at the heart of Soviet state centralization. It created the social milieu of polyvalent bureaucratic executives who could move easily from directing a factory to the regional administration, party apparatus, KGB, or university. Since the fall of the USSR, de facto *nomenklatura* appointments remain the mechanism of bureaucratic patronage.

Despite a widespread political prejudice, a *nomenklatura* is not an exceptional institution found only in "Soviet-type" or "totalitarian" societies. The Soviet *nomenklatura* cadres formed an elite group with a formal rank who were furthermore united by shared informal norms, patronage networks, as well as educational and career experiences. But so are the elite Japanese bureaucrats described by Chalmers Johnson or the French "state nobility" analyzed by Bourdieu.[23] In fact, to someone sufficiently familiar with both American business schools and Soviet-era party schools, the two types of institution might seem almost grotesquely similar in their recruitment patterns, social functions, interaction and consecration rituals, their peculiarly managerial kinds of rhetoric, and not least of all the energetic habitus of students aspiring towards executive careers.

The similarities are not incidental. The Soviet *nomenklatura* was perhaps at the far end of of the spectrum in regard to the extent of self-corporatization and bureaucratic autonomy from private capitalist and democratic political controls. Nonetheless it belonged squarely in the scope of modern bureaucratic practices just as the Soviet state belonged somewhere in the scope of developmental states. Like all state bureaucracies, the *nomenklatura* oversaw the flow of resources going to and from the central government. The peculiarity of the USSR lay in the power monopoly of the communist party apparatus, which possessed in a fused form political, administrative, economic and ideological control over all operations of Soviet state and social life in general.[24] This rendered the *nomenklatura* an imposing social body. The fusion of functions and despotic centralization also rendered it exceedingly rigid, self-insulated, and thus resistant to change. This organizational pattern, which ensured a comfortable life for the Soviet dominant class during the Brezhnev period, became their major liability in the rapid and uncertain transition such as arrived in 1989, when the *nomenklatura* fragmented rather than effectively ruled to their collective benefit. Nonetheless, let me stress again that these are morphological peculiarities of a species that belongs to the larger genus of modern bureaucratic executives. Probably they are all prone to accumulating various rigidities if they stay in place long enough.

There existed different levels of *nomenklatura* subordination. At the ground level, district party committees selected and assessed executives, such as small factory managers, collective farm chairmen, local police chiefs, and school principals. Mid-level appointments were the responsibility of the party apparatuses of provinces and republics. The Politburo and the extensive apparatus of the Communist Party's Central Committee, centrally located in Moscow, supervised the strategic appointments at ministerial level, in the security apparatus, and at the top echelons of such institutions as the Academy of Sciences and the Writers' Union. Also, the Central Committee had the power to appoint and supervise the provincial and republican committees that in turn enjoyed the same powers over the district committees that in their turn had similar powers over the ground-level party cells in the factories, military garrisons, schools and universities, hospitals, supermarkets, newspapers, and TV stations – whatever formal organizations were found in its territorial jurisdiction, with the exception of state units considered too strategically important to permit local interference. This hierarchy differentiated the *nomenklatura* along the dimensions of rank and institutional affiliation. Overall the system maintained a comprehensive ladder of bureaucratic ranks and subordinated spheres of competence.[25]

Bureaucratic agencies could be divided into two principal types: territorial (national republics, autonomies, and ordinary provinces, towns and districts) and sectoral (the various ministries, from defense and heavy industry to health and education). When the USSR collapsed, it fell apart along the borders of existing bureaucratic entities, as the national republics were declared independent – and thus effectively "privatized" in most cases by their native *nomenklatura* – and the post-Soviet industry was transformed into market assets and privatized, with varying degrees of success, by the erstwhile *nomenklatura* managers (see Table 3, page 327).

The collapse of the Soviet Union was primarily the unintended result of bureaucratic fragmentation caused by the defensive and opportunistic actions of various bureaucratic executives who began to appropriate state assets. With the prospect of revolution looming, they acted with a haste that verged on panic. The sovereignization of territories and the privatization of economic sectors, which started in 1989 and lasted into the mid-1990s, were the two default strategies of the *nomenklatura*'s escape from Soviet collapse. Their actions were conditioned by the location of the *nomenklatura* in the territorial or sectoral agencies of the Soviet state. Political assertiveness in the pursuit of each strategy depended on the relative weight of each agency vis-à-vis Moscow and on how much value the appropriated assets promised to bring on the political and economic markets. Thus the full-status national republics offered the best chance of international recognition, and the export-oriented oil and gas industry offered a bureaucrat the best prospect of rapidly becoming a millionaire (see Tables 1 and 3). Both strategies extended directly from the long-familiar mechanisms of bureaucratic patronage, turf separatism, and corruption.[26]

According to the official theory, the Soviet bureaucrats were akin to proletarianized specialists because their income should have consisted solely of wages and the fringe benefits of the workplace (supposedly just slightly better than the Soviet average). In reality, the *nomenklatura* always found ways to create various extra perks and rents, which stretched from hefty bonuses and special shops to outright bribes.[27] The opportunities for corruption, and the very determination of what would be considered corrupt and thus punishable, depended on intra-elite perceptions as well as one's position in informal patronage networks and location within the territorial or sectoral divisions of the state apparatus.

The levels of bribery were considered higher in the southern republics of the USSR, especially in the Caucasus and Central Asia.[28] Corruption was commonly attributed to the "Southern culture," which was patently the wrong explanation for what was nonetheless an empirically correct observation. To begin with, what shared "Southern" culture could exist between Moldova and Uzbekistan? But it is certain that both places had less developed industrial economies and thus a higher proportion of agriculture, including the "shadow" commodity production of fruits and vegetables that were exported internally and profitably sold at the markets of large industrial towns in Russia and the Ukraine. Corruption was greater in the Caucasus and Central Asia because in those national republics the *nomenklatura* enjoyed two advantages: ethnic ties that hindered Moscow's interference, and the institutionalized opportunities for exacting bribes from the cash-flows generated by the large predominantly agrarian smuggling economy that operated in the USSR's southern tier. When in 1989 Moscow's central government lost much of its previous redistributive and supervisory powers, the economy was monetized, and provinces were turned into bailiwicks, Russia also rapidly developed corrupt patterns of "Asiatic" proportions.

After 1991 the relations of bureaucratic rent flowed into post-communist privatization; in other words, administrative capital was converted into economic capital. To the extent that the social backgrounds of the new businessmen in the North Caucasus region can be known at all, my interviews and observations conducted in 2000–2001 indicate that perhaps two thirds were either themselves former *nomenklatura* or close relatives and clients.[29] There is considerable justice in the bitter words of a former engineer (and himself an enthusiast of market liberalism) who in the 1990s tried to run a private gas station: *If among your parents or in-laws there wasn't someone important, you may as well give up running a business in this town.*

In the early 1990s the Russian neoliberal reformers reconciled themselves in advance to what they foresaw as the inevitable triumph of the *nomenklatura* under any scheme of privatization. At the time one could routinely hear brash young economists in the intelligentsia salons of Moscow claiming that even if shares in privatized enterprises were thrown from an airplane over the city the factory directors would still have 90 per cent of them in their hands the next day. The neoliberal reformers candidly admitted the social injustice of insider privatization. But since these neoliberals were themselves another historical avatar of high-status radical intelligentsia, they also held to the teleological belief in the inevitability of progress that was typical of the revolutionary frame of mind. Thus the temporary injustice of *nomenklatura* privatization would eventually be redressed by the forces of the new market-driven revolution, just as the "inevitable" and "temporary" injustices of Red Terror or collectivization were to have been redressed by the accelerated arrival of a bright utopian future of universal emancipation and technical-scientific progress. Inevitably, privatization would shrink the state, create private businesses, and start the capitalist growth that would generate jobs, prosperity, a middle class, and liberal democracy.

Ten years later, in the early 2000s, a walk through the boulevards of downtown Nalchik, the capital of Kabardino-Balkaria, or in any big town in the Caucasus or in Russia, points to a very different reality. True, one can see the ostentatiously remodeled buildings of the private banks (which operate, however, mostly with government accounts), the expensive boutiques and restaurants, and the offices of private businesses whose nature often remains somewhat mysterious. Yet no less prosperity is projected by the buildings and – even more conspicuously – the guarded parking lots that belong to state agencies with direct economic powers: customs, tax, state security, anti-mafia police, even the pension fund and sanitary inspectorates. The post-Soviet state remains omnipresent not simply because private businesses tend to fail under the present hostile conditions; the state itself, for those who enjoy privileged access to it, has become the best and biggest source of economic profits and private protection.

PROLETARIANS, THE PRINCIPAL CLASS

Since the Soviet industrialization of the period between the 1930s and the 1950s, the majority of the population has been proletarian, according to the crucial index of wages (and pre-wage incomes, like student stipends, or the post-wage benefits, like retirement pensions) as the basis of household income (see Table 1, page 325). An enduring misconception equates proletarians only with factory workers. Certainly, they were proletarians, but so were rural workers in agro-industrial enterprises, office workers, technical staff, medical personnel, pilots, ordinary military officers, teachers, journalists, and many other kinds of employees if their livelihood depended on regularly paid wages. The comical curse from a classical Soviet film – *Let you live on wages alone!* – captured the essence of proletarian existence.

The power and omnipresence of the Soviet state engendered the peculiarly broad and homogeneous proletarian class that included the majority of Soviet citizens. In a fundamental sense, Soviet proletarians were the product of the socialist developmental state. They were born in state hospitals and grew up in state kindergartens and schools; many went to study at state technical colleges and universities; all males served in the military; most men and women worked full-time in the state enterprises and bureaucracies, lived mostly in apartments provided by the state, bought their food and basic goods mostly from state-run shops (even if occasionally from the back door); in towns they used public transportation, went to state-operated cinemas, stadiums, and cafés, and took vacations in recreational facilities belonging to the state or state-sponsored trade unions. At the workplace, and to a large extent when not at work, all Soviet proletarians – whether teachers, doctors, coalminers, or machine operators – were subject to bureaucratic control by a hierarchy of managers, planners, and Party officials. The "common" Soviet men and women – i.e. predominantly the state-dependent proletarians – subsisted on fixed wage incomes paid regularly (usually twice a month) over their whole lifetime, until eventually they were replaced by state pensions. Unemployment was virtually unknown. At the same time, a shortage of goods was a no less predictable condition of everyday life. Conditions were largely the same and the Soviet institutions isomorphous across the whole of the enormous territory of the Soviet Union, anywhere between the Baltic and the Pacific.[30]

All this lent a considerable predictability to the existence and expectations of the Soviet proletarians. They knew well the conditions and demands of their work and their rights, such as the free grant of an apartment.[31] They also increasingly understood the constraints on their lives: the bureaucratic ossification, corruption, economic shortages, meaningless official ideology, and they possessed a growing knowledge that analogous jobs in the West brought greater material rewards. Thus the official censors and the Soviet border guards came to be seen as the sole obstacles to a better, freer life in a bigger world.

The block on political struggle and professional institutionalization imposed by the Soviet regime encouraged the better-educated state employees to compete to distinguish themselves by accruing higher cultural capital. This process occurred on a massive scale after 1945, and was usually perceived as the emergence of the Soviet intelligentsia. During the period between the 1960s and the 1980s the Soviet Union was often described as the most well-read society in the world. Perhaps this claim was a bit romantic, and certainly it conformed to the image portrayed by Soviet propaganda; nonetheless there was a significant grain of truth in it. The books, music, films and other cultural goods considered "serious," whether classical or modern and cosmopolitan, were consumed avidly and in huge quantities.[32] From the late 1950s the Soviet Union experienced a tremendous expansion in the practices of high culture, the products of which were being consumed from an early age. Open to children and their parents were the extra-curricular schools of music, fine arts, film, ballet, and chess; they could take part in sophisticated sports like gymnastics and figure skating; there were theater studios, children's libraries, circles of aviation and rocket modelism, other hobby centers, and courses in foreign languages, geography, biology, the environment, and advanced sciences, as well as summer camps dedicated to boating, mountain walking, or archeology. All this was in part an extension of Soviet welfare provisions and an official ideology that carried a strong imprint of the Enlightenment. But the post-1945 boom in high culture practices was no less driven by Soviet citizens who were willing to invest considerable amounts of their time and, if necessary, money to secure the best and broadest education for their children.

Adults themselves actively sought to participate in high culture, which, given the character of the Soviet economy and state, often caused shortages. Hence there appeared the unofficial markets in books and audio records, and the enormous lines of people prepared to spend days and nights queuing to get tickets to the prestigious theaters and to cinemas during the international film festivals. The practices and products of high culture confirmed the Soviet specialists, intellectuals, and advanced workers as a group which could enjoy pride and prestige, even if they were politically disempowered and economically restricted to the usual proletarian existence. Moreover, the procurement and consumption of high culture fostered looser networks of personal connections and tighter circles of shared interests that at later stages could provide the basis for political organizing. In this milieu we find the circle of Shanibov's friends and former students.

The aspirations of state-employed intellectuals, specialists, and the highly skilled sector of socialist proletarians reflected their central position in the state's industrial hierarchy. Potentially, such a position could be a good source of social power. The emergent agenda of these upper levels of socialist proletarians can be described as broadly social democratic. Its central desires were the preservation of stable employment and benefits, with additional collective bargaining and a new electoral accountability for managers and the political elite. This meant the re-affirmation of what might be called the proletarian occupational capital, which translated into a demand for respect for a collective workplace power within the state industrial hierarchy and the desire that the skills acquired through education and experience be rewarded. The positional expectations and demands of socialist intellectuals were thus homologous to those of skilled workers in the high-status industries (armaments, the big "flagship" factories in the civilian sector, shipyards, and coalmines). Furthermore, the proletarians who were concentrated in the occupational neighborhoods, like the coalminers, and those who possessed concentrated occupational capital – electronics specialists or auto workers – were correspondingly more assertive and pro-democratic in their demands.[33] These attitudes prevailed in large cities like Moscow, Leningrad, Sverdlovsk, Novosibirsk, and the Ukraine's Kharkov or Odessa. Homology created the potential for joint political action from the intellectual and technically skilled proletarian specialists. These were the urban locales and social strata where Gorbachev's discourse of perestroika and glasnost found immediate support (See Table 2 and Figure 2, pages 326 and 334).

The broad commonality of the Soviet proletarian condition, however, did not easily translate into the broadest type of unified class action as exemplified by Poland's Solidarity. For the majority of Soviet industrial workers, an agenda of institutionalized occupational autonomy (i.e. genuine unionization) and political democratization might have seemed too daring, too abstract, or too distant to relate to their life interests and outlook. These workers were more likely to rely on the familiar forms of tacit bargaining on the shopfloor. The Soviet proletarians faced formidable barriers to collective action. The secret police and volunteer sycophants were omnipresent, and strikes were often put down with machine guns. Under Brezhnev the Soviet rulers switched to less brutal means of taming the workers. The key strategies for pacification were the ritualistic dissimulation of "unanimous popular politics," which served to prevent any actual politics, and, at the level of socioeconomic structures, the cultivation of a paternalistic dependency in the workplace. The distribution of goods and welfare benefits was largely tied to employment and was therefore controlled by factory administrators and the official trade unions. In this situation the workers were left with what James Scott famously called the weapons of the weak: subterfuge, evasion, indirect negotiation, or the classic East European jokes.[34]

In the aftermath of Stalinism the workers actually won a far better deal, though the benefits remained unevenly shared between various economic sectors and regions of the country. The overall effect was to disperse and tame potential industrial protests. Among the less skilled workers, especially the older ones, the prevalent political ideals could still be very authoritarian, even to the degree of maintaining popular Stalinism. These attitudes prevailed in particular in the less industrialized regions, like the Caucasus and Central Asia, where workplace paternalism and opportunities for smuggling were embedded in networks of ethnic and neighborhood patronage.[35] After 1991 the official conservative nationalisms propagated by the ruling *nomenklatura* of post-Soviet states tended to resonate with the dispositions of these lower-status and peripheral workers.

PROLETARIANIZED SPECIALISTS AND INTELLECTUALS

The Soviet proletarian class, as I have already stated, included substantial numbers of intellectuals and specialists. They were formally distinguished by the possession of diplomas of higher education. Most of them were in fact a special category of skilled worker performing non-manual labor tasks in the overall framework of Soviet state industrialism. This does not mean that all intellectuals had been proletarianized in the USSR, but the large majority certainly were.

Here lies perhaps a crucial difference between the Soviet intelligentsia and pre-1917 paragons like Leo Tolstoy, Chekhov, or, for that matter, Lenin, whose father had acquired through civil service the rank of a nobleman and owned some land, or Trotsky, who was the son of a wealthy miller. We seldom care to recall that the old intelligentsia usually had servants and an independent means of income – that is, independent from the state and private employers.

For this reason, in the analysis of late Soviet society we must substantially reduce the relative weight of the intelligentsia – the legendary East European category of the holders of symbolic and cultural capital who constituted themselves into an autonomous status group in opposition to officialdom. In the USSR perhaps only the celebrity artists and academics and, conversely, the marginal bohemians, could enjoy a freedom from state controls sufficient for them to behave like the old intelligentsia. These groups clustered only in the big high-status cities like Moscow and Leningrad, and, to significantly varying degrees, in the capitals of the union republics. But we are more concerned here with the lesser-status towns, like Kabardino-Balkaria's capital of Nalchik or Checheno-Ingushetia's Grozny. Such places normally lacked an autonomous intelligentsia. That is probably the main reason for their appearing so provincial, conservative, and inertial. Yuri Shanibov and his friends were employed in state institutions, received wages at the level equivalent to skilled industrial labor, and lived mostly in the same standard apartment blocs as the majority of Soviet proletarians.

On the other hand, in the sixties there emerged a growing number of people who claimed to be intelligentsia, and sometimes even displayed a moderately critical attitude towards the officialdom, but at the same time held positions in the field of bureaucratic power. These were *nomenklatura* executives whose careers advanced in the institutions of mass propaganda, intellectual production, research, and education. Their main function was indeed executive: to direct and supervise the formal state hierarchies that dominated such fields. Stalin laureate authors and the permanently elected bosses of "creative unions" would be a good example. The university rectors and provosts, the editors-in-chief of the newspapers, and the head doctors in hospitals all in fact belonged to the *nomenklatura*.

Much analytical and political confusion can be avoided if we recognize that the Soviet-era professional specialists were not at all professionals in the Western sense of a self-organizing guild whose membership brings privileged, independent incomes. In the USSR, the lawyers, medical doctors, educators, and journalists were rather university-educated specialists on the state's payroll. Normally, they were no more than diploma-credentialized and relatively better-paid proletarians. Like the workers, they were bound to state employment for the duration of their working lives, subordinated to a formal structure of bureaucratic management, and dependent on their wages. Given the leveling effect of Soviet mass education and the poorly differentiated wage grid that became the norm in the Khrushchev period, these specialists were distinguished from skilled manual workers only by their diplomas, the corresponding cultural capital, and perhaps a greater aspiration for increased professional autonomy from the ruling bureaucracy.

Many Soviet architects, jurists, teachers, professors, researchers, scholars, and medical doctors would undoubtedly have liked to belong to autonomous professional guilds with comfortable incomes, and to enjoy a freedom from the state (Table 2, page 326). Though they were to remain repressed for a long time, these aspirations maintained a potential for cultural and political mobilization, a potential realized in exuberant bouts of self-organizing during periods when the ruling regime attempted reforms. This is why the highly educated proletarianized specialists were in the forefront of anti-bureaucratic mobilizations after de-Stalinization and throughout the Soviet bloc. But the specialists and intellectuals could become a potent force only if they managed to mobilize larger sectors of the population, either on a class basis, as fellow proletarians, or as members of the same nation. That the two patterns of mass mobilization – class and nation or shared ethnicity – were not mutually exclusive is best illustrated by the example of Poland's Solidarity trade union in 1980.

Also, the potentially autonomous jurists, professors, researchers, and medical doctors were vastly outnumbered by the educated technicians who were without administrative powers – in the main the engineers. In the Soviet industrial hierarchy this group occupied an ambiguous position between workers and the *nomenklatura*. Many Soviet bosses had been engineers or agronomists at an earlier point in their careers. For admission to the party schools, the experience of three to five years on the shopfloor was a required rite of passage on the way into the executive class. The bureaucratic ladder of social mobility continued to operate throughout Soviet history, but with the onset of the famed Brezhnevite "stability of cadres," executive openings grew scarce. A typical character within late Soviet socialism was the disenchanted low-paid engineer stranded on the lower echelons of sprawling bureaucratic organizations and caught in an unenviable position between the demands of production and those of half-heartedly compliant workers.[36] The social frustrations of this group, however, rarely found political expression. Like workers, engineers were part of the same shopfloor compact: controlled by managerial paternalism and tamed by state subsidies.

There existed, however, a different way of translating a high cultural capital, professional skills, and position into quasi-professional sources of income and social stature. This was largely by means of what we would perceive as corruption. Such opportunities were not available to the majority of educated Soviet specialists, and particularly hard to come by for those groups who were bound to the dominant heavy industry, abstract research, ordinary bureaucracy, or the military. But many teachers and university professors could earn additional incomes from private tutoring, which could extend to taking bribes from students in exchange for better grades, especially in university entrance examinations. Medical doctors, and in particular the highly specialized ones like cardiologists, dentists, and gynecologists, enjoyed perhaps the best combination of income opportunities, occupational prestige, and safety.[37] Gifts from grateful patients and their relatives were considered perfectly normal – indeed in some national republics they were regarded as obligatory – although their value could equal a month's salary or even more. But cardiologists were hardly ever audited, unlike the managers of restaurants and shops; besides, the *nomenklatura* and police would also need their help. The lower non-*nomenklatura* managers and specialists in consumer-oriented industries such as retail commerce, food processing, hotels, travel, repair services, or fashion design routinely engaged in the barter exchange of goods and favors, or charged extra over the approved prices. State-employed lawyers and notaries typically expected that their clients would pay them directly at a rate higher than that set officially. Another kind of opportunity, conditioned by highly specialized skills and professional connections, was offered by the extensive "gray" markets in books, music records, domestic pets, collectibles, and antiques, or the black markets in jewelry, hard currency, and prestigious goods smuggled from abroad.

In Soviet times such activities were punishable by law, and could lead to the confiscation of personal property and imprisonment, which is why they normally required the protection of powerful patrons in the *nomenklatura* and police. In effect, the extra-legal professional activities of Soviet specialists generated a major source of the *nomenklatura*'s corruption rent. Little wonder then that the old bourgeois slogan *laisser faire* strongly resonated with many Soviet specialists who had been driven into a proletarian existence by the ideological prejudice of communist officialdom. But the fact remains that for the duration of the Soviet regime, they were proletarians with proto-bourgeois profits earned furtively on the side.

In sum, the university-educated proletarian specialists did not merely seek an opportunity to earn extra money and gain access to scarce goods. They sought to translate certain kinds of occupational capital into the consumption and symbolic display associated with the prestigious imagery of Western middle classes.

The inducement to behave in such a manner was strongest in big cities like Moscow, which had an exceptionally high concentration of bureaucratic and intellectual capital and was exposed to foreign examples. It was even stronger in the select capitals of national republics that had preserved the traditions of "civil society" dominated by old families that could be traced back to the pre-communist gentry, bourgeoisie, and intelligentsia. The actual number of old high-status families could be quite small, because communist repressions took a heavy toll and Soviet industrialization brought its own specialists in vast numbers. Nonetheless, the families of old prestige tended to monopolize the gatekeeper functions in the formation of high-culture fields and thus exerted a disproportionate influence. The members of such families served as an attractive example for the Soviet-era newcomers who were seeking admission into intellectual and professional elite. Thus the old families could preserve their own elite status despite the loss of political and economic power in socialist times.

For our purposes, we must remember that such prototypical "civil societies," structured around old elite families, existed only in some republics. They were virtually absent in Belorussia, much of the Ukraine, in Russia itself, and in Central Asia. The reason is mostly historical and world-systemic: these Soviet republics were either too peripheral to possess sizable Westernized elites before 1917, or such groups had been destroyed or drastically diluted in the Soviet industrialization. National networks of educated elites were found primarily in the three Baltic republics and to some extent in Moldavia and western Ukraine – all annexed to the USSR only in the 1940s and relatively close to the West both in terms of urban culture and geography. This was also the case in Transcaucasia, where these elites were mainly found in big towns such as Baku, Tbilisi, and Yerevan, whose pre-1917 traditions of national enlightenment flowed into the structures of Soviet nationality-building. It might be added that the substantial unofficial economies of Transcaucasia could better support the middle-class aspirations of Soviet-era specialists: the prominent professors and medical doctors from Georgia or Armenia often looked better off than their Russian counterparts. The Baltic republics, Moldavia, western Ukraine, and Transcaucasia were the exact locations where nationalist contention would emerge the strongest of all during perestroika. The causal link between the "civil societies" of educated elite families and the aspiration for greater national freedom from Moscow seems quite straightforward.

NATIONAL REPUBLICS

One of the defining characteristics of the Soviet state was the existence of numerous national republics and autonomies. If very briefly, we need to consider this peculiar institutional fact, to develop some ideas about its origin and function, and to try to understand its implications for the structure of classes and the patterns of contention.

The ethno-national Soviet federation emerged from the contingent and complex compromises made during the Civil War, which the Bolsheviks won in large part by gaining the support of various ethnic forces, or at least dividing and placating them.[38] The granting of centrally supervised administrative and cultural autonomy within bounded territories became, after 1919, the key strategy for incorporating non-Russian nationalities into the Soviet state. Once this strategy was recognized as a success (at the outset this was not at all evident to many of Lenin's comrades), the Bolsheviks began pursuing national autonomization pro-actively and with their usual energy in order to outdo the nationalist forces on their native ground. In many places the Bolsheviks created nations where none had existed before.[39] The nation-building strategy that was applied on the periphery of the former tsarist empire followed from the Marxist-Leninist idea of progress: backward peoples had to pass through this stage before they were ready to join the world social commune. For that purpose national republics were endowed with a panoply of formal institutions – national schools and academies, theaters and museums – intended to shape their modern, secular ethnic cultures.

Terry Martin argues convincingly that, contrary to formal appearances, the Soviet Union was not a federation but rather a large unitary state where power flowed through the central hierarchy of the communist party.[40] But when considering educational admissions and bureaucratic appointments within the non-Russian republics, Moscow deliberately favored members of the titular nationalities. The Soviet version of affirmative action worked well for nearly seventy years. The native communist cadres, whose outlook and careers were embedded in Soviet institutions, zealously guarded against "bourgeois" nationalism. This arrangement broke down only after 1989, when Moscow's sudden incapacitation became widely apparent and the national communist bureaucracies scrambled to find alternative sources of power. Thus the strategy of ethno-territorial affirmative action – once a major strength of the Soviet state – would shape how it collapsed.[41]

Its critics liked to dismiss the Soviet institutions of nationality as oppressive hypocrisy or mere ornamentation on the imperial façade. And so they were, to some extent. But as time passes, all institutions tend to acquire a life of their own. Those designed to develop the national cultures of the Soviet Union inevitably created numerous professional positions for national intellectuals. The jobs were respectable, relatively well paid, and not too demanding, all of which made them enviable.

Moreover the institutions catering to national cultures fostered tightly-knit professional communities of educated men and women who normally spent their entire lives in the same town: the capital of their national republic. This was because their credentials did not travel beyond the republic's borders. An engineer with a diploma from Lithuania or Kazakhstan could find a job anywhere in the USSR where there was a factory. But specialists in Uzbek poetry or Ukrainian dance would be unlikely to find their skills valued outside their homeland. Yet at the same time, the all-Soviet centralization of social fields and official rituals, like the congresses and festivals of national cultures, regularly brought together artistic intellectuals from the different republics. Moscow's intent was to affirm its centrality and foster Soviet internationalism. But these events also created occasions for national intellectuals to exchange their ideas and dreams, which, because of the homology of their positions, were remarkably similar despite the differences between the lifestyles and customs of places as far apart as Estonia and Azerbaijan. Little wonder then that in 1989–1991 many Azeri or Chechen nationalist documents appeared to be copied from the more advanced Baltic nationalist programs – they were in fact copies transmitted through the Soviet-era networks among national intellectuals.[42] The prospect of independence from Moscow promised to make the lesser national academies, universities, and museums into the central institutions of sovereign states with direct access to the world arena. As long as the power of the Soviet Union looked rock-solid, these remained dangerous dreams. But things would change in 1989.

THE SUB-PROLETARIAT, THE MOST AWKWARD NON-CLASS

The last of the three social classes does not even have a commonly recognized name in the terminology of social science, despite the fact that it arguably constitutes the largest and fastest-growing segment of the world's population, especially in peripheral urban and semi-urban areas. The definition of this class is mostly a matter of stating what it is not. This renders it a peculiar "non-class," bounded by multiple exclusions. The major structural condition of this awkward category is deruralization – the loss of village life but without a transition to an established urban lifestyle. These people are mostly those former peasants and their descendants who did not find a place in, or could not be absorbed and transformed by, the towns. In different countries they are variously called *lumpens, declassé, marginales*, the "underclass," the "bazaar crowd," or, as in the Middle East, just the "street."

The term sub-proletariat seems more appropriate to capture the contradictory reality.[43] The crucial difference between this class and proletarians is that, for them, wages (though occasionally earned) do not provide the basis of household income. Other incomes are derived from multiple sources: subsidiary backyard agriculture, unpaid household labor, the barter exchange of goods and services among households bound by ethnicity or neighborhood, "informal" (i.e. untaxed) trade, criminal activity, gifts, and charity provided by relatives, neighbors or traditional religious institutions (see Table 1, page 325).[44] Since the sub-proletariat is a very motley category that plays a significant role in our analysis of ethnic mobilizations, let me illustrate it with localized examples.

To a locally trained eye the sub-proletarians are distinguished by the details of their dress, speech, and behavior – all of which flagrantly violate middle-class conventions. Pinning the sub-proletarians to specific occupations and living quarters is usually possible, but tricky because of the instability of their life patterns. Estimating their group size and distribution from official statistics is next to impossible. While partially overlapping with the lower-ranking proletarians, they have for some reason failed to accumulate the cultural dispositions and occupational capital of an established proletariat. This could be because the proletarianization occurred too recently, or because some structural inducements (the higher gains from smuggling and seasonal labor migrations compared to regular wages) or cultural dispositions (the traditional prestige of trade compared to employment, patriarchal ideas regarding female labor) predetermine them to avoid factory work.

Sometimes people in formal employment could in fact be sub-proletarians. In Soviet times it was very difficult to fire workers or expel students for absenteeism, drinking, or even petty theft. The official policy (hated by the mid-ranking managers responsible for its implementation) prescribed the re-education of slackers and drunks rather than dumping them in the streets. But it is far from true to say that all sub-proletarians are unproductive and parasitical. In fact, many can be remarkably resourceful and resilient laborers, approximating in this respect to farmers or artisans. Indicatively, the version of the Russian language used as an interethnic lingua franca across the Caucasus contains distinct words for working in the sense of generic employment – *rabotat* – and working for oneself or one's own family, in which case it is usually called *hambalit* or *mantulit* – "working very hard," slogging, drudgery. Large numbers of sub-proletarians were found at the state and collective farms where the official wages could be woefully low. Most of the time the employment demands in state agriculture were regarded as a form of state-imposed *corvée*, a demand which was complied with, very reluctantly, in order to allow the collective farmers to devote themselves with full force to the permitted cultivation of small garden plots. Part of this household production was allocated to subsistence, and part could be sold at urban markets. Since the purchasing power of Soviet urban workers had been steadily growing over the decades while the official restrictions on travel had been slackening, the rural workers found it increasingly advantageous to concentrate on supplying the town markets, sometimes over great distances. (Of course, the tendency for rural workers to turn themselves into de facto truck farmers further contributed to the perennial labor shortages in Soviet agriculture, but at the same time it helped to alleviate the shortages of fresh produce in urban industrial areas.)[45] Besides, only the biggest and wealthiest collective farms offered their employees housing. The majority of villagers had to build their homes themselves. The practical and status need to possess one's own home (which was especially pronounced in patriarchal regions like the Caucasus) sent many men off to seek supplementary incomes in the seasonal labor migrations (*shabashka*), mainly in construction. Such self-organizing migrations were tolerated by the Soviet authorities because they helped to alleviate labor shortages at strategic industrial sites located as far away as Siberia.

Today in the Caucasus the empirical markers of sub-proletarian membership might include the chicken roaming in the backyard of a nominally urban house; a street stall at the front gate from which the old men or women sell cigarettes, chewing gum, or homemade pies; and the presence of many women and children of different ages. Sub-proletarians are not necessarily paupers from shanty towns, though certainly many are desperately poor. Today on the outskirts of any big city in the Caucasus, one sees ostentatious new houses with Mercedes-Benzes in the driveways.[46] The mansions and the cars are the flashy emblems of the violent entrepreneurs who have risen from the prison world and informal economy of the Soviet era.[47] Wealth is inseparable from risk, and a risky life is inseparable from hardship and breaking the law. Among the Caucasian sub-proletarians, between a half and two thirds of the adult males have journeyed to Russia as migrant laborers or market vendors, and upwards of a quarter may have spent time in prison.

The disorganized lives of sub-proletarians episodically offer various opportunities, though the associated risks might look excessive to people with more stable social positions. In the Caucasus such opportunities were and remain principally of two kinds: the semi-legal labor migrations to zones of higher wages (Siberia, Moscow, and now Western Europe), and various kinds of smuggling operation. In the Soviet command economy, transporting a basket of strawberries from the southern climes of the Caucasus and selling it for a hefty profit in a big industrial town in central Russia already amounted to smuggling. Such operations required toughness, support from Caucasian expatriates in Russian towns, and the purchase of official protection.[48] Ethnic contacts help to find lucrative opportunities, avoid trouble with the agents of the state, and reduce the risks of cheating. Such skills and connections, which extend beyond the state's notion of legality, are central to the social capital of sub-proletarians.

It is a precarious class in every sense. Its members' lives are permeated with brutality. A great deal of defensive aggressiveness is displayed in the dress and demeanor of males and in the "marketplace scandalousness" of many women. Domestic violence serves to reaffirm the fledgling patriarchy; street gangs become the default mode of socialization among adolescents; violent sports like boxing and wrestling serve to uphold the virtues of masculinity; vandalism against the symbols of the dominant order (be it a defenseless park bench or a toilet seat in a public restroom), seemingly unmotivated hooliganism, and occasional rioting all help to vent social frustrations. Sub-proletarian social beliefs are precariously suspended somewhere between the ritualistic religiosity of peasants and the secular confidence of urbanites. Hence the responsiveness of sub-proletarian masses to secular populist or religious fundamentalist cults.

Sub-proletarians catch the eye of foreign visitors who then tend to overgeneralize the spectacle in exoticized ethnic terms, as I tried to show in the field descriptions in chapter one. Ethnic or regional cultures are terribly slippery things to describe and analyze. Take for example the notorious propensity of North Caucasians for symbolic posturing, which leads them to do things like bring weapons to public rallies (which can obviously make a difference in a political mobilization). But who brings weapons to rallies? Certainly not women, and it is hardly likely to be bureaucrats, medical doctors, or middle-aged workers. It would be worth trying to disassemble the supposed unitary ethnic "cultures" into social fields and combinations of habituses, specified in terms of social class, gender, and other characteristics – something along the lines of Bourdieu's *Distinction*.[49] We might discover that ethnic cultures are not systems of norms and enduring traditions but very contentious turbulent arenas. The young sub-proletarian toughs who bring daggers and guns to rallies or the romantic sub-intellectuals sporting *papaha* hats might be hailed as true co-nationals, as happened in the North Caucasus during the street mobilizations of 1991 and 1992. But under more normal circumstances they might well be ridiculed: *Where do you think you are, at a folk-dance competition?* The situational attitude towards the young men and women who nowadays exhibit in their dress and behavior a special Islamic piety are even more contrasting and, more often than not, hostile, because the new Islamists are widely regarded as a sectarian minority hailing from the lowest ranks of society.

Bourdieu emphasized the limited time-horizon of social action for the sub-proletarian, which he saw as related to the generalized unpredictability and under-lying violence of their existence.[50] This observation meshes well with Stinchcombe's argument that institutionalization is what extends the range of the socially predictable future.[51] In modern British history, as Tilly shows in marvelous detail, the institu-tionalization of politics and proletarian classes changed the character of contention towards a lasting parliamentarization.[52] Class formation and institutionalization are not, however, steady and unilinear evolutionary processes. Moreover they are reversible, as is demonstrated today in the former Soviet countries where many prole-tarians are beginning to adopt sub-proletarian strategies for coping with hardship.

Proletarians and sub-proletarians occupy subordinate yet very different positions in the social structure. The two classes may clash over their vision of social reality, tastes, and dispositions, and their collective action can be radically different. A crucial distinction between the proletarians and the sub-proletarians may be found in how they relate to the state. For the post-Soviet proletarians, the state remains the key provider of social structure and benefits. Thus their prevalent strategy, in Albert Hirschman's celebrated term, is loyalty, despite the state's deserting them.[53] Sub-proletarians, by contrast, see the state as an inescapable nuisance, represented by greedy police and street-level officials, the "jackals." Individual exit is their daily sneaky strategy. But in times of state breakdown, the sub-proletarian masses can raise their collective voice and become the "street crowd."

NEW CAPITALISTS: A BRIEF UPDATE

Today the new capitalists emerge from the ranks of all classes, though to a very different extent and by various trajectories. The ruling bureaucracy could often make big gains by transferring their power into wealth. Just as the old *nomenklatura* was differentiated by administrative levels and area of bureaucratic competence, so the new oligarchs come in corresponding shapes and sizes, from those celebrity billion-aires who dominate throughout the whole country or over entire industrial sectors (finance, oil, metallurgy, timber), to those who are wealthy notables in their own provinces, down to big rich men in small towns.

The most adventuresome sub-proletarians made fortunes on the "gray" and "black" markets, where they could best use their extra-legal skills and connections. Later we shall encounter the prime example of the "vodka tycoons."

The capitalist success stories of former proletarians come in a distant third because these people remain enmeshed in what might be called the "sticky structures" of their industrial existence. Among former proletarians entrepreneurial successes are concentrated in the skilled upper strata, and are mainly intellectual and technical cadres who have struggled to transform themselves into independent professionals.

None of the new capitalist groups, however, moved too far from their original classes either in terms of social space or class dispositions and habitus. The *nomenklatura* capitalists are rich because they preserve many connections in the state bureaucracy. Successful medical doctors, lawyers, and financiers still cultivate the respectable image of intelligentsia, mostly in order not to fall into complete social isolation and to differentiate themselves from the crude and violent "*nouveaux* Russians." And the smuggling tycoons are rich because they remain, in effect, lucky bandits.

THE FORMATION OF GROUP INTERESTS

In recent scholarly controversies regarding social structures, many doubts have been expressed about, and criticisms leveled against, the straightforward equation of the objective economic existence of social classes with subjective class cultures and political interests. Such criticisms made a valid point. How do people establish the existence of common interests with other members in an impersonal aggregate that lies beyond the circle of immediate acquaintance? Are social classes always aware that they are classes, and do they really know what they are pursuing? To the latter question history supplies plenty of negative answers. Social classes are very far from always being self-conscious entities with a clearly articulated agenda. Many barriers must be overcome to forge a unifying cultural identity, and still more daunting tasks are involved in translating an acquired common consciousness into a coherent political strategy. This takes effort, the inventive use of existing resources, and time, which history may not be inclined to supply. In this section I shall provide only a brief sketch of what seems a reasonable approach to such questions. The following discussion is short in part to avoid boring the non-specialist reader, and in part in keeping with the same principle that is known to modern lawyers no less than to old-time mariners: the smaller it is, the more watertight it will be.

The political tasks of nationalist mobilizers might seem easier than those of class-based political campaigners. Purportedly, all they need to do is "awaken" the nation from slumber. How doubtful this assumption is has been demonstrated compellingly by the recent scholarship on nations.[54] As Benedict Anderson put it in the title of his widely cited book, nations are *imagined communities*.[55] This does not mean that they are someone's fabrication, as people misinterpreting Anderson's famous title are inclined to think. The transformation of nations into the quintessential political and cultural reality of the modern epoch required a great deal of contentious charged imagining that was done by the identifiable thinkers and activists who operated through the social processes and means of diffusion that in turn had been created by capitalism and modern states. Perhaps it is not mere coincidence that the groundbreaking works on nationalism written by Gellner, Hobsbawm and Ranger, and Benedict Anderson all appeared in Britain in the same year, 1983. They opened a booming intellectual field that seems now to be reaching its maturation. At the same time, the analogous debates on the construction of classes remained less active apparently because the subject matter was considered central to Marxism, which was a rapidly declining paradigm. This is a pity. The two debates, to stress it forcefully, were analogous mainly because their focus was on an analogous social process: how an impersonal aggregate of many people, whether a nation or a class, acquires the properties of a self-conscious agency that can construe its interests and act on them.[56]

It is heartening that the debates on class are flaring up again and this time promise to yield sophisticated and rigorous generalizations of the kind that were achieved in the study of nationalist discourses.[57] A good example is the ongoing sociological controversy caused by Richard Lachmann's deservedly lauded monograph *Capitalists in Spite of Themselves.*[58] Lachmann analyzed the ruling elites of the early modern West, who had started from feudal premises and, acting without a grand historical plan but rather in response to a myriad of local dilemmas, eventually evolved into capitalists – much in spite of themselves. Lachmann's empirically rich and theoretically sophisticated work thus dealt a major blow to the orthodox liberal and Marxist image of capitalist modernity as the result of political struggles by the rising bourgeoisie against the aristocratic Old Regime. Likewise the Soviet *nomenklatura* executives, hard pressed by the events of 1989 to act on a myriad of local dilemmas, transformed themselves into capitalists as well as into the leaders of newly independent states, and quite in spite of themselves.

Did this transformation serve the personal and class interests of the *nomenklatura*? Perhaps not entirely, considering the collective weakening of their geopolitical and status positions in the world-system. Yet at least we may be assured that the *nomenklatura* were acting to the best of their imagination and historically available possibility. But before 1989 could they have dared to imagine where they were heading? The answer must be no, despite what some of the newly successful men (and they are predominantly men) might wish to reveal now about the dreams they previously shared only with their pillow. Likewise it seems incontrovertible that many rebels at the time became rebels in spite of themselves. The example of our Yuri Shanibov is quite clear. Could this provincial instructor in Scientific Communism imagine that he would be leading pan-nationalist guerrillas in a war against Georgia, and that later some of his disciples would draw inspiration from the Islamist fighters in Afghanistan? Yet they did become rebels, and that being so, we must ask how and why it was.

Lachmann's theory is nicely parsimonious, yet we should also take seriously the criticisms made by Julia Adams, even if in doing so we threaten the neatness of our explanation.[59] Adams admits that her admiration for Lachmann's work is insep-arable from her utter frustration at his treatment of elites as given coherent entities endowed with unproblematic interests and the ability to pursue them. Lachmann's study seems so elegant largely because the author assumes that the rich and powerful know that they all share common interests and also know what they are doing, at least in the short run. Like many critics who insist on paying special attention to the processes of translating the objective and structural into the subjective and active, Julia Adams essentially leaves us there. We must hope that a reasonable degree of certainty in describing the dynamics of social structures and political contention will be regained at some later stage. Right now we must try to grasp how, out of numerous locally-embedded micro-conflicts and structurally constrained choices, there emerged the homologous conditions that coalesced into waves of action along the lines of class and nationality. If we can succeed in this, we have a potential theory; therefore let me restate the arguments more explicitly to open them to crit-icism and invite improvement.

The isomorphism of Soviet institutions engendered similar situations and tensions in the different sectors of the social structure and at the various levels that in Bourdieu's terms might be called fields of power, culture, etc. These situational tensions produced homologous aspirations, frustrations, and conflicts. Nonethe-less, they would remain limited to specific situations insofar as there existed little or no flow of information between the different sectors and social fields. A related condition was the lack of imaginable alternatives to the existing order. Soviet censor-ship was the key mechanism in this, and was intended to curb the flow of undesirable information and imagined alternatives.[60] But, like all mechanisms, censorship cannot last forever. It can be clogged up with work, broken in some historical accident, circumvented by resourceful subversives, or it might be partly dismantled from above by a reformist faction who face their own frustrations and therefore might seek broader discussion to formulate a way out. Once the information starts flowing and suddenly alternatives can be imagined and popularized, micro-conflicts coalesce in chains of resonance. From different sides people may begin to realize that they have something important in common, which enables them to organize and pursue their goals collectively.

It takes time, however, for this feeling of solidarity to be translated into practical mobilization and concerted action. In revolutions time flies very fast, spurred by the rapid succession of events. Revolutions are disorienting for all participants. Therefore people start looking everywhere for ideas that might guide them: they take inspiration and form in historical or foreign examples that seem relevant to their own struggle, or they reach back to their own experience that they refashion to fit the new goals (in the way Shanibov applied what he had learned as a young activist dealing with street toughs to the formation of guerrilla detachments). The relevance of an idea is judged mostly by the degree to which it resonates with the intuitive knowledge carried in what Bourdieu called habitus. It is that practical acumen that cannot extend far into the future because it reflects in unreflected ways the past experiences of individuals and social groups. This does not mean that habitus or intuition offers poor guidance. Blind they may be, but they usually work. As Charles Tilly observes, his elbow most of the time succeeds in instinctively closing the kitchen door when he returns home loaded with grocery bags. Accidents happen and the groceries occasionally get spilled on the floor, or closing the door may require a second, more conscious and concerted push.[61] Still habitus works most of the time for most people, even in the confusing and unpredictable situations of historical crises. If you will, we can call it muddling through. Since the dominant classes possess more resources to help them act on their intuitive understanding of their interests, in the end they often prove dominant once again, though perhaps dominant in a different form. What was once the European feudal class becomes the capitalist class in the Western transition to capitalism. Likewise the former communist executives (or their juniors) become something else, the owners of economic capital or leaders of national states. If not all of them, at least those who were nimble and better positioned succeeded because they had already been administering profitable enterprises like banks and oil fields (see Table 3, page 327). They knew how to play some tricks with Moscow in order to divert its unwanted interference in local bureaucratic affairs, and this knowledge, after 1989, enabled the Soviet bureaucrats to play the trick of a lifetime.

In such heady moments it appears that great personalities are making history, in other words, that human agency prevails over social structure. This observation pertains to a huge intellectual controversy regarding structure and human agency that is perhaps as old as the concept of a struggle between destiny and human will

– first expressed in the Mesopotamian epic of Gilgamesh and the Greek tragedies. Distilling a suggestion made in Immanuel Wallerstein's writings, we might be able to escape from the perennial conundrum of which is more important, human will or the conditions of life.[62] For this, the terms of our discussion must be placed in the time/space of human history instead of the timeless space of philosophical abstractions. Let us be more precise when trying to identify the historical moments and institutional locations in which human agency might liberate itself from structural constraints to shape the course of history. Evidently, this becomes more likely in moments of historical transition, when structural constraints are overloaded, eroded, battered, and imploding. But it is always a relative situation. Structures rarely fall apart completely, and besides, complete chaos would deny human agency the structural basis for exercising its plans or might undo that agency itself. The two sides of the equation are surely relational. Furthermore, let me add that the impression we gain may depend on our instruments. The greater the magnification, the more important do acts of human will appear. Researchers, mainly historians, who study in detail specific events and personalities, might be expected to see the object of their study rapidly moving through a dramatic series of human decisions. Admittedly, by making Shanibov's biography the leitmotif of this study, I consciously aimed to track developments at this more subjective, "voluntaristic" and dynamic level. But once we step back, the kaleidoscopic combinations of human acts and fleeting events may acquire a pattern that looks slower and pretty structural. This is, of course, what Fernand Braudel's distinction between *longue durée, conjoncture* and the time of events was all about.

MAPPING THE SOVIET COLLAPSE

We have now obtained a description of classes and key fractions in late Soviet society, of its institutional morphology, of shared aspirations and the potential for actualizing them in collective action. Bringing these threads together, let us attempt to draw relational charts of the social structure on which we are going to map the empirical processes that led to the collapse of the Soviet Union. Our portolan maps are Figure 1 (a, b, c), Figure 2 (pages 331–334), and the corresponding Table 2 (page 326). Admittedly, they might look even cruder than the old navigational charts and logs from the European Age of Discovery. The shapes, in the absence of precise topographical instruments, are drawn arbitrarily, and therefore the sizes of classes and class fractions are distorted, with workers being probably the most seriously underrepresented. I hope, nonetheless, that these sociological portolans

represent more or less correctly and, what matters to us most, relationally the landscape of late Soviet society. On these maps we can identify different locations, the
directions of historical currents, and the source of the tempest.

Figure 1 illustrates the three generic patterns of the revolutionary situations of
1989–1991. The first shows the restoration of *nomenklatura* powers in the renewed
oligarchic compact (1-a), which remains today the prevalent pattern across the
former USSR. Second there is the institutionalization of liberal "civil societies" and
markets (1-b), which is mostly evident in the three Baltic republics and, in part,
Russia (namely in Moscow and St. Petersburg). And third, Figure 1-c depicts the
messy state disintegration that has resulted in the massive mobilization of lower
and marginal groups, who are temporarily acting together with various defectors
and opportunists from the upper social strata in what in the Caucasus are usually
called "ethnic conflicts."

Figure 2 and Table 2, in different ways, represent the same idea. They chart relationally the prevalent social constituencies of three political projects and their
outcomes: the preservation of bureaucratic paternalism; the orderly change
(reform) of state and economic institutions, mostly to the benefit of groups
possessing the higher, relatively autonomous, and ascendant forms of capital; and,
lastly, the zone of rebelliousness indicates the groups that are most likely to engage
in various kinds of "rowdy conflict" where the degree of physical violence depends
on the availability of decentralized means of coercion, and which may or may not
be ethnically targeted. The homologies in Table 2 are depicted as the concatenation of affinities that arise out of analogous positions and constraints, which
furthermore result in affinities of disposition and aspiration. In other words, Table
2 helps us to see who might feel attracted to whom, and on the basis of what shared
traits, which then translates into who might support whom in the ensuing political
contention.

The key shape of Soviet organization was the pyramid (see Figure 1). The whole
of the USSR was essentially a huge pyramid consisting of many bureaucratically-
organized pyramids of two kinds, those of sectors and territories. The pyramidal
hierarchy of bureaucratic subordination was held together by the overarching apparatus of the Communist Party, the secret police, and the institution of *nomenklatura*
appointments. This organization originated during the Russian Civil War, in which
the Bolsheviks devised their revolutionary dictatorship. The vertically integrated
dictatorial apparatus was forcefully extended during the Stalinist industrialization
in order to gain central control over all economic assets and labor resources in this
vast country, and thus the formal bureaucratic pyramid came to encompass all

aspects of social reproduction. The extraordinary concentration of powers and resources in the hands of a dictator and central administration in Moscow was subsequently applied to catch up with the military-industrial potential of the core Western states. The result was not only the extraordinary Soviet victory in the Second World War, but also the achievement of an impressive degree of "development," in the contemporary sense of the rationally coordinated creation of industries, science, education, administration, public welfare, and labor force approximating to the core Western examples of the industrial epoch, such as Wilhelmine Germany or Detroit at the height of the "Fordist" industrial regime.

On this road, the Soviet state achieved rates of proletarianization perhaps unprecedented anywhere among the capitalist countries. This condition wasn't limited to the huge labor force engaged in industrial production. Those who would elsewhere normally be "self-employed" – lawyers, architects, poets, taxi-drivers, cobblers, hairdressers, and, importantly, peasants and farmers – went on the payroll of the various Soviet state bureaucracies. Only at the bottom level and on the fringes of this imposing state-industrial leviathan do we find populations who had been only partially incorporated in official institutions of employment, i.e. who remained sub-proletarian. The relative weight of sub-proletarian groups, however, could be quite large in the southern areas, like the Caucasus and Central Asia, that possessed fewer industrial enterprises, bigger agrarian populations, and thus usually continued with higher birth rates.

Located at the top of pyramidal structures was the *nomenklatura*, or the corps of bureaucratic executives formally invested by the supervising committees of the Communist Party. The majority of the *nomenklatura* felt very comfortable in their positions after the de-Stalinization of 1956 and especially after the arrival of conservative Brezhnevism in 1964 and the suppression of the 1968 movements across the Soviet bloc. These successive political shifts, effected by the *nomenklatura* themselves, made their existence safe from arbitrary persecution, stable in terms of career, fairly rewarding materially, and overall allowed an easing of the work pace and psychological pressure that had been the scourge of Soviet managers under Stalin. The urge to introduce reforms came from the activist minority of the *nomenklatura*, who, owing to their central positions, had to be concerned with the foreign power and prestige of the Soviet Union, or else felt that the immobility of Brezhnev's rule stifled their ambitions – which was mostly the case among the junior ranks of the *nomenklatura* and those in the technologically advanced industries (see Table 2).

The reformist *nomenklatura* could find impatient constituencies among intellectuals, university-educated specialists, and the skilled workers of large, capital-intensive enterprises, especially those located in big towns. Bourdieu's principle of homology illuminates why such an alliance looked natural. The upper proletarian strata possessed large concentrations of occupational and cultural capital. They felt stifled in various ways and believed that they could do much better if the regime gave them a public voice and the ability to organize and act legally as collective bodies. The artistic and scholarly intellectuals believed that their creativity suffered from censorship and the stringent checks on resources, information, and mobility imposed by the conservative bureaucratic institutions. Not without reason, the specialists who possessed highly detailed kinds of knowledge in their areas – lawyers, medical doctors, academics, architects, art appraisers, or frustrated inventors – commonly held that they could incorporate themselves into the middle-class professions if only the ruling bureaucracy would let them. The workers in capital-intensive and advanced industries wanted to obtain the legal ability to influence decisions concerning production processes, remuneration, and perhaps the selection of shopfloor management. In short, they sought to unionize independently of the bogus official trade unions. These upper fractions of socialist proletarians generated streams of cultural symbols and political projects that increasingly endowed these groups with internal cohesiveness and collective autonomy from the ruling regime. Thus their aspirations conformed to the ideals of civil society and democratization.

Still there remained the much larger body of ordinary workers employed in Soviet industries, offices, services, and agriculture who possessed neither a high level of occupational capital nor, as ordinary workers go, much cultural capital. This majority of Soviet citizens nurtured fairly prosaic aspirations, which were limited to their immediate social environments. This does not mean that they were doomed to docile inertia and could not mobilize in principle. The idea of better working conditions and wages, negotiated for them by independent trade unions, could not have been totally alien to ordinary workers. Many collective farmers, given their situation, would have welcomed the prospect of de-proletarianization, which would have allowed them to become independent farmers, perhaps united through some sort of genuinely autonomous cooperatives. And surely a great many workers would rejoice at the chance to punish a particularly odious bureaucrat in an election, once they believed that such a thing was possible. Certainly there exists empirical evidence of such tendencies spreading at the lower reaches of the Soviet class structure. But class organizing takes time, of which there was little during the accelerating run towards the Soviet debacle. It also takes a great effort, of a kind which the prospective political mobilizers on the democratic side did not make until the last moment because they had placed their hopes in President Gorbachev, who they presumed had the power to bring about all the necessary changes from the top.

Conversely, the mass of ordinary workers could and sometimes did form a constituency for the political projects of the conservative *nomenklatura*. Here we find another example of homology. The key to Brezhnev's conservatism was the combination of incremental material improvements, corporativist paternalistic redistribution, and the tacit toleration of various inefficiencies. The majority of the *nomenklatura*, especially in the middle ranks, felt comfortable under such a regime and preferred not to worry about its long-term consequences. And so perhaps did the majority of Soviet workers who had adapted to the less demanding work level and the limited expectation of goods distributed through the workplace under the control of benevolent bosses. This was, however, a predominantly passive accept-ance of the existing order. If it was to last, a counter-reform or conservative activist mobilization of Soviet workers still required a credible ideology, which the conser-vative *nomenklatura* patently lacked. Their repressive hypocrisy perhaps looked too transparent to workers and even to the *nomenklatura* themselves. And thus, because of both their embeddedness in the existing order and their lack of belief in it, the majority of Soviet citizens would remain politically passive throughout perestroika.

There remain the sub-proletarians, whom we locate at the fringes and interstices of the state-controlled industrial economy. This means that the sectoral agencies of the Soviet state contained few or no sub-proletarians. But the territorial agencies, especially the national republics in the lesser developed southern tier of the Soviet Union, are another matter. There the sub-proletarian component could be very substantial. Usually the sub-proletariat is a fundamentally non-political class. It has little stake in the existing order and not much to gain through its changing either. Therefore it is typical of the sub-proletarian habitus to try to avoid everything related to the state. Instead, their life strategies focus on the survival of individuals and fami-lies, achieved primarily through informal networking among friends, neighbors, and people of the same clan, religious group, locality, and ethnicity, especially when confronted with foreign and alien environments such as the big cities that serve as the destination of sub-proletarian migration. But sub-proletarians can invade poli-tics during moments of crisis when they feel that their group is threatened, that their erstwhile oppressors can be battered and humiliated, or there emerge unusual oppor-tunities to jump into the focus of public emotional attention, or to gain a new status and resources. If the sub-proletarians are rebellious in their motives when choosing to participate in politics, they are rarely democratic in their rhetoric and aims. Perhaps nowhere do these features of sub-proletarian contention emerge as glaringly as in ethnic conflicts. Sub-proletarian activism in ethnic conflicts is not the sole cause of violence, but it is certainly a significant factor.

For the purposes of our analysis, we will distinguish between two varieties of bureaucratic pyramid: the non-territorial sectors concerned with the economic, coercive, and welfare-providing functions of the state; and the territorial administrations, including the national republics and autonomies that were subject to the territorially bound Soviet variety of affirmative action. The creation of national republics was once a clever adaptation which, as we have seen, originated during the Civil War. This practice endured as a strategy to incorporate ethnic minorities in the Soviet state, and eventually it fostered loyal non-Russian elites who could serve as proxies in taming national separatism.

But just as the Soviet industrial bureaucracies tended to insulate themselves from unwanted interferences by Moscow, so the national republics gained a greater degree of bureaucratic insulation conducive to their becoming de facto sovereignties. During the Brezhnev period, it was only in exceptional cases that Moscow could replace the leaders of national republics, whose power now rested not only on their investiture by central authorities but also on the formidable patronage networks they had forged in their republics and territories. Additionally, many national republics developed cohesive nuclei of national intellectuals. This became possible either because the official institutions of national cultures began to acquire a life of their own, or because there already existed lasting traditions of national culture, which had been cultivated primarily by the families of the old intelligentsia and the newly educated entrants to the field of national culture who aspired to emulate the status and fashions of their predecessors.

Once Gorbachev's policies permitted the open questioning of the mid-ranking conservative *nomenklatura*, the high-status intellectuals in the republics could rapidly transform themselves into the leaders of emergent civil societies. Such societies originated mainly in networks of cultural intellectuals who had known each other for a long time and usually spent their entire lives in the same towns working in interconnected state institutions concerned with national history, culture, etc. Given that the coercive powers of the *nomenklatura* in the national republics were limited and entirely derived from the graces of Moscow, it is not hard to see how the civil societies shaped by national intellectuals could emerge as a formidable challenge to the national *nomenklatura*.

Nationalism seemed in this situation a natural choice because much of the institutional setting in the republics was already national. Politically, nationalism offered a big advantage compared to democratization and economic reform, because it could bypass the obstacles in the way of mass mobilization that were embedded in the paternalistic structures of Soviet industry. In fact, the same paternalistic patterns of workplace dependency that deterred the predominantly Slavic working class from action in the central regions of the USSR tended to encourage nationalist mobilizations in the national republics. The contrast between these radically divergent outcomes of essentially the same social pattern was due to the fact that the non-Russian *nomenklatura* and economic managers were more likely to defect, and could then use their authority and resources to sponsor rallies, strikes, and eventually referendums on national independence. The *nomenklatura* in national republics would start to defect after they saw that the actions of Moscow had become indecisive and erratic while locally the growing appeal of national intellectuals threatened to eclipse their power. At this point the Supreme Soviets of the national republics, whose function previously had been essentially to translate the decrees of Moscow into the local languages, began to recast themselves into national parliaments, and the junior *nomenklatura* appeared in the front rows of nationalist mobilization, even leading their employees and clients in public protests.

Still, the more probable result was what some political scientists call "pacted transitions," leading to national independence if not necessarily to democratization. By offering to form a political alliance, against Moscow or another nation, with national intellectuals, the former national *nomenklatura* obtained a good chance of staying in power. In some instances, such as in the Ukraine, Uzbekistan, or Tatarstan, the *nomenklatura* splintered and overpowered the weaker coalitions of national intellectuals, which resulted in an orderly but authoritarian transition to national independence (or quasi-independence as in Tatarstan). In the three Baltic republics the former *nomenklatura* remained in a broad alliance with the relatively numerous and organized national intellectuals, which resulted in democratization. It is primarily in the Caucasus that we find the empirical validation of a third possibility. The coalitions created and led by national intellectuals were able to splinter and overthrow the *nomenklatura*, but could not preserve state order. These revolutions drew much of their energy from the violent rebellions of sub-proletarians, but the same uprisings set them on the self-destructive path of ethnic violence. In the next chapter we shall see how this actually happened.

6

The Nationalization
of Provincial Revolutions

"The most perilous moment for a bad government is one when it seeks to
mend its ways. Patiently endured so long as it seemed beyond redress, a
grievance comes to appear intolerable once the possibility of removing it
crosses men's minds. For the mere fact that certain abuses have been
remedied draws attention to the others and they now appear more galling."

Alexis de Tocqueville, *The Old Régime and the French Revolution*
(Translated by Stuart Gilbert. Garden City; NY: Doubleday, 1955, p. 177)

What exactly went wrong with perestroika? I shall attempt to answer this question
here by combining macro-explanations with an in-depth look into national mobilizations in the Caucasus region and elsewhere in the USSR. The rise of nationalism
has featured centrally among the factors blamed for the failure of Gorbachev's
reforms, but the detailed analysis to follow should allow us to see the contentious
processes behind what was perceived in the contemporary political imagination as
an inevitable consequence of the existence of nationalities.

The national mobilizations at the time could be very impressive indeed. Out of
three and a half million Armenians then living in Armenia, probably a million,
which means close to every adult in the country, stood for days on end in the Opera
Square in Yerevan chanting the same demand – that the Armenian mainland be

[handwritten: Demand of Armenians]

reunited with the province of Nagorny Karabagh. The latter, despite being predominantly Armenian and separated from the Armenian republic by only a narrow strip of Azerbaijan's territory, had somehow been placed in the jurisdiction of Soviet Azerbaijan. In the Baltic republics of Estonia, Latvia, and Lithuania hundreds of thousands of people held hands to form a human chain extending from the border of Poland to the Bay of Finland. Rather than chanting overtly political demands that could provoke police repression, they sang the mighty choruses of national songs. And yet, through the songs, the key Baltic demand rang out loud and clear: they wanted to live in Europe, not the Soviet Union. Later in 1994, thousands of ordinary Chechens would sell their TV sets or cattle to buy guns on the black market and go to Grozny to face the advancing Russian tanks and infantry. The Chechens were fighting against what they saw as the repetition of Stalin's deportation of 1944, in which almost a third of their small nation had perished. Do we need any further evidence of the national determination?

However, we are not looking for evidence of mobilization. Rather we want to understand how millions of people could acquire – and later lose – the ability to speak in one powerful voice. We must open a Pandora's box containing many bewildering questions. Why did the Soviet nationalities suddenly begin to demand something that Gorbachev, Moscow, or what was simply called the "Center," could not deliver? Why were the first to do this so forcefully the Armenians, previously one of the most loyal nationalities in the USSR? And why did they express their demands through a nationalist discourse? Why did they not talk in terms of democratization, social reform, the devolution of economic decision-making, or ecology? All these issues did in fact feature in the political demands of the time, but they were subsumed in the demands of nationalism: no democratization, social reform, market-based autonomy, or ecological clean-up was considered possible as long as the key power remained vested in Moscow rather than in the national republics and provinces.

Why was it that in some republics of the USSR, mainly in the Caucasus, the words and images of national identity seemed to lead automatically to ethnic violence? And why was it that the violence was fratricidal in so many instances? Ethnic Russians were almost never the targets of the pogroms and mass expulsions that occurred in the non-Russian republics. Instead, hatred ran laterally, usually against neighboring nationalities where the victims and victimizers (which could be interchangeable categories) shared many traits of material culture, social status, even language and religion. In Tadjikistan during the civil war of 1991–1993, Tadjiks were slaughtering Tadjiks; in the Transdniestrian stand-off that briefly escalated into war in 1992 both sides were (nominally at least) Orthodox Christian and both included ethnic Moldovans, Russians, and Ukrainians; the Georgians and Abkhazes had much in common in their lifestyles and in some areas had lived side by side for so long that many families and whole villages couldn't tell which nationality they belonged to – in Abkhazia, it was normal to be bilingual or even trilingual; the Kabardins and the Balkars were both traditionally Muslim peoples that had lived on fairly peaceful terms for as long as anyone could remember; and even the Armenians and Azeris, despite differences of language and religion, still had a lot in common in terms of their social organization, family life, ethnic food, and folk music (Armenian intellectuals wished their common people had less Persian and more European tastes but they could do little to change what was served, played, and danced at weddings and on other such occasions).[1] This little anthropological overview suggests an almost rhetorical question: What clash of civilizations?

WRONG PREDICTIONS

First of all, it is necessary to explain why no significant violence occurred elsewhere.[2] This is a more puzzling question than it may seem. If back in the 1970s one had asked a Sovietologist to predict where the rule of Moscow might face the most serious nationalist challenges, the answer quite certainly would have been the Baltic republics, the western provinces of the Ukraine, and perhaps Uzbekistan.

Since the 1970s, a small but highly respected group of mostly French and British experts on Islam and Central Asia had been arguing that Uzbekistan could be the undoing of the USSR because of the rapidly growing population of Muslims who supposedly were aggrieved at their economic backwardness and the domination of Christian Russians, and inspired by the examples of their brethren in Iran and Afghanistan.[3] In fact Uzbekistan was among the last of the republics to leave the USSR, and even then it was pushed out by Yeltsin's Russia acting with the Ukraine and Belarus to abolish the union.[4]

Uzbekistan's exit from the USSR was remarkably orderly. Yet there were at least two serious episodes of mayhem on the road to unintended independence that possibly indicated the presence of much more disruptive and violent historical possibilities. In both instances, however, the violence was waged by Muslims against fellow Muslims rather than being a joint Muslim action against Christians or Russians. One was the 1989 pogrom against the Meskhetian Turks and the other a brief but quite bloody dispute between the Uzbeks and the neighboring Kyrgyzes in 1990. Information gathered during my visit to Uzbekistan in May–June 1990 suggests that the Uzbek–Kyrgyz violence was essentially a local clash between the two ethnic sub-proletariats who were connected to different networks of official patrons. Back in 1990 the administrative border between Soviet Uzbekistan and Kirgizia (now Kyrgyzstan) was poorly demarcated, which resulted in rival claims being made on land plots in the vicinity of the town of Osh in Kirgizia. This was located in the Fergana valley, the largest and most densely populated oasis in Soviet Central Asia. On the one side, the Kyrgyz town administration wanted to lease the adjacent land plots for the construction of private housing, which was intended to alleviate the problems of poor young Kyrgyzes and, as such projects usually go in this world, perhaps create a lucrative market in home construction and a flow of bureaucratic kickbacks. On their side, the Uzbeks had been using the same land for years in the shadow gardening-economy, because suburban plots lay outside the official monopoly of collective farms on agricultural land.[5] All the evidence suggests that the violence that claimed dozens and perhaps hundreds of lives had been anticipated, if not secretly planned (makeshift weapons had been produced beforehand at local factories). The permissive atmosphere for such acts was created by the violent outbreaks elsewhere in Central Asia and the Caucasus, in which Moscow had intervened only half-heartedly. The nearest example was the expulsion of Meskhetian Turks from Uzbekistan's section of the same Fergana valley earlier in 1989.

On the surface, this clash was also over the distribution of niches in the shadow agriculture market. The Turks, who under Stalin had been deported to Uzbekistan from Georgia's province of Meskhetia, came to concentrate on the household production of food crops and eventually its commercialization, where they competed with the native Uzbeks. In local opinion, the fact that the Turks were fellow Sunni Muslims and spoke a Turkic language related to Uzbek only made things worse: the Meskhetian Turks were in all respects just like the Uzbeks, only they considered themselves more industrious. There existed, however, an even more industrious community of ethnic Koreans. The Soviet Koreans had also been forcibly resettled under Stalin and subsequently translated their earlier survival strategies of household production and ethnic solidarity into success on the shadow markets. But they could not easily be attacked because, as an Uzbek informant put it, *Koreans are Europeans.* He meant that in the Central Asian context, Koreans were not considered fellow Asians by virtue of their not being Muslim. Did this mean that Koreans, like the Russians, enjoyed a special aura or Moscow's protection? Not quite. A well-informed Soviet Korean explained it differently (and exaggerated only slightly): *For years, we have been "feeding" fat bribes to Uzbek officials and police. Besides, they knew that we had been buying guns and that half a million Koreans would all fight ferociously for each other. For we are such a people!* Bravado aside, Koreans were probably safer because they enjoyed a higher local social status, more resources, and thus stronger patronage. As to the Russians in Uzbekistan, they were predominantly industrial specialists and workers, and thus did not compete for land or market niches with the Uzbek sub-proletarians.[6]

Whatever the reason, the selection of the Meskhetian Turks for victimization did not seem entirely random and the stories surrounding this pogrom point to the possibility that it was coordinated at some unknown level. A major conspiracy, however, seems unlikely. The internal politics of bureaucratic patronage in Soviet Uzbekistan had been in disarray since the early 1980s, when Andropov's faction in Moscow dispatched to this notoriously corrupt Central Asian republic a special team of police investigators with a broad mandate.[7] The external investigators uncovered pervasive embezzlement and bribery. Between 1982 and 1986, as reported by the contemporary press, the anti-corruption campaign led to the dismissal of more than 90 per cent of Uzbekistan's *nomenklatura* and a score of high-profile arrests and trials.[8] Andropov's anti-corruption purge was followed by another wholesale replacement of Uzbekistan's leadership under Gorbachev. Opinion in Moscow held it that the new Uzbekistani appointments had soon proved as corrupt and nepotistic as their predecessors because of ingrained Oriental despotism. The chief investigators, who claimed during perestroika the heroic status of "mafia busters," leaked to journalists what they considered particularly scandalous facts that for our sociological purposes provide a glimpse of the established neopatrimonial system of shadow governance. Intricate networks of corruption collected tributes from all sorts of shadow economic operations and syphoned resources upwards, possibly all the way to patrons in Moscow. This tributary mechanism generated sums in excess of what the Soviet Uzbek elites could actually consume, hence the fabulous hordes of cash and gold that the investigators had literally unearthed in the gardens of various officials and their clients. Of course, while the USSR lasted, it was difficult to open accounts in Swiss banks or build palaces. And besides that – as the daughter of a very high official told me – one would have a problem in Central Asia finding the skilled builders and materials required to make a good bathroom.

The illicit wealth accumulated in the middle and upper ranks of the *nomenklatura* in such republics could be used to arm private militias or foment violent mobilizations. But this does not mean that corruption itself was the cause of violence. Unless the pyramid of corrupt officials began to collapse, leading to unconstrained factionalism, corrupt patronage could preserve stability. In the end, the pogrom against the Meskhetian Turks was used to discredit and expunge the Uzbek leadership that had been appointed by Gorbachev a few years earlier.[9] In the wake of these events, Islam Karimov, the last First Secretary of Uzbekistan, and since 1991 its first President, came to power as the restorer of the previous order and defender of local interests. In this, he enjoyed strong support from the old *nomenklatura* networks.

After independence, the government of Uzbekistan forcefully revived the Soviet practices of censorship and police repression. Soon they imprisoned, drove into exile, or forced underground both the small democratic intelligentsia and the far more numerous sub-proletarian Islamists (who, after September 2001, the Uzbek *nomenklatura* could oppress as their supposed contribution to the American war on terror). The economy of Uzbekistan, including the heavily taxed market sector, still remains under government control. But evidently the preservation of economic controls and the ability to collect taxes spared the country the terrible slump experienced by many other former Soviet republics.[10] In Uzbekistan today, roads and imposing public buildings are being built and local factories are operating at nearly full capacity, almost as they were in Soviet times. Political power is in the hands of an authoritarian regime that consists of former Uzbek *nomenklatura* – though in order to express an appreciation of national glories, they ordered the statues of Lenin to be replaced with statues of Tamerlane.

Such continuity in the make up of power elites and state structures, at the expense of democratization and market reform, may be regarded as a practical way to maintain order and relative prosperity. This seems a plausible hypothesis as regards Central Asia. We find additional evidence in Tadjikistan, where attempted democratization, resisted by the entrenched *nomenklatura,* led to the calamitous breakdown of state power in 1991–1993 and a gruesome civil war. As the conflict spread outside the towns into Tadjikistan's countryside, the mobilizing platform of popular anti-bureaucratic contention shifted from the elite intelligentsia's program of secular democratization to a popular variety of political Islamism. However, the civil war in Tadjikistan was not an ethnic or religious conflict but rather an Afghanistan-style internecine struggle among various Tadjik warlords from different provinces.

Given such examples, one might conclude that there must be a strong, if conservative, authoritarian state to repress the demons of ethnic violence. But what then about the western Ukraine and in particular the Baltic republics, where the national mobilizations were as powerful and sweeping as in the Caucasus but the exit from the USSR turned out to be both peaceful and relatively democratic? Common opinion, once again, holds that this pattern was to be expected because the westernmost territories of the USSR were very different from Central Asia in being more "civilized," less corrupt, and almost European. The existence of significant differences between Uzbekistan and Lithuania seems undeniable. However, it is less evident that Lithuania was very different from, say, Croatia.

Speaking of ancient and not so ancient hatreds, the Baltic and western Ukrainian territories had fallen under Soviet rule as a result of the Second World War, and long after 1945 the Soviets had been fighting the tenacious guerrilla resistance of the Baltic "Forest Brothers" and the Ukrainian nationalists of Stepan Bandera. During the war, the nationalist guerrillas (some of whom were still alive and returned to politics in the late 1980s) received their weapons, uniforms, and not a little of their ideology from the German Nazis.[11] In other words, they were definitely European, but hardly civic nationalists of the 1930s–1940s formation. The fate of Ukrainian and Baltic Jews during 1941–1944 suggests that ethnic extermination was not an entirely foreign idea anywhere in the region. In addition, Stalin's secret police had deported to Siberia many thousands of families previously belonging to the bourgeoisie or suspected of nationalist sympathies, a fact which emerged in the 1980s as a major source of grievance. The Soviet military and industrial policies brought to the Baltic republics and western Ukraine large populations of ethnic Russians who settled in towns. After 1945 Moscow's rulers reconfigured many national borders. Germany's Königsberg became an odd exclave of the Russian Federation called Kaliningrad; the Austrian Lemberg after 1918 became first the Polish Lwow, then the Soviet Lvov, and then the Ukrainian Lviv; Poland's Wilno became Lithuania's new capital of Vilnius. The list of territorial transfers does not end there. If historical legacies of violent conflict, transborder irredentism, the presence of unwanted settlers, long-standing religious controversies, racial prejudices, and the popular spread of nationalism were all good predictors of ethnic violence, then the western Ukraine and the Baltic region should have been a congregation of demons.

Fortunately, somehow, they are not. In 1989 the Balt *nomenklatura* quietly gave up their communist ideology, opened their ranks, and peacefully blended with the ascendant national intellectuals. Acting together, they managed to channel the contention into the construction of nationally defined "civil societies." Local policing remained effective despite a number of serious provocations (including some by the retreating Soviet police). Markets were successfully presented as belonging to the Balt national traditions of self-sufficient farming as opposed to Russian despotism. The costs of transition to capitalism were shifted squarely on to the Russian urban settlers who had been caught in the Soviet-era structures of industrial employment and state-owned apartments and could not have a stake in the restitution of property confiscated by Soviet authorities back in the 1940s.

Moscow let the Balts go, disregarding the cries of Russian chauvinists. Neither Poland nor Germany raised irredentist claims to their territories. The Western governments and European institutions welcomed the arrival of three new mini-states, helped and encouraged their market reforms, and only once in a while lightly chastised the Baltic republics for their less than democratic treatment of their Russians. And while the Russian settlers grumbled, soon their children began to learn the national languages in order to pass the state examinations for citizenship. Doesn't it all look puzzling?

In contrast, ethnic violence broke out in Armenia and Azerbaijan, which is still more puzzling. Armenians had been arguably the most loyal Russian subjects since the days of the tsarist empire. The reason for this seems clear: Russian rule offered the Armenians some hope of survival. For centuries, they had suffered invasions, massacres, and deportations because their lands (historically much larger than the modern Republic of Armenia) happened to be situated on the ancient geopolitical fault-line between Anatolia, Mesopotamia, and the Iranian plateau. In the eyes of both the Armenians and many Russians the protective alliance was sanctified by their shared forms of Eastern Christianity (though the Armenians were not Orthodox they came very close). Quite a few Armenians rose to the heights of the Russian imperial service in the nineteenth century, and many more achieved impor-tant positions in the Soviet period – foremost among them were the long-serving premier Anastas Mikoyan and his brother, the builder of the Soviet MiG fighter planes (Mi stands for Mikoyan and G for Gurevich, the Jewish co-inventor). Under Soviet rule, the Republic of Armenia rose from dust and ruins to become one of the most prosperous territories with one of the best-educated citizenry. More than a hundred Armenians became generals and marshals in the Soviet army, and many more were found throughout the Soviet intellectual, artistic, managerial, and medical elites. During perestroika, two of Gorbachev's top advisors were Armenians: the economist Abel Agąnbeghyan and the political scientist Georgi Shahnazarov. (The latter happened to be a distant scion of a feudal family from Karabagh and there-fore many Karabaghtsi automatically presumed Shahnazarov to be their lobbyist.) In short, Armenians were very well integrated into the Soviet state structures, knew how to work them, and appreciated this beneficial situation.[12]

In Azerbaijan, the early industrialization based on the oilfields of Baku provided the platform for a large and robust urban elite with a distinctly cosmopolitan outlook. In the late 1950s and 1960s, for instance, Baku became a Mecca for alter-native jazz music in the USSR. Azerbaijan's rural areas remained substantially poorer and thus more "backward" and Oriental in character. But Baku overshadowed the hinterland. This marvelous town boasted an East–West flavor, prosperity, elegance, and not least of all an ethnically complex urban society. Nearly a quarter of a million ethnic Armenians had lived comfortably in Baku before 1989, alongside a million or so Azeris and many other ethnic groups, including half a million Russians and other Slavs, tens of thousands of Jews, Daghestanis, and quite a lot of ethnic Germans, Georgians, and Poles. As in Sarajevo before its catastrophe, the people in cosmopolitan Baku used to believe that their inter-ethnic tolerance and high-modern culture rendered the prospect of ethnic violence just about impossible.

True, there were many skeletons hidden away from sight. The collective psyche of the Armenians, for instance, was terribly traumatized by the horrors that their ancestors had suffered at the hands of Turkic overlords and Muslim neighbors. In 1905 and again in 1918 Baku was the site of horrific pogroms in which many thousands of Armenians and Azeris died. The Soviet period had not been entirely peaceful either. Occasionally, there were nasty fights, ethnic slurs could be heard, and competition for bureaucratic appointments or lucrative opportunities in the shadow economy sometimes assumed an ethnic tinge.

In retrospect, many commentators tend to take it for granted that Gorbachev's slackening of state controls released the demons of mutual suspicion and ancient hatred that led to inter-ethnic violence. I have already indicated that in some places where unrest would have seemed very probable it failed to materialize. Instead, ethnic violence erupted where it was much less expected. Therefore our exercise in deconstruction should not be limited to nationalist discourse and the re-invention of identities. First of all, other possibilities existed at the time of perestroika. They must be excavated in order to clarify how the nationalist mobilizations eventually prevailed. We should focus our microscope on the mundane details of administrative relations, social networks, class and group attributes, and various conflicting efforts to reshape the networks and reframe the goals that taken together produced the vector of nationalist mobilizing and violence between neighboring populations. Moreover the state must be a major factor in our analysis, not only because nationalism is a state-seeking program, but mainly because nationalism in the history of the Soviet disintegration became a possibility mainly because the state was itself in the process of collapsing.

We include in our analysis Armenia, Azerbaijan, and Georgia because these are the places where nationalism first emerged as a potent movement and rapidly acquired a violent character. We will keep in mind the Baltic and Uzbek counter-examples, but they will remain in the background since we are concerned here mainly with the Caucasus. We shall keep an eye on Moscow and its changing politics of reform, its democratization, and its eventual political stalemate. In this historical context we situate Kabardino-Balkaria and our hero, who was still called Yuri Shanibov at the time of the events recounted at the beginning of this chapter but, as he followed the general trend towards nationalization, had become Musa Shanib by the time of the events related at our chapter's end. Once again, small examples can be very useful in illuminating the dynamics of large historical processes.

PROVINCIAL POLITICS

During the long years of Brezhnevism, Shanibov, though politically driven into internal exile, did not remain in isolation. For many of his colleagues and former students Shanibov remained the man who had suffered at the hands of hypocritical conservative bureaucrats, essentially for trying to be a public intellectual, something they dreamt of, but did not dare to strive for themselves. Former student activists fondly remembered Shanibov as a symbol of rebellious youth and optimism. These sentiments and common experiences helped to maintain Shanibov at the center of a network that gradually acquired considerable social capital as the former student activists became journalists, industrial managers, lawyers, and junior academics.

The careers of these younger cadres, however, kept running into barriers put up by the locally dominant bureaucratic network, which since de-Stalinization had imposed and zealously maintained a near monopoly on all promotions. The Brezhnev-era practice of lifelong bureaucratic tenure considerably reduced vertical mobility in late Soviet society. The resultant structural tension translated into the differential of the activist versus the bureaucratic-rentier habitus that we find in provincial backwaters like Nalchik, no less than in Moscow. In fact, in small republics like Kabardino-Balkaria, the conflict was perhaps more acute because the blockages looked corrupt and highly personal. The importance of personal animosities was regularly emphasized in my interviews. The official network and that of the nascent opposition had to share a living in a small provincial world. Furthermore, as we have seen, the Soviet mechanisms of ethnoterritorial affirmative action bound ethnic cadres to their native republics because moving elsewhere would normally put them at a career disadvantage.

In 1986, a year after Gorbachev came to power, the individual frustrations of mid-career specialists developed a common focus and their first quasi-political expression when the position of First Secretary in Kabardino-Balkaria was taken by a complete outsider who had been transferred from Siberia. Three years later the local power elite would master the new political game and expunge the outsider in "democratic" elections. But at the time the appointment felt like a political earthquake. It was part of Gorbachev's sweeping purge that between 1985 and 1989 removed virtually all regional party secretaries.[13] Soon Gorbachev enacted his second political strategy, the promotion of debates called *glasnost*, which were intended to supplement the top-down reshuffling with public pressure from below. The exuberance of the glasnost period was manifested in the energetic display of both technocratic and intellectual activism. The homology between the two sets of aspirations and social actors created a link between Gorbachev's faction of reform *nomenklatura* and the educated upper factions of proletarians. These groups were now politically united against the conservative *nomenklatura* in the middle.

The particular expressions of glasnost-era activism depended on the opportunities that were being generated in Moscow, the central locus of the fields of power and culture. The innovations of the capital city were broadcast across the entire Soviet Union via Moscow's mass media, whose popularity in those years achieved stratospheric heights. For the duration of perestroika Moscow remained the center from which public issues were generated. There Gorbachev's top reformers opened an evasive dialogue with the recognized holders of the largest amount of symbolic capital, such as high-status academics and celebrity artists. The centralized dissemination of political debates that, once underway, the authorities could not easily control, accounts for the synchronized emergence of social movements and the symmetry of demands across the entire USSR, from the Baltic republics to Central Asia.

This synchronization created a sequence of demands that briefly resulted in a nearly universal polarization between "us," construed as anti-bureaucratic civil society, and "them," the entrenched *nomenklatura*. In the capital cities of the Soviet republics and provinces Gorbachev's campaign of politicization met with the same types of Soviet-made isomorphous institutions, social groups, and cleavages between activist reformers, conservative bureaucratic rentiers and patrons, and the usual undecided "swamp" in the middle. They were all avidly watching the developments in Moscow, albeit with each sector drawing its own conclusions and trying to respond to the rapidly changing situation.

The removal of Brezhnevite provincial prefects raised many different hopes. A few ambitious men from the junior *nomenklatura*, especially technocratic managers in their late thirties and forties, saw the removal of entrenched superiors and the official endorsement of open debate as a good opportunity for self-promotion and the advancement of their careers in ways that had previously been unthinkable.

This was a general trend across the USSR.[14] Such opportunistic behavior, however, was severely condemned by the majority of the *nomenklatura*. The perpetrators usually soon vanished from sight, though many later reappeared far away from their original positions, for example, as businessmen somewhere in Siberia or politicians in Moscow. Some daring political careerists became leaders of the revolutionary movements.

Boris Yeltsin presents arguably the biggest and luckiest example of such a defector; another example being his nemesis, General Djohar Dudayev, who in 1991 became the president of separatist Chechnya. Like Shanibov, Yeltsin and Dudayev had been born into the hard life of peasants after the war, and like their generation these men advanced in Soviet industrial society through the combination of newly opened opportunity, formal education and extraordinary determination. Unlike Shanibov, however, Yeltsin and Dudayev remained in the Soviet elite and rapidly rose to the top ranks: respectively, as the Candidate to the Politburo and as Flight General. Their careers advanced mainly on their reputation for being demanding and invasive managers whose brash style made them indispensable in difficult organizational situations. But when the climate of perestroika slackened the norms of *nomenklatura* behavior, such ambitious personalities often went beyond what their stolid comrades could swallow. The usual question as to whether they defected or were expelled need not concern us here. The real question is where these mavericks were able to go once they had been rejected by officialdom.

The rapid disintegration of the Soviet hierarchy offered several new opportunities. One was the nascent business entrepreneurship where revolutionary adventurism coupled with managerial expertise and personal contacts were a big asset. But before the massive privatization of the early 1990s, the pathways of the defectors from the *nomenklatura* typically led them into the ascendant political opposition where their previous high status and public notoriety directly translated into leadership positions. Besides, professors and artists usually proved inadequate when the amorphous movements began to develop organizational apparatuses or seized the state offices in elections and popular rebellions. The defectors treated political platforms opportunistically, which also made them more effective politicians than the ideologists from the intelligentsia. Virtually all of them, including Yeltsin and Dudayev, began during perestroika as reform communists, became generic democrats in 1989, and then, according to the changing times, morphed into anti-communists and market reformers. The successful *nomenklatura* mavericks who had returned to power in the post-Soviet successor states subsequently adopted a variety of nationalist rhetorics in connection with their new positions. But many were less

lucky. A disproportionate number fell victim to the political and business assassinations during the bloody nineties which must be related to the stormy personal
trajectories and risk-taking dispositions of the elite outcasts.

Overall, the *nomenklatura* continued through perestroika as a single body bounded
by its formal administrative competence, internal subordination, informal networks
of patronage, and shared norms and class habitus. Gorbachev's velvet purge of
1985–1989 unilaterally violated the key bureaucratic conventions set up during the
previous decades of Brezhnevism, such as job security, the toleration of inefficiencies, and the suppression of unwanted information. The campaign of forced
retirement and surprise replacements severely destabilized the local *nomenklatura*
networks and caused widespread feelings of apprehension and disorientation. This
came out clearly in my interviews with *nomenklatura* members. These people felt
needlessly victimized for bureaucratic practices that were regarded as the norm
during the Brezhnev period. They felt utterly humiliated by Moscow's approval of
journalistic investigations, which they regarded (not without some reason) as mere
opportunities for revenge. As one of the older executives put it: *We knew that a newspaper can be used to smash a fly, and now we saw that a newspaper can also smash a man.*

Up to this point, the provincial *nomenklatura* had felt powerless to resist and was
constrained by its own bureaucratic habitus and formal subordination. Therefore
they glumly endured. But Gorbachev's unilateral violation of *nomenklatura* taboos
was bound to elicit a response from desperate mid-level executives. Eventually the
example of the emergent national movements would offer them a promising
strategy by which to restrain the apparently arbitrary whims of Moscow. The key
elements of provincial bureaucratic defense would become the rejection of mavericks and defectors, the selective incorporation of nationalist ideologists from the
intelligentsia, the erection of political barriers around the ethnically distinct
republics, and the recasting of regional patronage networks into what were essentially the old-time devices that Americans call political machines.[15] In the end, the
nomenklatura's best strategy for survival proved to be loyalty to one's class and
patronage network, though no longer to the centralized state.

THE ALL-UNION SEQUENCE OF MOBILIZATIONS

Common opinion blames the disintegration of the USSR, as well as that of
Yugoslavia, on the hasty democratization that released the demons of nationalism.
This view is based on an important omission. In the USSR it took almost four years
of intense political activity – followed by the failure of reform rhetoric to maintain

its optimism in the face of sudden economic insecurity and the consequent break-down of central governance – before nationalism could move from the dissident fringes on to the center stage.

Let me sketch the sequence of public mobilizations during perestroika that occurred across the whole USSR. Here we do not need cautious qualifiers like "almost" or "roughly" when claiming that the process applied everywhere across the Soviet Union. The sequence may contain omissions in certain cases, and it could be compressed and truncated because some republics entered it belatedly or left early. Nonetheless it was exactly the same centrally created and synchronized succession of causes and movements.

In 1985 the first public mobilizations cautiously addressed a combination of offi-cially sanctioned topics and genuine public concerns with such social issues as alcoholism, the preservation of historic monuments, "informal" youth groups (hippies, punks, football fans), and the proposed reinvigoration of official public organizations like the Komsomol. In 1986, and especially after the Chernobyl nuclear disaster in May of that year, came a brief but tremendous efflorescence of the ecology movement. It had a strong case: in the wake of Chernobyl environ-mental concerns reached levels bordering on mass hysteria. Yet it did not directly challenge Soviet power, which made participation in the ecology movement not only honorable but also safe.[16]

At the same time neo-Marxist clubs sprang up that, emboldened by the rhetoric of Gorbachev, debated mostly the perennial issue of whether Stalin was necessary for Soviet development or whether Nikolai Bukharin offered a more humane alter-native in the late 1920s. This was essentially a resumption of the debates of 1968. The amnesty granted to imprisoned dissidents in November 1986 signaled a further extension of the debates to include non-Marxist themes of liberal democracy, human rights, and also nationalism.

Nevertheless for two more years, 1987 and 1988, dissidents of both the liberal and the nationalist persuasion would remain on the fringes because the rapidly expanding framework of official Soviet ideology took up most of the public's attention. Even in Armenia and Georgia, which would be engulfed by the strongest possible nationalist passions a couple of years later, while the release of nationalist dissidents was generally welcomed, the dissidents themselves were shunned by the mainstream national intelligentsia as unthinking radicals. A Georgian professor recalls that sometime in 1987 he saw a small parade of fifty or sixty high school students carrying the national flags of the independent Georgia of 1918 and singing patriotic songs. This paltry procession was led by two men in their fifties, Merab

Kostava and Zviad Gamsakhurdia, both celebrity dissidents.[17] The onlookers waved and smiled but nobody wished to join the marginal parade.

The focus of public attention in January 1987 was the officially sanctioned screening in all Soviet cinemas of *Repentance*, the complex and grotesquely tragi-comic film made in Georgia earlier that decade under the auspices of Eduard Shevardnadze, who was then Georgia's First Secretary. After a special screening before members of the Central Committee, the film was officially released and seen by millions of people across the Soviet Union. The event heralded the collective remembrance of the Stalinist terror – as Gorbachev and Shevardnadze had hoped it would. In effect, this coup on the part of official ideology marginalized the dissidents by incorporating in the Soviet discourse one of their strongest demands. Compared to the hypocritical and repressive atmosphere of the Brezhnev period, this seemed a major validation of the reformers' agenda.

Kabardino-Balkaria skipped some of the issues of mobilization typical of this early period and generally lagged behind in the later phases. In a place like Nalchik, one could find hardly any punks or hippies, and Yuri Shanibov was virtually the sole approximation of a Brezhnev-era dissident. Nonetheless the participation of Shanibov and his colleagues and former students was registered in the earliest debates on the reform of education and student life, the environment, and in the discussions of Stalinist crimes and the legacy of Bukharin. (For more on the issues and the participation of Shanibov's friends in public mobilizations, see Table 4, Second Period, page 328.) As in most parts of the USSR, both Chechnya and Kabardino-Balkaria had their own industrial plants that were polluting the environment and that, shortly after Chernobyl, the locals wanted closed. This was already a proto-nationalist cause: from the protection of beautiful nature against chemical pollution it was easy to move towards the protection of pristine national landscapes against soulless bureaucracies in Moscow.

Next would come the public committees of intellectuals set up to encourage the revival of ethnic cultures that at the time meant little more than folkloric festivals and the teaching of traditional etiquette in school. Later, such discussion clubs and intelligentsia committees began cautiously to suggest ways of dealing with the consequences of historical traumas. For the Balkars, one such trauma was the Stalinist deportation of 1944, which had not only killed nearly a third of the Balkar population but also left the survivors under the lingering stigma of having been Nazi collaborators during the war – which was, of course, a gross lie, for the Balkar village rebellions and desertions of 1942 had been mostly the reaction of peasants to the desperately chaotic demands of the Soviet authorities for recruits and food for the Red Army in the face of the rapidly advancing Germans.[18] For their part, the Kabardin intellectuals found their historical trauma in the Russian Caucasus war of the nineteenth century, which ended in 1864 with the tragic exodus of Circassian Muslim refugees (*muhajeer*) to the Middle East.[19] It was at this time in the late 1980s that the relaxation of the Soviet visa regime allowed descendants of the Kabardin and other North Caucasian muhajeers today living in Jordan, Syria and Turkey to visit the land of their ancestors. The majority of visitors observed a much stricter version of Islam than did the locals; they did not drink alcohol and they spoke in curiously antiquated dialects. But for these very reasons the diaspora Circassians seemed to the locals more authentic and untainted by the influence of Soviet modernity. Such visits often proved to be exceedingly emotional occasions, and supported the wild idea that one day the members of the diaspora could resettle back in the North Caucasus, as many of the visitors promised, thereby creating a much larger and ethnically purer Circassian nation.

In 1988 the first competitive elections – which at this time were held only within the Communist Party – brought the first taste of real politics. Officials were forced to campaign in earnest within party ranks for election to the Nineteenth Party Conference. Of course, they detested Gorbachev's initiatives, and quite a few officials at the time liked to draw ominous parallels between Gorbachev's rambunctiousness and the events that in 1964 led to the ousting of Khrushchev. Such predictions seemed to acquire validation in March 1988. The Moscow daily, *Soviet Russia*, which began to emerge as the leading mouthpiece of the conservative wing (and later, in the nineties, became the mouthpiece of Russian imperial nationalism), carried an impassioned op-ed letter ostensibly sent by one Nina Andreyeva, a humble schoolteacher from Leningrad. Its moralistic title, *I Cannot Renege on Principles*, said it all. Its publication was regarded as a signal for a change in political direction. On their own initiative, the local party authorities in many provinces began to sponsor public discussions of this conservative manifesto. The rector of Kabardino-Balkarian State University determined that the letter should be distributed to all faculty members and students and discussed in classrooms. But two weeks later came an authoritative rebuke in a terse editorial published in *Pravda*, the main newspaper of the Central Committee. The confrontation between the two texts signaled the beginning of an overt factional struggle inside the party. Soon afterward, Gorbachev, faced with the manifest intransigence of the party's silent majority, began tacitly to encourage the formation of "popular fronts for the support of perestroika" outside party ranks in order to foster a pro-reform majority.

The second half of 1988 (and in such epochs months matter) marked a break-through in popular political organizing, which now flowed from the intelligentsia's discussion clubs into the town squares. The first independent rallies were held under loyal slogans of support for Gorbachev and the reforms, but clearly displeased local bureaucracies almost everywhere. In Nalchik, the first rally attracted enormous attention despite the fact that only a few hundred people dared to show up. They were mostly students and intellectuals who had got to know each other at university. This was enough, however, to fill to overcapacity the small hall designated for the event by the authorities. Many people were left standing in the street. (The KGB officers, the petty party functionaries sent to watch the rally, and uniformed police were probably as numerous as the actual participants.)

In this situation, Shanibov emerged as a leader almost by default, after his fellow intellectuals pushed and nudged him, nervously joking about his reputation as a veteran oppositionist. He accepted the honor and, proving his abilities, approached the police directly to negotiate a change of location. Led by Shanibov and escorted by the confused police, the small crowd marched to the open-air summer theater located in a nearby park, where the first rally finally took place. In the recollections of those who took part, the speeches were a derivative mixture of Gorbachev's fuzzy reformist rhetoric and figures of speech borrowed from the progressive news-papers of Moscow. (Incidentally, as in many territories and republics of the generally conservative North Caucasus, the local authorities tried secretly to prevent the distri-bution of progressive newspapers from Moscow, which had to be smuggled into the region.) The very fact that a rally was being held that was not scripted by offi-cials had an electrifying effect. Shanibov, long a master of lecturing on the problems and prospects of socialist progress, was particularly impressive. Even his opponents acknowledge his oratorical skills. He soon became one of the most acclaimed speakers in town, learned but not didactic, witty and quite daring.

In spring 1989 the elections to the USSR's Congress of Deputies offered the local "civil society leaders" the chance of an incredible leap in status – to become parliamentarians. The conservative party apparatus, however, still enjoyed the power to include on the ballot only the usual collection of officials and a few token repre-sentatives of peasants, workers, and women. In this respect Kabardino-Balkaria did not prove politically backward because of its Muslim population, as some commen-tators speculated. The electorate of democratic reformers in Russia consisted of intellectuals, the non-*nomenklatura* managerial cadres, specialists, and skilled workers found in leading enterprises that enjoyed relative independence from local author-ities. But there existed few such enterprises in Kabardino-Balkaria. Furthermore in the union republics like Lithuania, Moldova, or Georgia the votes went primarily to the celebrities among the national intellectuals who possessed enough status to be able to look down on their compatriot bureaucrats. The cultural field of Kabardino-Balkaria was simply too small for such personalities to exist – the local university and a few research centers provided the only concentration of status intellectuals – and it remained for too long controlled by the same bureaucratic patronage network of the conservative *nomenklatura*. Within the university mavericks like Shanibov were relatively rare and thus easily isolated.

During the spring of 1989 Shanibov and his friends began to recognize the need to build a large political platform outside academia and perhaps along the lines seen in Armenia, Georgia, or in the Baltic republics. Two forthcoming symbolic dates suggested such an opportunity. First, the Balkar activists proposed to commemorate the forty-fifth anniversary of the deportation of their people in March 1944. Later in May the Kabardin activists convened to mourn the exodus of defeated Circassians following the final Russian victory in May 1864, 125 years earlier. This event attracted the activists of fellow Circassian nationalities, all speaking closely related languages but living in different autonomies: Adyghea, Karachai-Cherkessia, and Abkhazia. They were joined by Chechen and Daghestani activists. This was the beginning of the pan-ethnic alliance that would evolve into the Mountain Confederation. But it was initially construed as simply a public lesson in history intended to teach respect for the heroism and suffering of the nation's ancestors.

The ceremony became unexpectedly dramatic with the arrival of the police in heavy riot gear and armored cars. A well-known Kabardin semiologist of traditional etiquette – whose father was a Hero of Socialist Labor and the locally prominent chairman of a collective farm – approached the unnerved officials with a sermon expressing an attitude typical of the times: *Look what you guys are doing! Is this your idea of democracy? This is essentially a funeral. Don't you have any respect for our ancestors? Didn't your father and mine fight together against the Nazis? Dismiss your troops and join us, don't be fools, behave like Kabardins, like true Circassians!* The officials, however, were right to have suspicions, even if they were desperately unsure how to act on them. The commemoration of past victims focused the public's attention not only on the Russian tsars or Stalin but rather on all the injustices committed by the Empire against all the natives of the North Caucasus.

But let us not rush the account of Shanibov's conversion to nationalism. We need to avoid not only determinism but also its opposite, the assumption that political entrepreneurs are instrumental exercisers of free will and rationality. In retrospect it is tempting to see the nationalist shift during the fall of the USSR as either an explosion of primordial ethnic passions or, conversely, as the instrumentalist manipulation of political entrepreneurs. Both views have long intellectual lineages, dating back to such venerable figures as Herder (for primordialism), or Durkheim, Marx, and Engels. (It was the latter who invented the damning label "false consciousness" in frustration at the stubborn unwillingness of Polish workers to recognize that their exploiters were the capitalists rather than "those Germans.") Both views of nationalism can be illustrated with empirical data and certainly they command considerable support in the mainstream currents of social science. The instrumentalist view easily lends itself to rational choice formalization and, on the other hand, to humanistic ruminations about the construction of identity. The primordialist view is today more popular among journalists and politicians than scholars. Nevertheless in social science we find no less an example than Huntington's *Clash of Civilizations*.

The pitfall common to both primordialist and instrumentalist views is their streamlining of history. Because we – and the participants whom we interview – know the historical outcome, in hindsight the early manifestations of ethnic politicization seem more logical and loom larger than they ought to in the wider stream of perestroika-era movements. In this perspective all that matters about Shanibov is his exotic *papaha* hat, regardless of whether we decide to attribute it to the primordial Kabardin tradition or his rational decision to become a nationalist leader and warlord. Either interpretation means we need not care that Shanibov might have had a different life as a frustrated social reformer in which he got no promotions in twenty years and instead read banned books and listened to classical music or jazz.

The example of Shanibov's oppositional network seems typical of the lesser autonomous Soviet republics. The extensive event-analysis that Mark Beissinger compiled for the entire USSR offers substantive proof of this contention.[20] Beissinger found that the autonomous republics followed as a bloc and with a time lag the sequence of events in the full-fledged union republics of the USSR. The reason they were slower to change was the relative scarcity of organizational resources that could be deployed for political mobilization. In both the union and the autonomous republics nationalism took time to develop, and radicalized only after a series of public confrontations and violent incidents in which Moscow showed a glaring inability to restrain effectively spreading unrest. Our microscopic observations regarding this period are summarized in Table 4, Second Period (page 328). It shows something commonly known to contemporary activists yet too often neglected by analysts who focus on ethnic conflicts alone. Shanibov's oppositional network, which in this period began to expand beyond his original circle of friends, participated in virtually all contemporary movements in one way or another and the causes were very diverse. Nationalism prevails towards the end of the sequence, and only *after* Moscow lost control over central economic redistribution and local politics in the fall of 1989.

THE KARABAGH CONFLICT: OVER THE THRESHOLD OF ETHNIC VIOLENCE

We now need to look on the other side of the Caucasus mountains. In the three republics of Transcaucasia the nationalist breakthrough occurred significantly earlier, was much stronger, and more violent. First there was Armenia and Azerbaijan, as early as February 1988. Georgia followed suit in April 1989. The autonomous republics of the North Caucasus arrived at the threshold of nationalist mobilization and street violence only in 1991.

At the nodal point of 1988 divergent patterns of contention opened roads leading in two directions. One was civic mobilization for democratic socialism that, like in Poland, could lead to the liberal reconstitution of polities and the transition to capitalism. In this pattern, the high-status intellectuals remained in control of oppositional mobilization and the post-communist transitions were negotiated and predominantly peaceful. The alternative pattern was a nationalist mobilization directed primarily against neighboring ethnic groups, where a significant role was played by activists of marginal social status. This paved the way for the ethnic wars that plagued the Caucasus.

The first such war was the Armenian–Azeri conflict over the border region of Nagorny (or Mountainous) Karabagh. In the late 1980s, during the final years of the USSR, the general opinion was that back in the early 1920s the Bolshevik apportionment of national autonomies had been a devious plan intended to divide and rule, or to set ethnic "time-bombs" which would be set off by some future attempt at democratization. This appeared to be a strong argument because during perestroika, in the emotionally charged atmosphere of the public revelations regarding the totalitarian past, no decision attributed to Stalin could be justified. But perhaps Lenin or Stalin were not as far-sighted or, rather, their vision of the future differed very substantially from what was imagined by perestroika-era critics.

During the civil war of 1918–1920 Karabagh became a contested borderland between independent Armenia and Azerbaijan. Horrendous ethnic massacres had been waged during this period by the Azeri and Armenian nationalist armies with the involvement of their respective peasantries. The first reaction of the Bolsheviks after their victory in Transcaucasia was to attach the Armenian-populated parts of

Karabagh to neighboring Armenia, fully in accordance with the principle of national congruence. For the purposes of propaganda, this could be presented as another triumph of proletarian internationalism, which in no time at all could resolve the nasty problems created by "bourgeois" nationalists. In fact, this is how the Azeri Bolshevik leader Nariman Narimanov explained events to fellow Armenian toilers in November 1920.[21] This political line was still maintained at the opening session of the Bolshevik Caucasus Bureau (*Kavburo*) in July 1921; and then it was reversed overnight, between the first and the second sessions. For reasons that long remained mysterious, Karabagh ended up becoming an autonomous province within Soviet Azerbaijan.

Seven decades later, in 1988, the rebellion of Karabagh Armenians who wanted to join the mainland Armenian nation ignited the process that led to the disintegration of the Soviet Union. The conflict escalated after 1991 into a full-blown war between the once again independent Armenia and Azerbaijan. The unrecognized Armenian state in Karabagh is one of several currently "frozen" ethnic wars in the former USSR. Indeed it can look as if history is repeating itself and Stalin is grinning at us from beyond the grave.

The archival findings of Grigory Lezhava reveal a different picture of the events of 1921. Lezhava's account looks more complicated, contingent, and credible regarding what we know about the Bolshevik style of reasoning.[22] Dr. Lezhava discovered in the Moscow archives previously classified transcripts of telephone conversations conducted on a fateful night in July 1921 between various Bolshevik leaders in the Caucasus and in Moscow. As it turns out, the initial idea of transferring the Armenian enclave of Karabagh to Armenia was opposed from a totally unexpected corner – by the Georgian Bolsheviks. They argued that this plan would create a dangerous precedent for approving the secession of rebellious ethnic borderlands everywhere in the Caucasus. In particular, this would spell the end to Georgia's claims over Abkhazia, southern Ossetia, and the Armenian-populated district of Lori. This would be perceived by the majority of Georgians as the dismemberment of their nation, which the recently installed Bolshevik government of Georgia might not survive. The ultimate argument, it seems, was that the province of Adjaria would almost certainly end up under Turkish jurisdiction. Adjaria was home to the Georgian Muslim minority who at the time identified with Muslim Turks rather than the linguistically close, but Christian, Georgians. (The Adjarian identity today is Georgian as a result of Soviet secularization.) Batumi, the capital of Adjaria, was an important seaport and oil export terminal.[23] Its loss threatened the economic development of the whole of Transcaucasia.

Back in 1921, then, in view of extraneous considerations, the predominantly Armenian Karabagh was made the autonomous province of Azerbaijan because the Bolshevik leaders, once in power, decided to discourage ethnic secessions across the Caucasus. They believed that the solution to ethnic hostility lay in progress delivered by industrial development. Baku, the famously cosmopolitan capital of Azerbaijan, was the hub of Transcaucasia's early industrialism. In Soviet theory, it should have served as the engine of progress for backward regions like Karabagh and thus remove the causes of ethnic strife. In 1988 Moscow would arrive at the same conclusion once again. Gorbachev offered a huge increase in social and economic investment to address the problems of Karabagh, but ruled out the revision of internal borders.

The Armenians, however, would not accept the economic rationalism of this policy. To understand why, we need to look at how the modern Armenian nation came to be a cultural and political community. The Armenians possessed a strong sense of ethnic identity long before the appearance of modern nationalism, because they were a Christian minority united by their church in predominantly Muslim Ottoman and Persian realms. In the modern period the traditional esteem reserved among the peasants, artisans, and merchants for the Armenian clergy was reclaimed by the secular intelligentsia. Between the 1840s and 1914 the secular Armenian intelligentsia successfully recast a religious ethnic identity into a formidable national ideology. During the final agonies of the Ottoman empire Armenians suffered terrible losses in massacres sponsored by Turkish rulers who reacted with paranoid brutality to the growth of Armenian national assertiveness.[24] Memories of the 1915 genocide (which Turkey has been denying ever since) became the focal point of Armenian national consciousness. By contrast, the eastern Armenians had long been under Russian rule and therefore escaped an officially sponsored persecution of the kind experienced by their brethren in the Ottoman empire. Yet the Russian Armenians suffered their own heavy losses during the revolutions of 1905 and 1917–1920 in a series of murderous clashes with their Muslim neighbors who were later known as Azeris. The Azeris probably suffered just as much from the Armenian forces, who often proved better organized.

Such memories certainly help to explain Armenian behavior in the most recent wave of ethnic conflicts. The trauma of genocide produced among the victims' families and among their descendants an exceedingly strong yearning for moral catharsis. Some of the most powerful ethnic mobilizations in the Caucasus occurred precisely in such groups: not only the Armenians but also, to a lesser extent, the Azeris, and then the Chechens, Karachais, and Balkars who had been deported by Stalin, as well as the Abkhazes who felt perennially embattled in the face of the much bigger Georgian nation.

But ethnic memories do not determine absolutely the future of a people. We must note two important factors that can produce a significant variation in national discourses and politics. First, retribution is not the only possible form of catharsis. Nearly a third of Belorussians were killed during the German occupation in 1941–1944, but a salve was found for this tragedy in the Soviet glorification of Belorussian partisans, which allowed for a steady stream of public rituals, various forms of compensation, and, not least, a sustained cultural production focused on the heroism of the wartime generation. In Chechnya shortly after the revolution of 1991, as I mentioned in chapter one, the nationalists themselves renamed a square in Grozny after Nikita Khrushchev, thus stressing the existence of a virtuous Soviet leader alongside Stalin's nation-killers. For the Crimean Tatars catharsis was at last found in their belated return to the ancestral land from which they were banished under Stalin.

Second, historical memory is a form of discourse that can have no material consequence unless it is linked to a chain of organizational resources and social mechanisms. The Caucasian Greeks, many of whom were also deported under Stalin, possessed neither an autonomous state nor a national church in the USSR (because they were placed under the Russian Orthodox hierarchy) or any other organization that could focus and channel individual traumas into some political goal, and hence no Greek mobilization has ever taken place. Instead, many Caucasian Greeks accepted the invitation of the government of Greece to emigrate to a country that was effectively foreign to them. Therefore we need not get fixated on national traumas, even though we must recognize the extraordinary emotional power of such memories. We are going to concentrate rather on the political processes and resources that determined national memory in Soviet Armenia and Karabagh.

Armenian national solidarity in the USSR had been building up in successive cycles since the late 1950s. The cycles were produced by the emergence of a new educated urban generation, whose creative members competed in the cultural fields of Soviet Armenia. (The mechanism of symbolic competition in the Khrushchev-era field of national culture was outlined in chapter three.) The popular resonance found by the works and thought of Armenian intellectuals, most of whom were then quite young, proved very strong, and indeed irrepressible, for several mutually reinforcing reasons. First, as early as the late nineteenth century the traditional Armenian veneration of learned priestly careers had been translated into an extraordinary respect for higher education, which caused a massive influx of people into the ranks of the intelligentsia. This small republic boasted a rich intellectual environment, including many world-class celebrities, like the chess champion Tigran Petrosian, the astrophysicist Victor Hambartsumian, or the composer Aram Khachaturian. In addition, Armenia's cultural resources and nearly a third of the republic's population were heavily concentrated in one big town, Yerevan.

In the 1960s and 1970s, pre-nationalist mobilizations appeared in nascent form on the streets of Yerevan during the funerals of national celebrities such as Khachaturian or the soccer triumphs of the local team, pointedly called Ararat – after the mountain which towered over Yerevan and yet stood just across the border in Turkish territory.[25] Thus Armenian mobilization on the street in early 1988 appeared spontaneous and natural – the rituals and rhetoric would have been familiar to all the inhabitants of Yerevan, which put them in sharp contrast to, say, the atomized Muscovites.[26] Furthermore, the long history of the Armenian people and the trauma of the historically recent genocide produced an exceptionally strong feeling of ethnic cultural cohesiveness that provided Armenian intellectuals with reference points, causes, and an avid audience. Lastly, the Armenian national ideology did not explicitly contradict the official Soviet ideology, because the Young Turk genocide of 1915 was certainly not a Soviet crime, and the Armenian diaspora outside the USSR was traditionally pro-Russian and (much unlike other émigré communities) generally supportive of Moscow's rule.

The Karabagh issue emerged in November 1987, when the series of emotionally intense revelations about the crimes of Stalin was reaching its peak.[27] In this context, a group of top-ranking Armenian intellectuals wrote an open letter to Gorbachev in which they blamed Stalin for placing Karabagh under the jurisdiction of Azerbaijan. Therefore, they argued, in the spirit of democratization and socialist internationalism, Karabagh should be reunited with Armenia. The effect of the letter was profound. For the Armenians, the question of Karabagh encapsulated all their historical sorrows and became the symbolic substitute for the much larger trauma of the 1915 genocide and the loss of historically Armenian lands that remained under Turkey's control. Such a transposition seemed natural insofar as the Azeris shared with the Turks a closely related language and were Muslims (though they were Shiite, whereas the Turks were Sunni, such subtleties didn't much matter).

In Azerbaijan a rapid counter-mobilization mirrored Armenia's challenge. From their side, authoritative Azeri academics and authors wrote a letter in response to that from the Armenian intellectuals, appealing to the friendship among the peoples and against "certain irresponsible provocateurs unworthy of being called intellectuals." The two letters, copies of which were widely circulated and soon published by eager journalists in the official newspapers of Yerevan and Baku, placed the respective officialdoms in a very awkward position. Both in Armenia and Azerbaijan the First Secretaries at the time were hangers-on from Brezhnev's epoch who, fearing their imminent removal, preferred to avoid attracting Gorbachev's attention and therefore opted for inaction.

In the meantime, the top Armenian and Azeri intellectuals, by writing letters on behalf of their national republics, effectively put themselves forward as their countries' leaders, at the expense of the embattled First Secretaries. This inspired a great number of lesser intellectuals, such as ordinary journalists, scholars, and self-styled publicists, to try to follow suit. They rapidly discovered that Soviet censorship was inactive and started to compete to come up with ever more radical arguments and rhetoric. This opened an escalating war of public pronouncements and newspaper publications between Armenia and Azerbaijan. This seems a crucial factor – the Soviet state first lost control in the symbolic arena in the republics of Armenia and Azerbaijan. Moscow would eventually try to shore up the collapsing structures of authority in Transcaucasia, but this was done too clumsily, indecisively, and too late to control the rapidly developing popular mobilizations.

All other causes were abandoned immediately. The oppositional Karabagh Committee that emerged in Yerevan consisted almost entirely of young academic activists who just a few days earlier had been picketing an environmentally hazardous chemical plant or writing articles on educational reform. Now the activists looked more like a government in waiting, and, indeed, they would soon become the government.

In April 1990, when the Armenian mobilization was at its peak, I spent a day observing the anteroom of one of the leaders of the Armenian Pan-Ethnic Movement, with whom I happened to have friends in common from graduate school in Moscow. The long line of visitors to this former historian included a woman who complained about her husband's heavy drinking and two fat and sweating policemen who were looking for a stolen car, presumably commandeered for the "national struggle." All around Yerevan cars without license plates were being recklessly driven by young men sporting beards and Rambo-style vests and headbands. They belonged to an assortment of volunteer paramilitaries with names like the "Crusaders," the "Armenian National Army," or "King Tigran the Great Brigade." A rising politician, with a small party of his own and formerly an electrical engineer, admitted that his party's militia were boys from his native village.

The fact that four other members of this party's executive committee were also electrical engineers had a simple explanation – they had all studied together. Another factor that helps explain the way that parties were formed is the topography of Yerevan. One party was created by educated men of approximately the same age, all in their thirties, who lived along the same metro line and thus got to know each other traveling to and from the rallies downtown.

Things were different in Karabagh itself where native intellectuals were not sufficient in number and did not possess the stature to effectively claim the political leadership. It was the mid-ranking local officials in Karabagh who saw an opportunity to break loose from the oppressively corrupt patronage network of Azerbaijan. Also, the national cause immediately accorded them a heroic status among their fellow Armenians. In July 1994 I was in Karabagh and had an unusually candid conversation with Robert Kocharyan, who was then the Chairman of Karabagh's State Committee for Defense (which deliberately mimicked the title Stalin had adopted during the Great Patriotic War of 1941–1945).[28] Kocharyan's biography provides a good illustration of the dilemmas faced by the Armenian *nomenklatura* in Karabagh. After mandatory military service, he tried to get into the university in Baku, but lacking connections and the money to pay for tutoring he was failed twice in the entrance examinations. So instead Kocharyan took a correspondence course for a degree in engineering from the Yerevan Polytechnic, but once qualified could not get a job in Armenia because he lacked connections there as well. Besides, he knew Russian and the Karabagh dialect of Armenian but felt uneasy speaking, let alone writing, in the literary Armenian of Yerevan. A smart and energetic careerist, Kocharyan managed to advance in his native province to the rank of First Secretary of Karabagh's Komsomol (Young Communist League). When he turned thirty-six, it was time to leave the youth organization, but no openings were available for further promotion within the *nomenklatura*. Since 1974 Karabagh had been dominated by a tight circle of officials, who were ethnic Armenians but had all been appointed from Baku and owed allegiance to Azerbaijan. They did not even speak Armenian, because in multi-ethnic Baku everybody communicated in Russian. Moreover, they were personal clients of the mighty Heydar Aliyev.[29] In 1987 Gorbachev retired Aliyev from his Politburo position, and it was then that the native Karabagh *nomenklatura* decided to act.

Kocharyan admitted that it all started as a carefully planned, albeit provincially naïve, bureaucratic insurgency. In November–December 1987 the ethnic Armenian officials from Karabagh secretly traveled to Moscow seeking, through ethnic ties and bureaucratic acquaintances, to acquire patronage in Gorbachev's circle. Back in

Karabagh, the insurgent bureaucrats directed their administrative resources to sponsoring popular rallies. They hoped that, in the new spirit of democratization, these rallies would provide Gorbachev with evidence of popular support for the administrative transfer of the Autonomous Province of Nagorny Karabagh from the Soviet Socialist Republic of Azerbaijan to the Soviet Socialist Republic of Armenia – a simple decision, they thought, especially since Gorbachev's key political advisor, Georgi Shahnazarov, was also from Karabagh. An old nurse at whose home I stayed, and who seemed an improbable rebel, was genuinely surprised at my question about her decision to participate in the first protest rallies: *How could I not? Surely I am an Armenian. Our nation has suffered so much in the past, and besides it was our party secretary from the hospital who told us to go to the public meeting, just as usual.*

Robert Kocharyan, however, admitted with a chuckle that if the first rally had met with KGB repression, he would have run home, shut the doors and blinds, and hoped that they hadn't noticed him. Precisely because no serious repression followed in the wake of the first, or the second, or the tenth rally, or even after the Armenian and Azeri villagers began fighting each other with sticks and later with shotguns, Kocharyan began to realize that Moscow might cease to be relevant to their conflict. The older Karabagh *nomenklatura* could not admit such a possibility and stayed firm in the belief that their conflict with Baku would be mediated by the "Center" in Moscow. At this time Kocharyan began to make secret preparations for a real war, and this foresightedness, he claims, is what allowed him to become leader despite his relatively young age.

Given the themes of democratization and the denunciations of Stalinism, which dominated Soviet political discourse during 1987–1988, the overwhelming majority of Armenians considered their demand eminently justified and indisputably loyal to Moscow and Gorbachev's reforms. They could not comprehend how the omnipotent and sympathetic General Secretary could hesitate in granting them their wish. In Moscow, however, the Armenian demand presented a major dilemma. Granting it would risk provoking similar demands from all over the Soviet Union and could derail the key agenda of disarmament on the foreign front and economic reform at home. To deny the Armenians' wishes, however, threatened to enflame the protests, which is what eventually happened. Ordering a massive repression would have reactivated precisely those parts of the KGB and party apparatus that Gorbachev did not trust, remembering as he did the fate of Khrushchev.[30]

Counter-rallies were organized in Azerbaijan almost immediately. They too appealed to Gorbachev and to the new spirit of democratization, and also invoked the constitutional norms that, among other things, prohibited the changing of borders without the republic's consent. Soon rallies in the central squares of big towns became regular events in both republics, providing the urban populations with a locus for intense emotional expression and political socializing, to the extent that, according to my data, even the local Azeris during the first few weeks could not help but attend the Armenian rallies in Karabagh. Some Azeris even spoke publicly in support of Armenian demands as they extolled inter-ethnic friendship, democratization, and socialist internationalism.

Azeri speeches at Armenian rallies in Karabagh could be regarded as an attempt to build new mechanisms of inter-ethnic cooperation to complement those that already existed. Many such mechanisms exist in any sphere of life where different ethnic groups come into contact. In the past, sedentary Armenian peasants regularly engaged in ritualized exchanges of their agricultural produce for the cheese, yoghurts, and animal hides that were supplied by the Turkic and Kurdish pastoralists. According to local tradition, Christian neighbors were invited to hold little boys in their laps during the Islamic ritual of circumcision, which made such Christians *kirva*, statutory kin.[31] It is somewhat ironic that the Soviet bureaucratic institutions which were intended to develop the national republics largely prevented such interaction. In Yerevan many Armenians admitted to me that they had never spoken to an Azeri in their life. The opportunity to do so had simply never arisen because the Armenians living in Armenia attended Armenian schools and worked in the company of fellow Armenians. Although some Azeris were found in Armenia before the expulsions of 1988, they lived in villages. To obtain a higher education, these Azeris traveled to Azerbaijan and afterwards usually stayed there. The Azeri and Armenian *nomenklatura* and intellectuals mingled mostly in Moscow, at the party school and university. Such contacts created personal ties but proved very fragile in the face of national mobilizations. As a ranking Azeri official complained to me in 1989, *I tried calling my old classmates in Yerevan to ask them what the hell was going on, but they told me that one of them now carries a gun. Armenians have gone mad!* It took the upper-class Azeris a little longer to develop attitudes of radical rejection because they still lived alongside Baku Armenians. There exist many testimonials that during the Baku pogroms of 1990, Azeris, including nationalist intellectuals, helped to hide their Armenian friends and neighbors from the enraged crowds. Even during the Karabagh War of 1990–1994 we can find anecdotes that attest to an enduring sympathy between the two ethnic groups. For instance, an Armenian colonel after a battle could call his Azeri counterpart on the radio and, politely addressing him in Azeri, ask him to remove his snipers for the night. The Azeri colonel, greeting his enemy in Armenian, agreed that if they were now killing each other in battle, the least they could do was allow their soldiers to relieve themselves in the bushes without anyone getting killed with his pants down. These two officers had once attended the same military academy in Baku. In 1994 Robert Kocharyan told me that, of course, he knew of many such episodes at the front and regarded them as normal, even useful. If in the beginning of the conflict, said Kocharyan, his foresight was to prepare for war, in the end it would be necessary to prepare for peace. This, however, remains a distant prospect.

The emotional energy of the public rallies in 1988–1989 served to override the personal-level mechanisms of cooperation between the nationalities, just as they served to mightily reinforce the sentiments of national solidarity. The urge to participate and share in the ebullient emotions must have been irresistible.[32] Let me illustrate the point with two vignettes from this period that Levon Abrahamian, an anthropologist from Yerevan, recorded in his fascinating diary.[33] The first is in fact a traditional joke transformed to reflect the new political reality. A young man is asked by his parents why he is spending so much time away from home at the rallies and refusing to get married. The son replies: *I must marry an Armenian girl, right? But all Armenians are one family now, so how can I marry my sister?* The second story is an urban legend. In the huge rallies held at the Opera Square in Yerevan, an inconspicuous balding man in a good suit, evidently a godfatherly figure from the underworld, climbed on the platform and patiently waited for his turn at the microphone. When he finally got his chance, he said: *Esteemed Armenian People* [the new opening line that had replaced the Soviet "comrades"], *forgive me, for unlike the rest of the speakers here, I am not going to make a speech. I am not even going to introduce myself, because those who need to know me, they know me already, and the rest needn't. All I wanted to say is that if in this holy moment for our nation a single wallet disappears in this square or an apartment is burglarized in the town, those who commit this sacrilege should know that we have very long arms and will get them wherever they are.* The legend claims that in the following weeks the Armenian police dealt only with traffic accidents.

The latter story marks the symbolic entrance of sub-proletarians into the new mass politics. Certainly not all violence can be blamed on the sub-proletarian habitus. The disdain of intellectuals towards this awkward non-class tends to result in their criminality being exaggerated. Nonetheless it is indisputable that the sub-proletarians, especially the young males, were increasingly found in the forefront of street violence during the nationalist mobilizations in Armenia, and perhaps more so in Azerbaijan. Sometimes they deliberately subverted the orderly political campaigns favored by the urbanite intellectual leaders.

Volcanic mobilizations produced a momentous reversal of social statuses in both republics. In Azerbaijan a rowdy crowd heckled a top party official who tried to read his typewritten speech in Russian, the prestigious language of multi-ethnic Baku that dominated in the elite fields of administration and higher education. "Speak Azeri, bastard!" chanted the unshaven rustic-looking men, asserting the symbolic value of their vernacular.[34] In harmony with these acts of low-culture defiance was the appearance of Khomeini's portrait at rallies in Baku. Before the Russian annexation of Transcaucasia in the early 1800s, Azerbaijan had for many centuries been an Iranian province. The majority of Azeris are Shiite Muslims, as are the Iranians. The Russian-educated Azeri intellectuals had hoped that Shiite religious "obscurantism" had been left behind a century ago.[35] One such intellectual, a specialist in medieval Islamic art, interrogated a man carrying Khomeini's portrait about the basics of Islamic theology and Iranian politics and discovered a complete ignorance of these subjects. The purported Islamist could not even tell the difference between the Sunni and Shia creeds. That was, however, beside the point. The stern charismatic features of the ayatollah conveyed an emphatic message of undifferentiated native protest against everything that the Azeri man carrying the portrait was certainly not: a powerful bureaucrat, an Armenian professional, or an urban secular Azeri intellectual. (A picture of Osama bin Laden, widely displayed nowadays from Indonesia to Senegal, carries essentially the same message of violent rejection and retribution.)

Meantime in Armenia, sometime in early 1990, a video made for the nightly news captured a typical volunteer detachment preparing to leave for the hills of Karabagh.[36] The boys stood in formation in the schoolyard. Before taking the oath, they sang the battle songs of the nineteenth-century anti-Ottoman insurgents. Despite the fact that many wore their hair long and wore blue jeans rather than uniforms, they could march and hold their Kalashnikovs pretty much like real soldiers. Little wonder, for in the Soviet Union all boys and girls were taught basic military skills in special classes starting in the seventh grade. Most of these young fighters had until recently been among the less successful students from an unprestigious school situated somewhere on the dusty outskirts of Yerevan. The day before, many had been considered hoodlums and street trash. But now they stood symbolically next to the legendary heroes of the nation's tragic history: from the valiant knights of prince St. Vardan Mamikonian, who faced the Persian battle elephants on the field of Avarayr in AD 451; to the fedayeen guerrillas of Andranik-pasha, who had fought the Turkish soldiers and the marauding Kurdish tribesmen during the last years of the Ottoman empire and in 1914 had joined the

Russian army as the Armenian Volunteer Division. A priest led the young men in the Lord's Prayer and blessed the detachment, urging them to be worthy of Armenia's Christian martyrs. The school principal, tears in her voice, came out to bless the fighters and begged them to forgive her their bad grades. The detachment's commanders were two young intellectuals, a physicist and a historian, both exuding solemn romanticism. The physicist was the first to die, in leading an assault on Azeri positions. The historian would return morally shattered by the death of friends, by the atrocities he had witnessed, and by his failure to restrain his own fighters, pleading in vain that Armenians were a "civilized Christian nation." An Azeri prisoner was gang-raped, which had nothing to do with presumed Oriental barbarism, nor was it a random act of brutality. It was a socially degrading ritual taken directly from Soviet prison life, a key socialization mechanism for Brezhnev-era sub-proletarians.[37]

The previously maintained taboo on crowd violence was first overcome in a pogrom that happened in the Azerbaijani town of Sumgait in February 1988. This grim event was seen at the time as the consequence of a devious conspiracy, masterminded by the KGB intent on derailing democratization, or by mythical pan-Turkic and pan-Islamist secret cells, mafia, or some other nefarious organization.[38] Yet the evidence that I have seen and gathered conforms to the analysis of Edward Judge, who studied in detail the late nineteenth-century Jewish pogroms and concluded that a pogrom need not be organized.[39] The conditions that lead to such an event could be the ineffectiveness of a police force who are not trained to deal with massive rioting, the inflammatory pronouncements of popular figures – whether officials or journalists – and the kind of provocative circumstances that might arise during public mass rituals. The latter might be a Russian Orthodox procession at Easter that passes by a synagogue in Kishinev in 1903, or an Azeri political rally in 1988 in the sprawling, grimy, and socially undesirable suburb of Sumgait, at which somebody spread rumors of Armenians harassing and murdering Azeris.

Such a rumor, whether intentionally spread or not, sent enraged groups of young Azeri workers and sub-proletarians (judging by the court descriptions of the defendants) to seek out the apartments of local ethnic Armenian professionals – ostensibly to empty those apartments for Azeri refugees and the poor. Over twenty people were killed and hundreds were brutally beaten, including elderly women. Not all of the victims were Armenians. The Sumgait pogrom produced the first exodus of refugees who streamed into Armenia. In the opposite direction came ethnic Azeris who had been expelled from Armenia. (This aggrieved and dispossessed mass of refugees, mostly country folk, added an important element of instability to Azerbaijan's politics in the following years of revolutionary upheaval and war with Armenia.)

In 1994 I also interviewed in Karabagh the local senior statesman, Musheg Ogandjanyan, who from 1963 to 1974 had been the Chairman of Karabagh's Executive Committee (*oblispolkom*, or provincial government) and during the late 1980s was Azerbaijan's government minister and lived in Baku. In contrast to the overwhelming majority of Armenians, Musheg Ogandjanyan dismissed the idea of there having been official Azeri planning behind the Sumgait pogrom: *Public opinion has certainly been prepared by the violent talk in the newspapers. There could have been some sort of gang-like organizing among the street rabble, but at Azerbaijan's Central Committee? Nonsense! I was there. Bagirov* [then the First Secretary of Azerbaijan] *came to my office begging me, as an ethnic Armenian, to help him to apologize before the Armenian people and to restore inter-ethnic peace in the republic. His face was dirty-green from fear, and saliva was dripping from his mouth. In previous times, Moscow would not have forgiven even a much smaller failure in the area of nationality policies. Bagirov was hoping that they would just expel him from the Party, because he really feared that they would sentence him to death.*

This statement from a highly placed former official helps us to appreciate the amount of damage caused by Gorbachev's contradictory reactions in the aftermath of the first pogrom. Bagirov was eventually retired and a few of the chief perpetrators of the Sumgait pogrom were put on trial, but this slow process was soon overtaken by the tempo of events and further mobilizations. Evidently the General Secretary felt caught between the Armenians and the Azeris, both of whom were very loyally calling for Moscow's arbitration and both expecting a zero-sum solution in their favor. Moscow's confused and indecisive response to the violence in Sumgait expanded by default the structure of political opportunity. Street violence and radical nationalist rhetoric were no longer taboo. If the first pogrom was probably not anyone's plan, the subsequent violent episodes would have at least been pre-structured by the expectation of acting with impunity, and were sometimes deliberately orchestrated.

GEORGIA: THE COLLAPSE OF A CORRUPT DEPENDENT STATE

We now move our focus to Georgia, where both communist power and the organizing of a liberal opposition were simultaneously destroyed in what was essentially a deliberate provocation. In April 1989 a previously marginal group of Georgian nationalist dissidents, who were predominantly bohemian intellectuals, staged a new kind of protest in the main square of Tbilisi. It followed the conventions of a funeral vigil: priests and prayers, lots of flowers, candles, and many women dressed in black, all mourning the fate of the Georgian nation, and in particular the plight of Georgians living in the autonomous province of Abkhazia.

In the years of perestroika, public gatherings in Tbilisi had become normal occurrences. Until 1989, however, the rallies had taken a form familiar from the celebrations of soccer triumphs or the friendly street encounters of urban intellectuals from the circle of "good families" – mostly the descendants of the great number of yesteryear's Georgian gentry, who in Soviet times translated their status into higher education and prestige occupations.[40] These earlier rallies in Tbilisi were dominated by speakers who were cultural celebrities. They talked generally about democratization and the devolution of power from Moscow to the national republics. Both goals were meant to make the Soviet bureaucracy more accountable and allow the intellectuals a greater role.

The mournful vigil of April 1989 brought a significant change in the rhetoric, cultural disposition, and social status of participants. Many of them spoke with various rustic accents, predominantly the Megrelian patois spoken in the western Georgian provinces and Abkhazia. Zviad Gamsakhurdia, though himself originating from among the gentry and a very polished man, also belonged to the Megrelian sub-ethnic group of the Georgian nation. The typical participants of the vigil were described by local witnesses as middle-aged women, probably teachers, librarians, and other sub-intellectuals from small towns, or else simply housewives, and unshaven men who might have been market vendors, farmers, or truck drivers. The urban intelligentsia no longer felt comfortable at the rally; they considered the speeches bizarre and extremist, and gradually they started to leave.[41]

This nerve-racking vigil, continuing round the clock, put great pressure on the government officials under whose office windows it was taking place. Fearing another Karabagh, Moscow (though it remains unclear who exactly was responsible for this) decided to break up the vigil by force. A regiment of paratroopers recently withdrawn from Afghanistan had to be sent because the Georgian police proved reluctant to use strong-arm tactics against their fellow countrymen – the vigil's stress on martyrdom probably worried them too. The soldiers moved to clear the square in the middle of the night, but they still encountered a large agitated crowd. A combat variety of tear gas was used and, to make up for their lack of batons, the soldiers were told to beat the protestors with military-issue shovels that, as it turned out, inflicted serious wounds. In the ensuing stampede and mayhem, at least nineteen protestors died and hundreds were injured, most of them women.

If the first communist regime to abdicate de jure in Eastern Europe during 1989 was Poland, Georgia's was the first de facto abdication in the aftermath of the April outrage. Gorbachev pleaded ignorance (he was abroad during the crackdown) and took no measures in any direction: neither admitting personal responsibility nor sanctioning a more severe repression of the nationalists. In a customary gesture, several Georgian communist leaders were sacked. The soldiers were withdrawn into barracks and the police were nowhere to be seen. Predictably, the funerals of the victims turned into huge political rallies. The Georgian newspapers, despite still formally belonging to the Communist Party and the government, were full of indignant commentaries and demands to punish the perpetrators, and were soon calling for the creation of a genuinely Georgian government. All this convinced the Georgian *nomenklatura* of Gorbachev's irrelevance to their survival. With the exception of a few die-hard Stalinists who loathed Gorbachev for his indecisiveness (but could do no more), the majority felt confused and close to panic.

A major weakness of the Georgian *nomenklatura* – and, to varying extents, of all the *nomenklatura* regimes in the Caucasus – was the lack of a strong bureaucratic ethos that, in revolutionary situations, might have enabled them to assume the guise of dispassionate and competent technocrats (which is what saved the majority of the *nomenklatura* in the Baltic and Central European socialist countries). Once the moral legitimacy of the national government was destroyed and Moscow failed to offer effective support, the ensuing fragmentation of the state could be rapid and spectacular. The reason for this weakness was both historical and structural. Ever since the Russian colonization of Georgia in 1801, Tbilisi (then called Tiflis) had served as the base for the Russian-imposed administration and military command in the Caucasus, which offered the native noblemen many opportunities to derive comfortable incomes at Russia's expense. Under Viceroy Vorontsov in the 1840s, it became official policy to try to accommodate native noblemen in the bureaucratic service.[42] In the nineteenth century Tiflis was notorious for its relaxed work schedules, the abundance of sinecures, and a festive atmosphere which so many Russian visitors found charming (or despicably slothful, depending on their disposition). In Soviet times, Georgia maintained – indeed many Georgians cultivated – its image as a land of excellent native wines, elaborate cuisine, perennial sunshine, courteous manners, and easygoing attitudes.

The political economy behind this pleasant image rested on a steady flow of official subsidies from the Soviet budget and the large unofficial profits derived from the advantageous climate that made Georgia exceptionally attractive as a tourist destination and the privileged supplier of fruits, vegetables, and wines. (All this was happening, let me remind you, in the Soviet Union, where the urban industrial population was generally deprived of both sunshine and fresh produce.) The distribution of unofficial incomes in Georgia, and to a varying degree all over the southern republics of the USSR, was channeled through the unofficial institutions of corrupt patronage and the ubiquitous shadow economy. Doctors and teachers expected "gifts," traffic police regularly stopped motorists to exact cash "dues," shop attendants rigged the weights and kept the small change, and even the drivers of state-owned buses charged twice the official fare during rush hour. The lives of those who did not enjoy such petty monopolies or have access to patronage could be miserable indeed.[43]

We have no systematic data about corruption in the Soviet era, but informed people suggest that in Georgia and elsewhere in Transcaucasia the position of district party secretary was as a rule sold to the prospective office holder. The price varied between fifty and a hundred thousand rubles during the Brezhnev period and could go still higher in particularly lucrative districts. In general, it worked as follows. First, a prominent local family raised the money and lent it to the ambitious relative seeking office. By itself the money was not enough – one needed the proper credentials and connections, and the opportunity. Having purchased the desired position in the party apparatus, the new office holder would begin to repay his debt by appointing relatives and clients in lucrative subordinate local positions: chief of financial inspection, chief of police, manager of cooperative shops, collective farm chairman, director of a building materials factory, etc. In turn these lesser officials would establish various illicit operations under their control to skim off the funds and enrich themselves, and they paid regular bribes to their superiors to ensure patronage and protection.

The neopatrimonial principle that structured both the governing elite and the intelligentsia in Transcaucasia also helps to account for the extreme political fragmentation that occurred after the collapse of Soviet order. In 1990, more than seventy political parties competed for power in Georgia; Armenia acquired at least nine "national armies" and a dozen political nuclei featuring in their names various combinations of the words "democratic," "constitutional," "national," "party," or "movement"; and in Azerbaijan, the leaders of the Popular Front located in Baku admitted that they had little idea as to who exactly constituted the groups proclaiming themselves branches of the Popular Front in various smaller towns and rural districts of Azerbaijan, and that it seemed that these groups were pursuing local agendas and often consisted of members of elite local families and their clients who were aggrieved at a particular familial network in their district.

This system looked thoroughly deviant from the normative standpoint of a rational bureaucracy. It was certainly an internal failure of the Soviet state, which did not have the reach to regulate the affairs of Transcaucasia and Central Asia. The neopatrimonial pattern of corruption proved very resilient, albeit unstable in its internal elements, because bureaucratic cliques were continuously feuding over coveted positions. Moscow might periodically crack down on the corruption by removing the upper echelons of officialdom in national republics. In this way in 1969, with the help of the KGB chief Yuri Andropov, the entire government of Azerbaijan was removed after the reputedly honest and capable young chief of Azerbaijan's KGB, General Heydar Aliyev, had been appointed to lead the purge. Four years later, in 1973, a similar move by the KGB and Moscow in neighboring Georgia brought to power another police general, Eduard Shevardnadze. Both young leaders replaced great numbers of corrupt officials with their own corrupt clients. The problem was institutional and cultural, and not a matter of personal wickedness. Aliyev and Shevardnadze, both shrewd politicians, realized that their primary aim had to be to placate Moscow while consolidating their local power base by appointing loyal clients who, in order to rule and deliver, would have to indulge in the deeply entrenched practices of corruption. Officials who denied sinecure appointments to their relatives would lose the support of their family networks, and thus the inadequacy of formal political and bureaucratic institutions ensured that such honest officials would be eaten alive by rival families. Besides that, the ethnic cultures of the region, much as in the Mediterranean, laid special stress on conspicuous consumption as proof of social status. The office-holder who could not provide for his relatives and guests the "proper" level of entertainment, gifts, and favors would be judged a scrooge and a miserable failure.[44]

In such a setting the state might seem useless, if not downright parasitical, to most people. Many Georgian officials themselves did not appear to behave like the organizers of economic production or providers of public goods – if anybody's concern at all, things like the provision of electricity, roads, and schools were considered Moscow's responsibility. Georgian officials often behaved more like old-fashioned gentry than managers and bureaucrats. The result was a particularly brittle state that would collapse instantaneously once its power stopped flowing from central government and the population lost the last vestiges of fear or trust in the authorities. The restoration of the state then presented an intractable problem that, in the opinion of a rapidly growing majority, required nothing less than a miracle – national independence, perhaps.[45]

The Georgian *nomenklatura*'s abdication from political power can be seen as a spontaneous act of defense. In effect, it constituted a mass defection away from the official position in the political field and over to its extreme opposite after the state in Soviet Georgia suddenly lost its legitimacy and could no longer receive effective protection from Moscow. A review of electoral lists and bureaucratic appointments under the new anti-communist regime shows a surprising number of mid-ranking former communist officials and many of their children among the rising ultra-nationalists. Apparently the Soviet-era bureaucrats sensed that among the high-status intellectuals, the majority of which was liberal and moderately nationalist, they would face too much competition and ridicule. Instead, the defecting *nomenklatura* jumped on the bandwagon of the radical secessionist movement, whose bohemian leadership patently lacked administrative skills and whose huge, ecstatic, and predominantly sub-proletarian following offered the best bet for electoral victory.

The high-status intellectual elite found themselves politically outflanked and ideologically disoriented. The old government that they were trying to make civilized, accountable, and rational had suddenly disappeared. Erupting from below was a tremendous social movement of almost millenarian zeal whose icon was the former dissident Zviad Gamsakhurdia. This movement seemed to the intellectuals more like an irrational mob. It was then that the stellar Georgian philosopher Merab Mamardashvili, an all-Union celebrity, uttered his last famous aphorism: *If this is the choice of my people, then I am against the people!* Shortly afterwards, Mamardashvili died of a heart attack. In hindsight this seemed like the symbolic death of the Georgian intelligentsia and their mission to create a "civil society."

THE FAILURE OF ALL-SOVIET DEMOCRATIZATION

We now shift back to the all-Soviet perspective, where we must try to answer three questions. Why did Gorbachev and his faction of elite reformers fail to act against the spread of ethnic violence in the southern republics? Why did the oppositional democratic intelligentsia of Russia fail to establish alliances across the borders of republics that might have tamed nationalism and shifted the contention towards a civic agenda? Finally, why did the nationalist mobilization spread from republics like Armenia and Georgia, where a formidable nationalist potential already existed, to republics like Kabardino-Balkaria, where such potential was significantly weaker?

The answer to the first question seems obvious. Gorbachev did not trust his security agencies, believing, probably with good reason, that the repression of the rising nationalist movements would end all reforms, and at any rate finish his political career. In turn, the security agencies did not trust Gorbachev, especially after he forbade the use of major force in the Karabagh conflict and left exposed to public investigation the generals who had commanded the Tbilisi operation in April 1989. The options that remained to Gorbachev were a matter of finesse and evasion, and he could perform masterfully in this area. The last Soviet reformer apparently hoped that his efforts would soon produce a more dynamic and attractive union state. In 1989–1990 Gorbachev concentrated on the accelerated appeasement of the West in the hope of gaining in the near future the political and economic benefits that were expected from this. Thus he chose to move forward towards what he considered the strategic goals of Soviet renovation and to leave aside those problems that at the time appeared intractable.[46]

In 1989 Gorbachev sponsored the creation of a semi-competitively elected parliament – the USSR Congress of People's Deputies – but allowed it no real power. In taking this precaution he only created more trouble for himself: the Congress acquired a very loud voice but had little responsibility. In the end, the emperor himself suddenly looked naked. The new Congress, which was first convened in June 1989, turned out to be, in effect, a huge grievance-articulating device whose sessions were broadcast live by Soviet TV and radio and avidly watched and listened to across the USSR for a whole month. For added effect, the speeches were published verbatim the next day in the leading newspapers. This produced the Soviet equivalent of the *cahiers de doléances* of the French Revolution – a compilation of grievances. The first session of the new parliament became an incredible marathon of claim-making that culminated in a revolutionary situation.[47]

Demands of all kinds were directed at the summit of political power – at Gorbachev – who was presiding in person at the Congress. Caught in his own improvised game, he had to listen. He endlessly made promises suggesting that more resources would flow to the very diverse groups and territories that the claimants presented as their constituencies. This was the continuation of the Brezhnev-era practice of bureaucratic bargaining and corporate patronage, but now vastly magnified and made public. Gorbachev had to act in the old fashion insofar as the political system remained, on the surface, rigidly centralized, and he was ostensibly the omnipotent chief executive who had proclaimed himself the reformer of all irrationalities and evils in the realm.[48] Yet the struggling Soviet budget, despite rapidly growing borrowing abroad, could barely deliver on its usual obligations, let alone on Gorbachev's new promises. Moscow had already decided not to use its sticks, but now it had lost its carrots as well.

The second question, regarding the sudden failure of the Soviet liberal opposition, cannot adequately be explained solely in terms of Moscow politics or the personal traits of the leaders. Perhaps this is the reason why it has been rarely asked, let alone answered. Most authors jump from the parliamentary confrontations, street protests in the national republics, and the coalminers' strikes of summer 1989 right to the ascendancy of Yeltsin and the dissolution of the Soviet Union. Of course, one hears that the sheer size and ethnic complexity of the USSR stood against the "velvet" pattern of the Czechoslovakian divorce or a version of the marginalization of nationalist radicals in Hungary and Poland. This usual explanation is not wrong but it is too superficial. It still needs to be explained why the great size of the Soviet state made such a difference.

The immediate factor was the exceedingly shallow nature of those networks that might have had some potential to form the basis of an all-Soviet civil society. The exceptional reach and symbolic power of Moscow's television during the years of glasnost entirely bypassed what Sidney Tarrow calls the "capillary work" of movement organizing.[49] In other words, the ephemeral TV communication network that spread out in one direction, from center to provinces, did not translate into an extensive network of face-to-face contacts producing the personal commitment and solidarity that could have been utilized in political organizing. When in June 1989 it came to an open clash at the newly elected USSR Congress of People's Deputies, the democratic faction that had gathered around the celebrities – like the dissident Academician Sakharov or the *nomenklatura* defectors Yuri Afanasiyev and Boris Yeltsin – failed to elicit a strong and sufficiently coordinated show of support outside Moscow. The psychological reasons given for this widespread failure are based on irrefutable assumptions regarding provincial inertia or on a caricature of totalitarian *Homo soveticus*. A less metaphysical causation must be possible. The high-status Moscow intelligentsia enjoyed enormous media exposure, but they lacked a countrywide network like Poland's Solidarity that could rapidly identify the nuclei of local organizers and deliver to them a plan of action together with the organizational resources required to execute it.[50]

Shanibov, in one of our conversations, frankly admitted that he admired the Academician Sakharov and envied the high-profile democrats in Moscow. But from his position in Kabardino-Balkaria *they looked no closer than the Moon*. In other words, Shanibov's turn to nationalism came after he despaired of becoming usefully associated with the oppositional celebrities on the rise in Moscow, who addressed their pleas and criticisms to Gorbachev instead of building up political support down in the provinces. Such grass-roots support would have probably appeared within a few years as the celebrity democrats began on the one hand to lose their faith in Gorbachev and on the other to attract a nuclei of younger and once totally obscure activists, many of whom later proved to be capable political organizers. Time, however, was running out fast. Once again, if only such nuclei and networks had existed since 1968 or 1980 – as they did across the Central European socialist countries – things might have been different. But in the USSR, the mobilizations of 1968 had been terminated in embryo.

Interviews with Shanibov's associates and similar activists from neighboring regions (Krasnodar, Adyghea, Stavropol) reveal short-lived attempts to forge at the local level the kind of intellectual–worker alliances that characterized Poland's Solidarity. But one way or another, all such efforts proved ultimately futile because the workers, usually aggrieved at a specific boss or factory policy, met the outsider activists with a certain degree of distrust. Many workers favored the familiar tactics of shopfloor bargaining, or suspected that the intellectual activists sought to use them for self-serving electoral purposes.

This attitude could have changed had the intellectuals proved themselves politically useful to industrial workers. But, once again, there was very little time for that. It seems that in the case of Shanibov's associates, who were predominantly ethnic Kabardins, nationality became an issue because many workers were Russian. In short, we see the familiar obstacles to class mobilization. One of Shanibov's lieutenants summarized their conclusion: *Unfortunately, our people proved too backward for European social democracy. Since we did not want to go back home and listen to the music of Vivaldi again, we had to find the political language that our people could understand.*

In effect, the conflicting political forces that emerged during perestroika tended to restrain each other. The conservative *nomenklatura* still possessed considerable power, but their political program was wholly nostalgic, as they demonstrated blatantly in the last-minute coup attempt of August 1991. Gorbachev's reformers were experts at bureaucratic infighting but proved unprepared for an open political struggle. They called on and then failed to harness their potential constituencies among the intelligentsia, progressive technocrats, and skilled workers. On their side, the elements of the democratic intelligentsia failed to provide an effective leadership for the emergent popular opposition. The national civil societies of the Baltic republics had already turned their backs on the Soviet Union and were looking towards Europe. And the nationalist leaders in Transcaucasia were trying to ride the tigers of the mobilization they had let loose.

The political impasse lasted for two whole years, from the emergence of the revolutionary situation in summer 1989 until the desperate reactionary coup of

August 1991, which opened the way to the dissolution of the USSR; and the turmoil continued in the successor states for several more years. Instead of the revolutionary reconstitution of state powers, the Soviet Union experienced a stalled revolution that eventually fragmented into a myriad of revolutionary situations at the level of the union republics and provinces. Thus unlike Poland or Hungary – though perhaps not unlike Yugoslavia – the revolutionary situation in the USSR became an extensive, state-destroying morass.

Once the overarching formal network of the Communist Party had effectively disintegrated by the end of 1989, state power was segmented along the lines of administrative units. The proletarians suddenly lost the central target of their claim-making and, eventually, the state-industrial structure that defined their existence as a class. All politics became local, not excluding Moscow, where Gorbachev's USSR government in June 1990 found itself challenged by Yeltsin's Russian Federation government. The emergence of dual power in Moscow had a very disturbing effect: the all-Soviet command economy fell apart.[51] Provincial governments, using their ability to directly control economic assets, resorted to the defensive hoarding of resources and local rationing.[52] Many bureaucrats began looking for an escape route as the fall of communist regimes in Eastern Europe became a mighty catalyst. All this created the conditions for truly massive mobilizations at sub-union levels, especially because informal networks of the necessary density existed mostly inside the provinces and republics. The contentious politics of the 1989–1991 period were now fought out in town squares and in the new parliaments of the republics. Since many of the Soviet territorial units were defined by titular nationality, their politics acquired an increasingly nationalist slant.

THE DYNAMICS OF KABARDIN AND BALKAR POLITICS

We have already seen how in the three republics of Transcaucasia, Soviet democratization unleashed the dynamics of political competition that led to the rise of nationalist contention and violence. It had started with a new opportunity to rapidly acquire symbolic capital through public pronouncements made outside and in spite of the official framework. The benefits of such opportunities were accessible mainly to university-based intellectuals like Shanibov and certain categories of specialists (lawyers, economic managers) who were adept in giving and writing public speeches. The intellectuals and junior technocrats, however, needed a device to translate their newly gained symbolic stature into political ascendancy, and the easiest way to do this proved to be through identifying and exploiting grievances that involved whole ethnic communities. This move bypassed the obstacles involved in forming political alliances based on a social class (i.e. that of the industrial worker). Once highly emotional issues had emerged and obtained public resonance in a constituency, the slower-moving and more orderly efforts to institutionalize social movements and parties could be easily outflanked by the anarchic mobilization of large rallies and "street crowds." The presence of sizable subproletarian sectors in the Caucasus made violence more likely. In fact, violence in its symbolic and brutally physical forms became the weapon of politically weak and socially marginal groups. Violence, waged in the near absence of state controls, rapidly escalated on each side of the contested boundaries. One of its effects was to make those moderate reformers – higher-status intellectuals, technocrats, and professionals – who had a stake in the orderly transformation of the polity and social structure appear irrelevant if not even unpatriotic.

And yet, even then there was not an automatic, unilinear progression towards nationalist politics elsewhere in the Caucasus. Ethnic conflicts grow from – and can subside back into – the ordinary flow of power, network structures, and the tensions of social position. So what factors *did* ignite the ethnopolitical situation in a territory like Kabardino-Balkaria, which was controlled by a strong network of local *nomenklatura*, possessed only an embryonic "civil society," and moreover had no history of ethnic animosity? Emulation alone would not produce such an effect unless the contemporary examples of larger union republics managed to resonate with something occurring locally. What was occurring locally in Kabardino-Balkaria?

First, let us look briefly at the earlier perestroika-era movements, which had faded away and, on the surface, had absolutely nothing to do with ethnic grievances (see Table 4, Second Period). What happened, for instance, to the contemporary mobilizations around the issues of ecology or "problem" teenagers? A micro-investigation based on interviews and a close reading of the newspapers of the day indicates that the shifts in rhetoric followed not only the Moscow-generated structure of opportunity but also local connections leading to old and new resources. At its outset, the ecological movement in Kabardino-Balkaria comprised two types of activist. One was the devoted Green-like individual, who would commonly be an ethnic Russian scientist or engineer. The other was a native Kabardin or Balkar intellectual, whose education was mostly in local history and the humanities, and who thus normally assumed a secondary position in the movement.[53] The more cosmopolitan scientists had professional contacts in Moscow, could speak competently on the issues, and, later in the 1990s, learned how to write successful grant proposals to Western foundations. Alas, by that time ecology was no longer a public priority. We find essentially the same trajectory in the evolution of social movements for the reform of school education and for dealing with the problems of unruly teenagers. Both sets of issues are increasingly seen in ethnic terms as the activists begin to claim that only the revival of ethnic traditions can cure the problems of modern education.

Later during perestroika activists of Kabardin and Balkar nationality found causes where their credentials and connections seemed more relevant – initially within typical national awakening movements in the pre-political sense, as described by Miroslav Hroch.[54] The intellectuals whose careers depended on the state-sponsored institutions of ethnic culture collectively sought to expand the size and prestige of their field. Fully in accordance with the Soviet practice of affirmative action, they loyally begged officials to direct more resources to local museums, theaters, and universities. One novelty brought about by democratization was that national intellectuals now also used discussion clubs, newspapers, and television to foster "awareness" and mobilize their co-ethnic constituencies.

In this process, national intellectuals competed among themselves, a competition which was especially fierce between aspiring juniors and established seniors. The process rapidly moved the antagonists towards the polarization of their political stances. Senior national intellectuals relied on their administrative connections and the formal symbolic capital derived from official positions, which placed them in the moderate-conservative camp. According to the logic of opposition, the juniors had to be radical and populist, which led them to broaden and dramatize their claims. Ethnic cultures were soon portrayed as being on the verge of extinction in the face of threats ranging from air pollution to the lack of traditional filial respect among teenagers. All problems were then blamed on Moscow's aloofness and the servility of the local *nomenklatura*. It was now only a short step from here to claiming that Moscow's policies amounted to cultural genocide, which sought by different means to continue the crimes of Stalinism and the devastation wrought by the tsarist armies during the nineteenth-century conquest of the Caucasus. Still later in the 1990s this discursive trend further translated the same claims into Islamist invectives against the Godless mechanistic civilization of the West.[55]

BALKARIAN SEPARATISM AND KABARDIN COUNTER-MOBILIZATION

In popular opinion the 1944 Stalinist deportation of the Balkar people lent immediate validity to the claims that Moscow was engaged in "cultural genocide." As in

Chechnya, and in the Baltic republics that suffered similar deportations, the issue was easily turned into a collective grievance because virtually every Balkar family had lost someone during the exile of 1944–1957. Calls to investigate the old crimes of Stalinism soon grew into a demand for reparations. But instead of electoral success and the compensation expected, the Balkar opposition and even the *nomenklatura* candidates discovered with dismay that after the first round of the first competitive elections to the Soviet parliament in 1989 they had failed to win a single seat. This was a totally unexpected result brought about by the new political conditions.

Previously all multi-ethnic territories of the USSR had followed the unwritten "Lebanese protocol," according to which each nationality tended to be allotted a different rank of appointment. Normally, in Kabardino-Balkaria the top positions in all bureaucratic hierarchies would belong to ethnic Kabardins, their first deputies would be Balkars, and the second deputies or leading specialists would be Russian or from some other ethnic group. In the first competitive elections, where the old ethnic quotas were no longer honored, the Kabardins and Russians won while the Balkar minority's share suddenly looked like it would dwindle to nothing. This was to be expected as the Balkars represented merely 9.6 per cent of the republic's popu-lation.[56] Nonetheless the sudden loss of group power proved to be a cause of ethnic unity. Nearly all of the ninety thousand Balkars, led jointly by their *nomenklatura* and intellectuals, poured into the streets of Nalchik. One of the participants (a teacher) recalled: *The sense of urgency was tremendous – it seemed that if we failed to make our demands heard now, our people would lose out for ever in the new democracy.*

The solution seemed obvious, and soon the Balkars began to demand a republic of their own; that is, a polity where it would be certain that every election would be won by an ethnic Balkar. After all, that is generally the purpose of state institu-tions: to increase one's chances of political and economic success in the future. Traditionally, the Balkars lived in the upper mountain reaches close to the edge of glaciers. This small population call themselves *Tauleri*, which means literally "the mountaineers." Because they were few and militarily weak, they had to live in the upper mountains, which is the poorest ecological niche in terms of agriculture. However, in more recent times it had become apparent that the snow-covered mountain slopes were excellent for skiing, and that together with the beautiful Alpine meadows they could generate a considerable income from tourism. Balkar separatism threatened to take away what was now considered prime real estate. Furthermore, the Balkar activists were suggesting the partition of Nalchik, the only sizable town in the area, which they claimed as their capital too.

Traditionally, the whole Balkar people lived in five villages located in adjacent mountain valleys.[57] But in 1957, after their release from exile, the majority of Balkars did not return to their impoverished native villages, settling instead in the vicinity of Nalchik. On their side, the local authorities hoped that the resettlement would address the Balkar grievances over the properties lost in the Stalinist deportation and help to keep the community under state control. By the 1980s, however, the high birth rate among the Balkars had made them a more sizable minority in Nalchik and its environs than anyone had expected back in 1957. In addition, the increasing scarcity of well-paid industrial jobs forced a disproportionate number of Balkars, as the more recent arrivals in town, into sub-proletarian conditions. This led to them being caricatured as rough, rowdy hillbillies whose men lounged around the streets and spoke too loudly and whose women thronged the marketplace selling roasted sunflower seeds or homemade sweaters and socks. The stereotype is not entirely incorrect because many Balkar men (in the depressed 1990s as many as 90 per cent) were indeed underemployed and thus the women had to work at the lower end of local markets selling cheap snacks or items knitted from the wool of the goats traditionally kept by Balkars.

Predictably enough, the prospect of a separate Balkaria with a capital in Nalchik provoked strong objections among the majority of Kabardins, and hostility between the two peoples began to escalate rapidly – despite the fact that historically the Balkars and the Kabardins had lived together peacefully. This was when the erstwhile social reformer Shanibov became the Kabardin nationalist leader Musa Shanib. The challenge of Balkar separatism finally overrode the barriers to a truly mass mobilization, and the focus of politics now shifted from class to ethnicity (just as the comparable threat of Karabagh Armenian secession had earlier nationalized and radicalized the contention in Azerbaijan). In the beginning, the politics of perestroika had involved only the *nomenklatura* and upper strata of specialists, intellectuals, and some of the most skilled workers in the biggest towns. In one of Gorbachev's televised encounters with the Soviet people, an ordinary Russian worker compared perestroika to a storm deep in a taiga forest: the treetops bend and crack, but on the ground the tree trunks stand thick and solid and the stormy winds blowing above can barely be heard down below. This metaphor applied in provincial Kabardino-Balkaria just as much as anywhere else in Russia. But now the prospect of Balkarian separation threatened virtually everyone in the small republic who was not a Balkar, and these people wondered if one day soon they would wake up to a new political reality, where their chances in life would be unknown but no doubt worse than they had been. The Kabardin intellectuals no longer needed to

cultivate ethnic awareness or persuade their compatriots to attend classes in traditional etiquette or ceremonies commemorating their dead ancestors. People
streamed into the streets and town squares of Nalchik at the first call because a
credible danger to their normal life had now appeared.

Fearing the worst, Kabardin officials hurried to extend their help to the Balkar
members of the local *nomenklatura*. In the end, they succeeded in getting a few of
the Balkar representatives elected, even though it required some personal sacrifices
from the Kabardin bosses and a little manipulation of the electoral process. To a
large extent this is what official speakers in Nalchik mean when today they praise,
in a somewhat opaque fashion, the "wisdom, self-abnegation, and steadfast commitment" of their republic's leadership to "inter-ethnic peace and justice" despite the
"provocateurs" and "the difficult conditions imposed by the times."

NATIONAL SEPARATIST PROJECTS

The Balkar example illuminates the process that broke the back of the USSR.
Political reform disrupted the existing configurations of bureaucratic patronage and
created unforeseen outcomes. The incapacitation of Moscow, and particularly the
destruction of the Berlin Wall, suddenly made the prospect of quitting the USSR
seem realistic. National independence served as a very effective platform for popular
mobilization. It was also an attractive collective incentive for aspiring politicians and
bureaucrats of the new nations. These popular enthusiasms and elite aspirations
were nurtured by the confident assumption that leaving Russia behind automatically
meant joining the West. In the larger historical picture, national independence became
a means to achieve the integration into the capitalist core that perestroika had failed
to bring about. Characteristically, the first to leave were the republics that enjoyed the
highest levels of socioeconomic development and relative cultural and geographic
proximity to the West: the Baltic republics in the USSR; Slovenia and Croatia in
Yugoslavia, and the Czech Republic in the former Czechoslovakia.

The Baltic example started a chain reaction of secessionist movements inside the
USSR. It ran all the way to the Balkar ethnic referendum that in 1991 unanimously
decided to carve out a Balkar republic separate from the Kabardins. (As in many other
non-Russian republics, the local ethnic Russians were caught in the middle without
a clear, legitimate platform on which they could mobilize. Feeling abandoned by
Moscow, they remained mostly silent or started to emigrate.) In 1996 another Balkar
referendum, the result of which was almost as one-sided, rescinded the declaration
of independence after its futility became widely obvious. The Balkar *nomenklatura*

settled their differences with their Kabardin counterparts, the common people got tired of mobilizing, some of the more sensible Balkar activists accepted various official positions, and the remaining radicals were muzzled by the courts and through police action.[58] But in 1991–1992 the standoff between the mobilized Balkars and Kabardins had brought the republic to the brink of state breakdown, and possibly a civil war.

THE COLLAPSE OF THE USSR: ACCIDENT INVESTIGATION REPORT

In a preliminary way, we can summarize our findings regarding the collapse of the USSR in the following sequence. Mikhail Gorbachev, who came to power in the spring of 1985, represented the younger, activist faction of the top *nomenklatura*, located predominantly in the agencies responsible for superpower functions: diplomacy, the KGB's foreign directorates, advanced science, weapons production, and capital-intensive civilian industries. The reformers sought to rationalize and invigorate state governance, particularly in the areas where central planning had been failing, such as in technological innovation or the diversified production of consumer goods and quality foods. A related concern was bureaucratic corruption and other forms of rent-seeking among those in office, and the enclosed nature of the mid-level apparatuses governing the Soviet territories and economic sectors. Both practices had become tacitly tolerated norms of bureaucratic behavior during the "stagnation" period of Brezhnevism. Geopolitically, Gorbachev's faction sought to reduce the costs of the arms race against America, and to a lesser extent China, as well as to solve the problems posed by the maintenance of East European socialist regimes and the growing number of the USSR's Third World clients.

The reformers devised a two-pronged political strategy. Externally, they successfully appeased the West by agreeing to what, by the standards of the previous decade, were major concessions. The appeasement was to pave the way for increased foreign investment, the transfer of technology, and trade. Domestically, the reformers sought to incorporate into the restructured official ideology the demands of the 1968 movements for "socialism with a human face." This included the criticism of past abuses (during the periods of both Stalin and Brezhnev), the public discussion of acceptable policy alternatives, the relaxation of censorship and border controls, and eventually the gradual introduction of market mechanisms in the economy and competitive elections in politics. The domestic reform was also successful insofar as it put considerable pressure on the entrenched mid-ranking *nomenklatura*, allowed for the recruitment of younger managers and public intellectuals into the reformist regime, and strongly resonated with the aspirations of educated specialists and higher-skilled workers. Moreover, domestic liberalization produced some positive feedback regarding the foreign agenda.

All this meant that the Soviet Union began to incorporate itself into the core of the world-system primarily through its association with Western European governments and economic interests. The ascending phase of Gorbachev's perestroika lasted four years, from spring 1985 to spring 1989, during which it seemed that the USSR could eventually become a more democratic, peaceful, and prosperous state – perhaps like Spain after the death of Franco.

The pinnacle and breaking point of perestroika was reached during the summer of 1989. Gorbachev convened in Moscow the first semi-competitively elected all-union parliament but denied it any real power for the obvious reason that such a body could have produced a totally new government and legislated for a change of regime (as happened in Poland). The parliament contained an influential minority of democratic intellectuals and reformist technocrats who had despaired at Gorbachev's caution and evasiveness, and who could have tried to impose a new government anyway. But this would have required a massive popular mobilization outside the parliament.

First of all, Gorbachev's faction remained too enmeshed in the symbols and images (no less than the fears) instilled in the wake of Khrushchev's abortive reforms – the failure of which was the formative experience of Gorbachev's generation. Besides, the Soviet reformers were still *nomenklatura* executives, who relied on familiar tactics of bureaucratic manipulation, and thus regarded the public contenders that their own efforts had brought forward as upstarts and dangerous interlopers. Therefore Gorbachev, like many well-meaning reformers who have ended up provoking revolutions, failed to support forces that he considered too radical, despite their sharing essentially the same ideas and goals.

On their side, the democratic opposition did not have the time to mature ideologically and organizationally. They lacked the precedents, the networks of grassroots activists, and the institutionalized resources that had been created elsewhere in Eastern Europe by the popular mobilizations of 1956, 1968, and the early 1980s. Furthermore, the sheer size of the Soviet Union and its compartmentalization into many administrative territories and ethnic republics presented daunting obstacles to political mobilization that were not found in more compact and unitary states. The democratic opposition managed to build serious bases mainly in Moscow and Leningrad, while failing to extend a political organization to almost anywhere else in this huge country.

There remained a reactionary alternative, which resided mostly in the Soviet military, the watchdog wings of the KGB and the ideological apparatus, and among the captains of obsolete industries who commanded the allegiances of paternalistically dependent proletarians. These forces might have produced a Soviet Vendée. Throughout perestroika bureaucratic resistance remained mostly tacit, though it presented a formidable brake on any concerted effort to change the situation. The reactionary bloc, however, completely lacked the credible counter-agenda that might have allowed it to become an autonomous political force. Even they saw that by 1989 a simple return to a Brezhnev-style regime was out of the question. Besides, this flank of Soviet politics had been discredited after years of glasnost revelations and the public admission of failures (such as the inability to match the American military build-up under Reagan, the quagmire in Afghanistan, and the notorious shortages of quality goods and food). When the Soviet reactionaries finally acted in the coup attempt of August 1991, it only demonstrated their impotence.

The *nomenklatura* reformers, the democratic opposition of intellectuals and technocrats, and the reactionaries thus kept each other in check. Instead of instituting the quick and decisive revolutionary measures that create new regimes in such historical moments, all three camps at Moscow's summit of power engaged in bewildering forms of symbolic posturing. The stalemate created a protracted revolutionary situation that lasted for two whole years, until the dissolution of the USSR in December 1991. Revolutionary chaos still existed after the Soviet collapse. The ethnic civil wars in Moldova, Azerbaijan, Georgia, and Tadjikistan were in fact the continuation of the all-Union revolutionary process. Likewise lesser conflicts such as the Chechen national revolution, the Ingush–Osetian clashes, or the Balkar attempt to secede from Kabardin domination were the aftershock of the same revolutionary breakdown of the Soviet state that had continued in fragments until 1993–1994. In Russia itself, this period of total uncertainty lasted until Yeltsin's violent dissolution of the transitional parliament in October 1993.

During this period multiple contenders appeared and tried to claim state power, but nobody succeeded. It was then that all-Union governance began to unravel, and the immediate effect was the breakdown of the centralized economy. For the first time during perestroika the effects of political struggles became a direct threat to the structures of everyday life everywhere in the USSR. Earlier in perestroika the removal of old bureaucratic notables primarily affected the *nomenklatura* and the specialists standing at the threshold of *nomenklatura* appointments, which was probably 10–15 per cent of the population. The democratic rhetoric of glasnost resonated with the intellectuals, educated specialists, and skilled workers who comprised between a third and, in some big towns, half or more of the population. Perestroika and glasnost generated waves of optimism. But increasing shortages and the disarray in consumer markets (including the shadow ones) suddenly dampened hopes and threatened the whole Soviet population.

After 1989 the situation became rapidly-changing and chaotic on all fronts. At this time the first millionaires began to emerge openly, their wealth having been gained predominantly on the shadow market. Following the traders, a new generation of violent entrepreneurs – gangsters, rogue policemen, ethnic mafiosi – made their spectacular appearance. It is hard to overestimate the effect of the televised overthrow of the communist regimes in Eastern Europe during autumn 1989. Things were falling apart indeed. In sum, all this produced the impression that the rules and taboos of the past were null and void. Outside Moscow and especially in the national republics, different forces devised their own strategies for surviving the breakdown, propelling nationalism to the center stage.

The predominantly conservative regional *nomenklatura* began to erect protective barriers around their jurisdictions and to recast the networks of bureaucratic patronage as political machines. This was justified as the defense of local and ethnic-national interests. The immediate success of this strategy (judged from the narrow perspective of those in power) is manifest in the prevalence of former communist bosses among the leaders of the newly independent states. The long-term economic and social costs, however, have often been staggering.

The intellectuals and specialists who had become active in the democratic politics of perestroika, and who now saw the demise of their idols in Moscow, began to advocate democracy and economic reform through national independence. The most successful examples of this kind are found in the Baltic republics, where mass mobilizations began early and were fuelled by deeply ingrained national sentiments, central to which was a tendency to identify with Europe rather than Russia. In this region, national revolutions succeeded rapidly and rather peacefully – despite prior predictions of violence, which had been based on factors like territorial irredentism and the presence of sizable Russian-settler minorities. The prospect of European integration, however, played a major role in "civilizing" Baltic nationalism. The Russian minorities had to reconcile themselves to second-class status in exchange for being allowed to stay in what were now becoming Western countries. It needs to be added in particular that state capacity in the Baltic republics was preserved and perhaps improved during the revolutions. This was possible because the local officials, who were less involved in corruption and nepotism and thus more rationally bureaucratic, could easily switch their allegiance to the national "civil societies" constructed by the intelligentsia and to European institutions. Democratization offered the former national *nomenklatura* the prospect of regaining state power in a new capacity as popularly elected officials at the next round of elections, which is what they might have expected to happen after the politicized intellectuals had proven their incompetence in state management.

In Central Asia an orderly and mostly peaceful exit from the USSR was possible for quite a different reason. Here state capacity was also preserved or reconstituted after 1989, but this was made possible through the emergence of strong national patrons from the ranks of the former *nomenklatura*. Their power relied on networks of elite patronage, some old and some new, that were solidified by the tributary and redistributive mechanisms usually called corruption. The political radicals and various elite mavericks were exiled or incorporated into the institutions of newly independent nation states, and the disruptive potential of the sub-proletarian masses was checked by the imposition of coercive authoritarian regimes. The suppression of sub-proletarian revolt was then justified in terms of secularism, modernity, and progress because the Central Asian sub-proletarians mobilized mostly on the platform of a puritanical Islamic variety of social justice and traditionalism.

In Tadjikistan, where the program of *nomenklatura* authoritarianism and national sovereignty had failed to restrain the elite mavericks and sub-proletarian masses, the immediate outcome was a horrific internecine war in which many external forces tried to intervene. After much bloodshed during the early 1990s, Yeltsin's Russia and Karimov's Uzbekistan imposed on Tadjikistan their joint de facto protectorate. This created conditions for the slow reconstitution of the national government out of the elements of the democratic and Islamist opposition and the former *nomenklatura*. It grew to be weakly authoritarian and perhaps more than usually corrupt because Tadjikistan's government of reconciliation, lacking effective means of coercion, had no other choice but to buy the compliance of various local officials and former warlords. In addition, because the government of Tadjikistan had almost entirely lost its capacity to collect taxes and instead subsisted on foreign aid, it had to buy internal peace by providing its new officers various sources of rent and tribute, such as the private control of an advanced aluminum plant built in Soviet times or mafia-style operations centered on drug trafficking from neighboring Afghanistan.

Finally, the third set of successful nationalist mobilizations and revolutions arose in Moldova and predominated in the Caucasus. The typical outcome here, however, was ethnic conflict and wholesale disaster. Intellectual leaders rapidly managed to create national "civil societies" by using some kind of big local grievance, usually associated with unrelieved historical trauma and/or a competing neighboring nationality, to mobilize the masses. The composition of societies in the Caucasus made a crucial difference. On the one hand, there existed large, even outsized concentrations of high-status national intelligentsia, who were historically rooted in the urban middle classes and comfortably incorporated in Soviet institutions for the promotion of modern national cultures. This made Armenia, Georgia, and Azerbaijan (mainly Baku) comparable to the Baltic republics. On the other hand, and unlike the Baltic region, in the Caucasus there also existed very large sectors of various types of sub-proletariat. The reasons were structural. The region remained only partially industrialized. Attractive industrial jobs were scarce and often monopolized by the established urban proletarians, including the ethnic Russian settlers. Besides that, occupations in the large shadow economy, the officially tolerated seasonal labor migrations, and commercialized semi-private agriculture normally promised better returns while largely preserving the traditional patterns of family and ethnic community. The political activism of sub-proletarians, who in the Caucasus mobilized mostly on the platform of radical nationalism, added force to the movements initiated by the national intelligentsia. But sub-proletarians also brought their own rowdy habitus into the arena of political mobilization, which was something the intelligentsia leaders could not control. The national movements thus rapidly acquired a radical and violent aspect. Furthermore, intellectuals of marginal, dissident, or Bohemian status could incite and hoped to channel towards their own goals the rowdiness and emotions of the sub-proletarian masses.

Last but not least, the state structures in the Caucasus were highly dependent on central government in Moscow, yet this dependency was skewed and favored provincial clients who enjoyed institutionalized corruption and embezzlement. During Soviet times the Caucasus exhibited an odd combination of Central Asian style corruption and the Westernized aspirations of the *nomenklatura* and intelligentsia. These aspirations were expressed in the symbolic markers of Westernism such as stylish patterns of consumption and an elevated view of themselves (Armenians proudly considered themselves the first Christian nation, Georgians were notoriously called the French of the Caucasus, and the educated Azeris styled themselves after modern Turkey). The result in each case was a very brittle state that was too corrupt to be bureaucratically efficient or respected by its own population, yet at the same time possessed too many educated and ambitious elites to permit the government to be reconstituted as a despotism.

In 1989–1990 the structures of the Soviet state in the Caucasus unraveled very rapidly and were left irreparable. A major cause was the panic and massive number of defections among the families of corrupt *nomenklatura*. They felt politically exposed, betrayed by Moscow, and effectively without leadership. Meantime the massive entrance of sub-proletarians into the politics of national revival directed contention towards violent radicalism and anarchic anti-statism. State paralysis and the continuous presence of rowdy crowds in the streets changed the whole political environment. Given Gorbachev's own dilemmas, these developments served to cut off the local political arenas from the Soviet "Center." Virtually from the outset of the mobilizations Moscow lost its local levers and so its ability to interfere effectively. But the same factors of state incapacitation and violence in large part served to dash any hope for the rapid arrival of political and economic stabilization from the West. In contrast to what had happened in the Baltic republics, Western involvement in the Caucasus seemed too difficult, costly, and unpromising (even Azerbaijan's oil did not help). The national elites, whether they were aspiring intellectual politicians or energetic elements of the *nomenklatura* seeking new opportunities, faced a nasty choice between total defeat and the dangers of trying to capitalize on the disorderly situation. Since there were many such elites and they competed ferociously, the struggle between them became another major factor in the perpetuation of disorder and violence.

Thus the destruction of the communist regimes in Transcaucasia did not produce a swift reconstitution of states. To the contrary, these states were severely undermined and would remain very weak and prone to breakdown for years to come. What was once the shadow economy became the dominant type of economic activity, while politics and state structures themselves acquired a distinctly shadow-like quality.

7

The Scramble for Soviet Spoils

"No one ever really liked the state, but the great majority had permitted its powers to grow ever greater because they saw the state as the mediator of reform. But if it cannot play this function, then why suffer the state? But if we don't have a strong state, who will provide daily security?"

Immanuel Wallerstein, "Social Science and the Communist Interlude"
The Essential Wallerstein (New York: New Press, 2000, p. 385)

In the wake of 1989, structural constraints loosened dramatically and actors could no longer securely predict the consequences of their own decisions. This indeterminacy in social structures and in the minds of individuals did not mean, however, that human agency could now reign supreme in the shaping of history. As the Soviet state was breaking apart, the scramble for fragments of its political and economic assets became increasingly turbulent. The course of events could turn on such small contingencies as timing, personal acquaintance, contemporary social "mood," or one lucky move. The broken and chaotic system of relations nonetheless formed a maze that allowed only certain pathways.

The combination of overt bureaucratic rigidity and locally brittle state structures eroded by corruption created perhaps the main set of historical constraints. In a severely disorganized environment it proved very difficult if not entirely impossible to democratize the structures of state governance and maneuver economic assets towards collectively rational goals. A constructive agenda of this kind would have required strong institutional bases and a clear, long-term political vision.[1] Instead, the goals became limited to the nearest horizons in terms both of time and of social participation. In other words, the old *nomenklatura*, the aspiring oppositionists, and the emerging private entrepreneurs could pursue only the immediate stakes, which promised them either a grand scoop or complete disaster, and in this they relied on circles of friends, relatives, and clients. Trust became a variable circumstantial category, and political constituencies were now recruited on the traditional basis of common locality and ethnic group.

At the unstable and superficial level of history that Fernand Braudel in a rather derisory manner called the "history of events," we will encounter in this chapter instances of high drama – including assassinations, prison-breaking, and revolutionary mobs storming government buildings. Braudel was playing at being a maximalist when he famously proclaimed that "events are dust."[2] From the standpoint of human existence, the divergence of historical events between someone's success or failure in seizing state power at an opportune moment could make a difference as big as that between war and peace. In the long run, however, Braudel was right in stressing the enduring power of structures. The self-destructiveness of the pathways to be examined in this chapter was not the result, as has been supposed, of the irrationality of ethnic traditions or deep-seated hatreds. Structurally formulated, the question should be this: What processes and constraints created the new peripheries which emerged from the collapse of the Soviet state? If, in the course of just a few years, millions of people who had enjoyed a standard of living comparable to that in Southern Europe could end up enduring a degree of insecurity and misery more typical of Central America or Africa, this must be a pretty big question.

The historical bifurcation that occurred in the wake of the revolutionary situation of 1989 confirmed the enduring power of structural differentiation into the semi-periphery and the periphery in the modern world-system.[3] Those locations that had been semi-peripheral before the communist interlude – namely, the belt of countries winding from Estonia via Poland and Hungary to Slovenia, and thus all adjacent to the capitalist core – reverted to semi-peripheral development after 1989.[4] None of these countries really achieved the power and prosperity of core states, but at least they became directly associated with the core's (mainly West European) political and economic institutions, though in a more or less subordinate position (i.e. they became semi-peripheral). In the meantime, the larger group of post-communist countries – geographically extending from Albania, Bosnia, and Bulgaria, via Romania, to the Ukraine, Belarus, and across much of Russia to the south (excepting the largest cities, which became semi-peripheral enclaves), and east to the Caucasus and Central Asia – emerged from the collapse of communist dictatorships with typically peripheral features.

In this chapter we empirically investigate a number of pathways along which locations in the Caucasus returned to the periphery after the disintegration of the Soviet developmental state. These are the national revolution in Chechnya, the ethnic civil war in Abkhazia, and the twice-failed revolution in Kabardino-Balkaria, which resulted in the quasi-restoration of the oligarchic *nomenklatura* regime (see Table 5, page 329). Musa Shanib played a leading role in all three instances. The miraculous events surrounding Georgia's autonomy of Adjaria also provide an analytical counterpoint to Abkhazia, and perhaps to the far more notorious tragedy of Bosnia-Herzegovina.

A look at Chechnya, Abkhazia, and Kabardino-Balkaria will provide us with a good overview of the post-communist periphery. Previously Chechnya had been heavily industrialized and dominated by the large and largely Russian city of Grozny. Abkhazia did not have much industry nor did it have big towns. Rather, before 1991 it possessed an extensive and very lucrative informal economy based on subtropical resorts and the commercialized agriculture of citrus fruits. Kabardino-Balkaria stood somewhere inbetween these two examples, though it was closer to Chechnya in terms of industrialization and urbanization. During the 1990s in Chechnya the state structures were wrecked altogether following the revolution and the war; in Abkhazia the state structures were half-wrecked as a result of the separatist civil war against Georgia; and in Kabardino-Balkaria, after an acute crisis, the old state was restored under Moscow's tutelage, albeit imperfectly and on such a greatly reduced scale as to make its future breakdown probable. We now come full circle back to the themes of chapter one and should be ready to answer the question as to what caused the divergence between the revolutionary processes in Chechnya and Kabardino-Balkaria.

Beyond this question, which is of undeniable importance for our political theories, looms a much larger one: Why was it that all these places, even those like Adjaria and Kabardino-Balkaria where violent destruction was avoided, ended up so impoverished, rapidly deindustrialized, and marginal to global markets? In short, what made them all peripheral once again? This question is too big to be dealt with adequately in this chapter, yet it is also too big to be entirely ignored. Therefore we need to take at least a brief detour in the following section in order to examine the nature of the contemporary periphery.

THE RETURN TO PERIPHERY

The sources of socioeconomic backwardness have been at the center of many theoretical and political controversies. In the 1960s an influential school of radical scholars tried to relate socioeconomic "underdevelopment" to the structural dependency of the Third World – which they called the periphery – on the "advanced" Western countries, or the core. This opened a promising theoretical venue because it managed to connect the trajectories of disparate countries and regions in a holistic model of relations evolving over time.

The early formulations of dependency theory, however, often suffered from a crude economic and political determinism that provided good political slogans instead of nuanced analysis. The original explanation for the peripheral condition was European colonialism, i.e. the direct political domination and pillage of resources, as happened in Spanish Peru or British India. But the acquisition of state sovereignty by the former colonies of Latin America in the 1820s and Asia and Africa after 1945 proved that colonial domination offered an insufficient explanation. From the 1950s to the 1970s analytical efforts focused on such factors as the lack of modern education, industry, infrastructure, or the imperialist policies of the West and the exposure to unequal exchange with former metropoles. But the example provided by the former socialist countries that in the 1990s reverted to peripheral status seems to contradict many of these previous academic attempts to explain the failure of certain states to "develop." It turned out that a country can be a sovereign national state, possess an educated population and a large industrial economy, have spent many years in a mercantilist autarchy resisting unequal exchanges with the West, and in the end still re-emerge with typically peripheral social patterns. As such, explaining the diversity of the outcomes of communist developmentalism in the former Soviet bloc and China is today a major analytical challenge.

Two decades ago, arguing against simplistic theories of Third World dependency, the French economist Alain Lipietz suggested that it was not the West that was deliberately underdeveloping the Third World.[5] Lipietz rather pointed to the structural differential between the metropoles of capitalism and the peripheral outliers in the world distribution of economic, military and cultural resources. This "objectively existing" situation tends to create the games in which the peripheral elites might rationally seek individual profit at the collectively irrational cost of underdeveloping their own countries. The post-Soviet countries provide many glaring examples.

Beyond the immediate level of events where political intrigues and transborder economic machinations occur, the source of trouble remains invisible from the standpoint of ordinary humans or, for that matter, of commentators on current politics, because ultimately the source is to be found in the impersonal, highly abstract and historically inherited structural constraints embedded deeply in the morphology of the capitalist world-economy. Indeed they have originated in the Western military and economic expansion of the past centuries. Times have changed but, *mutatis mutandis*, the structures of world inequality evidently remain a durable condition. And thus even without anybody's conscious intervention, the dynamic "power games" resulting in the reproduction of peripheral underdevelopment continue to emerge at new historical junctures. This is where the world-systems analysis begun in the 1970s by Immanuel Wallerstein, Samir Amin, and Giovanni Arrighi offered a major theoretical advance. There is, however, much to be done in order to connect the insights of the world-systems perspective with theories operating at other levels of causality. Here, let us try to sketch what such bridges might look like from the world-system level to quotidian observable reality.

The Soviet Union forcefully imposed its isomorphous institutions of political and economic governance and a bureaucratic-industrial social structure on a vast expanse stretching from the Baltic to the Pacific.[6] The *nomenklatura* and national intellectuals, the district party committees and collective farms, the same sets of government ministries and state universities existed in Estonia as well as in Georgia or Uzbekistan. However, anybody familiar with realities on the ground could expect a collective farm or district committee in Estonia to differ significantly from its counterpart in Georgia in terms of its internal norms, interaction rituals, and social functions. The practical difference between these Soviet institutions might be attributed to the character of insider bureaucratic networks, the types of resources and strategies of appropriation, and the actual "style" of power that would be shaped by their embeddedness in the local cultures and social structure.

This variation certainly must not be portrayed in absolute terms that perpetuate the bad old reification of a civilization chasm between East and West. For instance, the process through which Soviet order disintegrated in Azerbaijan mirrored the feverish contention in Armenia and Georgia, but for better or worse the fate of Azerbaijan differed from the patterns of Central Asian republics. Contrary to the long-standing predictions of area experts and to contemporary political rhetoric, the Islamic heritage and Turkic and Iranian cultural affinities of Azerbaijan played a relatively negligible role in its post-Soviet transition. What mattered most was the centrality and size of Baku, Azerbaijan's capital, which since the late nineteenth century had harbored a large industrial sector and a vibrant cosmopolitan intelligentsia. After all the debacles of the 1990s, Baku emerges today as the site of a very active political contention that may yet be conducive to the institutionalization of democratic politics. Azerbaijan's smaller towns and countryside, however, remain a great unknown.

Periphery seems a better analytical concept than any "clash of civilizations" model because its relational nature resists the reification of cultural traditions, which has been both a widely held prejudice and a scholarly fallacy. "National" culture is a complex, historically acquired and therefore changeable set of practices. Moreover, culture is a domain that does not exist independently from the fields of power, economic production, and social hierarchy. What modernization theorists used to construe as the cultural traits associated with backwardness, appear in a more materialist perspective as being primarily the function of three factors.

First is the lower degree of the state's penetration into society. Put differently, peripheral states are lacking in what Michael Mann has called "infrastructural power"; conversely, they are in a situation Joel Migdal famously described as "strong societies and weak states."[7] Such states often resort to crude violence against their citizens precisely because they have few better means available. Alternatively, weak states must rely on the complex web of self-serving functionaries, venal office-holders, mercenaries, and local notables. In the absence of effective central supervision, these subordinates would attempt to consume almost all duties and taxes that they collect. As a result, the options of central government are reduced to begging for foreign aid or bank loans, or trying to monopolize the available lucrative exports where the concentrated mineral wealth, such as oil, seems the greatest.

The periphery is a zone where state penetration is superficial, often imposed from abroad, and where state structures thus have little staying power. It is a zone where the control of state office usually hinges more on personal ties than on formal bureaucratic promotion, and such office is construed as primarily a self-serving sinecure. Scholars influenced by Max Weber call this pattern of rule neopatrimonialism, or the familial ownership of public office.[8] Neopatrimonialism, as we saw in the previous chapter, can erode the structures of a modern state and render them brittle. The combination of superimposed modern institutions (formal governments, parliaments, even electoral procedures) and the essentially neopatrimonial pattern of rule makes the peripheral states look dysfunctional. And indeed they are inefficient with regard to the supply of public goods that we normally associate with the modern state: the basic security of the citizenry, their welfare, education, roads, etc. But these states are, nonetheless, quite effective mechanisms for producing wealthy rulers in poor countries.

The second factor is that modern economic enterprise finds states that cannot deliver effective regulation, coordination and protection to be adverse environments. Officials in these states tend to embezzle whatever their budgets allocate for public projects and to regard businesses as prime objects of extortion. The result is that national economies are polarized with, on the one hand, the sectors controlled by big foreign investors and local oligarchs who possess sufficient power to buy-off or restrain the greedy officials; and, on the other hand, the majority of the common populace who are reduced to the precariousness of subsistence, irregular employment and petty trade – or what the Peruvian sociologist Aníbal Quijano generically described as *la economía popular*.[9]

The third set of conditions pertains to the social structure of peripheral "backwardness," and this closes the causal loop. The domestic balance of power is vastly biased against the impoverished dominated classes who can find few resources to mobilize and press their demands on the rulers, oligarchs and provincial notables. The economic structure leaves little space for the formation of middle classes and proletarians who could in theory challenge the existing regimes and lead to their transformation into something popularly accountable, restrained by law, and less predatory. Educated middle classes and fully-formed proletariats do still emerge, because no modern economy can function entirely without such classes, but they remain a minority usually isolated in the globally-connected enclaves that are located in capital cities or specific sectors. Thus these classes cannot realize their potential as agents of orderly political change because they are numerically small, spread thinly over the social hierarchy, limited to their enclaves, vulnerable to repression, or are bought off with incomes considered enviable by the local standards of poverty.

Sub-proletarians are probably the largest class found in the contemporary periphery. They are rapidly replacing peasants as the age-old structures of village life disappear all over the world.[10] The massive presence of a de-ruralized but not yet urbanized sub-proletariat produces an impression of enduring archaic traditions, or anomie and a mob mentality. The peasants and sub-proletarians can on occasion rise in rowdy protests that usually take inspiration from a populist myth of secular or religious variety. But such rebellions rarely result in a constructive transformation of state and society, least of all when they are not conjugated with the political projects of better educated and disciplined groups capable of advancing a political vision. Therefore the citizens of peripheral states either accept being subordinated to rulers who are themselves subordinate players in the world-economy and international politics, or else, left to their own devices, they attempt to emigrate to the core countries, which to many seems the best option.

To summarize, the periphery is the zone where there are too many "corrupt" officials bound by family, ethnic, and other forms of patronage instead of Max Weber's ideal-typical bureaucrats who are bound solely by loyalty to an institution and a rational legal code. Economic activities are polarized between big enterprises that internalize their protection costs, and scattered small units operating at the level of households. There is too great an unstable de-ruralized population made up mainly of unruly sub-proletarians, and there are too few disciplined proletarians and university-educated specialists who favor orderly, long-term contention and tend to institutionalize their collective gains in the structures of political citizenship and modern welfare.

Inevitably, this description is a simplification that sacrifices actual historical complexity for the sake of generalization. Nonetheless, I believe it sets us on the right track in analyzing the consequences of the Soviet collapse. The biggest complicating fact is that during the twentieth century there have existed a great number and variety of developmental states whose efforts were directed at overcoming the condition of socioeconomic backwardness. The Soviet Union was one of the earliest and longest-lasting examples of a developmental state, and up to a point it had been a big success. But today developmental states are things of the past. (Once again, the continuing evolution of communist China presents an extraordinarily big complication, but it seems exceptional.) Back on the agenda is the analysis of backwardness, which calls for a critical re-examination of the concept of periphery.

Despite the risk of committing another gross simplification, I want to claim that today the periphery is not a zone of imperialist domination. Fundamentally, it is an area of various structural weaknesses, and weakness invites misfortunes. Among them may be a vulnerability to foreign economic exploitation, but more commonly there exists a vulnerability to predatory behavior by native elites. The latter may find it in their own interest to pursue strategies conducive to the draining of resources, the erosion of states, and deindustrialization. These elites are neither suicidal nor irrational, at least not if considered individually. Certainly, such people know what political power means in their corner of the world. But collectively, they are poorly articulated as a cohesive, self-reflective dominant class, which is indeed their major weakness. Too many among the peripheral elites possess particularist interests and allegiances, often reaching outside the state's borders. Comprador traders are a good example.

If we wanted to characterize the pure form of such peripheral states in just one word, it might be *irresponsible*. Externally, today's peripheral states are not particularly concerned with their military survival because they are sheltered from the threat of stronger foreign predators. In contrast to the past, since 1945 the right of conquest has been effectively excluded from the code of international behavior. The fact that America and Europe reserve the right to take military action to counter what are described as threats to collective security and human rights, overall serves to ensure the security of weak states that demonstrate a willingness to comply with the norms imposed by the "international community," i.e. the core states.[11]

Internally, contemporary peripheral states can afford to indulge in varying degrees of irresponsibility towards their citizens. Their notorious institutional incapacity is a pretext rather than a cause for their offering very little in the way of public services such as education, health, law enforcement, or roads. The problem is the detached autonomy of peripheral states from their own citizens, who do not matter much either as military recruits (because these states do not fight big wars), or as tax-payers (because these states derive their resources externally from aid, debt, and monopolies on export trade).[12]

Few people might be surprised by the observation that contemporary peripheral states draw their military security and financial resources from outside their boundaries, i.e. that they heavily depend on the political and economic structures of the world-system. But this observation carries huge analytical and political implications. In the 1970s and 1980s some scholars complacently suggested that while states like Mobutu's Zaïre might be grotesquely venal and ruled by pompous despots, so was absolutist France under Louis XIV. These scholars believed that modernization takes time, but that all countries nonetheless should eventually arrive at the modern stage similarly to the evolution of European states. On a practical level, this debate reached a kind of resolution with the tragic fate of Zaïre (nowadays once again called Congo) where the state, after being badly eroded over the decades by Mobutu's pillaging, has altogether collapsed into a myriad of "ethnic" conflicts and marauding warlords.

In the meantime, historical sociologists and political scientists who were inspired by or worked in response to the breakthrough formulations of Perry Anderson, Stein Rokkan and especially Charles Tilly, succeeded in advancing a robust theory of modern state formation in Europe.[13] The new theory singled out two intertwined trends as being chiefly responsible for the evolution of modern states: the continuous warfare that simply weeded out states that had failed to raise standing armies and create extensive bureaucracies; and the growth of taxation that fed the expansion of state armies and bureaucracies. Revolutions in the final account served to rationalize modern states, and democratization emerged as a sustained mechanism for negotiating the extraction of resources from the population in the form of taxes and conscripted soldiers. But if today the states found on the periphery are drawing their military security and financial resources from without, and disregard effective governance from within, then we must conclude that they are not recapitulating in any significant respect the historical trajectories that have shaped the modern West: neither militarily, nor economically, nor politically and institutionally.[14] They are a different species existing in a very different historical environment. To push this biological metaphor further, these states are not developing predators, like their presumed European predecessors; they are rather parasites or scavengers.

No doubt the erstwhile developmental states, especially in their ascending phases, often pursued their economic and political goals at the expense of horrendous cruelties. Yet the collapse of state developmentalism was fraught with different but perhaps no lesser cruelties. The modern state is especially important in those places where capitalism can be expected to be very scant, or too volatile, or subordinated directly to serve foreign interests, or to be downright predatory, or all of the above. States still matter. The key problem is that the current deterioration of the former developmental states in Eastern Europe is not merely an accident. It is the result of two principal struggles waged in the aftermath of Soviet disintegration. One was the *nomenklatura*'s shift to neopatrimonialism as they sought to preserve their privileged positions even if, as in Lampedusa's famous line, everything had to change in order to stay the same.[15] The second was the popular rebellions that, especially when conducted by the sub-proletariat, could sometimes destroy but could hardly ever rebuild states. These theoretical observations should make clear the historical horizon as we now plunge into the chaos created by those struggling for the spoils of the disintegrating Soviet state.

MOSCOW'S DUAL COUNTER-STRATEGY

In the second half of 1989, Moscow responded in two very different ways to the breakdown of its control over Eastern Europe and the republics inside the USSR. Eastern Europe and, eventually, the Baltic republics had to be written off because a return to coercive control there would have jeopardized Russia's own prospects of integration with the West. Hence the permission given for "velvet" transitions after 1989.

But in remoter areas like the Caucasus, Tadjikistan, and Moldova, Moscow opted for covert subversion by making itself a backstage participant in the unfolding conflicts. Moscow's new goal was to inhibit separatism by almost any means, including pretty dirty ones, for which reason it preferred to use various proxies. In large part, it paralleled Belgrade's strategy in the wars of the Yugoslavian succession: the beleaguered central government sponsored coups and separatist rebellions within the secessionist republics.[16] It remains unclear as to what extent Gorbachev sanctioned this strategy, because he made a great deal of effort to distance himself from the dirty tricks and their bloody consequences. But the question will weigh heavily on the judgement of future historians.

In the USSR, the first national republic where the *nomenklatura* fled or defected to the nationalist opposition was Georgia. Owing to its ethnically mixed population and history, Georgia could have faced half a dozen internal separatist rebellions. Not all of them actually emerged. Georgia's borderlands contained several rural districts populated predominantly by ethnic Azeris and, elsewhere, by ethnic Armenians. But these generally impoverished districts did not possess the special status of ethnic autonomy and therefore had few structures that could be utilized as alternative governments in separatist mobilization. Besides, neither Azerbaijan nor Armenia, absorbed in their war over Karabagh, wished to prosecute another war against Georgia. Lacking the internal or external resources for a mobilization, these districts remained quiet.

Separatist rebellions on Georgia's territory flared up only in those borderland areas that did possess autonomous governments and that also received covert aid from Russia. Three such autonomies existed in Soviet Georgia. One was Abkhazia, which we shall look at later in this chapter. Another was South Ossetia, which enjoyed, in addition to Russian aid, the support of co-ethnic North Ossetia, a larger autonomous republic on the Russia-controlled northern slope of the Caucasus ridge. But precisely because there existed a North Ossetia, Georgian nationalists insisted on calling "South Ossetia" something else – "Samachablo," for instance, meaning literally the dynastic domain of the Georgian Machabeli princes; or "Shida [Inner] Kartli," implying that it was a mountainous extension of the medieval Georgian kingdom of Kartli. These explorations in historical geography belong to the category that Pierre Bourdieu called symbolic violence and, as we shall see, symbolic may become actual violence once the guns have been dispersed widely enough and the people begin to feel that arms are their best protection.

The Georgian anticommunist intelligentsia, who in 1989 were on their way to political power, formulated the goal of returning to the "embrace of European Christian civilization," transforming Georgia into an independent liberal nation-state. Virtually all factions of Georgian "civil society" featured in their programs pledges to abolish the ethnic autonomies, which they portrayed as "divide and rule" imperial institutions imposed by the godless Bolsheviks. This message was literally driven to the minorities via motorcades carrying radical Georgian politicians and busloads of their supporters who would visit the autonomous outliers of Georgia to stage their rallies. Such propagandistic caravans pursued three goals. Back in the streets of Tbilisi, these expeditions were accorded the heroic status of a crusade – that is, they generated a symbolic variety of political capital. They also generated political capital directly by engaging the participants in a common cause. They sought to "awaken" the local Georgians who lived inside the autonomies and turn them into political supporters of the new nationalist parties who promised to eliminate Russian and communist bureaucratic controls (a cause popular among farmers engaged in the informal economy) and to elevate the status of their fellow Georgians above that of the "undeserving minorities." Finally, it goes without saying that such expeditions were a show of force intended to prepare the minorities to part with their "Bolshevik entitlements" and accept the unitary Georgian nation-state. By the logic of political polarization during the run-up phase of conflict, the dramatic radicalization of Georgian nationalism equally served to radicalize the politics of minority groups. Wherever possible they now sought internal political unity and outside protection against the threat of Georgian national independence.

HEROIC SULTANISM IN ADJARIA

Besides Abkhazia and South Ossetia, there existed in Georgia a third autonomous region, called Adjaria. It was the only autonomy of its kind in the USSR, because it had no titular nationality, that is, officially there were no "Adjarians" in Adjaria. We have briefly encountered this name when discussing why in 1921 the Bolsheviks decided to attach Karabagh to Azerbaijan: they were afraid of losing its oil terminals in Batumi. The population of Adjaria could be considered Georgian in every respect – linguistically, culturally, and historically – except that Adjaria had for centuries been an Ottoman province and its population had converted to Islam. From the standpoint of Georgian nationalism, whose symbolic foundations lay in the legends of a Christian resistance to barbaric Muslim invaders, the special status of Adjaria was an abomination. Likewise the Greek or Serbian nationalists could not concede that a part of what they would have otherwise considered their people could have betrayed Christianity and joined the Turks. As the history of modern Greece or the recent bloodshed in Bosnia can attest, such perceived incongruities between nationality and religion can have very nasty outcomes.

Back in 1921 the Bolsheviks granted autonomy to Adjaria in a concession intended to placate Turkey and the Muslim natives of Adjaria. But after seventy years of Soviet experience, the descendants of Adjaria's Muslims had become over-whelmingly secular and thus came to identify with the Georgian nation rather than the Turks. The "Adjarians," however, were detectable because many still preserved the Muslim first names that had been passed down through the generations. The powerful revival of Georgian nationalism put them in a very ambiguous position. In 1989, Zviad Gamsakhurdia went to Batumi with a huge escort of ecstatic supporters where, speaking at the local stadium, he urged: *Adjarians, remember that you are Georgians!* This awkward reminder troubled many "Adjarians," who concluded that they were not, after all, regarded as true Georgians.

Nationalist discourse aside, the apprehensions of Adjaria's traditionally Muslim natives received material confirmation when Zviad Gamsakhurdia, already acting as president-elect of Georgia, appointed new prefects and other officials to Adjaria. The new rulers were drawn mostly from among bohemian intellectuals (their leader, a painter, had served two years in a Soviet prison for what he described as dissi-dence but the locals remembered as a restaurant brawl) and *nomenklatura* defectors to radical nationalism. Moreover, they were predominantly Christians from Georgia proper with few social ties locally. Immediately upon arrival, the new government set out to divide the spoils, awarding their friends and clients the most lucrative positions at the seaport, customs, licensing agencies, tourist hotels, and restaurants. (Most of the time, the new nationalist leaders held court at their favorite seaside restaurant rather than in government offices.) The resistance of the old officials was overcome by violence – the communist governor of Adjaria was dragged out of his car and savagely beaten by "unknown" assailants. The same young Georgian nationalists soon acquired guns and declared themselves a "National Guard."

In terms of identity construction, Adjaria presents a curious case. Its natives, desperate for protection, grabbed whatever ideological symbols they could find that suggested an opposition to Georgian nationalism. But what could such symbols be for a barely defined, sub-ethnic group that discovered a common interest in defending their small province from rapacious and arrogant outsiders? First they clung to the official Soviet ideology of Marxist-Leninist internationalism. Long after the virtual self-destruction of the Georgian Communist Party, communist candi-dates still prevailed over the nationalists in the first democratic elections in Adjaria. But since the communist alternative to nationalism appeared to be a lost cause, there began to emerge a revived and politicized Islam. Strange spectacles were witnessed as bearded old villagers appeared at rallies in Batumi to pray under red banners as factory brass bands played Soviet anthems, just like at May Day celebrations. Under the circumstances, communism and Islam had really just one thing in common –

they were both anathema to Georgian nationalists.

Adjaria seemed to be moving rapidly towards becoming another Bosnia. But the descent into violent conflict was suddenly stopped by what local legend now regards as a bullet sent by God, and which we shall call historical contingency. In what was described as a spontaneous gunfight during a heated cabinet discussion, the newly appointed leader of the Georgian nationalist government in Adjaria was shot dead by his local deputy, Aslan Abashidze. (Another bullet, claims the legend, passed so close to Aslan's neck that the skin over his jugular vein was burnt, but Allah saved the local hero.) Previously Abashidze had been a Komsomol apparatchik and school principal. More recently he had served as Deputy Minister of Urban Services, overseeing barbers, cobblers, and plumbers. Admittedly this was not a prominent bureaucratic post, but it was certainly a lucrative one. Abashidze had no qualms about admitting that he was "not exactly poor."[17] He also happened to be the grandson of Memed Abashidze, a respected Adjarian Muslim aristocrat (*bek*) who had been a leading socialist-federalist politician from 1917 to 1921, and later in Soviet times a devoted educator of his people. Memed-bek had been executed on Stalin's orders in 1936.[18]

Enlightened local patriotism and the art of political maneuvering evidently ran strong in Abashidze's family. Upon coming to power, *batono* (Sir) Aslan managed to abort the investigation of the shooting and muffle the reaction of nationalists. He bought off several local nationalists and gave politically modest but comfortable positions to the former communist leaders in Batumi. The Islamic elders were ceremoniously escorted back to their villages, and money was generously donated for the restoration of both the mosques and various Christian churches in Adjaria (Georgian, Armenian, Russian, Greek, and even Polish). Moreover, in pursuing his policy of paternalistic consensus, Abashidze never tired of insisting that Adjaria would never secede and must remain an unalienable part of Georgia. However, under Abashidze Adjaria rarely contributed taxes to the central budget and it built up a formidable militia, which was prudently called a police and customs corps rather than an army. When in 1992 Georgian nationalist paramilitaries attempted to invade Adjaria, they were met at the border river by a compelling display of Adjaria's "police" supported by heavy armor and artillery lent by the commanders of the Russian garrisons near Batumi. (On every 8th March, the International Socialist Women's Day, Aslan Abashidze respectfully sends fruit baskets and flowers to the wives of all the Russian officers stationed in Adjaria.) This explains everything – Aslan Abashidze, a benevolent sultanistic ruler, had successfully prevented the transformation of Adjaria into another Bosnia by astutely turning it into a Russian military protectorate.[19] In May 2004 Abashidze was forced to flee to Russia by a combination of threats from Georgia's new youthful and energetic president Mikhail Saakashvili, and the internal rebellion in Adjara where apparently many people became fed up with the comprehensive monopoly held by Abashidze's family on all appointments and lucrative opportunities.

A chance glimpse I got of the inside of Abashidze's garage provided evidence (namely, his son's Porsche and an assortment of armored Mercedeses) of his new wealth. His grandchildren were studying at English boarding schools. The patronage network of Adjaria, reconsolidated by Abashidze, seemed to be doing just as well, mainly through its profits from the border trade with Turkey. Criminality is very low now because in the new era one in ten men join the police (a major source of patronage and employment), and the professional thieves, so legend has it, left the country after a frank conversation with Abashidze. In short, it is a small example of an Uzbekistan-like pattern of authoritarian order. Adjaria's economy, however, has suffered the same dislocations that troubled all of Transcaucasia. There are very few jobs outside Abashidze's police and state apparatus; the oil stopped flowing to Batumi long ago; factories once connected by production processes to their counterparts all over the former Soviet republics have not been operational for years; the tourist hotels are permanently occupied by Georgian refugees from Abkhazia; cows roam the boulevards and beaches; and crops of tangerines and tea can be taken outside of Adjaria only with great difficulty. According to an unconfirmed local rumor, an American businessman, who was claiming to be Hillary Clinton's brother, tried to organize the export of nuts – the most lucrative produce left in Adjaria – but for some reason it did not work out. At one of the obligatory banquets I attended, a local notable rose to say that his dream was to see the train from Batumi to Moscow run again, and the man who made it happen should receive a golden statue at the railway station square! But so far, only thick grass and saplings cover the rail tracks, since the war in Abkhazia cut the connection to Russia. But in Adjaria, all is forgiven Aslan Abashidze as long as his small bailiwick is spared the fate of Abkhazia.

THE MOUNTAIN CONFEDERATION

We now turn to the analysis of less happy patterns of state breakdown in Abkhazia.[20] Before the Soviet disintegration, this small territory on the coast of the Black Sea profited from its exceptionally lucrative shadow market. After all, precious few subtropical resorts or tangerine plantations existed in the USSR. For decades, the control of these profit sources had been the object of Georgian–Abkhaz rivalries at all levels, from local government down to gangsters and individual farmers.

The situation resembled Szelényi's "socialist entrepreneurs" operating in an institutional setting where the Soviet era entrepreneurial opportunities depended on ethnic networks.[21]

An Abkhaz farmer felt more confident in dealing with an Abkhaz official or policeman not simply because they shared a common culture and language, but primarily because they shared strong ties of ethnic kinship that allowed a farmer to put more social pressure on the individual state officials and policemen in order to counter their official duties, such as the forced acquisition of tangerine crops at state prices. In short, Abkhazes could reach a deal more easily – and usually at the expense of state interests – because among this small nationality virtually everybody was each other's relative, neighbor, or friend.[22]

Interviews with old residents provide compelling evidence that the actual situation in the Caucasus, especially in the countryside, differed from the picture of uniform communist governance painted by official reports and no less by mainstream Western Sovietologists. In Abkhazia, ever since de-Stalinization in the mid-1950s, collective farms had tolerated their workers cultivating large family-controlled groves in exchange for their delivering a share of their fruit crop which would allow the local officials to fulfill centrally imposed plan quotas. The collective farm workers could then sell what remained of the crop at the markets of big towns in Russia. The monopolistic profits, accumulated from the 1960s through to the 1980s, are visible in the splendid two-story mansions that predominate in the Abkhazian villages.

Save for moments of forceful intervention, Moscow's rule was normally mediated by overlapping patronage networks within the administrations of republics, towns, and districts. Everywhere in the Caucasus, government appointments were subject to Soviet affirmative action, which had a direct effect on the subtle multilevel negotiations that took place regarding the relative proportions of trade in the official and the smuggling economy. The fusion of local state and economy, both in the official and unofficial sectors, created plenty of occasions for conflicts that were essentially economic yet inevitably also "nationally relevant."[23]

Abkhaz–Georgian rivalries recurrently burst into the open during periods of political transition in Russia and the USSR: in the Civil War in 1918–1921; in the collectivization and purges of 1936–1939; during de-Stalinization in 1956; in the socialist democratization movement of 1967; during the Brezhnev-era dissidence of 1977–1978; and during perestroika in 1989.[24] In other words, for generation after generation the structural tension engendered by the patterns of land tenure, shadow markets, and Soviet nationality policy in the distribution of state offices have reproduced the Abkhaz–Georgian clashes at every historical juncture. Thus the new clashes were well-rehearsed and their escalation into a separatist war in 1992 looked automatic and even perfectly "natural."

The Abkhazes numbered less than a hundred thousand against more than four million Georgians. This included a quarter of a million ethnic Georgians inside Abkhazia, some of whom were treated as locals. In some villages the populations were mixed to the extent that everybody possessed a native fluency in both the Georgian and Abkhaz languages (as well as Russian, the lingua franca), and inter-marriages were fairly common. In such villages people often felt puzzled when asked about their nationality.

But there were also quite a lot of ethnic Georgians who had been moved to Abkhazia between 1938 and 1952, ostensibly under the agrarian development plan of the Soviet Georgian authorities. In fact, as the pattern of new settlements clearly reveals, they were relocated to fill Abkhazia with a population that would feel more loyal to Georgia. This might be explained by the fact that Beria and Stalin, after all, were both Georgians. Most of the time their loyalty was to themselves and Soviet power, as they understood it. But as to the Georgian issues of national faith, Stalin and Beria could behave as true nationalists, though we need not speculate here whether their motives were affectionate or manipulative. Perhaps nowhere was this fact more apparent than in their treatment of Abkhazia, which in Georgian national legend was regarded as the cradle of medieval Georgian statehood and culture, a bit like the Serbian image of Kosovo.

On their side, the Abkhazes remembered that the resettlement of Georgian collective farmers in Abkhazia began after their beloved Bolshevik leader Nestor Lakoba mysteriously died in 1936, shortly after having dinner with Lavrenty Beria – Georgia's leader at the time and later the head of the Soviet secret police. Like many Caucasian Bolsheviks, Lakoba started out as an honorable bandit persecuted by the tsarist police, and his friendship with Stalin dated to the times they had spent in the revolutionary underground. While Lakoba was the Bolshevik leader of Abkhazia, the Abkhazes were spared collectivization because he could plead with Stalin to deal gradually with particularly backward nationalities. But after 1936 collec-tivization struck with a vengeance, and with it came the landless peasants from central and western Georgia, whom the Georgian authorities settled separately in newly built villages. After 1989, these settlements would become the focal point of nationalist mobilizations and violence. The agrarian problems and state policies were reflected in popular memory as generalized ethnic hostility: *The Georgians came here to take our land.*

After 1989 the prospect of competitive elections and market reform appeared as a direct threat to the Abkhazes. Their predicament and their united response to the rise of Georgian nationalism were structurally similar to Balkar separatism. The Abkhazian separatists, however, enjoyed Moscow's covert support. Besides, the economic stakes of the post-Soviet transition were much higher in Abkhazia. The logic of a social power structure built on bureaucratic patronage along ethnic lines clearly suggested (to paraphrase the famous Westphalian principle): *Whose the administration, theirs the privatization*. Translated from the Latinized legalese, this principle meant that the vastly outnumbered Abkhazes stood no chance against the Georgians in the coming competitive elections, and thus could expect to lose their power over state appointments in Abkhazia. This prospect meant furthermore that, in the looming privatization and the capitalist economy that would follow, the Abkhazes were also going to lose control over their citrus groves and resorts. Proof of this came in June–July 1989 when, while Gorbachev's First Congress of People's Deputies was in session in Moscow, the Abkhazes and Georgians rioted in Abkhazia's capital of Suhum (or Sukhumi) where, incidentally, the ethnic Abkhazes represented just 7 per cent of the urban population. Among the immediate causes of the trouble were disputes over admissions to the local university – where the Abkhazes, as titular nationality, enjoyed disproportionate representation – and such symbolic things as the use of different alphabets and place names on road signs (which were regularly vandalized by one side or another). For example, the final "i" in words like *Suhumi* made them sound Georgian, therefore the Abkhaz nationalists demanded that their capital be called *Suhum*. Moscow reacted by sending police reinforcements but, fearing further violence, instructed them to do little more than stand between the opposing groups, in the manner of UN peacekeepers.

In the hot August of 1989, Musa Shanib and other national activists from across the North Caucasus, including the young Chechen poet Zelimkhan Yandarbiyev, were invited to Suhumi/Suhum for the founding congress of a new pan-ethnic alliance. This meeting was sponsored by the Abkhaz officials, who paid all the expenses. The Abkhaz language represents a distinct branch in the Circassian linguistic sub-family. The ethnic kinship of Abkhazes and the indigenous peoples from the northern slopes of the Caucasus such as Kabardins, Adygheis, and, still more distantly, the Chechens, was not a popularly accepted fact until quite recently because the languages were as distinct as English and Swedish or Russian, and because the mountain geography and the patterns of traditional social organization, focused on clans and small villages, had long prevented close contacts among these peoples. Only in modern times was the connection identified by the linguists and anthropologists who studied the Caucasus, and only in the 1960s did this fact enter the local textbooks. Since then, however, the broad commonality of language, culture and history has been celebrated at various scholarly gatherings and artistic festivals that brought together the Abkhazes and the North Caucasians. These gatherings had mainly served to demonstrate that in combination these nationalities were not that small. But now the celebrations of a common cultural and ethnic identity moved to embrace the politics of pan-nationalist solidarity. The goal was to bolster the claims of the Abkhaz separatists against Georgia with the political construction of a surrogate co-ethnic mainland in the North Caucasus, and thus pointedly outside Georgia.[25] On their side, the national activists from the North Caucasus found a rallying point in Abkhazia and were able to benefit from the resources provided by Abkhaz officials.

Shanib proposed calling the new political alliance the *Assembly of the Mountain Peoples of the Caucasus* (Assembly became Confederation in 1991). The word "Mountain" neatly excluded the valley-dwelling Georgians while putting the Abkhazes in the same category as highlanders like the Chechens and Kabardins. (Strictly speaking, several distinct minorities among the Georgians were traditionally highlanders, while the majority of Kabardins and Chechens actually lived in the more fertile valleys and foothills, but this complication was left unnoticed.) By virtue of his having named the alliance and his seniority, Musa Shanib was elected the Confederation's first president. The political project looked grandiose – the union of the native peoples from Daghestan, Chechnya, and Kabardino-Balkaria to Abkhazia on the Black Sea. The ghosts of Imam Shamil's rebel state of 1834–1859 and the short-lived Mountain Republic of 1918 were to obtain another chance in history.

When the Georgian police tried to disband the confederation's meeting, a team of athletic and unmistakably Slavic men, dressed in oddly identical suits, emerged from a back room. Shanibov does not feel too shy about this kind of support: *Whether the KGB or the military Spetsnaz, they were a real help, and as long as our goals coincided it would have been prudish and downright stupid not to use it.* In contrast to the many conspiracy theorists that imagine intricate plans seamlessly executed, we ought to recognize that these contemporary intrigues were much more chaotic and contingent. To begin with, it was not clear during this period who was in control in Moscow, where a number of claimants to state authority had emerged. The politics of the time became a rather disjointed game, in which sides pursuing quite different goals thought that they were shrewdly exploiting each other.[26]

Admittedly, in this whole affair Shanib was a bit of an imposter. He had come to Abkhazia to represent the Kabardin people, though at the time he was simply a notorious democratic intellectual back at home. He returned to Kabardino-Balkaria wearing a *papaha* hat that symbolized his position as the president of a mysterious pan-national confederation that, in reality, was no more than a freshly created club of oppositional backbenchers. But then much of the politics and emerging business deals of the time were also really just novel improvisations bordering on bluff.

The glasnost-era press helped enormously in spreading the sensational news about the Confederation and Shanib's eloquent and occasionally bombastic pronouncements regarding the creation of a "peaceful common Caucasian Home." However fraudulent this attempt to create symbolic capital might seem now, at the time it did not look exceptional: in many instances writers and junior academics were indeed becoming heads of state. The reputation and resources Shanib derived from Abkhazia enabled him to create the organizational nucleus of the Kabardin National Congress, construed as the local chapter of the Mountain Confederation, but which consisted largely of the usual network of his friends, colleagues, and former student activists. Since several among these men had won good positions, they could use their offices as a resource for further nationalist mobilization: university professors and students were the activists; journalists reported on the events involving Shanib and debated the program of national democratization; and managers could provide buses to take the participants to rallies. In the words of one of them, *We had finally found a language understandable by less-educated people.* The events in neighboring Georgia and the East European revolutions dramatically changed perceptions of what was possible. Indeed nationalism was no longer a taboo; it was the only game in town.

In 1990 two new conditions suddenly propelled Shanib to the forefront of Kabardin nationalist politics: the perceived threat of Balkar secession, which provoked the united counter-mobilization of the Kabardins, and the next round of elections, which were now to be held for seats in the parliaments of the republics. Just as happened previously in the republics of Transcaucasia, nationalist ideology in the North Caucasus now subsumed and sidelined all other issues such as democratization, economic reform, education, or ecology. Nationalist organizations sprang up all over the region, and soon began to split into competing factions. Though at first ephemeral, these organizations were soon gaining resources and militant recruits from the wavering elements of the *nomenklatura* and, on the opposite side, from young sub-proletarians entering the political contention.

THE DEALS OF ETHNIC POLITICS

After 1989 even some of the most cautious and conservative men among the territorial *nomenklatura* in the Soviet republics began to sponsor in various indirect ways the creation of national movements. Their goal was to deflect oppositional pressure and channel it into vertical bargaining with the patrons in Moscow. This tactic developed directly from the Brezhnev-era corporativist bargaining for centrally allocated resources. Adding a new twist, the officials in Soviet republics now claimed that they urgently needed more power and goods from the center in order to contain the nationalist radical fringe. But as Moscow continued to lose strength and local bureaucratic or market-based rivalries became openly expressed, the focus of contention shifted to lateral competition with neighboring ethnic groups. In contrast to the vertically polarizing politics of democratization that opposed the "people" or "civil society" from below to the communist ruling elite from above, the new lines of political alliance crossed class boundaries as the nationally defined fractions of the *nomenklatura* sought to present themselves as defenders of their respective regions and nationalities.

In the meantime, from the marginal spaces of the state socialist hierarchy there emerged a powerful sub-proletarian militancy. The prospect of gaining new kinds of social, symbolic, and economic capital motivated sub-proletarians to engage in nationalist activism. The toughness and cultural "backwardness" of those in this class, who primarily spoke native languages and often came from traditionally religious families, was suddenly to their advantage in the new kind of nationalist mobilization. As we saw in Armenia, yesterday's school dropouts were tomorrow's fighters for the nation. Meanwhile, a successful smuggler, racketeer or a corrupt petty official could transform his gang and clientele into an ethnic militia and support an eloquent professor like Shanib, who promised to become state president. The violent entrepreneurs, chasing the new opportunities created by the weakening of the state and the chaotic transition to the market, readily saw their profit in forging alliances across class and status divides that a few months earlier would have seemed unthinkable.[27]

For their part, the national intellectual politicians who were in the ascendant in 1990–1991 sought alliances with the local *nomenklatura* and sub-proletarian entrepreneurs because they needed access to their client networks. Clearly, this offered a more effective means of securing new political capital than the abstract and now discredited liberal rhetoric of Moscow's intelligentsia. The new provincial legislators rewarded their sponsors and allies by issuing various legal privileges related to privatization. This new practice created a whole set of acute conflicts and prompted clashes over executive implementation. Who gets to own a private shop or gas station? Who can obtain the license to export oil or non-ferrous metals bought at the domestic Soviet prices of the planned economy and sold for dollars at world market prices? Moreover, who gets the right to issue the privatization and export licenses: the old appointed government or the new elected parliament – and is that in Moscow alone or also in the republics? Or perhaps, there would appear some totally novel "National Congress" whose licenses would also grant special rights.

The repertoire of political action soon included ballot forgery, smear campaigns, assassinations, and mob violence. Networks of local solidarity and patronage were activated by spreading rumors, sending messengers from house to house, calling on elders playing backgammon in front of the mosque, providing transportation to the sites of protests downtown, and distributing food and petty cash to the participants, etc.[28]

Shanib was not allowed to run for a seat in the local parliament in 1990. Instead he proclaimed the oppositional Confederation and its local chapters to be the only true representative of the North Caucasus nations. This claim did not seem very credible because the real power clearly remained in the hands of the local *nomenklatura*. This situation suddenly changed in the last week of August 1991. The failure of the reactionary putsch in Moscow, which was intended to restore the USSR by the means of repression, instead precipitated its dissolution. With their communist patrons in Moscow suddenly gone and Yeltsin's oppositional bloc appearing triumphant, the conservative rulers in the North Caucasus suffered a terrible loss of confidence. A leading local democrat (and former archeologist) only slightly exaggerates: *If, in those days, we had rolled a guillotine into the town square, the* nomenklatura *would have obediently lined up for execution.*

But instead of revolutionary terror, what ensued was a political spectacle worthy of Kafka. Indignant activists of the Kabardin movement set up camp in the square in front of the government building and declared a hunger strike in protest against the reactionary coup in Moscow and its local supporters. They did not know that the government of Kabardino-Balkaria had already fled in panic. It was some time before the intrepid youths entered the building and found only bewildered police guards and a few clerks dutifully reporting to work. The astonishing news, however, failed to change the minds of the hunger strikers. The organizers of the protest insisted on following democratic procedure, although they could not say exactly what that might mean under the circumstances.

The simplest explanation, suggested by participants and observers, is that nobody expected the fall of communist power to be so sudden and that the opposition was caught morally and organizationally unprepared to seize power. This might be true. There is, however, one consideration that complicates this explanation. It brings us back to the discussion of why the attempted democratic opposition to Gorbachev at the 1989 Congress of People's Deputies had failed to elicit a strong show of support from outside Moscow. Two years later, in 1991, the nuclei of local democrats, like Shanib's network of friends, colleagues and students, had matured into a variety of political movements. These revolutionary forces, however, still remained uncoordinated, divided between various provinces of Russia, and lacking a clear vision of their political goals and strategy. By default, the activists in the provinces put their hopes in Yeltsin's government of the Russian Federation and political patrons from the ascendant opposition in the Russian transitional parliament elected in 1990. But Yeltsin himself vanished from sight for almost two months shortly after the August coup attempt. Observers speculated that the Russian President must have been deep in his cups after the nervous pressures of the coup – though that remains speculation. What is clear, however, is that Yeltsin and his advisors were themselves at a loss when trying to determine the political course that would lead them away from chaos. Only later, in November 1991, did Yeltsin resolve to push for the dissolution of the USSR and the introduction of neoliberal shock therapy in Russia in a desperate attempt to catch up with Poland and other former communist countries of Central Europe en route to joining the capitalist West.

Autumn 1991 was truly a frightening period. Severe economic shortages were threatening the country with starvation during the coming winter. The Soviet army was immobilized and in danger of disintegrating. Its weapons and former soldiers fuelled ethnic conflicts in places like Karabagh, which were now escalating into genuine wars with artillery barrages, tank raids, and trenches. The reluctantly victorious revolutionary alliance that had gathered around the charismatic figure of Yeltsin in Moscow was engaged in a series of political improvisations that were to a large degree vacuously democratic declarations (laws, decrees, grandiose promises unsupported by action or resources), and in part ad hoc experiments in devising new institutions and making political appointments intended to preserve some kind of governance in the country. Because the burden of dealing with chaos was suddenly theirs, the new Moscow felt very ambivalent when considering requests for support coming from provincial democrats – in Moscow, they often did not know who these people were or what the situation really was in their provinces. Instead, Yeltsin's new Center responded with vague calls to maintain constitutional order. An important voice in this rather dissonant chorus was that of the Speaker of the Russian Parliament, Ruslan Khasbulatov, a professor of economics and an ethnic Chechen to whom the appeals from the North Caucasus were directed almost automatically. It was Khasbulatov's mantra that the constitution must be observed.

The protestors in Nalchik finally resolved to write to the former communist government asking it to stay in office until free and democratic elections could be held, and to Moscow, asking it to ensure the fairness of the coming elections in Kabardino-Balkaria. It took the messengers a whole day to find the former communist government, whose key figures were finally located in a village bearing the official name of "Kyzburun Number 3."

The government returned, the Supreme Soviet reconvened to schedule elections for January 1992, and thus passed the first revolutionary situation in Kabardino-Balkaria. Four candidates competed in the elections for the newly created presidency. The Balkars boycotted the elections because only Kabardins were running. The intellectual from the democratic opposition did not get through to the second round because even to his supporters the elderly professor of philology looked unconvincing as a prospective ruler for such stormy times. The internal attempts to replace the failing candidate with a more energetic oppositionist also failed due to acute factionalism. Within the revolutionary bloc the liberal professors competed against each other; the intellectuals collectively opposed the uneducated outsiders whom they accused of populism; and everybody suspected the maverick defectors from the *nomenklatura* of harboring dictatorial ambitions.

In the final count the presidency went to Valeri Kokov, a former communist boss, temporarily the speaker of the local parliament, and a seasoned cadre from the old *nomenklatura* network that had dominated in Kabardino-Balkaria since the late 1950s. During the intervening four months, Kokov had mobilized almost the whole *nomenklatura*, or rather they lined themselves up behind Kokov as the figure who promised to restore order in a desperately chaotic situation. This was a typical pattern across much of the former USSR, as for instance in Uzbekistan. After a moment of uncertainty and great fear, the former *nomenklatura* realized that their survival no longer depended entirely on Moscow and began to act independently.

Usually they were successful. In Kabardino-Balkaria, however, Kokov's regime would still have to weather a second and much stronger revolutionary tumult several months after the first.

Among the autonomous republics of the Russian Federation, only in Chechnya (which in mid-1991 was still the twin republic of Checheno-Ingushetia) was Moscow's implosion in August 1991 followed by a successful revolution. The communist-era establishment in Grozny was overthrown entirely and, in one instance, an influential figure was literally defenestrated. The possibility of a revolutionary outcome in Chechnya arose from the peculiar composition and proportions of its social and demographic structure and from Chechnya's recent history to which we must now turn. The pattern of Chechen revolution provides us with an analytical contrast to the events that shook Kabardino-Balkaria and Abkhazia later in 1992.

THE PRESSURE-COOKER OF CHECHNYA'S DEMOGRAPHY AND SOCIAL STRUCTURE

When in 1957 the Chechens were allowed to return from exile, locally they remained under the stigma of a "disloyal nationality" and in private they were still being accused of treasonous collaboration with the Nazis. In reality, this served as a pretext for urban racism. In the 1945–1956 period, while the Chechens were away, the post-war reconstruction of the oil industry had attracted skilled Russian workers and specialists to the city of Grozny. They subsequently established a de facto settler monopoly on all spheres of town life.

No ethnic Chechen cadre was ever promoted to a top position in the Checheno-Ingushetia ASSR until 1989. The village mosques had been destroyed after the deportation of 1944 and were not allowed to be rebuilt in the 1960s and 1970s despite the fact that in neighboring Daghestan nearly a hundred mosques operated. This policy served to drive the Chechen and Ingush Islam underground, into the tightly-knit mystical fraternities of the Sufis, which only strengthened the religious tradition instead of eradicating it. To add insult to injury, in one of Grozny's squares stood a statue of Viceroy Yermolov who had founded the town in 1818 as a colonial fortress, in Yermolov's own words, to "lock the Chechen beasts in their wilderness until they starve and come to beg for our order and civilization" – and which the progressive Russian poet Alexander Griboyedov enthusiastically called "the drumbeat Enlightenment" (*barabannoe prosveshchenie*).[29] In 1982 the predominantly settler Russian government of Checheno-Ingushetia held the celebrations of the bicentennial of Chechnya's "voluntary joining of Russia" which even by the contemporary Brezhnevist standards looked scandalously hypocritical and pompous. These and other violations of Leninist nationality policies and Soviet affirmative action were cited repeatedly by the sincere communists among the Chechens and Ingushes who had been writing letters to the Central Committee in Moscow. But after the arrival of Brezhnevism Moscow rarely bothered to intervene in the local affairs of patronage.

The situation in Soviet Checheno-Ingushetia thus stood apart from the rest of the Caucasus and in some ways rather resembled Algeria under French rule. A large modern town populated mostly by the European settlers dominated the countryside populated by the traditionally Muslim natives. In the 1980s the Chechens comprised only 17 per cent of Grozny's population, but comprised a majority of 54 per cent in the republic as a whole. Many Chechens found themselves driven into a semi-proletarian existence on the outskirts of Grozny and in the sprawling villages. In contrast to the industrial cities, in such locations the state provision of employment, housing, and welfare benefits remained minimal – which only served to perpetuate among the Chechens a widespread distrust of the state after the deportation. This also helps to explain the large size of Chechen families, typically consisting of three or more generations, and the inordinately high fertility rate of the lower-class Chechens. In my interviews it came out clearly that besides the demographic strategy of pulling together resources, which is common in peasant and sub-proletarian households, at the level of cultural subjectivity the larger Chechen families sought to recover the human losses of deportation. Bearing more children was proudly regarded as a patriotic obligation. Despite the deaths of probably a third of the 244,000 people that made up the entire Chechen population at the time of the 1944 deportation, by 1989 the Chechens numbered nearly one million people, which made them by far the biggest native nationality in the North Caucasus (Kabardins, the second largest nationality in the region, numbered half as many as the Chechens).

Additionally, two demographic facts should be taken into account. The Chechens comprised more than half of the population of Soviet Checheno-Ingushetia and thus were the only titular nationality in the North Caucasus that formed a majority in their republic. This provided the Chechens with the confident belief that Chechnya should belong to them. Second, the high birth rates in the three decades after the exile ensured that the Chechens remained a predominantly young population, in contrast to the rapidly ageing Russians and also, to some extent, the Kabardins.[30] When in the 1990s it came to popular mobilization and war, many young Chechens were available for recruitment. Furthermore, many among these men of fighting age were poorly educated and jobless.

The expansive demographic dynamic is directly related to the high structural unemployment in Soviet Checheno-Ingushetia. When the Chechens and Ingushes returned from exile, there were twice as many of them as there were jobs available in the republic (even including the least desirable employment on collective and state farms). Structural unemployment continued and actually got worse towards the end of Soviet period because the industrial growth had been slowing down. In the mid-1980s, according to official estimates, 40 per cent of the rural labor force received wages below subsistence level, while close to 60 per cent of adult women had no formal employment at all.[31] By the official statistics of socio-economic development, Checheno-Ingushetia ranked in last place among all the republics and national autonomies of the USSR. Unofficially, however, the situation on the ground looked somewhat different. The Chechen villages boasted many brick houses with modern amenities and furniture, colour TVs, expensive Oriental rugs, and privately owned cars. Much of this family wealth was hard-earned in labor migrations and the smuggling economy, in part because the colder climate did not permit the Chechens to rely on the lucrative household agriculture that in the 1960s had become the basis of popular prosperity in the southern Caucasus.

Each year an estimated forty thousand males left Checheno-Ingushetia in unofficial labor migrations, traveling as far as Kazakhstan and Siberia (where many had preserved contacts since the time of their exile). Typically they found temporary jobs in construction, mining, and agriculture. This created the social mechanisms of recurrent chain migration that directed the lower-educated Chechens and Ingushes towards specific economic sectors and geographic locations where they formed fluid expatriate communities. In addition, many young Chechens graduating from school sought higher education elsewhere in the Soviet Union rather than facing the local settler racism and usual corruption in the entrance examinations at the universities of Grozny. Many of them succeeded and came to occupy prominent positions outside their homeland. Examples are Dr. Salambek Hadjiyev, the last USSR Minister of Oil and Chechnya's ill-fated Premier during the Russian occupation in 1995; Ruslan Khasbulatov, professor of economics in Moscow and Speaker of Russia's transitional parliament from 1991 to 1993; and the Air Force General Dudayev. Usually such prominent personalities were revered as role models or well-placed patrons back at home, and thus potentially exercised a significant political influence on local affairs.

The labor migrations from Chechnya followed an age-old tradition. The high-landers of all mountain countries, always constrained by the poverty of their natural environment, had been compelled to seek additional incomes either as seasonal agricultural workers (shepherds, harvesters) or as guards, military mercenaries and traditional bandits like cattle-rustlers. When the patterns of migration could be regularized, many migrants developed dual households, living part-time among the compatriot migrant men (and sometimes consorting with the local women) but invariably also trying to preserve a traditional family, or at least a cemetery spot, back in their ancestral village. The labor migrations engendered a special sub-culture whose norms and rituals chiefly pertained to the internal organization of migratory teams. The teams usually gathered around a seasoned man who was invested with quasi-parental authority and responsibilities. The members of the team formed the male peer group, essentially a fraternity, sometimes with internal ranks based on seniority or the recognition of individual merits. The traditional bonds of clan kinship, village community, and religious congregation provided an added strength to the internal discipline and cohesiveness of such teams. Yet otherwise the factors of cohesiveness could be obtained in surrogate paternity, peer friendship, and the ethnic solidarity of rural men temporarily finding themselves in a culturally alien environment and working together towards shared goals.

What matters for our focus on the Chechen revolution and war is that such labor teams provided a modular and transposable pattern of micro-organization which in a changed situation could be put to quite different purposes, such as forming a chapter of a nationalist movement or a guerrilla band. In my field observations, the best-organized fighting units in the recent Caucasus wars were found not only in Chechnya but also in Mountainous Karabagh, whose Armenian population, although Christian, shared with the Chechens a similar pattern of labor migration and the profound faith that they were fighting to save their nation from a repeated genocide. Needless to say, like virtually all Soviet male adults, the Chechen and Armenian fighters possessed the requisite technical competence for battle having been previously subjected to the Soviet army draft. It would be useful to investigate how much of a role labor migrations and military service might also have played in the wars of Yugoslavian succession.

Along these lines we might also build a rational explanation for the extraordinary success of the Chechen mafia in the late 1980s and the 1990s, during the marketization of Russia. In terms of their socio-demographic composition and cultural background, the Chechen and other southern ethnic mafias in the new Russia do not look very different from those groups involved in ordinary labor migrations. They are mostly made up of young, poorly educated, and jobless Chechen men who, individually or in small tightly knit groups, went far from their native villages looking for employment or higher education. Some village lads, like Beslan Gantmirov or Shamil Basayev, proved ill prepared for the university and flunked out. Or they could not find the desired jobs because the construction industry and agriculture, which were the traditional Chechen occupations for previous generations, had grown highly competitive with the massive influx of newly impoverished migrant workers from republics such as the Ukraine and Moldova. Instead of sinking into penury or returning home as miserable failures, these Chechen youths found or fought their way into the dangerous but fabulously lucrative and romanticized arena of violent entrepreneurship. The traditions of clan solidarity, Chechen masculinity, and ritualized violence surely played a big role in enabling them to do this, providing a ready set of skills that were advantageous in the criminal underworld.[32] Yet it would require a lot of detailed research to discover what mechanisms transported traditional social institutions into the marketplaces of postcommunist Russia. The Chechen national character continues to captivate the imaginations of Russian and Western journalists and not a few scholars. But these superficial ethnic accounts overlook the fact that Chechnya is no longer a mountain clan society.

THE CHECHEN REVOLUTION

In 1989 Gorbachev's removal of the Brezhnevite apparatchiks and the general climate of democratization finally allowed the small elite of Chechen cadres and educated urbanites to break through the "glass ceiling." On the coat-tails of the ascendant Chechen *nomenklatura*, several competing factions of ambitious junior intellectuals also rushed to claim positions in the emergent local polity. Their shifting ideologies were copied from the standard textbook of perestroika-era politics: first ecology, then democratization, then the preservation of ethnic folklore, and only later, radical nationalism. They followed exactly the same sequence and mechanisms as in Kabardino-Balkaria. And just as easily, the intellectual "upstarts" were brushed aside insofar as common Chechens were bound by their dependency on elite patrons. Politically checked at home, Chechen radicals, like the poet Yandarbiyev and the journalist Movladi Udugov, allied themselves with Shanib under the umbrella of the Mountain Confederation.

The Chechen *nomenklatura* was momentously discredited by its collusion with the abortive putsch of August 1991. For a few weeks in September and October, the

Chechen intelligentsia, together with pragmatic industrial managers, struggled to occupy the power base deserted by the corrupt, conservative bureaucrats. But the low-status radicals, now led by the maverick General Djohar Dudayev, outflanked the emergent liberal-conservative pact by maintaining at the same time a continuous, unruly and inevitably carnivalesque mobilization of crowds in the streets of Grozny.

Where did these people come from? From as far away as the upper mountain villages and from as nearby as the sprawling semi-rural suburbs of Grozny. The more people attended the rally, the more compulsion others felt to attend. It grew exponentially. Zelimkhan Yandarbiyev, a leading participant, provides in his memoirs an estimate that on August 19, the first day of the State of Emergency proclaimed by the putschists in Moscow, only a few dozen core activists gathered in the main square of Grozny. They came, as Yandarbiyev admits, mostly because sitting at home waiting for arrest felt intolerable. Many more chose to hide. On the second day, when the indecisiveness of the reactionary junta became noticeable, several hundred activists attended. On the third day, after it had been announced that tanks were ordered away from the streets of Moscow and Gorbachev would soon return to the Kremlin, more than two thousand people came. Next day it was many thousands, and then it became an avalanche.[33] Even if Yandarbiyev's numbers are imprecise, his description perhaps accurately captures the general dynamic.

The rallies in Grozny became a major focal point of emotional attention. First, there was a moment of enormous relief after the reactionary putsch in Moscow had failed. Only two months earlier, in the Russian presidential elections of June 1991, Yeltsin had received in this republic the overwhelming majority of votes and nearly 98 per cent in the ethnically Ingush rural districts. The Chechens and the Ingushes trusted the electoral promise of the Russian democrat leader that he would complete the "rehabilitation" of the two nationalities and give them long overdue compensation for the losses and sufferings of Stalin's deportations. In retrospect it seems almost unbelievable that for several months in 1991 the majority of Chechens strongly associated their fate with that of Yeltsin. During the putsch days, the rumor spread that a large fleet of empty trucks had been spotted near the border of Checheno-Ingushetia. In all probability, this was a usual Soviet practice of amassing transports during harvest time at collective farms. But to the Chechens and the Ingushes this ominously resembled the fleet of Studebaker trucks that back in 1944 had been used in their deportation. Second, the failure of the coup attempt was universally greeted as the end of communist rule. In the words of the participants, it suddenly felt possible, indeed urgent to shed the old shameful stereotypes and humiliations, to go openly in the street and shout: *We are Chechens! This is our country!* This was exactly what Ernest Gellner named as the key emotional motivation of nationalism – the affirmation of group dignity.[34]

Many participants came to the continuous rally on their own. Others were transported by buses. The buses were sent by Chechen industrial managers and the new private businessmen, including some of quite shady quality, who were equally seeking to earn political capital in the new situation. In addition, the managers could provide the flatbed trucks to serve as a podium as well as the loudspeakers ordinarily reserved for the May Day parades. Factory guards and the retainers of gangster businessmen were also both useful in blocking the street traffic to create space for the rallies.

In the summer of 1991 the usual forty thousand or so seasonal laborers were unable to leave Checheno-Ingushetia because the Soviet economy was collapsing and their migrant jobs had suddenly disappeared. These men were aggrieved, puzzled by the turn for the worse, and prepared to listen eagerly to Dudayev and other radicals when they explained that the labor migrations outside the republic had in fact been part of a devious plan by Soviet authorities to humiliate and assimilate the Chechen nation. If Chechnya became independent, explained future president Dudayev, it would use its oil to create jobs and prosperity for all its citizens in their home country, and thus the nation would be reborn. It was a simple and powerfully inspiring discourse that sounded strangely reminiscent of the national liberation and developmentalist programs of the 1950s and 1960s. Dudayev indeed behaved and spoke like Nasser, Sukarno and scores of other progressive Third World generals before him.[35] His favorite argument, however, was to compare Chechnya to Estonia, where until 1991 he had been commander of the Soviet Strategic Air Force base: If a small Estonia after many centuries of tsarist and communist oppression could become an independent nation and join Europe, why couldn't Chechnya? The combination of Dudayev's military demeanor and visionary message elicited an exuberantly hopeful and proud response from the common Chechens that no liberal reformers or communist conservatives could ever hope to match.

Dudayev won in the field of popular rhetoric first, but his victory was gained not by words alone. Every gain of the street mobilizers brought them new resources, which emboldened them still further. The seizure of the local TV station gave the radicals a major propagandistic tool, and the storming of parliament and other government buildings denied the Soviet-era elite their symbolically legitimate spaces. As in Eastern Europe, the signal success of the revolutionary crowds was the capture of the KGB headquarters. But the Chechen crowds also opened the prison, whose inmates immediately formed an armed movement called *Nïyso* (Justice).[36]

An additional blow to the old state structures was the separation of Ingushetia proclaimed in September 1991 by a convention of village officials, intellectuals (teachers), and specialists (veterinarians, agronomists). Ingushetia was created out of three rural districts that had no towns. Besides the simple fact that Ingushetia's villages were too remote for any authority to ban the secessionist gathering, the haste of these rural politicians was impelled by two calculations. First, as they openly proclaimed themselves, the Ingushes did not want to become a minority in an independent Chechnya. Second, there was a factor they did not admit to openly: the radicalism of village notables in Ingushetia outflanked the more powerful and higher-status Ingush officials and intellectuals who lived in Grozny and other towns and preferred to monitor events from afar. These low-status rural radicals intended to solve the problem of the lack of towns in newly proclaimed Ingushetia by demanding the partition of Vladikavkaz, the nearest big town and the capital of neighboring North Ossetia. Many fellow Ingushes had settled near Vladikavkaz after the return from exile in 1957, and they believed they possessed historical rights to this land.[37] Thus the parallels with Balkaria were almost exact. Just as the Chechen revolutionaries went further than their Kabardin equivalents, so the Ingush separatists went further than the Balkar separatists. In this experiment the outcome was an actual civil war, fought over a week in November 1992 in the predominantly Ingush suburbs of Vladikavkaz. Hundreds died in these clashes and tens of thousands of Ingush residents were expelled from North Ossetia. The victory went to the more numerous and better-organized Ossetins, whose republican leaders additionally enjoyed a privileged access to Moscow via official channels and personal patronage. The Ingush disaster, occurring less than a hundred miles away, certainly played a significant role in the de-radicalization of the comparable project of Balkarian separatism.

During these revolutionary days in 1991, prominent democratic politicians from Moscow had been visiting Checheno-Ingushetia one after the other. They sought a compromise in the troubled republic that would essentially give Moscow a degree of control over local events. In accordance with the principle of homology, the Moscow visitors, themselves now statesmen, felt a closer affinity to the more "serious" men in the Chechen political-technocratic-cultural establishment than to the rowdy street crowds and their populist leaders. But the Chechen reformist establishment was rapidly losing ground. The influential Speaker of Russia's Parliament, Ruslan Khasbulatov, himself a Chechen, remained in Moscow during the revolutionary turmoil of autumn 1991. But he was surely engaged in extensive backstage negotiations, seeking to ensure that the next ruler in his homeland would be loyal not only to Russia's new democracy but also to Khasbulatov personally.

All these hasty and contradictory attempts at political manipulation profoundly alienated Dudayev and other radical Chechen leaders because they felt, perhaps with good reason, that they were not considered qualified to run postcommunist Chechnya. Like the Ingush village notables who had been radicalized by the perceived arrogance of prominent Ingushes from big cities, the Chechen revolutionary leaders were radicalized by their fear of being discarded once the higher-status politicians in Moscow and Grozny no longer found them of use. Disregarding Khasbulatov's mantra of constitutional order, the maverick Dudayev decided to consolidate their political gains by speedily organizing elections for the new president and parliament of Chechnya. In this, Dudayev was enthusiastically supported by the radicals, many of whom we have already encountered in chapter one: poet Zelimkhan Yandarbiyev, young journalist Movladi Udugov, former engineer turned museum curator and democratic deputy Lyoma Usmanov, rogue policeman and leader of his personal militia disguised as the "Party of the Islamic Path" Beslan Gantamirov, drop-out student Shamil Basayev, minor apparatchik in the Komsomol and Dudayev's distant relative Salman Raduyev, as well as former convict and talented autodidact Yusup Soslambekov, and, of course, our frustrated social reformer and professor manqué Musa Shanib. When at Khasbulatov's suggestion the Russian parliament in Moscow declared the coming Chechen elections unconstitutional, Dudayev answered that Chechnya was not in Russia's jurisdiction. Instead of submitting its sovereign decisions to the judgment of Moscow's legal scholars, Chechnya first of all wanted to conclude a peace treaty with Russia (Dudayev borrowed this demand from Estonia) to end what he described as the Three Hundred Years War between the Russian Empire and the Chechen people. On 27 October 1991, Djohar Dudayev was elected Chechen President with 85 per cent of the vote, though the Chechen liberal opposition contested the validity of the elections. On 2 November, Chechnya declared its independence.[38]

In Moscow at the time, Russia's President Yeltsin was scrambling to wrest controls from the dying USSR presidency of Gorbachev, which explains the pathetically uncoordinated show of force against the separatist rebellion in Grozny. On 9 November several planeloads of military police were flown into Chechnya to enforce the state of emergency declared by Yeltsin's government on the same night. Dudayev immediately appeared on Chechnya's television with a very emotional appeal to the nation and a warning that the Stalinist deportation was about to be repeated by the new rulers of Russia who had betrayed the ideals of democracy and national self-determination.

Dudayev's claim might have sounded hyperbolic to an outside observer, but it did not to the majority of Chechens. The sad aphorism of Milan Kundera – small nations know they can disappear easily – held a brutal truth for the Chechens. At the time of these events, one in three Chechens was a survivor of Stalin's deportation. Everybody knew and many directly remembered how on 23 February 1944, in just one day, the Soviet secret police and army troops herded the whole nation into cattle cars and shipped them off to exile. This was the bureaucratic effectiveness of Stalinism at its murderous high. The mountain villages that during winter could not be reached by automobile had been annihilated by aerial and artillery bombardment. Scholars and experts must take seriously the psychological imprint left by genocide on the nations whose self-protective reactions might otherwise seem wildly excessive. This observation pertains to the Christian Armenians and Serbs, or to the Israeli Jews, no less than to the Muslim Chechens. It is not a matter of civilization or religious traditions, it is rather the urge to overcome the trauma of collective victimization in the past and secure survival in the future – the mighty sentiment of *Never Again!* Exactly because the collective emotions of the post-genocide syndrome are exceedingly strong, they usually serve to the political advantage of extremists.

On the night of 9 November 1991, Yeltsin's thoughtless declaration of a state of emergency in Chechnya had the opposite effect to that intended: it instantaneously unified the Chechen nation and destroyed the political prospects of all those in Chechnya who for any reason had criticized Dudayev's declaration of independence. When the first military plane touched ground, it was immediately surrounded by armed Chechen rebels and thousands of civilian protestors. The dispirited troops, who had not been provided with clear orders or firepower, surrendered on the promise that they would be allowed to leave Chechen territory. Upon learning the news, the Russian parliament voted by an overwhelming majority to rescind the state of emergency in Chechnya and to censor President Yeltsin for reverting to totalitarian methods. For added propagandistic effect, the Chechen revolutionaries insisted that the expeditionary force leave on buses, which turned their departure into a slow parade amidst jubilant crowds. The botched operation became the first major humiliation of Yeltsin's presidency, and one that Musa Shanib, who was there, likes to attribute to himself and his Chechen comrades. It seems, however, that Yeltsin's problem was still Gorbachev, as much as it was Shanib or Dudayev. The police already reported to the Russian President, but Yeltsin had not yet acquired from Gorbachev the command of the former Soviet army and its arsenals. As a result, the Russian police had arrived in Chechnya armed only with anti-riot shields and batons. They were met by rebels with plenty of Kalashnikovs and even tanks.[39]

The military forces of the Chechen revolution were created out of the "body-guard" retainers of shady businessmen, Chechen gangsters, romantic students, and eager sub-proletarian youths who gathered spontaneously under the exotic banners of the Party of the Islamic Path, the National Guard, the Society of Former Inmates *Niyso*, etc. Weapons were looted from military arsenals or bought from corrupt officers of the collapsing Soviet army. In fact, the weapons were so plentiful that an open-air market had emerged in Grozny where for the price of a TV one could purchase a grenade launcher or machine-gun. The spectacle of such an uncommon market (and its noise, as the guns were tested on the spot by prospective buyers) never failed to captivate visitors to Dudayev's Chechnya, and evoked romantic images from Tolstoy's stories or, among the West European visitors, comparisons with the Corsicans and Basques. President Dudayev himself promised that the independence and democracy of the Chechen Republic of Ichkeria would be safeguarded by the universal arming of its citizenry – and he called it the "Switzerland model."

In reality this meant that the Ichkerians took into their own hands the protection of their property and life. The new rule did not apply equally to all citizens but only to those who were socially and psychologically prepared to rely on force and on the support of their relatives and friends. Chechen males of rural and sub-proletarian background found themselves at an advantage over the urban higher-class population, and especially over the Russian settler workers and specialists. Many violent crimes committed by the Chechens against the ethnic Russians were pecuniary in nature rather than manifestations of Chechen racism or religious intolerance. The Russians and, incidentally, quite a few urban Chechens, became easy prey for those who might want to take their money or apartments. In addition, the sub-proletarians and peasants possessed far more relevant skills and resources to survive the collapse of Soviet state economy. They could rely on subsistence, barter, migrant remittances, and the smuggling trade (the end of Soviet-era border controls opened many new opportunities in international smuggling). To them, the old state had little relevance anyway, and they had oftentimes considered it a nuisance. By contrast, the engineers, teachers, or oilmen who had previously worked for the state enterprises and were accustomed to regular wages, social protection, and, not least of all, the presence of police, were generally at a loss for what to do.

Unsurprisingly then, the unilateral proclamation of Chechnya's independence triggered an exodus of ethnic Russian specialists and virtually the entire Chechen elite.[40] Already in 1992 and 1993, before the Russian military invasion and war, an estimated two hundred thousand urbanites, mostly ethnic Russians, emigrated from this lawless enclave. Perhaps nearly as many Chechen cadres, former officials, intellectuals, and workers left their homeland "temporarily" to seek jobs elsewhere in former Soviet lands. The exodus had the effect of physically removing from Dudayev's Chechnya virtually all claimants to political power except those who procured their living by the gun.

THE LONG DECAY OF THE CHECHEN REVOLUTION

Arthur Stinchcombe defines revolutions as "periods in which the rate of change of power positions of factions, social groups, or armed bodies changes rapidly and unpredictably. Revolutions then come to an end to the degree that political uncertainty is reduced by building enough bargains into a political structure that can maintain these bargains."[41] By this measure the revolution in Chechnya has had a very long aftermath, passing through a violent ebb and flow, and may be still going on. Stinchcombe summarizes the structures that may produce decreases in political uncertainty as conservative authoritarianism (or "Thermidor"), independence, occupation government, totalitarianism, democracy, and *caudillismo*. In the last decade, Chechnya has moved in all of these directions but stopped short of following any one to completion.

Chechnya is an obvious exception to the general tendency of conservative authoritarianism that swept across other post-Soviet countries, including Kabardino-Balkaria. Until August and even November 1991 (Yeltsin's botched state of emergency) such a pattern seemed to be Chechnya's likeliest future, but in the revolution's aftermath the prospective forces of *nomenklatura*-oligarchic restoration had fled the country. Dudayev's unilateral proclamation of independence, however, failed to install a credible government possessing the necessary political, coercive, and economic resources because Russia imposed a blockade and, perhaps more consequentially, prevented the international recognition of Chechnya. Thus no foreign aid, loans, or investment could be obtained to finance Dudayev's regime. For the same reason neither totalitarianism nor democracy could emerge, since both, in their own ways, are difficult things to build and maintain in the absence of functioning bureaucratic institutions.

The Russian military invasions have already twice failed to impose an effective occupation government. In 1995–1996, Moscow sent back to Grozny the remnants of the old *nomenklatura* overthrown four years earlier. But these men proved incapable of winning political support locally because in popular opinion they were associated with the brutality of Russian soldiery, from which they could offer no protection. They could not offer much in the way of economic or social benefit either, because the money which Yeltsin's government had earlier allocated for the civilian restoration of the war-ravaged country vanished somewhere between the various offices in Moscow and in Russian-occupied Grozny.

The second Russian occupation that began in 2000 took a different approach by amnestying and inviting as junior partners various defectors from the Chechen armed resistance. The biggest such name was Ahmad Kadyrov, formerly the chief Islamic authority (mufti) under the separatist president Dudayev and, incidentally, the same man who in 1995 had declared jihad on Russia. Kadyrov, who belonged to the traditional Sufi Islam, has subsequently found himself in a deadly conflict with the emergent Islamic militancy that drew its puritanical inspiration and material support mainly from Saudi Arabia and recruited among the disillusioned Chechen fighters in the first war, such as Shamil Basayev's force. It seemed for a while that Putin's government had astutely pulled off a coup by enlisting Kadyrov as Chechnya's new proconsul and turning his private army into the new state police. But Kadyrov proved to be worse than a puppet. On the one hand, this figure possessed the typical liabilities of foreign-imposed puppets: he came to be widely despised as a corrupt and self-serving politico with little influence on the Russian generals. On the other hand, Moscow was apparently trapped by its own bet on Kadyrov and thus had to turn a blind eye on his misdeeds. Kadyrov quarreled viciously with the political partners and civil administrators whom Moscow had been trying to impose on him. Instead, the former mufti relies on a closed clientele of his relatives and on his own security force. The courageous journalists and human rights activists who still work in Chechnya blame the majority of nightly disappearances on the political and commercial operations conducted by Kadyrov's private army-turned-police and commanded by his infamous son. In the Kremlin, they apparently still hope that the death squad tactics may eventually eliminate the Chechen resistance. But the most recent proliferation of terrorist attacks in Chechnya and Russia seems to provide evidence to the contrary. The well-informed Russian journalist Anna Politkovskaya describes the new generation of fighters as a non-political "third force," whose attacks are fundamentally the acts of family revenge for the close relatives who had been murdered by the Russians and Kadyrov's military.[42]

The example of post-revolutionary Chechnya comes closer to *caudillismo*, which Stinchcombe himself recognizes as looking "too much like a continuation of the uncertainty of revolution to seem like an ending."[43] Other scholars call it warlord politics.[44] In this volatile and violent pattern political leaders and followers are tied not by any formal rules regarding social and moral obligations between governments and the governed, but by the unstable personalized pyramidal networks through which *caudillos* have to truck and barter, often violently, with their clients and competitors for the resources to run a government. By analogy with the mafia violent entrepreneurs, we might call this pattern "violent neopatrimonialism."

After the revolution the state in Chechnya could not be restored. In 1992–1993 Dudayev's separatist government survived by granting various smuggling monopolies to its strongmen and allied warlords. Attempts to reclaim these monopolies for the state budget and the embryonic Chechen army provoked ferocious resistance. Dudayev's regime found itself isolated both internationally and domestically, because of the Russian diplomatic and economic blockade, and because his unrecognized state could not deliver on either its promises or its threats. By default, Dudayev chose to increase his calls for national unity in the face of what he was describing as the imminent war with Russia. This eventually became a self-fulfilling prophecy.

Furthermore, the neoliberal shift in the global environment took away the key state-building resources previously available to Third World developmentalists. With the end of the Cold War, progressive generals and exotic guerrillas lost the structural opportunity to play on superpower rivalries, and the deep political recession of the Western Left rendered much remoter the expectations of international solidarity and aid to national liberation movements. Moreover, in the new world situation, such regimes as Dudayev's could not find a workable state-building ideology. The twentieth-century activist program of peripheral state-building (i.e. "national liberation") centrally prescribed the nationalization of key economic assets. With the disappearance of the national developmental model, Dudayev had to pay lip-service to market liberalism in the hope (though rapidly vanishing) that this might help bring about the international recognition of Chechnya just as it did for Estonia. Meanwhile the warlords were taking over Chechnya's oil wells and refineries by force, which left the prospective state-builders of Chechnya faced with the alternative of zero revenue or joining the game and themselves behaving like the warlords. While President Dudayev and his shrinking circle of loyalists were still hoping to create a national army and issue national passports and currency, their numerous and well-armed opponents gained access to global smuggling operations that grew explosively during the early 1990s, and thus obtained another major source of cash. The up-and-coming warlords no longer needed the government because they had their own means of violence and, with their newly acquired capabilities, could create their own economic opportunities.

The Russian invasion in 1994 provided, for a while, the cause for national unity. But the war gave rise to many new guerrilla bands and autonomous field commanders. The covert Russian sponsorship of various Chechen auxiliaries, renegades, and rogues was another major source of new warlords. Some of them were purely entrepreneurial and no more than gangsters; others, like Shamil Basayev, pretended to possess some kind of political agenda. Among the latter category some were later known as Islamic terrorists. Under the pressure of the Russian invasions, and for reasons of internal legitimation, some of the most radical (and violent) among the Chechen guerrillas developed ideological, military, and financial links to Middle Eastern oppositional networks. Possibly these included al-Qaeda, although the role of Osama bin Laden seems to be overplayed by Russian propaganda, which since September 2001 has thus sought to justify the brutal and endless "antiterrorist campaign" in Chechnya.[45]

In the 1990s Chechnya experienced catastrophic deurbanization and deindustrialization, which began with the effects of economic isolation, violent lawlessness, and the flight of educated specialists, and was later compounded by the destructive war. The remaining population of Chechnya is estimated at only a half or even a third of the pre-1991 figure.[46] Apart from the men with guns, the people caught in the endless and multi-sided war are now overwhelmingly made up of ruined farmers, former workers, and low-level specialists, plus the sub-proletarians – destitute people with nowhere else to go. They sustain themselves with the faith provided by the idea of national resistance to the Russian occupation and, since the mid-1990s, the project of gaining social order and spiritual confidence through an activist, puritanical Islam. The religious distinction marks the chasm between the Chechen resistance and the Russian occupiers, but the project of Islamic salvation has also served to dramatically divide Chechen society itself. The rise of the new militant ideology turned on its head the relationship between the previously low-status rural Chechens, who stayed and continued fighting, and the no less numerous but now invisible secular urban Chechens, who have been undone as a social group with the destruction of the towns and are today scattered outside their homeland.

In the early 2000s, Chechnya remained far away from peace and stability in any institutional form. The first Russian invasion in 1994–1996 was accompanied by serious domestic and international protests. The Russian army fought half-heartedly in a war for which it was ill-equipped morally and technically, and the Chechen resistance enjoyed a truly popular character. All this combined to produce the improbable victory of Chechen guerrillas, who in August 1996 took Grozny in a surprise attack and forced Yeltsin's government (represented by the gruff and energetic General Lebed) to sue for peace. But, despite the promising beginning in early 1997 that was described in chapter one, Chechnya failed to pacify internally. Field commanders like Shamil Basayev abandoned the nationalist civilian government in utter frustration and reverted to a guerrilla lifestyle at their village bases, justifying their actions with reference to the new Islamic radicalism, calling for the liberation of fellow Muslims in other republics of Russia and throughout the world, and thus prophesying and indeed helping to bring about another war.

Desperate for resources and isolated internationally, the second Chechen President, Aslan Maskhadov, elected in 1997, could offer neither jobs to civilians nor a credible military force against the warlords and bandits. Ironically, Maskhadov proved insufficiently corrupt and ruthless to consolidate effectively a regime of personal sultanism, which would have been a more realistic course of action given the situation. Previously, Maskhadov had been a Soviet artillery officer, and universally recognized as one of the best. He earnestly tried to recreate in Chechnya the professional military discipline and civil legal order that to him formed the basis of normal life. But the odds were against President Maskhadov, who, judging by his later interviews, felt increasingly defensive, aggrieved, and disoriented, blaming his troubles on the machinations of Moscow if not on an international conspiracy of the American CIA and the Zionists.

In August 1999 Shamil Basayev, together with the commander of the Arab Islamist volunteers, Khattab, launched a military offensive in the neighboring republic of Daghestan in what many believed to be an effort to solve the problems of Chechnya by exporting their Islamic revolution. The cynical version claims that Basayev had been bribed by the Russian political manipulators who needed this war to make Putin president and thus assure a smooth succession after Yeltsin. But seeking to account for the convoluted events in Moscow during 1999, this explanation ignores that by many indications Basayev had indeed nurtured the hope of creating a larger state with more resources and direct access to the brethren in the Middle East.[47] The Islamist fighters were emboldened by the emergence in Daghestan of several Islamic "governments" at the village level whose fundamentalist policies resembled those of the Taliban. To explain what social forces support such policies, let me only mention that the young activists of "purified" (Salafite, or what hostile outsiders call Wahhabite) Islam prohibited the lavish weddings that heavily taxed family resources, banned alcohol, drove away the police and subjected criminals to the full harshness of *sharia* law, fought official corruption, and ensured "fair prices" at local markets. Even without the orders, claimed the witnesses, the prices at local markets fell by almost a third apparently because the expulsion of extortionate police and petty officials had dramatically reduced the transaction costs. The Daghestani villages under the Islamists' control began to attract shoppers from all over the region.[48] These villages incidentally were not at all small places in remote mountain areas, as some journalists described them. They were large villages in the foothills that possessed locally significant markets and where a majority of men were engaged in long-distance labor migrations as itinerant traders or truck drivers rather than in agriculture. Thus the villages were typical sub-proletarian concentrations suspended between declining traditions and the vagaries of the new markets, and no longer able to count on the support networks of the Soviet state.

However, in the traditionally deeply Muslim Daghestan, pro-Russian sentiments proved surprisingly strong, in large part because many Daghestanis feared, not without reason, that Basayev and Khattab were adventurers who had simply come to claim power in Daghestan, to take away the control of lands and the region's major economic opportunities such as smuggling along Azerbaijan's border or poaching the caviar sturgeons in the Caspian Sea. The extremely negative impression left on Daghestanis by Salman Raduyev's raid a few years earlier (described in chapter one) certainly played a big role. Last but not least, the Islamists coming from Chechnya and the Arab countries brought a very different version of Islam. The young militants regarded as near idolatry the Sufi mysticism that had traditionally been the creed of the Chechens and Daghestanis.

Basayev's invasion was easily rolled back in a couple of weeks, but in the following September its negative effect on Russian opinion was vastly magnified by mysterious explosions in residential high-rises in Daghestan, Moscow, and elsewhere in Russia that the authorities immediately blamed on Islamic terrorists. These events created broad political support for another Russian invasion of Chechnya – this time described as an "antiterrorist operation" – and the election of the tough, sober, and, as he is often described, "Germanic" former KGB colonel Vladimir Putin as the second Russian president after Yeltsin.

Four years later the war in Chechnya is still dragging on. Despite a very cruel campaign aimed at eliminating the Chechen fighters and their supporters, the Russian forces have failed to end the resistance and to capture or kill either Basayev or Maskhadov (who, staying true to his army instincts, had hailed the resumption of war as a return to political clarity). Likewise Moscow has failed to rebuild the state structures and industrial economy in Chechnya, relying instead on a combination of military occupation and the auxiliary force of various Chechen defectors who, despite being granted Russian military rank and state titles, essentially remain the same warlords whose small private armies facilitate their nefarious businesses.[49]

KABARDINO-BALKARIA: THE DIVERSION OF THE REVOLUTION

By contrast, a visitor to Kabardino-Balkaria today may get the impression that nothing has ever troubled this beautiful mountainous backwater since Brezhnev's time. On the surface, there are few traces of the revolution led by Musa Shanib in September–October 1992, which was inspired by the Chechen example and was nearly successful.

Generally speaking, the Autonomous Soviet Socialist Republics (ASSRs) of Kabardino-Balkaria and Checheno-Ingushetia (before October 1991) may look as if they were deliberately constructed for comparative analysis. The two places are located next to each other but were always separate republics inside the Russian Federation. They are of a manageable size that allows a researcher to identify and meet in a matter of weeks the majority of the important actors, participants, and uninvolved but informed observers (of course, only so long as these people do not disappear – as they are disappearing in Chechnya now). Their titular nationalities have similar histories and cultural traditions. The social structures have differed only in details and relative proportions although, as we shall see, the proportions of classes and the configuration of political patronage can make a significant difference in moments of chaos. The sequences of events, up to a point, look remarkably similar. Like the Ingush minority in what before September 1991 was joint Checheno-Ingushetia, the Balkar minority in Kabardino-Balkaria proclaimed their withdrawal from the previously shared administrative unit. The last communist ruler, the Kabardin Valeri Kokov, resigned under pressure from street protestors, and the republic's Soviet-era parliament announced that it would dissolve itself. Former officials on all sides began to defect to the street rebels, taking with them their administrative resources. Alternative centers of political power emerged, and the opposition began arming militias. But then, they stopped. In Shanibov's own words: *Had we gone to the end, today I would probably be some sort of dictator and this place would be as uncivilized as Chechnya. Of course, most of our bureaucrats are thieves but without them there can be no civilized life.*

Local observers and Shanib himself unanimously attribute these different outcomes to ethnic character – of course, the sensible and ceremonious Kabardins, unlike the Chechen hotheads, knew where to stop. Many North Caucasians see a special mystical irrationality in the Chechen style of waging war or practicing Islam.

This opinion is supported by authoritative quotes from classic Russian authors like Lermontov and Leo Tolstoy, who as young officers both fought against the Chechen tribesmen in the 1850s and left us their romanticized portraits of the noble natives. The history of the nineteenth-century Chechen resistance and the Kabardin cooperation with the Russian empire probably matters, but, let us ask, through what transmission mechanisms do the effects of history reach into the present? The literary constructs matter in a rather direct way, but not because they provide accurate descriptions but rather because Lermontov's poetry and Tolstoy's prose serve as a favorite source of ethnic pride in the North Caucasus where everybody has studied Russian classical literature at school.

Perhaps Tolstoy would have had little use for sociological hypotheses, yet, for us, there is compelling evidence that the divergent trajectories of the North Caucasus republics are primarily attributable to variations in two conditions: a) the class structure (the difference in the number of sub-proletarians, and the degree of cohesion among the ethnically articulate power elite); and b) the time lag marking the opening and closure of opportunity. The chronological reconstruction of the unfolding events in Grozny, Nalchik, and Moscow clearly points to a time lag as the proximate cause. In this context, however, time is always a social category that measures how long it takes for a process to unfold or wind down. I have already tried to explain why the revolutionary mobilizing in Chechnya could be so instantaneous and emotional, and why it brought with it a great deal of violence. Here I shall offer several hypotheses regarding why the analogous mobilizing among the Kabardins was slow to emerge, why it was not as emotional except for a brief period of time, and why the state authorities held their ground and managed to deflect the revolutionary violence, directing it instead into neighboring Abkhazia.

In the Soviet period the Kabardins had always dominated the government offices of their homeland. Possibly this could be explained by two historical hypotheses. First, the old Kabardin culture of feudal allegiances translated well into the ethos of bureaucratic and military service. Indeed the Kabardins had been relatively overrepresented in the Soviet officer corps since the 1940s. In their republic, the Kabardin native cadres had been in control since around the same time, and since de-Stalinization there had been a remarkable continuity and stability (alternatively, ossification and lack of mobility) in the local power network. After their return from exile in 1957, the ethnic Balkar representatives had been judiciously incorporated into this network where they enjoyed the right to occupy the number two positions in every formal office and hierarchy. Secondly, and perhaps more importantly, in Kabardino-Balkaria the Soviet nationality policy really seemed to operate as it was intended insofar as only very few ethnic Russians seem to have held positions of power. This impression could be the result of the cohesion and continuity maintained over the years in the local power network which effectively resisted the outsiders. The bureaucratic parochialism was able to endure because in Kabardino-Balkaria there was no oil or other truly big industry and thus no equivalent to Grozny's urban settler enclave in Soviet Checheno-Ingushetia. There were many ethnic Russians in Kabardino-Balkaria but they were dispersed over the whole republic, many living in small towns and villages such as the historically Cossack settlements. What matters is that there were few settlers competing for office with native cadres.

The time lag separating the revolution in Chechnya and the mobilization in Kabardino-Balkaria had historical and structural reasons. Put simply, it was more difficult to mobilize the Kabardins against their power elite because too many among the Kabardins were themselves in the establishment or close to its members. There was no historically recent national tragedy that could readily offer the shared strong emotions comparable to that among the Chechens. Once again, this condition is constructed and subject to change. Hence the efforts of Kabardin and other Circassian historians and literary figures to succeed in making immediate ("awakening") the tragedy that had been suffered by the ancestors of North Caucasus peoples in the nineteenth century, during the Russian campaigns of imperial conquest and the exodus of *muhajeer* refugees to the Middle East in the 1860s. The Balkars, of course, had a much more recent trauma inflicted by their deportation in 1944, and in fact their national movement mobilized as rapidly and emotionally as in Checheno-Ingushetia. But the separatist aspirations of Balkar minority ran into the hostility of Kabardin majority which defused rather than strengthened the revolutionary thrust.

The passage of time clearly made a big difference in the reactions of Moscow. Shanib's revolutionary attempt in Kabardino-Balkaria gained momentum a whole year after the successful revolution in Chechnya and its secession. Yeltsin, who had been struggling to supplant Gorbachev during the autumn of 1991, now found himself facing the challenge of provincial separatism and preserving the Russian state. Yeltsin soon overcame democratic prejudices, consolidated his control over the former Soviet resources, and resolutely threw Moscow's support behind the Kabardin *nomenklatura* in order to prevent another Chechnya. His help was gratefully accepted.

However, the suppression was ineffective as the popular mobilizations, both Kabardin and Balkar, gained momentum through 1992 while the Russian state was badly disorganized in the wake of the Soviet collapse. Kabardin revolutionary mobilization flared up with a vengeance in August 1992 when Georgian warlords treacherously invaded its fraternal ally Abkhazia. The war provided a tremendously emotional occasion. The first Kabardin volunteers – mostly romantic students, scholars, and a few former military officers – immediately left for Abkhazia to help to organize the defense. Their arrival played a crucial role in inspiring the Abkhazian resistance – the Abkhazes no longer felt isolated and alone in the face of Georgian invasion.

Meantime large crowds were gathering in downtown Nalchik. They were met with tanks, soldiers, and police. But evidently, as happens in revolutions, the sheer determination of the protesters overpowered the unprepared troops, who retreated into government buildings. The revolutionaries seized a number of helmets, shields, truncheons, and a few machine-guns. This emboldened them even further. *I could not believe myself doing it, you know, climbing on the tank in the street, banging on the armor and demanding that the soldiers give their guns to us* – recalls one of Shanib's lieutenants, a junior professor in thick, goggle-like glasses.

Kokov's victory in the presidential elections of January 1992 destroyed many illusions. The opposition realized that they should not expect Yeltsin's Moscow to provide leadership in the process of transforming the old order and instead they had to maintain the popular mobilizations and, perhaps, use revolutionary coercion. In early 1992 Shanib made a secret trip to Chechnya in a bread-delivery minivan, in which he intended to smuggle back to Kabardino-Balkaria fifty guns intended to be a "seed grant" of sorts. The tactics of looting army arsenals were already well known. The military officers would either be bought with hefty bribes or intimidated by the presence of angry crowds and gunmen, or likely both: after accepting the bribes, the officers still liked to put on a show in case their venality should lead to a court martial.[50]

Shanib had no money to buy guns, therefore he hoped to seize them by force, in which case fifty Kalashnikovs would be the necessary first step. But President Dudayev refused to hand over any weapons. Pointing to the window, he asked if Shanib wanted his Nalchik to become like Grozny, pervasively armed and anarchic. It is difficult to judge Dudayev's sincerity in this episode. Possibly, he was afraid of angering Moscow because he still hoped to reach a compromise. Or perhaps the rebel general simply did not trust Professor Shanib. There is a third possibility related to the desire of the Chechen leadership to take control of the Mountain Confederation. Chechnya, after all, was the only component of the Confederation to separate from Russia, and on this merit Dudayev considered himself the rightful leader of the movement for the larger pan-Caucasus state. This sort of tension has been well documented in the histories of other international revolutionary movements: the role of the Soviet Union in the Comintern, Nasser's Egypt in Pan-Arab nationalism, or Castro's Cuba in Latin America.[51]

Shanib, however, was undeterred by Dudayev's refusal. Revolutions are historical moments where the strangest improvisations can suddenly change the course of events. In Nalchik, Shanib received a fax from Yusup Soslambekov, the Vice-President of the Mountain Confederation and one of the leaders of the Chechen parliament.[52] The fax contained a draft of an official statement from the Confederation denouncing the Georgian invasion of Abkhazia and including various clauses that Shanib at first dismissed as the product of Soslambekov's Chechen bravado. The Confederation henceforth declared it open season for hostile acts on Georgian territory and all Georgians in the North Caucasus were to be interned as hostages until Georgian troops withdrew from Abkhazia. What forced Shanib to change his mind was the crowd in the street. He then added a famous paragraph giving marching orders to the "volunteer peace-keeping battalions of the Mountain Confederation," which sanctioned the use of force against anyone who tried to prevent the Confederation's forces from going to Abkhazia. Since Abkhazia had borders only with Georgia and Russia, the last line of Shanib's order meant in effect attacking the Russian border guards and police if they sealed the frontiers with Abkhazia. Of course, there were neither guns nor battalions, but as Shanib put it, *a serious bluff must be carried to the end.* But in a revolutionary situation can anyone, even those who appear to be behind it, know what is a bluff?

Several days later on the Trans-North Caucasus highway the Russian traffic police stopped a convoy of two trucks and several cars. The young men traveling in them demanded they be let through because they were the volunteer battalion of the Mountain Confederation. When the startled police refused and called for reinforcements, the commander of the volunteers declared that on the orders of the Mountain Confederation's President Musa Shanib the police were to be taken prisoner and would be shot if they tried to escape. The young commander was Ruslan Gelayev, later one of the most notorious Chechen guerrillas. He forced the traffic policemen, and some town officials who had arrived on the scene, to escort his convoy to the mountain pass on the border with Abkhazia.

Similar incidents were occurring across virtually all the republics of the North Caucasus, especially in Adyghea and Karachai-Cherkessia, where the ethnic affinities to Abkhazes were felt most strongly — these neighboring territories were populated by fellow Circassians. Groups of young men, armed or barely armed, and calling themselves the volunteer battalions of the Mountain Confederation, were springing up all over the place. Some scaled the mountains on foot, performing astonishing feats of endurance. Others traveled to the Abkhazian border by cars and buses, hoping either to ford the border river Psou or to camp at the Russian checkpoints and demand they be let through – or else they would earnestly put into action the orders of Musa Shanib. Still others stormed into the main squares in the capitals of their native republics to set up volunteer registration booths and demand that the authorities give them guns and transport to allow them to defend their Abkhaz brothers against the Georgian bullies. In short, the pan-Caucasian revolution was suddenly taking off with Abkhazia providing the spark.

In Nalchik, Shanib was invited to the republic's Ministry of Internal Affairs, ostensibly to discuss how to avoid further clashes between the protestors and the police. Instead, Shanib was asked bluntly whether the Confederation was a social movement or a would-be state. If it were a movement, then it must apply for registration with the appropriate Russian agencies. But since it had declared war on the now sovereign state of Georgia and had begun to arm its own battalions, the Confederation and its leader must be trying to create an independent state – which was a violation of the Russian constitution. This interesting theoretical discussion ended in Shanib's arrest. He was escorted to the courtyard, put in a covered truck full of soldiers, and driven at high speed to a helicopter waiting at the airport.

Shanib escaped several days later. Journalists in Moscow are cynical about the escape, which they see as the consequence of secret bargaining. Indeed, the arrest of Musa Shanib presented Moscow with a dilemma typical of revolutionary situations: as a free man, he was dangerously active, but keeping him in jail made him a hero. The news of his arrest produced a huge outburst of indignation in Kabardino-Balkaria. The government building was besieged in earnest – there was to be no more intelligentsia nonsense about hunger strikes. And this time, the government did not flee. Instead, President Kokov and his *nomenklatura* reportedly donned helmets, bullet-proof vests, and armed themselves. This might have looked like the Kabardin tradition of aristocratic masculinity re-emerging dressed in modern body armor. But curiously, one of Kokov's lieutenants rather cited the example of the last stand of Salvador Allende during the 1973 coup in Chile: the famous last photograph of Allende in a helmet was commonly known in the Soviet Union. Whatever the cultural inspiration, the decision to arm the bureaucrats was a very strong statement directed to many sides: to the protestors, to President Yeltsin, and no less to the bureaucrats themselves who had literally been forced into combat gear. In their own more than symbolic message, the protestors in the meantime drove two fuel tankers into the square and threatened to burn "the den of thieves," i.e. the former regional headquarters of the Communist Party, now called the government palace. From inside the building, the Russian police general Kulikov (later Minister of Internal Affairs in charge of the first war in Chechnya) threatened that if the square was not cleared by 21:00, he would send out his elite "Alfa-force," and these military professionals would eject the crowd barehanded. Kulikov was obviously ignorant about the local culture. Immediately, all sorts of athletes – wrestlers, boxers, martial artists – veterans of the Afghan war and simple hooligans began to line up for the fight. The volunteer who kept the list of these waiting combatants stopped counting at six hundred because a larger number was considered unfair to the "Alfa-force." Tens of thousands of spectators and supporters assembled around the square waiting for action.

Shanib's own version of his escape seems credible enough, because it contains many details betraying the sheer disorganization and plain bureaucratic idiocy predominant at the time in the post-Soviet coercive structures. For their part, the cynical journalists have to explain why Moscow or anyone else needed to let Shanib escape when they could have simply rescinded his arrest in a legal manner. To cut the story short, Shanib was flown out of Kabardino-Balkaria by helicopter and moved almost every day from one town jail to another, but all in the same region. In some jails, the police chiefs treated him apologetically and almost like a guest; in others he was roughed up and put in stinking cells with common criminals. There was no consistency in his treatment and there were no interrogations. Finally, Shanib was driven in a police car to Rostov, a big town in southern Russia. The trip took more than a day, in part because a tire blew and it took a couple of hours to replace it on the road. When the policemen were working on the tire, a car with Chechen license plates pulled over beside them. The police turned pale and reached for their pistols, but the Chechens did not know that Shanib was inside the car. They had just stopped to offer help. The convoy arrived in Rostov after midnight and found the prison gates closed. The two colonels accompanying Shanib took his papers, went into the service entrance, and disappeared for more than an hour. Evidently they were not expected. In the meantime, the exhausted driver began to nod off. Shanib carefully opened the door and walked away; at first pretending that he desperately needed to take a leak, he soon sped off towards the brightly lit main street – he had known the area around Rostov prison well since the time he had been a district attorney in the 1960s. Shanib guessed that the police would first look for him in the darker back streets and courtyards, which proved to be correct. Pretending that he was a drunk returning home late, he made his way across town to an old friend's apartment, borrowed some money, and immediately went straight back to Kabardino-Balkaria by private car and bus. It was not quite like the escape of Petr Kropotkin from Petropavloskaia fortress in St. Petersburg, and nothing like the Count of Monte Cristo's adventures, which in my opinion makes it more credible than the conspiracy theory of journalists, which probably repeats the version "leaked" by the police themselves.

Whatever the reality, the details of Shanib's escape help us to appreciate the disarray that afflicted the Russian state in 1992. Politically, it did not matter whether Shanib escaped or was let go. He returned to jubilant crowds in Nalchik, who carried him on their shoulders to an improvised rostrum. Shanib told the story of his arrest and escape (which immediately became a legend embroidered with various romantic details) and urged the protestors to carry on their campaign until the government of *nomenklatura* thieves and Moscow's minions resigned and let the peoples of the Caucasus freely decide their destiny. But first, Abkhazia must be defended!

The proposed military expedition to Abkhazia offered a safety valve to the besieged *nomenklatura*. At some point the officials in the North Caucasus began to plead with Moscow to let the volunteers go to Abkhazia. On its side, the government in Moscow was expecting rebellions. From the outset, the neoliberal reformer Yegor Gaidar called his cabinet a "suicidal bunch." These young economists thought of themselves as implacable revolutionaries and in fact a couple of them had famous Bolshevik ancestors. Their optimistic plan was that while neoliberal "shock therapy" would be very painful to the population, it would nonetheless erase the Soviet-era distortions and jump-start the motors of economic growth, leading the country to join the advanced capitalist nations. What mattered at present was to survive the period of market transition, when popular rebellions were to be expected.

As regards Yeltsin, he had inherited the secret operations of the Soviet era after coming to power in Moscow. At the very least he did not object to their continuation in what the security experts in Moscow regarded as Russia's exposed flank in the south. Yeltsin's renewal of covert support for the Abkhazian rebellion against Georgia was a gamble that smacked of desperation. But in 1992 he could be concerned only with short-term goals.

THE SEPARATIST WAR IN ABKHAZIA

State officials from across the North Caucasus dispatched the volunteers to Abkhazia with a blessing. This move served two purposes: it exported the revolutionary challengers while at the same time punishing newly independent Georgia, which had threatened to become a hostile neighbor. This seems Machiavellian, but it was actually a split-second gamble. In those days of galloping hyperinflation, the threat of industrial and infrastructural paralysis, and chaotic confrontations with the Russian parliament, neither Yeltsin nor anybody else could plan ahead further than the next few days. Yeltsin, caught in a stand-off with the Russian parliament and probably still hopeful of the promised miracle of neoliberal shock therapy, was simply buying time. For his part, Shanib hoped that by accepting Russian weapons he was making a tactical concession that could earn for the Confederation the strategic lever of its own army forged in battle.

Shanib was allowed to form the Confederation's battalions of "peace-makers" on the understanding that they would leave at once for Abkhazia. Whereas the earliest wave of volunteers had to trek secretly over glacier-covered mountains on the border with Georgia, or else fight their way there like Ruslan Gelayev's detachment, Musa Shanib and his soldiers traveled to Abkhazia in a long column of buses, escorted by Russian military helicopters. Overall, some 1,500–2,000 Kabardins fought in Abkhazia at various times. The monument to the war dead in Nalchik lists fifty-six names, but probably as many died from causes not directly related to military engagement, in accidents and fights, most of them after the war ended. The exact social composition of this force is unknown. However, interviews with participants indicate that, expectedly, the overwhelming majority were young veterans of the Soviet war in Afghanistan and sub-proletarian toughs among whom, typically, a great many were semi-professional wrestlers or boxers – these martial sports enjoy an exceptional popularity in the North Caucasus, especially among the sub-proletarians.

In Abkhazia, I studied the old lists of various ethnic battalions: Ossetian, Adygheian, Cherkessian, and Chechen. (The commander of the latter was Shamil Basayev.) Among the several things that caught my eye, the first was the homogeneity of Basayev's detachment. With few exceptions all the men were born between 1967 and 1973, i.e. they were 19–25 years old during this war. They nearly all came from only three districts of Chechnya, two in the mountains near Basayev's native village of Vedeno, and the third that of the city of Grozny. But there were also two ethnic Russians, and possibly an ethnic German or Jew, and a man who, judging by his birthplace and appellation, was probably a Volga Tatar. They could have been friends, or mercenaries, or more likely just adventurous romantics with some connection to Basayev dating from before the war, perhaps former fellow students from Moscow. Only one member of the detachment had a higher education, though some listed vocational college (*technicum*) diplomas. The documents attempted to follow the formal language of Soviet institutions. However, the receipts, logs and combat orders, written in Russian, contained glaring mistakes – for instance, the word airplane (*samolet*) was spelled according to the phonetics of the Caucasian accent as *samalot*, something like "eirplain" in English. Yet it is striking that the lists were meticulously kept and formal orders were issued – just like in the real Soviet army, where many of these men must have served shortly before.

It is furthermore very indicative that among the former volunteers whom I had a chance to interview, a disproportionate number grew up in families with three or more children. This size of family was very unusual for urban Soviet society, but it is more typical among farmers and sub-proletarians in the Caucasus. It seems that mothers with several sons were more likely to give their blessing should their children want to go to war. I have already discussed this hypothesis and the possibility of testing it in chapter one.

Abkhazia looked set to become for the North Caucasus nationalists what the Spanish Civil War was to the Western Left, or Afghanistan in the 1980s and 1990s was to Middle Eastern Islamists. It was above all an opportunity to participate directly in the type of romantic insurgency politics that was impossible in the home countries of these soldiers, to acquire fighting skills and political capital, to create support bases and forge cross-border alliances that might ultimately allow the struggle to spread to the native lands of the volunteers.[53]

Nearly half of Shanibov's volunteers came from the supposedly blockaded Chechnya. The Chechen "Abkhazian" battalion led by Shamil Basayev was indubitably trained and equipped by Russian special forces (*Spetsnaz*), reportedly by the same instructors who in Soviet times used to train Palestinian and other Third World guerrillas. Later in 1994 the "Abkhazian" battalions of Shamil Basayev and Ruslan Gelayev became the backbone of the Chechen guerrilla resistance to the Russian invasion – this was a serious instance of blowback from the secret Abkhazian operation.

In an important new development, the Confederation's forces received aid and volunteers from Turkey and Middle Eastern countries, primarily Syria and Jordan, where sizable minorities trace their descent from the legendary Circassian Mamelukes and the Muslim refugees (*muhajeers*) from the Russian imperial conquest of the 1860s. The common Ottoman legacy and the Islamic religion provided the symbolic framing for this transnational alliance.

There were also very practical reasons for the growing salience of Islam in wartime. From the first day Shanib and his lieutenants had struggled to instill discipline in their fighters – to justify, for instance, the ban on alcohol and to impose corporal punishment. It seemed natural in this context to invoke the norms of *sharia* law. With the first deaths in combat, questions arose regarding which rituals to use in the burials. Starting with the charismatic Chechen commander Shamil Basayev, the younger war leaders also started to shift the movement's ideology towards Islam, the more so because it stood opposed to the professed Christianity of the Georgian nationalist paramilitaries. This sort of warrior's pragmatism, however, must not be regarded merely as manipulation. The Islamic rules had originally been formed in the time of Muhammad in order to regulate the lives of his soldiers.[54] A further incentive in this regard would have been the fact that the North Caucasian volunteers felt unsettled at receiving Russian backing, especially in the company of their Middle Eastern comrades, and wanted to accentuate their common Islamic identity.

In the Islamic revival Shanib proved a failure. He was too much of a Soviet-made secular intellectual to appear natural when performing Islamic rites. Besides, historically, the more aristocratic Kabardins have never been as deeply affected by Islamization as have the anarchic peasant Chechens, who bore the main brunt of the nineteenth-century highlanders' Holy War against the Russian Empire. At first in subtle ways, a symbolic rivalry began to emerge between the Chechen and the Kabardin volunteers, which, since times of violent conflict do not favor moderation, the Chechens won by being more radical in everything from their battlefield behavior to their religious practice.

The war in Abkhazia became the darkest period in Shanib's life. His only son was mysteriously murdered outside the battlefield, possibly by political rivals. Shanib himself was grievously wounded by a stray bullet. (The guard outside his office accidentally dropped his machine-gun on the floor, and, for reasons of either carelessness or bravado, had not bothered to use the safety catch. The accidental burst of bullets went through a wall and hit Shanib and an Abkhaz general in the legs.) The injured leader was first treated by Abkhaz doctors who failed to cure the wound. His treatment was then taken on by an ethnic Kabardin volunteer from Syria. He employed a traditional herbal medicine whose recipe had been preserved in the family since their expulsion in the old times. These romantic treatments healed the flesh and helped Shanib to partake in national mythology, but afterwards the damage to bone tissue forced him to spend almost two years in Russian military hospitals. While slowly recovering, he began his extensive reading of Bourdieu's books, which had for the first time been translated into Russian.

In effect, the wound put an end to Shanib's political career. But even before that, he was already on the way to becoming a political irrelevance as younger and more ruthless field commanders, like Basayev, took control of military operations and

finances. Shanib was relegated to the role of public ideologist and diplomatic negotiator in charge of relations with political patrons in Moscow. But many such patrons
also happened to be Russian nationalists or populists entrenched in the transitional
parliament, and they were becoming increasingly vociferous opponents of President
Yeltsin. It was getting very difficult to navigate the murky and turbulent waters of
Muscovite politics, an area where Shanib had already suffered quite a few failures.

On the ideological front things did not look much better either. Shanib was
espousing the secular ideology of pan-Caucasus unity and national liberation, which
ran against the trend towards Islamization. More importantly, dangerous rifts were
beginning to emerge between the Chechens, who perceived themselves to be
exporting their own brand of anti-Russian revolution, and the Circassian volunteers (Adygheis, Cherkess, and Kabardins), many of whom were dreaming of an
ethnic Greater Circassia rather than the regional Mountain Confederation. The
Abkhazes themselves grew weary of the political projects of their allies and especially of their Islamism – the Abkhazes observed the pagan rites of their ancestors,
worshipping at sacred trees and ancient graves, and offered only a token appreciation of either Islam or Christianity. (Indicatively, after the war, the new mosques
built by Middle Eastern volunteers were abandoned and several were blown up.)

Moreover the Abkhazes were becoming worried that the Islamic component of
their war jeopardized the more tangible military assistance they received from
Russia, and that the North Caucasian volunteers might stay for good. The main
source of apprehension, according to many interviews with the Abkhazes, was not
that the volunteers would outnumber them – in fact, after the expulsion of a quarter
of a million Georgians there were plenty of empty houses and Abkhazia was
severely depopulated. The real problem was that many volunteers, especially those
who arrived later in the war (the war eliminated a great many idealistic nationalists,
many of them former students, who had arrived in Abkhazia with the first wave
of rescuers), were so lacking in idealism that they were little more than looters and
common criminals. The war was accompanied by atrocities on all sides. Looting,
executions, torture, arson, and rape all played their part in the escalating spiral of
vengeance and mass delirium. The Abkhaz President Dr. Vladislav Ardzinba, who,
earlier in his career had been a respected historian of the proto-Hittite mythology,
plainly admitted to a journalist that rape and the plunder of conquered towns had
been in the laws of warfare since the Bronze Age.[55] Though that might be so, it
means that the irregular militias in the recent civil wars had failed to generate the
discipline, spirit, and extensive hierarchical cohesiveness that ought to distinguish
modern militaries and guerrilla forces. The failing was both moral and institutional.

It seems that the warlords, who lack the incentives of ideology and promotion, tend to reward their fighters by allowing them to rape and pillage.

The Abkhazes, feeling cornered and facing, as they believed, wholesale extermination, fought with determination and unity. For the same reason they occasionally displayed a paranoid brutality in searching for spies and traitors in ethnically mixed villages and families (and many of them were mixed) or even among the "purest" Abkhazes. Such acts looked more like archaic witch-hunts – symbolic struggles for the violent purification of the social body that might look familiar to anthropologists and cultural historians.

On the other side, the invading Georgian forces were badly disorganized and politically disunited. The lack of discipline seemed to be a much bigger problem for these fighters. The cause was not dissimilar – the Georgian paramilitaries resembled warlord bands more than a regular army. However, in this case, the particular historical culture of Georgian warfare might have been a factor. Generally, people fight as they work or play, which in theoretical terms means that the social habitus remains a consistent principle in generating activities ranging from work to leisure and to war. The Georgian nationalist volunteers often behaved at the battlefront like aristocratic warriors, performing valiant and spectacular acts of dashing bravery. But by the same token aristocratic sloth and indiscipline reigned in the rear. The former Georgian fighters with whom I had a chance to speak after the war admitted that much of their time had been spent enjoying the wine and food they had gathered, or just looted, from nearby homes (many of which belonged to fellow Georgians), that orders from superiors were routinely challenged, that sometimes half of their units would be away at home, perhaps taking back as "trophies" TV sets and rugs, and nobody wanted to sully their hands digging trenches or repairing old Soviet tanks.

Through their determination and with the help of foreign volunteers and Russian backers, the Abkhazes eventually prevailed in the war. But its ending was exceedingly gruesome. Despite their numerical advantage, the Georgian nationalist forces were routed and driven out of Abkhazia in October 1993. In the following days the advancing Abkhazian and Confederation troops forced out of Abkhazia virtually all the ethnic Georgians – nearly half of the republic's pre-war population. There were many personal and micro-vendettas in this campaign, which were not necessarily ethnically motivated. According to one credible witness, after the fall of Abkhazia's capital Suhum, the commander of a locally-formed ethnic Armenian unit (nearly eighteen per cent of Abkhazia's native population had been ethnic Armenians and many of them joined the Abkhaz effort) sought out and murdered nearly a dozen medical doctors and professors, along with some of their family members, regardless of the fact that many of the victims belonged to the local Armenian community. Before the war, this commander had worked as an ambulance paramedic (and, reportedly, used to sell painkillers on the black market) and aspired to become a medical doctor himself. But he had been failed twice by the medical examination board whose members paid for this with their lives.

It would be misleading, however, to think of this kind of behaviour as merely atavistic brutality. The general pattern suggests the existence of a premeditated strategy that sought to maximize the public effect of terror. The Chechen battalion under Shamil Basayev, acting in a more orderly fashion, executed only Georgian males known or found to possess membership cards for Georgian paramilitary organizations – yet these cards had been freely issued by the paramilitaries, who promised that, on the payment of membership dues, the bearer of a card would be able to use it as a privatization voucher in the coming land auctions.

Whatever the specific motives and modes of execution, this ethnic cleansing was not an outburst of irrational rage. Like all terror strategies, it could be called a weapon of the organizationally weak – the intent of which is to maximize the effect of a force of limited capability. A small irregular military that had no power to police the conquered Georgian civilians sought to drive out the potentially hostile population, and thereby in the long run to change the demographic balance, through acts of conspicuous brutality. Such acts forced the Georgian population to flee from the zones that the small Abkhaz and volunteer army had conquered but could not hope to police effectively.

In the end, all sides lost out. Russia failed to secure its Caucasus underbelly from either real or imaginary threats, and its actions only suceeded in providing a training ground for Basayev's Chechen fighters. The Georgian regime of Shevardnadze, instead of regaining control over its territory and state, suffered a costly defeat in Abkhazia, followed by another civil war. Politically, however, Georgia was able to check Abkhazia's victory. The international norms of state recognition operate by consensus, and can often be blocked by the veto of the state facing the secessionist bid. Under such a blockade, the once prosperous Abkhazia is now a landscape of burnt-out seaside cafés and citrus groves overgrown by weeds.

THE GOVERNORS' RESTORATION IN RUSSIA

In 1994 the Kabardin volunteers returning from Abkhazia discovered a new political reality. In the brief civil war of October 1993, President Yeltsin had liquidated the opposition entrenched in Russia's transitional parliament and thus emerged as the unchallenged ruler. The bloody events of October 1993, swiftly followed by the adoption of a new constitution with huge powers allocated to the near-imperial presidency, in effect ended the long revolutionary situation in Russia.

In the meantime, the separatist regime in Chechnya was rapidly decaying and increasingly looked like a charade; it was widely expected to collapse on its own – which would probably have happened even without Yeltsin's fateful decision to speed up the process.

Kabardino-Balkaria was once again firmly under the control of Valeri Kokov and his reconsolidated bureaucratic network. The Balkars held another referendum and, in a decision that was as unanimous as the one that preceded it, rescinded their own demand for a separate republic. Nationalism was now a spent force across the region. The politics of the Russian provinces, including Kabardino-Balkaria, came to be dominated by regimes of bureaucratic restoration enmeshed in corrupt oligarchic patronage. Let us now see how this configuration emerged.

Once the USSR was disbanded in December 1991, Yeltsin's weak new government had to deal with conflicting pressures at three levels: the West expected an increased openness to global capitalist flows in exchange for IMF loans; Moscow's neoliberal technocrats and financiers aspired to become a "comprador intelligentsia"[56] mediating between global capitalism and Russian industries; while the former communist governors were still in control in the provinces. Industrial proletarians and managers, who had once dominated the Soviet economy, utterly failed to constitute class-based political forces. The managers, still guided by their Soviet-era connections and habitus, lobbied Moscow to have the flow of resources continue, but the revenues available to the Russian government dropped to almost a third of their previous level.[57] The prospect of massive bankruptcies undermined the bargaining and redistributive powers of the managerial corps and weakened the resolve of proletarians. It was exactly what the neoliberal economic reformers were hoping for: bankruptcies and top-down restructuring that would attract outside investors. But there was little actual money flowing from Wall Street and very few goods, other than mineral resources, that could be exported on the world market.

The provincial governors faced the immediate sociopolitical consequences of neoliberal reform. Without having to read Polanyi's 1944 classic about "double movement," the governors fell back on their old political habitus and inherited networks of bureaucratic patronage, which were now deployed against the looming market destruction of the substance of their provincial societies. If one knew the actual political economy of state socialism, such a turn of events would not have been a surprise. But the neoliberal reformers operated on the assumption of invariate market laws that were presumably independent of historical legacies and geographic location. Unlike in Latin America, however, in the USSR the institutional fusion of politics and economics embodied in the Communist Party apparatus made the provincial first secretaries pivotal actors in both fields. Yeltsin's Constitution of 1993 acknowledged the power of governors by automatically granting them seats in the upper chamber of Russia's new parliament. The latter became the governors' club and a convenient platform for political lobbying and alliance-making. The *sui generis* senate reproduced the essential features of the old Central Committee, minus the token representation of workers, peasants, and women.[58]

Learning as they went along and emulating each other, the governors devised two key arrangements. The first was the nominal self-privatization of enterprises under the existing management in order to gain full control of resources. Second, the governors led the industrial managers in building networks of barter exchange that assured the survival of bankrupt enterprises despite their frozen bank accounts.[59] It also bound industrial managers and workers powerfully to their governors and cut down on the local resources flowing to Moscow.

Depending on local context, towards the mid-1990s the provincial governors developed several intersecting strategies for market subversion, but here we need not be concerned with specific variations because the outcome in each case was essentially the same: a protectionist and inherently corrupt political capitalism controlled by neopatrimonial strategies.[60] In effect, while the Central Bank in Moscow was demonstrating compliance with the IMF's demands for monetary austerity, the provincial authorities created various monetary substitutes (chits, wechsels, locally circulating bills of exchange, transferable tax obligations) which allowed for local de facto devaluations that assured the survival of near-bankrupt enterprises and thus reasserted the centrality of the governors to their key regional networks. These networks were held together only by what might be called the trust of despair. These generally ineffectual arrangements looked acceptable only by comparison with the wholesale ruin they were designed to avert. The tenuously established barter schemes were fraught with a myriad of conflicts, rampant corruption, and the asset-stripping ploys of individual managers trying to escape to places like Spain, Cyprus, or Bahrain. Hence the continuous refrains in the speeches of Kokov and many other provincial governors in the 1990s included vague calls to stick together and not to rock the boat, and expressions of conservative, nationalist doubts about globalization.

In the absence of effective law enforcement, private protection and adjudication proliferated widely. At first, the new strains of organized crime developed out of the diversity of social groups that possessed the requisite cohesion and violent skills: prison fraternities, associations of professional thieves, bands of rogue policemen and former soldiers, sub-proletarian teenage gangsters, athletes discovering the new uses for their physical prowess and team spirit, and ethnic mafias. Competing ferociously for the turf, they all rushed to claim their stake in the emerging ultra-lucrative market of private protection. But in the later 1990s, as the local political machines acquired more cohesion, the mobsters' rule was rolled back and the survivors were relegated to specific niches at the lower tiers of the private protection and adjudication markets. This did not mean, however, that the rule of law prevailed. Rather, the police, former KGB, and the officially licensed protection agencies won a larger share of economic flows and essentially claimed the same niche as the racketeers who were offering protection for a fee.[61] The size of these fees and the availability of protection, however, directly depended on the governor's office.

The stolid figure of Valeri Kokov remained central to the renewed sociopolitical compact in Kabardino-Balkaria. Like most Russian governors of the 1990s, he forged a powerful network of paternalistic dependencies that hinged on his bureaucratic office. Already in 1992 and 1993, while Shanibov's volunteers were away in Abkhazia, Kokov had reached a durable compromise with Yeltsin's administration in Moscow. Kokov's trump card was Chechnya – if the new government in Moscow wanted to avert another separatist rebellion in the predominantly Muslim republics, it had to forgo its liberal prejudices and accept a deal with the old communist prefects. Through multiple deal-making, Kokov transformed himself from a fledgling communist official into a fatherly statesman, the embodiment of local patriotism and conservatism. Moreover, he came to be regarded in Moscow as a prudent partner – though a little prone to get carried away with his personality cult. Kokov's new power rested on his exclusive position in several networks: he had access to Moscow's government offices for political and redistributive power (thus, through Moscow's graces, Kabardino-Balkaria gained access to profits from Russian exports of natural resources and foreign credit); he enjoyed alliances with fellow governors through the Federation Council (the Yeltsin-era senate); he had control over the officials who staffed the provincial state apparatus and, through them, control over the local flows of resources; and his patronage extended selectively to the local populations according to the status and relative importance of various groups. Moreover, Kokov carefully cultivated and monitored the emergent "business community." The majority of businessmen were former *nomenklatura* or close relatives and clients. Some were in fact Shanib's former students, who during perestroika reached the threshold of the *nomenklatura* but tried to leap ahead by supporting the revolutionary contention of 1991–1992. Subsequently, they defected by accepting flattering offers from the official establishment. The remainder of the new capitalists rose from the criminalized smuggling economy with the connivance of venal officials.

THE DECLINE OF THE PROLETARIAT

By the end of the Soviet period the economy of Kabardino-Balkaria rested on industrialized collective farm agriculture, holiday and health resorts built around mineral spas, non-ferrous metallurgy based on the locally mined molybdenum ores, and enterprises related to the military-industrial complex. All four economic branches depended directly on central coordination and investment from Moscow (the spa resorts were also reliant on the tours organized by Soviet trade unions), and thus they were among those worst hit by the precipitous abandonment of central planning for the sake of the transition to a market economy. Nonetheless, the formal end of central planning did not result in the launch of market mechanisms, because the scale, character, and specialization of Soviet-made industrial assets did not allow privatization to go ahead easily. What was to be done with the molybdenum used in smelting tank armor and armor-piercing warheads when the Russian government could not afford to spend anything on the military and watchful Western governments would not allow such products to be exported to the Third World?

The workers in these semi-defunct industries, even in the rural areas, continue to depend on their workplace for the basic conditions of life. This dependency has many material forms: monetary wages, although paid only sporadically; fodder and fertilizers distributed by collective farms in lieu of wages; enterprise-operated kindergartens; and basic services like heating and running water, which are supplied to residential highrises from the industrial boilers of nearby plants. Yet the dependency goes far beyond material benefits to encompass all the key aspects of social reproduction, including identity, social status and expectations, family life, and everyday interactions.[62] The occupational capital of proletarians is collective-dependent and embedded in their workplace: an operator of a blast furnace must stay close to his furnace and among his co-workers. From the time of Stalinist industrialization, the Soviet enterprises were intended to become the melting pots that would recast former peasants into modern Soviet men and women, the nuclei of new communities, and thus the tangible expression of Soviet civilization in action.[63] But any civilization entails the caging of its subjects, to use a favorite precept of Michael Mann.

Millions of former Soviet citizens found it impossible to break with their modern industrialized lifestyle. During the 1990s Russia's GDP fell by more than 50 per cent, and may have dropped even lower in Kabardino-Balkaria; according to official statistics real wages decreased in 1991–2000 by 60 per cent. Nevertheless, employees continued to report to work though they hadn't been paid for months (this plague of Russia's proletarians during the 1990s in fact served to reduce wages through rapid inflation, and in many cases it allowed unscrupulous managers to use the temporarily withheld wages as capital in short-term speculations). Strikes, nevertheless, were rare and mostly symbolic, lasting only three days at most. The old factories continued to operate at a quarter to half of their capacity without any qualitative retooling or change in management.[64]

Three compensatory mechanisms served to mitigate the misery that was widespread throughout the populace (though all three pushed the proletarians closer to a sub-proletarian condition). The first is the subsistence agriculture that is practiced on small plots of land around towns and in backyards. Cows and sheep can be seen grazing even in the public parks of Nalchik. The second is the petty cross-border trade that has grown explosively in the last decade, during which it has become possible to travel by charter plane to Istanbul, Beijing, or the duty-free zone of Abu Dhabi. Each year an estimated thirty to forty million Russian citizens, mostly women, import cheap merchandize, literally by the bagful, to resell in open-air markets. It is a precarious and sometimes dangerous trade, but it is one of the few available opportunities to supplement the household income. The third compensatory mechanism is the mutual help offered variously by relatives, neighbors, and close friends. But the networks necessary for this can break down, as reflected in the commonly heard complaint that friends and relatives (in Nalchik these two generic categories encompass very wide circles) today are no longer as close and reliable as they used to be. Although instances of selfless generosity still abound and are praised, many people seem afraid that those who may claim them as relatives or friends in these times of hardship may stretch their resources too far. This fact is common knowledge, of course; therefore even those who are experiencing severe hardship feel reluctant to ask for help and would rather assiduously hide their misery.

Survey data from the 1990s consistently show that in Kabardino-Balkaria, as elsewhere in Russia, the most common concern among the populace (40–50 per cent) was the economic depression.[65] Next to this ranked the social anxieties related to structural instability: street crime, the deterioration of public education, career instability, substance abuse, the dissolution of the family, poor health, and old age. Concerns with the preservation of ethnic culture, national pride, and religious values came much lower, at around 10 per cent or slightly less.

Here we encounter a paradox. Overwhelmingly the people are afflicted by economic and social problems, but if they participate in any political protests they are predominantly nationalist in expression. It is very wrong to say – however often we might hear it – that these people are apathetic, lacking in civic consciousness, provincial, corrupt, and unable to act collectively. The same people a decade earlier were deeply engaged in the debates of perestroika. This puzzle is very important. Part of the answer must be that unemployment remains low, strikes or popular protests are minimal, the routines of daily life continue, and in general after the bout of market reforms the scene has reverted to something oddly resembling the days of Brezhnevism – which Michael Burawoy dubbed Russia's industrial involution.[66]

A larger part of the explanation, however, might be as follows. The shadowy and ruthless intra-elite politics of the new epoch left the majority of the post-Soviet population mystified, cynical, and feeling powerless – alas, not without reason. In the 1990s, the circle of political contenders was sharply reduced to factions of neo-*nomenklatura* officials and oligarchic entrepreneurs. The intellectuals and proletarians no longer mattered either as protestors or as the producers of material or symbolic goods. Profits and power were now generated not in industrial production but in financial speculation and trade exchange linked to global flows.

THE VODKA REBELLION

All large programs of mobilization have now been discredited: socialist developmentalism, proletarian social democratization, the quest for national independence, and the neoliberal promise of markets – each of them has had its moment in recent years and all led to cruel disappointment. The social classes that were once at the center of civic mobilizing – intellectuals, specialists, industrial workers – have now fallen mute. Yet all was not quiet for there still remained the sub-proletarians, those who were mostly excluded from official patronage. This group relied on their own networks, which could be mobilized for political purposes and in ways expressive of the local sub-proletarian culture. This could be clearly seen in the recent bootleg wars that produced the largest political mobilizations in the North Caucasus since the collapse of the USSR.

The end of the Soviet monopoly on alcohol produced a fabulously lucrative, fragmented, and violent market. The majority of vodka capitalists were socialist-era black marketeers and street toughs who, true to their roots, continued to live in the same sub-proletarian quarters. The vertiginous albeit inherently criminalized careers of the vodka capitalists are much-discussed success stories – a success which saddles this newly wealthy group with a hefty obligation to display generosity. When building themselves ostentatious walled mansions, the post-Soviet *nouveaux riches* in the Caucasus usually cannot neglect to pave the whole street, or to provide natural gas lines for the neighborhood, or build a new mosque and sponsor respected elders on the pilgrimage to Mecca.

For a while, Moscow turned a blind eye to the booming production of bootleg vodka in the North Caucasus, which, according to various estimates, claimed at least a half and perhaps as much as two thirds of Russia's vodka market. Moscow's passivity was in part due to the usual bureaucratic corruption and lack of oversight, but also to a politically motivated apprehension at unsettling the balance in the volatile region bordering on Chechnya.

In 1998 Russian border guards suddenly began to enforce in earnest customs duties on the heavy trucks carrying raw alcohol from western Europe via Turkey and the porous frontiers of independent Georgia. The likely reason was the severe fiscal crisis of the Russian government in the wake of the East Asian financial melt-down that precipitated both the collapse of Russia's speculative market dealing in government bonds and the end of IMF credits. Another plausible hypothesis which circulated at the time claimed that the operation was sponsored by the influential mayor of Moscow, Yuri Luzhkov, who was acting on behalf of the embattled alcohol industry located in the Russian capital. The enforcement of customs regulations and duties initiated a year-long standoff at the border check-points, with hundreds of heavy trucks carrying raw alcohol blocking the mountain highways. During this period the border guards were regularly fired upon from the mountaintops, scores of hostages were seized by gangs, notorious bootleggers were mysteriously assassinated, and bombs exploded in town markets. However, it is impossible to determine with certainty which of these violent events stemmed from the vodka wars, or indeed who actually won in this inchoate and opaque struggle. Several prominent bootleggers, quickly learning a new strategy of escape from their violent predicament, used elections to run for various offices across the region, from city mayor to federal parliament and gubernatorial seats. For the ruling bureaucratic cliques of the North Caucasus, the political activism of the rich and popularly admired bootleggers posed an unexpectedly dangerous challenge. It was defused by begging Moscow for help. Federal prosecutors readily brought criminal charges against the politicized smugglers.

In the Republic of Daghestan, this provoked the two Hachilayev brothers (both former boxers and celebrity smugglers) to launch an abortive rebellion that was proclaimed as the beginning of an Islamic revolution. The Hachilayevs' rebellion was crushed by the Daghestani police with the help of "angry citizens," who were in reality the private ethnic militias of various state officials. One of the brothers was killed, another escaped to Chechnya where he posed, for a while, as a leader of Islamic jihad. During the second Russian invasion of Chechnya in 1999, the surviving Hachilayev once again changed sides and, for services that remained unknown, has earned Moscow's pardon.

The mysterious conflict eventually abated. The vodka industry, though shaken, continues to provide the region with its main source of cash, which is redistributed through networks of bureaucratic patronage and private charities. Yet since 2000, Putin's centralizing regime has apparently improved tax collection by intimidating the smugglers and accentuating the dependence of regional elites on Moscow.

EPILOGUE

Today, Yuri Shanibov (who has now reverted to this more conventional name) is an internal exile once again. He lectures and tries to write in order to gain his long-overdue full professorship, joking that if they once again deny him a promotion, he will stage another revolution and become President – without saying of which state. And, just as in his youth, he is back to waging campaigns for university reform. The institution in which he works is dilapidated and overcrowded because the local authorities insist that more students are enrolled to keep the youth off the streets, but cannot provide adequate funding. When funds were provided to renovate the public toilets (which, as in many post-Soviet establishments, were in a shameful state), the new Turkish plumbing fixtures were vandalized almost immediately. Shanibov sighs: *Many of our students do not really belong in a university, or they feel that this sort of education is totally unpromising, but what can we do?* The curriculum and teaching methods have remained essentially unchanged since the 1950s. One of Shanibov's initiatives is to introduce student evaluations of courses, which is opposed by many professors.

The Mountain Confederation was reduced to a ghostly existence shortly after the Abkhazian war ended in 1993. It became clear that for the foreseeable future there would not be an independent state of free highlanders from Daghestan on the Caspian to Abkhazia on the Black Sea. The wretched examples of Chechnya and Abkhazia, the only segments of the putative Mountain Confederation where the national separatists gained political power, helped to discredit the idea on which it was founded. Also, much moral damage was wrought by the Ossetian–Ingush bloodshed over disputed land, during which the Confederation proved entirely unable to mediate and prevent the conflict between these two highlander peoples. The projected return of millions of ethnic Circassians, the descendants of the *muhajeers* of the 1860s, from the Middle East to their ancestral lands in the Caucasus has never materialized. Only a few hundred such descendants did come back, and most of them soon left again because they discovered that in reality their ancestral lands had become, in their view, too Soviet and culturally alien. Likewise the returnees, after several generations spent in the Middle East, appeared to their Caucasian brethren too much like Arabs or Turks. The formative experiences of modernity drew the Circassian communities apart.

When the war flared up in Chechnya in the last week of December 1994, the Confederation was effectively undone. Its last ally in the higher echelons of state power, Russia's Minister of Justice, Kalmykov, who was an ethnic Circassian, proved to be the only member of Yeltsin's cabinet to make good on his threat of resignation. But Kalmykov's resignation, despite its political resonance, remained an isolated act. Besides, it robbed Shanibov of his last channel of influence in Moscow. At the ground level, only a handful of Confederation fighters went to Chechnya. They were either the die-hards who had become professional soldiers in the Abkhazian war, or adventurous sub-proletarian youngsters who had missed their chance to fight the first time around. The intellectuals remained virtually silent and deeply ashamed by their political impotence

The Russian invasion of Chechnya in 1994 failed to elicit feelings of outrage and solidarity comparable to the reaction to the Georgian invasion of Abkhazia in 1992, probably because there is a limit to how long people can stay in a state of collective agitation. By December 1994, the turmoil started by perestroika was in its ninth year. Hopes of a miracle (delivered by democratization, national independence, or market transition) had been dashed, and the new post-Soviet life brought forth brutal dilemmas of individual survival.

The veterans of the Abkhazian campaign returned to their native suburbs. Many of them altogether vanished from sight and a few developed addictions. Several were assassinated in gangland-style affairs, including Yusup Soslambekov, Shanibov's successor at the head of the now insubstantial Confederation. Others became small merchants, shuttling to and from the Middle East; many others formed private protection agencies, which are a quasi-legal form of protection racket that exist in the gray area somewhere between the police and the purely criminal gangs. And a small but not insignificant number of the veterans became devoted Muslims. They did not, however, feel drawn to the established mosques, which were dominated by traditionalist elders. The young veterans yearned for a less ritualistic, more vibrant, and life-enhancing faith of the sort they had experienced with their Middle Eastern comrades during the Abkhazian campaign. An important distinction between the conformist and the newly resurgent Islam in the North Caucasus lay, of course, in matters of doctrine: the local traditionalists belonged to the Sufi mystical orders while the dissidents adopted the puritanical Wahhabi theology and practice recently imported from Saudi Arabia, Pakistan and Afghanistan. The religious distinction thus directly flowed from the organizational hierarchy and sources of funding. In one regard at least, the Islamic charities of the Middle East that first reached directly into the Caucasus in the mid-1990s created the same patterns of local emulation that were created by Western non-governmental organizations. To obtain positions in the local chapters of foreign NGOs, and therefore access to their material resources, symbolic recognition, and international travel, local staff members had to adopt the language and the rituals of their funding agencies. This does not mean, as the hostile propaganda likes to claim, that the young Caucasian Wahhabis sold out to foreign money. Wahhabism (or, as the adherents prefer to call it, the Salafite or "pure" doctrine) offered the young militants a platform from which they could attack the traditionalist Islam associated with Soviet-era official institutions. The new converts found in this an opportunity to constitute themselves into a separate group of distinct status and powerful internal solidarity that could claim to represent a facet in the worldwide movement for the renovation of faith and the moralistic reordering of social affairs.

In sum, the cultural and ideological differences between the Western non-governmental organizations concerned with education or ecology and the Islamic charities from the Middle East may be huge, yet their organizational dynamics seem remarkably similar. A key difference lies primarily in the social status of the local staff: the secular Western NGOs almost exclusively attract local English-speaking intellectuals; the Islamic charities attract the sub-proletarians and sub-intellectuals. For the latter categories who possess very little cultural capital, the Islamic charities are in fact the only accessible international organizations.

In two interviews with people who had traveled to Islamic schools abroad I heard stories of encounters with Osama bin Laden. He was described with great awe as a saintly ascetic who had quit a life of privilege and corruption for the caves of

Afghanistan. One of Shanibov's former volunteers, who is now held by the American military in the prison camp at Guantanamo Bay (I omit his name), provides a very explicit example. His mother is a Russian, and his father, who was a native North Caucasian, left them long ago when his son was just a baby. The mother had no education and worked as a janitor or laundress. The young man joined the volunteer brigades going to Abkhazia, where he was attracted to the Middle Eastern volunteers, converted to Islam, and was eventually invited to study at a religious school abroad. He probably ended up in Afghanistan, like several other essentially homeless and socially disaffected young men from the region, following the international networks of Islamic militancy.

It seems, however, that the wave of Islamic piety has already broken after its brief and rapid rise between 1995 and 1998. In 1997 I recorded the story of a Kabardin intellectual and once prominent nationalist whose seventeen-year-old son declared his intention to fast during Ramadan and study the Koran. When the puzzled father, who was a completely secular scholar and whose own father had been a devout communist, asked the son to explain himself, the answer was a condemnation of the period in which they were living: *When your generation were young, you could look forward to going to university and becoming engineers, doctors, pilots, or scholars. What is left to us? Drugs or envying the vodka tycoons? No, we must go back to the roots of faith, to something pure.* The same young man in 2003, however, became an engineer, largely thanks to the efforts of his parents. He has recently married and become a father. The engineer's salary, however, is less than a hundred dollars a month (and the prices in Kabardino-Balkaria today are at global market levels). The young specialist practices Islam, although much less conspicuously than before.

Contrary to alarmist predictions that cited ethnic traditions and the historical precedent of jihad, Kabardin society was not swept up in religious fanaticism. Though silent and profoundly tired of mobilization, the educated urban proletarians remain prevalent in the social structure, which, at least so far, has retained its modern secular outlook. The rest was accomplished by the police repression that followed the September 1999 apartment block bombings across Russia, which Moscow officials blamed on the North Caucasus Islamists, and especially after President Putin allied himself with America's "War on Terror."

Nevertheless future rebellions are not at all implausible. The ruling regime in Kabardino-Balkaria, like almost everywhere in the emerging post-communist periphery, is precariously suspended in a web of personal deals that periodically become tangled. One of the most robust generalizations formulated by the comparative sociologists of revolutions finds that regimes of the "sultanistic" variety are especially susceptible to being overthrown.[67] Disruptive events like bouts of market volatility, a succession of big patrons from within, or interventions by stronger political actors from without (like Moscow's crackdown on bootleggers or the "War on Terror") always threaten to aggravate feuds among the peripheral elites. Such crises in the future will create opportunities for radical contenders who up to that point have remained dormant. But will they be revolutionary forces, or rebels with a different cause?

There is now plenty of empirical evidence to suggest that the latter is more likely. Consider the events of the last decade in countries as different as Afghanistan, Algeria, Nepal, Sri Lanka, Peru, Colombia, or even Chiapas; or consider the frightening dynamics of more than a dozen collapsing states in sub-Saharan Africa; the former Yugoslavia's Kosovo and Macedonia; the formerly Soviet Uzbekistan and Tadjikistan, and also Chechnya. These examples indicate that the likeliest contenders would be ethnic separatists, various kinds of fundamentalists, or the type of smuggler warlords who emerge from peripheries within peripheries: rural and suburban sub-proletarian slums and the immigrant ghettos of core capitalism.

The possible targets of contention constitute a big problem. With the extinction of the whole sector of old socialist doctrines, there is no longer any rational theory to explain the current world situation and to offer alternatives. A vast majority of post-Soviet men and women have been left wondering what hit them. By default, conspiracy theories and the wildest mythology no longer belong in the fringes; they are in many instances the people's main explanation for the events of recent years. This helps to explain the recent spread of anti-Americanism and anti-Semitism, both of which are new to the Caucasus. That these social phobias are new cannot be doubted. If anything, for the generation of the Second World War, Americans were allies against the Nazis, while younger people were fascinated by exotic Hollywood films, jazz broadcasts on Voice of America, and American consumer goods such as smuggled Levi's jeans. Official Soviet propaganda was too much a matter of ritual to impress anyone with its diatribes against American imperialism; even party propagandists themselves did not buy it. As to the Jews, in the Caucasus they have traditionally been accorded perhaps the best treatment anywhere in Europe and the Islamic Middle East because here they were just another among a great many different ethnic and religious groups. The new anti-Semitism, it must be emphasized, has nothing to do with any actual Jews who live nearby. At that level relations are usually still good, a fact illustrated by the following touching story. A few years ago in a Circassian village, an old Jewish bachelor who had been a respected veterinarian died. The local elders convened to discuss the matter with the mullah and concluded that the dead man deserved a decent burial. But since nobody knew how Jews ought to be buried, he was given an Islamic funeral at the village cemetery in the expectation that his relatives, if they could ever be found, might eventually perform the proper Jewish rites. This example does not seem too surprising even to people who might otherwise make rabidly anti-Semitic pronouncements: the actual Jew was a good neighbor in this life; those Jews who seek to manipulate the world belong to a totally different dimension of mythology. Thus anti-Semitism and anti-Americanism gain hold where it would be futile to look for any specific cause in the tensions of local interethnic relations. The mythology of the diabolical American–Israeli plot to dominate the world is fed from both Russian and Arab sources, and it emerges now as a way to explain current humiliations and otherwise totally incomprehensible miseries. For example, the war in Chechnya is widely believed to be the result of American and Israeli manipulation intended to destroy the glorious Soviet Union and later Russia and, on the other side, the Chechens, who are believed to be the toughest Muslim fighters in the world.

The current prevalence of destructive, non-revolutionary contention derives from generalized systemic conditions: the absence in contemporary geoculture of legitimate ideological alternatives, and the end of the geopolitical competition of the Cold War. These conditions deny potential revolutionaries the resources of political recognition and international solidarity that were enjoyed by the national-liberation guerrillas of the 1950s to 1970s. What remains as bases of contention are various networks of a predominantly local character and traditional solidarities embedded in ethnic and religious communities (which can be carried far across state borders by modern communications). A related condition is the relative weakness of dependent peripheral states whose legitimacy and coercive powers are eroded by the very same foreign dependency and corrupt practices that sustain the ruling regimes.[68] At this point globalization, namely the global forces structuring these new forms of dependency, becomes a major potential cause of future ethnic conflicts.

So far Kabardino-Balkaria remains quiet politically. But most of Shanibov's veterans are still in their thirties and maintain their war-time camaraderie. Today their personal example, their war stories, and their networks provide one of the few positive patterns of socialization capable of appealing to the sub-proletarian adolescents who are coming of age in an unstable post-Soviet environment.

THEORETICAL REPRISE

Possibility

.

"Try not to judge our Yuri too harshly. During his whole life he has been fighting for really the same principle: self-governance. Only the reference groups of his self-governance projects have been shifting."

The Dean at Kabardino-Balkarian State University on his Professor Shanibov

"It seems to me inconceivable that the application of systematic thought to the improvement of the way we do things will stop."

Arthur Stinchcombe, "On Softheadedness on the Future"
(*Ethics* 93, October 1982, p. 118)

This man's story sounds much like Latin America in the twentieth century! – exclaimed my Argentinean friend. *In our wars, these kind of Shanibovs were found on each and every side* – said a sociologist who nobly persists in calling himself a Yugoslav. A Norwegian anthropologist who had spent most of his life studying Sudan and Yemen commented as follows: *Three generations ago, young educated Arabs challenged the existing hierarchy of power from the positions of technical Westernization and liberal constitutionalism; a generation ago, such agents of change were revolutionary nationalists and Marxists; presently, however, they would rather speak as Islamic revivalists against the moral corruption of Arab rulers and their subservience to America.* The life trajectory of Musa/Yuri Shanib(ov) has echoes with many similar stories of contemporary intellectuals from the countries that came to be called the Third World or now simply the global South. But how robust are these comparisons? Put differently, does this Shanibov's twisted biography illuminate historical patterns of larger import and, if indeed so, what are these patterns?

The answers to such questions require disciplined generalizations. Here we shall engage in a final effort to weave the various threads together in an attempt to discern new and broadly applicable insights that might be gained from the story of Shanibov and Soviet experience. Meaningfully construed generalizations can prevent superficial and false comparisons. Still more importantly, generalizations can lend explanatory power to analogies that may be genuine but are invariably partial – straight parallels being hard to find given the complexity of the social world. China, after all, is not Russia, and Russia is not exactly like Brazil, or Turkey, or South Africa. But looking from a certain angle, we may discover striking and possibly informative similarities. The source of light that makes these similarities visible and meaningful is social theory.

This book offers only a heuristic, or a provisional theoretical nucleus. A larger explanatory theory may be developed in the future through a collective transdisciplinary effort. Here my primary goal is to demonstrate by what theoretical means one might excavate the complex empirical reality behind the common clichés of "totalitarianism," "post-communist transitions," "failed states," "ethnic politics," or the "rise of globalization." In the introduction I employed the metaphor of an archeological dig that cuts a narrow trench across a promising site in order to reveal the stratigraphy of historical layers, indicate the hidden structures, and suggest directions for a more detailed excavation. But the near past of the Soviet experience is a huge buried edifice, in relation to which our job cannot be merely one of excavation. It is also necessary to clear the thick dust that envelops the site of catastrophic collapse.

In doing this, we face two hurdles. The first is the dearth of empirical knowledge, since the communist *nomenklatura* assiduously buried the facts in secret archives, misrepresented them, or else simply ignored them, fearing their potential for exposing the yawning discrepancy between the *nomenklatura*'s ideological claims and the reality of their rule. Since 1989 the archives have been opening up, and in many instances the witnesses of past events could still be interviewed. Thus, the scarcity of empirical data is relative and transient. The second, much larger, problem is epistemological in nature. It pertains to the inherited structures of knowledge that organize professional research, generate its topics and concepts, and prescribe common ways of validation, presentation, and interpretation. These structures of knowledge emerged from the late nineteenth-century institutionalization of social science into separate disciplines, where the economists lay claim to an intellectual monopoly on theorizing processes of material production and monetized exchange, where political scientists seek to formalize in "mid-range" theories the operations of political power, where historians normally focus on the manageable pieces of the documented past, and where sociologists, an intellectually promiscuous lot, then try to pick up the rest.

Moreover, the established structures of knowledge are sanctioned and informed by the powerful binary ideologies left over from the Cold War: in particular, the deep-seated antinomy between liberalism and its political opponents, who until recently had been mostly Marxists of various stripes. The antinomy goes back not to the symbolic dates of 1945 or 1917 but all the way back to the aftermath of the pan-European revolution of 1848. These binary lenses belong to the core of what was generically called modernity. Since the Soviet Union embodied one of the geopolitical and ideological poles of the opposition, in relation to its history the old Cold War perceptions – currently taking the form of conservative triumphalism and leftist despair – maintain an exceedingly strong sway.

In this concluding chapter I shall attempt three clarifications in succession. First, I offer a substantive summary that places the Soviet experience and the sequence of Shanibov's changing positions in a larger world-system perspective. The question to be answered in this section might be stated simply: What was state socialism, and how did it begin, evolve, and end? Second, I shall summarize the synthetic theoretical approach that emerges from the study of Shanibov's life. The question here can be expressed as: How can we rationally study individual human fortunes in relation to global transformations, and how can we make such research useful for dealing with collective choices? Finally, I shall dare to speculate regarding future possibilities. If the retrospective summaries of the first two sections constitute different kinds of mental map, one of the USSR in the world-system and the other of current academic production, my hypotheses regarding future possibilities pertain rather to what I would call the intellectual compass. We are currently facing huge and hugely consequential theoretical, political, and ultimately moral choices. The small region of the Caucasus offers but one stark example of a rising global dilemma currently subsumed under various familiar rubrics such as ethnic conflict, bad governance, lengthy economic depressions, new epidemic diseases, drastic damage to the natural environment, transborder terrorism, organized crime, refugee exodus, or the new racism directed against the peoples of "Southern" cultures and religions, especially Islam. All these are facets of a global dilemma stemming from the *durable social breakdown* which has already affected vast swaths of the world-system and threatens to spread further, penetrating even into the core zones. In such times, expanding the scope of realistic political options – realistic insofar as we can indicate the correlation of forces and possible mechanisms for realizing these options – becomes no less integral to the scholarly enterprise than perfecting our theories. As such I shall here attempt not only to push my formulations to the limit but also to make them accessible to readers who are not social scientists by vocation.

TRAJECTORIES OF SOVIET DEVELOPMENTALISM

The life story of Yuri Muhammedovich Shanibov provided us with a thread running through the decades and allowed us a series of microscopic observations. But such observations will not become fully intelligible and generalizable without drawing the relevant macroscopic connections. The bitterly bewildered question which is so commonly heard these days across the former Soviet lands – *What evil hit this place?* – will not obtain a rational answer without reference to the big structural transformations spanning the long and intense twentieth century.

At around 1900 and as late as the summer of 1914 the world appeared securely dominated by the Western imperial powers. This was the outcome of the preceding century when for the first time ever the whole planet came to be encompassed by a single world-system, as one after another the non-Western areas succumbed to domination by Western states. The Caucasus, for instance, was joined to the modern world-system much like the rest of the future Third World: it was conquered militarily between the 1800s and the 1860s, and subjected to colonial capitalist modernization between the 1870s and the 1910s through the creation of settler towns, railroads, ports, tax agencies and police stations.

The unprecedented expansionary force of the nineteenth-century West derived in large part from its pioneering the national state organization. This meant much more than the innovation of nationalist ideology acquiring official status after 1870. The national state fostered legal bureaucratic authority, industrial bases, currency, universal military conscription, and the institutions of national citizenship, education, and welfare that had effectively tamed and incorporated the multiple class contradictions of the early industrial era. This is why in the twentieth century the non-capitalist developmentalists would pin their hopes on reproducing in their countries the national state along with industrialization. From the capitalist standpoint, the national state represented an attractive trade-off between protection and the adventuresome vagaries of the cosmopolitan trade and finance that had characterized capitalist operations in earlier epochs. The core club of the "civilized powers" was not only highly exclusive but, like the capitalist markets themselves, internally competitive. Therefore the development of national states in the West proceeded apace with the competitive extension of several colonial empires outside Europe.[1] But in 1914 competition among the core states resulted in a horrific geopolitical implosion resulting in three decades of utter chaos in the economic, ideological, and political structures of capitalism.[2]

The Russian revolution of 1917 was among the earliest reactions to the self-destruction of the nineteenth-century capitalist order. It was also one of the most consequential because the Russian Empire contained elements of core Western society alongside a sea of agrarian backwardness and a variety of colonial situations. Furthermore, because Russia was a state of continental size it could effectively resist geopolitical pressures and support an extraordinary experiment in economic autarchy. The Bolshevik takeover of Russia, however, did not ignite a chain reaction of socialist revolutions in the core capitalist countries, as was hoped, and even more so feared, at the time.

The political structures of the core zone proved capable of absorbing the shocks of the 1914–1945 period of turmoil. Internally, this was accomplished by abandoning, after some struggle, the nineteenth-century faith in self-regulating markets, and devising instead the innovative hegemonic compact of Big Government, Big Business, and Big Labor that translated across the different Western countries into such familiar adaptations as mass party democracy, the welfare state, Fordism, Keynesianism, and the New Deal.[3] Geopolitically, capitalism was in fact inadvertently helped by the outcome of the Russian revolution – the military force of the newly industrialized Soviet Union canceled the antisystemic Nazi attempt to impose a 'New Order' through a coercive world empire. After 1945 the USSR was accommodated in the Cold War dispensation as the familiar and sufficiently rational foe whose presence played an important ritual role in contemporary capitalist ideology and politics.

The most consequential impact of the Russian revolution was on the areas that after 1945 became called the Third World. In the penetrating statement of Geoffrey Barraclough, "never before in the whole of human history had so revolutionary a reversal occurred with such rapidity ... When the history of the first half of the twentieth century – which for most historians is still dominated by the European wars and European problems – comes to be written in a longer perspective, there is little doubt that no single theme will prove to be of greater importance than the revolt against the west."[4] Just as the French revolution meant one thing in France (i.e. a succession of chaotic struggles resulting in the Napoleonic rationalization of state structures) but quite a different thing for the rest of contemporary world (a tremendously inspiring liberation message and a build-up of military and political pressure on all remaining absolutist regimes), so too the Russian revolution perhaps also accomplished one thing in Russia (a huge build-up of the state's coercive, extractive, and organizing capacity) but had quite a different impact on the structures of the world-system.[5]

With the example of successful revolution and rapid industrialization in what became the Soviet Union, the possibility of indigenous insurgent forces elsewhere taking over the political and economic structures of European colonialism, and turning these structures into the foundation of new national states became eminently realistic. The next goal of non-Western insurgents would be national development, which was understood as the use of local resources (previously extracted for the profit of foreign capitalists and their comprador collaborators) for the purpose of fostering modern industries, mass education, and, not least of all, new armies capable of protecting national sovereignty. National development opened dazzling prospects for collective and individual advancement, as the numerous indigenous cadres were recruited into the rapidly expanding structures of developmental states, and these states would themselves move dramatically upward in the world hierarchy of power and prestige. The program of revolutionary developmentalism, conceived in terms of socialism, national liberation and their numerous hybrids, thus appealed especially to those groups of modern educators, professionals, technical specialists, junior officers, and bureaucrats located in the peripheral countries. Their individual careers and social group aspirations were often stymied, and they generally felt humiliated and alienated by the "underdeveloped" conditions of their countries, yet such groups were also potentially best positioned to provide political leadership and formulate the agenda for popular movements of protest, especially when geopolitical and economic turmoil put pressures on the core countries and weakened the constraints.[6]

Given the mounting number of precedents, in 1917, and especially after 1945, the national liberation trend greatly worried the Western political leaders. In response, they felt compelled to formulate and support with actual resources a less disruptive, "moderate" alternative that envisioned voluntary decolonization, economic aid, and the creation of various international organizations such as the United Nations which (at least in theory) could serve the purposes of collegial world governance and a new economic order between the nations.

In the space of only a generation, by 1955–1965, the world outlook and balance of forces appeared very different from the situation before 1914. The Soviet Union under Khrushchev turned to embrace Third World developmentalism and openly proclaimed its dual goal of overtaking the capitalist West in industrial production and popular welfare while preserving peaceful coexistence in geopolitics, and extending broad alliances with the newly liberated national-developmental states (i.e. achieving a new world order while preventing the horrors of another world war).[7]

And that was not all. By various demographic estimates, sometime in the 1950s the global proportion of people living in towns for the first time exceeded – and rapidly proceeded to overtake – the proportion of people who lived in the countryside. At the same time the material networks of modern science and technology extended into the remotest places. A great many people on the planet, and virtually all Soviet citizens, now came to live within the reach of paved roads, health clinics, schools, electrical grids, and TV broadcasts. As Eric Hobsbawm put it: "For 80 per cent of humanity the Middle Ages ended suddenly in the 1950s."[8]

Let us now recapitulate the key arguments regarding the Soviet trajectory in chronological order. (The sequence is formally presented in Table 6 on page 330.) My central theoretical claim is that the Soviet developmentalist trajectory, the original and the longest of its kind, can be also viewed as a coordinated set of hypotheses applicable to the whole range of twentieth-century developmental states, especially those resulting from revolutions and other anti-systemic rebellions. This does not mean that any particular Soviet trait must find its exact replica in states as different as Turkey, Mexico, Vietnam, Mozambique, or Yugoslavia. The hypotheses should be rather treated as vectors along which we can build rational explanations and account for the variety of national developmental experiences in the twentieth century. In this way, we might work towards an understanding of the present world situation and our possible futures.

Before 1917 the Bolsheviks were a small but tightly organized faction of devoted full-time revolutionaries drawn mostly from the alienated intelligentsia. The alienation of the educated middle classes was the result of their being caught between an absolutist bureaucracy still dominated by aristocratic ranks, and the lack of modern markets in which their education credentials might be converted into professional incomes. Certainly not all the Russian intelligentsia suffered equally from the lack of careers and incomes. Those who occupied more comfortable positions would normally strive for liberal reforms rather than join the revolutionary underground. But in a predominantly agrarian country, with a politically repressive regime and a deeply alienated population, the revolutionaries could potentially tap on vastly larger reserves of mobilizable discontent than could the liberal reformers. The Bolsheviks emerged from the political culture of Western social democracy, but they considered the Second International's standing prescription of gradual incorporation into the structures of liberal states as an irrelevance, for the Russian Empire was not such a state. Neither were countries like China or Turkey, in relation to which the Bolsheviks' quarrel with the Second International looked perfectly justified.

At the same time, the Bolsheviks resolutely proclaimed their intention to resist the fate of the Paris Commune. This deeply ingrained disposition became the generating principle of Bolshevik politics. Hence their improbable combination of messianic zeal with ferocious pragmatism. In 1918, after a brief period of revolutionary euphoria, the realm of the now defunct Russian Empire was plunged into a horrific civil war, accompanied on its several fronts by ferocious peasant revolts and ethnic massacres. During the course of the civil war, the revolutionaries, now called the communists, developed out of their party structures their own Red Army and secret police, together with the economic, propagandistic, and administrative apparatuses that in sum became the Soviet state.[9] A new pattern of governance emerged with dictatorial powers that self-consciously emulated the war economy of Wilhelmine Germany. The Bolshevik insurrection thus succeeded by adopting the weapons of the enemy. The justification for merging the dream of Karl Marx with the Realpolitik of Bismarck and Lüdendorf was found in the Bolshevik conviction that their organization was now in the vanguard of world liberation and that thus their defeat would be a setback for historical progress. The combination of strong collectivist charisma with the centralized bureaucratic expropriation of Russia's vast resources made possible the Bolsheviks' glories as well as their infamies.[10]

The pro-market decade of the New Economic Policy (NEP) may appear as either a different face of Bolshevism or else as a deviation from the original revolutionary ideals. In fact it was neither. The Bolsheviks' embrace of the gold standard orthodoxy during the 1920s flowed from the same revolutionary combination of bureaucratic pragmatism and messianic expectation. Many Bolshevik intellectuals of the time could have become leading economists and sociologists had they not already been practicing revolutionaries. They knew about how the world works as much as they knew the advanced social science of the age – and let us recall that in the 1920s beliefs in the modernizing power of free markets were experiencing a worldwide return before the great slump. But by 1929 the hopes for foreign investment and domestic peasant-driven market revival had been exhausted. In the 1930s the Soviet state embarked on a quest to build a modern industrial base without capitalists. A major factor in this decision was the expectation of another world war. Soviet developmentalism thus became fundamentally military-industrial in character.

The architecture of the Soviet state was determined in the main by the three institutions that had most contributed to the Bolshevik victory in the civil war: the centralized and all-encompassing *nomenklatura* system of political-bureaucratic appointment; the forced mobilization of economic resources and manpower for the war effort; and the establishment of national republics. Stalinism flowed directly from the institutions, policies, and cadres forged in the Russian civil war.[11] There is no merit in culturalist and psychologizing explanations that variously invoke the Russian traditions of despotism, Stalin's paranoia, or Bolshevik messianism. Equally, there is little merit in leftist arguments against Stalinism as being a deviation from Lenin's legacy or even a counter-revolution. Hypothetically, a different successor to Lenin might have proven less murderous than Stalin. This might have saved many lives, yet it is doubtful that Soviet industrialization could ever have been less despotic, because its character seems fully determined by the war-economic configuration of the Soviet state, its antagonistic relation to the peasantry, and the contemporary geopolitical context. Nonetheless – to extend the counterfactual – a less terroristic regime might have later facilitated a less oppressive political climate in the USSR. Could this have led to a more democratic and orderly overcoming of the Soviet developmental dictatorship? "Possibly" seems the only possible answer.

To restate it as a positive theoretical proposition, the purges and the personality cult did not grow out of Stalin's head but rather from the newly achieved centralization of political, military, economic, and ideological structures. Historically, such a degree of centralization – usually achievable only in the aftermath of revolutions, wars or similar upheavals – has in turn produced its charismatic embodiment in great hero/villain figures such as Napoleon in one historical situation or Atatürk, Mussolini, Perón, Mao, Tito, Fidel, Nasser, and Khomeini in their different but broadly comparable situations. It remains to be investigated whether there may also exist a special receptiveness to such national-statist rituals in predominantly agrarian populations during periods of rapid socioeconomic restructuring. The terroristic and "totalitarian" tendencies of twentieth-century developmentalism flowed from the same conditions: the unusually high autonomy of a state apparatus constructed in the brutal ordeals of revolutionary struggle and yet to accumulate binding obligations to any particular group in the subject society; the tremendous concentration of all powers in the same apparatus; and the burning desire to validate the developmental project and past sacrifices by delivering at a historically unprecedented rate modernizing victories on all fronts even at the cost of new sacrifices.

The Soviet state was an extraordinarily prolific proletarianizer. To some extent, this was due to its Marxist belief that socialist modernity was to be achieved by proletarians, and therefore peasant masses had to be recast into urban and educated industrial workers.[12] But ideology alone seems a weak explanation. The extraordinary ambition of the Soviet state in the realms of industrial production and warfare demanded the rapid and massive production of educated industrial personnel and their concentration in towns. The state proceeded to expropriate and smash all autonomous bases of social and economic reproduction, which in the Soviet conditions of the 1930s and 1940s meant a brutal assault on peasant households. Almost by default (once again, ideology alone seems a weak explanation), the state found itself sponsoring wholly new institutions capable of organizing social reproduction in workplaces and residential quarters along the modern patterns: new public and even private rituals (secular weddings, funerals, New Year celebrations), mass education, healthcare, sports and entertainment and, though in earnest only after Stalin's death, mass-construction housing, mass vacations, and the extension of the pension system into the countryside.[13] All this, coupled with the tremendous social mobility experienced during industrialization, the war, and the post-war economic expansion, in sum produced a strong impression that socialism had been actually achieved. In this historical situation Yuri Shanibov grew up – as did millions of other peasant children who did *not* stay peasants – including my parents as well as prominent figures such as Mikhail Gorbachev, Boris Yeltsin, and Djohar Dudayev.

A strong tendency toward democratization first emerged after the death of Stalin. It was the paradoxical extension of two concurrent processes of class formation that both originated with industrialization. The first was the self-normalization of the *nomenklatura* bureaucracy, which could not be achieved without scrapping the terroristic machinery of Stalinism. The peculiarity of state socialism was that the threat to civilian control came not from the traditional military, but from the secret police force personally – and thus arbitrarily – controlled by the dictator. With the death of Stalin and the ousting of Khrushchev – the last civil war Bolshevik to be in command – the Soviet *nomenklatura* gained their paradise. Intra-bureaucratic collegiality and stable tenure of office replaced the charismatic dictatorial management of Stalinism. The inhuman work pace of previous regimes was over, deadly purges were no longer a threat, and Cold War became a familiar mode of international relations. Significant concessions to popular consumption could be now afforded thanks to the industrial base gained in the previous decades and, after 1973, the windfall of petrodollars.

The second source of democratization was the historically rapid emergence of a large industrial proletariat including millions of university-educated specialists. In a very real sense, these were the children of the Soviet epoch whose forward-looking social expectations, dispositions, and lifestyles were more closely associated with the developmental goals of Soviet state than with the village horizon of their parents' generation. In addition, the Soviet industrialization exerted a powerfully homogenizing effect in the fields of gender and inter-ethnic relations. As such, communist affirmative action was able to achieve its objectives – it integrated a great many women and non-Russians like Shanibov into the rapidly expanding structures of Soviet industrial society. It must be stressed that affirmative action proved a success not merely because of the ideological commitment but mainly because it was an important part of the massive industrial proletarianization. Cumulatively, it contributed towards the very broad and egalitarian citizenship which emerged in the 1950s.

The symbolically and often actually orphaned children of peasants, however, were not the hapless "human material" of Stalinist industrialization. They were a highly activist and optimistic generation who advanced their individual and collective fortunes in the framework of post-Stalinist Soviet ideology. Education and general modern acculturation seemed to them the best way of achieving confidence and higher-status positions in the new urban setting. Indeed, the expanding postwar industries and state bureaucracies rewarded skilled labor and activism. Taking the official communist ideology at its word, the Soviet proletarians obtained a cultural framework for their institutionalization as a class and for laying claims on the ruling bureaucracy. Thus they emerged as an active and conscious "class for itself" despite the harsh ban on independent political organizing. The process occurred mostly through the panoply of micro-initiatives that sprang up during the late 1950s. Shanibov's volunteer crime-prevention and campus self-governance programs were such examples. The younger Soviet workers and specialists sought to civilize their newly-gained social worlds, maintain the social mobility predicated on the merits of skills and education credentials, and make the distribution of material and cultural goods more generous and accessible in a broadly egalitarian manner. In effect, it was a diffuse struggle of new proletarians against the formation of a new ruling class.

A major vulnerability inherent in the Soviet *nomenklatura* order remained the scandalous contradiction between its official ideology and its actual practice. The ruling communist parties could not afford an open confrontation with their workers. Instead they prevented the emergence of politics through symbolic violence, which consisted of censorship, the hypocritical dissimulation of mass politics, and cultural and administrative controls on workers' consumption. Nevertheless, this created a durable, very broad, and homogenized structure of contention. The key demand of the proletarian class was that the hypocritical bureaucracy live up to its ideological promises of social justice, welfare, and rational regulation; in this their organizing framework was provided by the institutions of Soviet industry, education, and national territorial units. Thus a predominantly proletarian social structure and the effects of bureaucratic de-Stalinization spreading to the rest of society in the 1960s contributed to sustaining the USSR's relatively equal citizenship.

The next step was the emergence of what Charles Tilly considers the two crucial aspects of democratization: a) binding consultation of citizens in regard to state personnel and policies, and b) protection of citizens from arbitrary state action.[14] Already in the 1960s both criteria were met most of the time, albeit tacitly. The *nomenklatura* were reluctant to use overt repression for fear of reactivating the previous excesses of the secret police. Therefore they avoided provoking conflicts with socialist proletarians, since contentious meetings, letters of complaint, and even strikes against unpopular officials and policies were common enough in the tightly policed USSR, not to mention satellite Poland.

The contemporaneous national revival associated mostly with the emergence of younger, romantic artists and scholars from the non-Russian Soviet republics followed essentially the same vector of anti-bureaucratic resistance. It took the official ideology at its word and thus created a powerful symbolic weapon of anti-authoritarian resistance. Nationally-defined symbolic capitals concentrated around new nativist positions in the field of culture that came to be objectively opposed to the stolid administrative capital on the side of officially-promoted culture. National sentiments, in the context of de-Stalinization, stood for something authentic, creative and popular, as opposed to hypocritical, sterile and official. They also allowed the new urbanites to reconnect emotionally with the past of their ancestors and reflect with pride and love upon what only very recently had been regarded as backward peasant customs. Here we can see especially clearly that emotions associated with national cultures are not necessarily conducive to political nationalism. The symbolic revival of vanishing ethnological practices and dialects was rather another way of civilizing the urban industrial environment, fostering humanizing rituals, and constituting the social capital of the new educated classes. Thus national sentiment became a source of democratization.

Still, as Perry Anderson reminds us, "the secular struggle between classes is ultimately resolved at the *political* – not the economic or cultural – level of society."[15] On this count, the diffuse power of the Soviet workers and special-ists regularly proved weaker than the bureaucratically concentrated power of the *nomenklatura*. The surges of Soviet proletarian contention were made possible only by the factional splits within the reigning bureaucracy during de-Stalinization in the 1956–1968 period and again during Gorbachev's perestroika of the late 1980s. The recent nature of Soviet proletarianization, the official suppression of social communication, and perhaps also the sheer size of Soviet Union, all contributed to the fact that despite a very broad commonality of institutional conditions and perceived interests, collective action of a potentially democratic nature remained geographically limited to big cities like Moscow and Leningrad, the factory towns where worker protests occurred, and the capitals of national republics where it existed mostly among the national intelligentsia. All this ensured, at least until 1989, that a political democratic movement from below could emerge only in response to the opportunities extended from above – and when such opportunities were closed down by the consolidation of the *nomen-klatura*, the bases of popular movements could be rapidly undone – as happened after 1968.

The long internal shut-down during the reign of Brezhnev forced frustrated reformers like Shanibov to devise various adaptations, inevitably make compro-mises, and simply try to live on. What remained to them was jazz, yoga, the guitar ballads of Vysotsky and Okudjava, the films of Tarkovsky, Wajda, Bergman, and Fellini, the prose of Hemingway, Remarque, and Saint-Exupéry, or perhaps collecting the faded lithographs, copper jars, old daggers, and other such artifacts from the rapidly disappearing traditional life of their ancestors. In their consump-tion of such high-culture products the higher-educated and more urbane fractions of the Soviet workforce constituted the new intelligentsia. The mutual interests, sympathies, and strategies of symbolic and material exchanges (such as the procure-ment of prized books or records) made possible in virtually all towns of the Soviet Union numerous networks and partially overlapping circles of friends and acquain-tances. This was the beginning of oppositional "civil society."

But since the intelligentsia opposition was associated with the practices of high culture, it seemed irrelevant if not offensively pretentious to the proletarian majority who remained generally patriotic and loyal to the regime, if also very skeptical regarding its specific bureaucrats. The regime's response was to increase the real wages of ordinary proletarians (or decrease the real demands on their productivity), mostly at the expense of higher-skilled groups to the extent that the official remuneration of engineers, lawyers, and medical doctors, etc., could be lower than the wages of machine operators, nurses, or waitresses. The result was an increasingly alienated intelligentsia and a fairly complacent working class majority. The complacency, however, was only relative. Moreover, it was bought at a high price in terms of budget expenses, damage to work and civic ethics, resistance to innovation, and steadily decreasing productivity.

But this was only one of the big structural problems that would eventually undermine the Soviet Union. Besides the escalating consumer subsidies and toleration of inefficiencies intended to placate the proletarian masses, I have already identified two further sources of huge costs incurred by Brezhnev's regime of conservative stabilization. One was the geopolitical self-aggrandizement sought through the arms and space race with the US, and the collection of client states in the Third World. Due to its superpower status, the Soviet expenses were exceptional, yet the nature of the costs were not. Many other developmental states also acquired outsized militaries and embassies abroad, mostly for the purposes of prestige and to satisfy internal bureaucratic constituencies.

The second source of high cost seems in fact to be a universal feature of developmental states. It derives from the structural ability of sprawling bureaucracies to subvert the central command and control in many subtle ways. In the absence of price-setting markets, an unofficial press, competitive elections, or legal openings for popular contention, the rulers of developmental states had few institutional ways of reliably knowing the worth of their own subordinates, and could do little to change the policies if bureaucratic corps disliked the idea. Stalinist purges or Khrushchev-style megalomaniac campaigns were then the chief but still utterly wasteful mechanisms for inducing bureaucratic compliance. Once the Soviet *nomenklatura* liberated themselves from such scourges, they also became free to pursue the parcellization of bureaucratic turfs resulting in administrative and economic stagnation. The reform-minded factions of the Soviet elite thus found tempting the idea of democratization insofar as it might put pressure on the vested interests of the *nomenklatura*.

A linear extrapolation of historical trends suggested the likelihood of the institutionalization of political democracy within the lifetime of Shanibov's generation. Potentially, this kind of evolution might have resembled the democratizations of southern European countries like Italy, Greece, or Spain. The reform-minded elements among the Soviet ruling elites eventually accepted such a prospect because it promised them an advantageous way of dismantling the obsolete developmental dictatorship, and the possibilty of joining the European core states on honorable terms. This was essentially the Spanish route after the death of Franco.[16] Instead, the outcome was the totally unexpected implosion of the Soviet state.

During Gorbachev's reform, the Soviet state acquiesced in all sorts of demands for social autonomy but tried to defuse them by using the standard tactic of promising an increased flow of material and symbolic benefits to the claimants. But the perceived acquiescence of the new political leadership only induced an escalation of claims that eventually overwhelmed the USSR's central government, whose legitimacy still depended on its redistributive power. Gorbachev's government had especially bad lack at the quirky level of contingency: the costs of the Chernobyl disaster, the Armenian earthquake, and the falling oil prices wrecked the central budget and forced Moscow to run up a ballooning foreign debt. Moreover the structural militarization of Soviet industry prevented an easy conversion to the production of consumer goods that might have generated a substantial flow of cash into the state coffers. As a result, the central government rapidly lost its ability to deliver on promises as well as on threats. This was not, however, quite the end of its legitimacy, but only because Gorbachev still remained the charismatic focus of popular and international hopes elicited by his bold policies.

At first, Gorbachev's rhetoric of perestroika and glasnost spread from Moscow a vague but powerful message of renovation that resonated locally amongst circles of educated urbanites. Soon the resonance became much stronger as outspoken celebrity intellectuals in Moscow offered an attractive example for provincial emulation. Furthermore, Gorbachev's campaign to remove conservative Brezhnevite executives in the middle echelons opened up the prospect of extraordinary administrative promotions based on youthful energy, on meritocratic criteria, and, soon, on success at the ballot box. Ordinary workers also rejoiced at the punishment of corrupt, arrogant bosses and the opening up of public discourse (best evidenced in the stratospheric rise in subscriptions to democratic newspapers), though only as long as the structures of employment and consumption appeared secure. These different constituencies of democratization were still growing until about 1990.

National aspirations during the early years of reform (1985–1988) remained subsumed under the more general agenda of correcting all the wrongs of past Soviet governments. The first breakthrough of nationalism was achieved accidentally in Armenia and Azerbaijan, where it began as a petition movement asking Moscow to correct in rather minor ways an internal administrative border. Nationalist contention grew violent and eventually turned anti-Soviet for three mutually rein-forcing reasons. First, the emotional power of the Karabagh issue proved, for historical reasons, incredibly strong in Armenia and, by a mirroring effect, also in Azerbaijan. Second, the emergence of such strong emotions led to a competitive struggle in which lower-status intellectuals (beginner journalists, scholars and such) sought to overtake their more established peers by proffering ever more radical formulations, and where sub-proletarians could turn their native accents, religiosity, male peer networks, and rowdy habitus into nationalist assets. Finally, Gorbachev and Shevardnadze evidently regarded their own security forces as being a bigger threat than peripheral nationalism.

When the Soviet rulers finally resolved to use force against the protestors in Georgia, they discovered that nationalist sentiment can radicalize exponentially in consequence of public violence and the entrance into politics of millenarian sub-proletarian crowds expecting miracles in the near future from national independ-ence. Still worse, it turned out that the state structures in the Caucasus and Central Asia were liable to disintegrate momentarily both because they were too dependent on central government for the delivery of public goods as well as coercion, and because the locally prevalent patterns of shadow markets and neopatrimonial control had fostered in the less industrialized Soviet republics a gentry-like officialdom lacking bureaucratic discipline, internal cohesiveness or popular legitimacy.

Frustrated sympathizers of Gorbachev often blamed him for failing to dismantle the communist party when the time was ripe for formalizing a reformist social-demo-cratic faction capable of focusing the efforts of diverse and still formidable anti-authoritarian constituencies while leaving the *nomenklatura* conservatives scram-bling to present a credible alternative in open competition. But the last General Secretary remained himself thoroughly a product of *nomenklatura* advancement, and thus hostage to his habitus and position. Gorbachev's tragedy was that of many old-regime reformers who have unwittingly ended up provoking revolutions. The intermediate outcome of Gorbachev's own boldness was an emotionally-charged political and ideological crisis which invalidated the familiar strategies of bureau-cratic manipulation, dashed the original expectations of the reformers, and destroyed many elite connections. By default, the rising new leaders, who were not or were no longer bound by their belonging to the *nomenklatura*, found themselves at a consid-erable advantage in claiming the political initiative. At this unstable point a single successful speech could make one's political reputation. Thus, the example of the *nomenklatura*-outcast Yeltsin or, for that matter, the long-standing activist intellectual Shanibov, and several other leaders of national rebellions in the Soviet republics.

The character and outcomes of revolutions across the Soviet bloc depended on the local features of class structure, the rapid opening and closing of political opportunities, and the nature of mobilizable emotional issues and organizational resources. The construction and propagation of emotional causes was chiefly the function of creative intellectuals and scholars who were particularly concentrated in the capitals of national republics. The resources were delivered by opportunistic national *nomenklatura* who realized that their association with Moscow's control had become a liability. The force to such mobilizations was provided by the common people, and here the shape and proportions of the social structure mattered crucially. The established urban population of workers, intellectuals, and technical specialists is notoriously difficult to mobilize, especially when socially mature cohorts prevail in the demographic distribution. But if such mobilizations tend to be slower, they are also orderly and aim at achieving longer-term goals that may be institutionalized in the political mechanisms of democracy. Political pacts between national intelligentsia, defecting *nomenklatura*, and disciplined popular movements of the kind just described allowed the westernmost former socialist states, from Estonia to Poland and Slovenia, to escape from the Soviet Union relatively peacefully.

By contrast, the Caucasian sub-proletarians brought into politics their rowdy habitus and typically short-term expectations that all too easily translated into explosive bursts of collective violence against the nearest identifiable targets. The extreme forms like riot and pogrom might seem despicably irrational, yet at closer investigation they do not appear entirely random. Ethnicity in Soviet times played a salient role in granting or denying access to power, whether through formal administrative appointments or personal connections and back-door bribery. Therefore it should not look surprising that in the less-industrialized southern zones of the USSR, especially in the Caucasus, violent contention by the dispossessed and insecure broke out along ethnic lines. Sub-proletarian contention is also class struggle, even though it may often look like ethnic or religious rebellion. Yet evidently not all struggle by the dispossessed carries a liberating potential. Ethnic conflict is truly a weapon of mass destruction that for many years after leaves a poisonous fallout.

The bitter irony is that with the dramatic weakening of the USSR central government, the organizing framework of democratic contention was also weakened dramatically. The proletarian democratic agenda, embedded in the structures of state employment and supported by the occupational capital of specialists, intellectuals, and upper fractions of workers, began to look increasingly unrealistic as it was no longer evident what agency could deliver on their demands. In late 1989 the social-democratizing politics of perestroika lost their relevance. The locus of contention became fractured and localized. The Soviet Union fragmented after the protracted revolutionary situation of 1989–1991 (in some places lasting until 1993 or even longer) in which the contending forces stalemated each other. When nobody could win, everybody might lose.

In the end, the Soviet Union was not taken apart by ambitious intellectuals: they served merely in the ideological vanguard. Nor should we blame the "nationalities" that were themselves fields of internalized social struggle rather than unified actors. And even the violent sub-proletarians and bandits had to wait for the state's incapacitation before rushing to grab a share of the excitement and spoils. The actual destruction was carried out by mid-ranking *nomenklatura* who sought to escape the looming collapse of the centralized state by grabbing whatever assets they could, whether economic enterprises or the territorial governments of republics and provinces. This process relied heavily on existing networks of local patronage. These had to be reconfigured *en marche*: selectively opened to nationalist ideologists from the local intelligentsia; made ready to incorporate the ascendant mafiosi and warlords who delivered from below the coercive, political and economic resources that no longer flowed from above; and at the same time insulated to bar interventions from Moscow and from neighboring competitors. It is immediately noticeable that the Soviet Union fell apart precisely along the lines of bureaucratic turfs in its territorial and sectoral agencies. This fact remains most telling.

State structures disintegrated at a time when rational regulation along with legal and social protection seemed most vital in negotiating the return of former socialist countries into the capitalist world markets. The loss of geopolitical leverage hurt the pace and terms of capitalist integration even among the best-organized states of the former Soviet bloc that existed at its westernmost edge. Elsewhere the post-communist landscape was dominated by small organizations that could, always only very imperfectly, provide their own protection and economic opportunities. These organizations were of three intermeshing kinds: diminished bureaucratic cliques struggling to consolidate their control in successor states and provinces; private businesses based on former state property that typically behaved like gangs; and the actual gangs of various origin that typically behaved like businesses. The rest of society was suddenly demobilized if not atomized by the drastic loss of economic and physical security followed by the disintegration of structures that could connect the people and foster solidarities beyond the circle of one's immediate acquaintance or shared ethnic identity. Later in the 1990s power concentrated in the hands of provincial governors and presidents of republics who fell back on their old *nomenklatura* dispositions and connections, and those state structures that remained more or less intact at local level. The restorations, however, remained very limited because the post-Soviet rulers had neither resources nor serious incentives to prevent the popular immiseration, the de-industrialization, or the scandalous accumulation of private wealth by commercialized politicians, their allied oligarchic capitalists, or enterprising gangsters and warlords. All this meant a devastating recoil to a peripheral situation after all the sacrifices, achievements, and hopes of previous generations.

The operations of limited restoration can be illustrated with the saddest example of Chechnya, situated squarely at the far violent extreme in the much broader pattern of post-communist politics. Putin's political operators tried to impose in this region, as everywhere else, a provincial government of obedient ex-*nomenklatura* clients. The latter, however, do not and cannot operate as normal bureaucrats because a) the state is too weak to provide an adequate flow of public goods or to systematically identify and punish violations of bureaucratic principles, i.e. various forms of "corruption"; and b) despite Putin's efforts at quasi-dictatorial centralization, the Russian state remains too weak to organize anything adequately, even repression. The state in this situation becomes more of a label rather than an institution, although the label is valuable because, as the richest of Russia's new oligarchs, Mikhail Khodorkovsky, has learned since his arrest in October 2003, the formal stamp of authority can provide a lawful-looking veneer to what was otherwise purely personalistic coercion in the dispute over economic and political resources. To that extent the state remains a valuable asset, but by itself it cannot ensure the comforts of even its own agents. The latter are taking care of themselves by using state office to devise personalistic, unstable, and often astonishingly immoral schemes. In short, it is a dire case of neopatrimonialism disguised as a state. Everywhere, President Putin's overarching central machine has to buy with various favors the compliance of local political machines. In Chechnya this also means that the local clients are allowed to operate by heavy reliance on death squads instead of the more usual (but still typically dirty) tactics of dealing with opponents.

The Chechen opposition is not totally unusual, however incredible such a statement might sound. The Chechen separatist leaders are still former "democrats" from the 1989–1991 period: former journalists (Udugov), poets (Yandarbiyev, who was assassinated on February 13, 2004 as he was leaving the mosque in Qatar where he lived in exile), alienated state servants (former colonel Maskhadov), erstwhile romantic students (Shamil Basayev, who is apparently still alive despite many announcements of his death), or various other start-up entrepreneurs and sub-proletarian activists who have seen the prospect of self-realization in nationalist politics. The opposition has been weakened by eroding popular support (in fact, the loss of any hope in oppositional politics) and continued violence. Faced with this situation, elements of the Chechen opposition then may try to defect to the "state," as many of them have, but just as many fail to find safety or a livelihood by turning to Moscow, to a considerable extent because there can exist only so many political sinecures. Other elements of the outlawed opposition either emigrated abroad (either to the West or the Islamic Middle East, depending on personal dispositions and contacts) where they try to build political structures in exile or, if they stayed (mostly fighters of lower social status like Shamil Basayev), engage in desperately violent acts of terror that have no hope of defeating the far larger military forces of occupation, but at least serve to discredit Moscow's claim to victory. Meanwhile the ordinary population is left suffering on all sides. As elsewhere, the popular strategies of survival are vested in various combinations of subsistence, refugee and labor emigration, petty trade, and whatever remains of wage employment.

Across the whole post-Soviet realm the damage wrought by the economic and social depression seems so massive that it is hard to conceive how the popular constituencies for democratization and non-oligarchic market dynamism might recover in the short- to mid-term. Instead, the majority of former Soviet republics emerged with an internal polarization of wealth and power, and an external connection to the world-system, that are distinctly reminiscent of the Third World.

The 1990s fashion for neoliberal reform was dictated largely by the perceived need to secure Western recognition and financial access. But with the consolidation of new regimes, and the growing cynicism of post-communist elites regarding the West's willingness or ability to change things, this was replaced by the new fashion of conservative official nationalism. Another revealing trend is that of the dynastic succession of political office, where power is transferred within the ruling family, as in Azerbaijan, or else to successors anointed in the *dedazo* fashion of Mexican politics, as in the presidential transition from Yeltsin to Putin. A coup with or without popular support remains another possibility, as evidenced in Georgia in November 2003 where the ailing ruler was overthrown by impatient former clients.[17] Sultanism, coups, and corrupt competitive politics advance as the three typical patterns of the new politics. The neopatrimonial machinery may to some degree be disciplined and rationalized, as Putin may yet achieve in Russia. This route seems not entirely incompatible with economic growth, but perhaps only growth of a dependent variety if the country's resources are large enough both to enrich the ruler's circle and foreign investors, and still leave something to build modern roads and skyscrapers, at least around the capital city – in the manner of Suharto's Indonesia or many Latin American countries. Genuine economic growth in combination with "crony capitalism" is not a historical possibility open to the former Soviet republics because they lack the critical combination of conditions that served as a basis for the East Asian economic resurgence: robust rural markets, a large and productive workforce, an effective bureaucracy capable of strategic planning, and privileged access to the consumer markets of core capitalist countries.[18] Where then is there any hope? I shall return to this question in the final section. But first we must consider what kind of social science is needed to answer such questions.

MAPS AND COMPASSES

This section is necessary in order to account for the theoretical tools that were used in building my explanations, as well as mentioning some that were avoided. It provides a retrospective look at how the "Complex Triangulations" of chapter two translated into the rest of the book. The purpose, however, is not professional pedantry. It is rather an appeal to those social scientists who might join the debate on how we might synthesize the breakthrough formulations made since the 1960s, during the early "Golden Age" of macrohistorical sociology. Using the example of my own search for theoretical explanations, let me attempt another clarification regarding how we might move towards a new, reasonably holistic and more encouraging understanding of the social world. In this, the relational network method seems to be the key, and Bourdieu's passionate variety of sociological rationalism provides us with a major example.

One of Pierre Bourdieu's major contributions was to demonstrate practical ways of bridging the gaps in social analysis that had traditionally separated the realms of culture from the material bases of human existence. By introducing into the study of culture the analytical metaphor of a field structured by mutually related positions and social capital, Bourdieu was not only able to bring culture into the study of social hierarchy and political economy, but – a still greater achievement – he brought the operations of political economy and the hierarchical dimension of class back into the study of culture. To achieve this, Bourdieu had to fight relentlessly, not merely due to his pugnacious kind of intellectual habitus, but mainly because he had chosen to fight singlehandedly on several major theoretical and political fronts: against the mechanistic determinism of the erstwhile Marxism, the various strands of positivism and structural functionalism (which returned reincarnate, with a vengeance, in metatheoretical movements such as rational choice theory), as well as against the discursive solipsism of post-modernist commentary.

Yet Bourdieu was not merely a sociologist of culture. His intellectual ambition was much grander and in fact holistic. The ongoing philosophical debates in Bourdieu's writings centrally pertained to his own "unthinking" (in Wallerstein's apt expression) of the nineteenth-century paradigm of social analysis, especially the deep-seated yet false antinomies of structure and agency, micro- and macro-, objective and partisan, nomothetic and idiographic. Analogous efforts since the 1960s have constituted the main thrust in the search for a new paradigm in social science. Bourdieu, however, belonged to the first rank of pioneering thinkers who explicitly sought, and might yet succeed, in revolutionizing not just specific theories but our fundamental concepts and ways of "asking our questions regarding the social world."[19]

For my particular purposes, Bourdieu's influence was crucial in at least three respects. First, the theoretical notion of symbolic and, more broadly, social capital could be used to capture the ambiguous position occupied by the intelligentsia and other educated specialists in the Soviet social hierarchy, as well as their repressed political aspirations which led, when the political structure allowed, to explicit demands for democratization and later to the embrace of market reforms or nationalism. The combination of social capital, habitus, trajectory, and field may seem a deceptively simple toolkit, the use of which is fraught with the danger of oversimplifying – especially if Bourdieu's ideas at some future point become textbook material. Nonetheless the level of elegant operationalization achieved by Bourdieu must be acknowledged as a major strength of his work.

Secondly, Bourdieu rescued the concept of class as a key sociological concept, after it seemed destined to fall into disuse along with Marxism. In addition, he suggested ways of overcoming the analytical antinomy between classes and status groups that had animated a long-lasting but fruitless debate between Marxist and Weberian scholars. The intersection between the planes of material production and exchange and the planes of varying social capital provided the basis for my model of Soviet social structure (sketched in Table 1, page 325, and presented in terms of its political dynamics in Tables 2 and 3, pages 326 and 327, and the four Charts, pages 331–334). The multi-dimensional nature of capital, and the operations by which its particular forms are converted by social agents and transported from one field into another, created the analytical possibility of mapping social transformations at both the individual and aggregate levels. Such transformations include 1) the conversion of the communist *nomenklatura* into a bureaucratic executive estate, and later into the dominant political-economic class of the post-communist

restoration; 2) the project of the dominated educated specialists to constitute themselves as a new intelligentsia, followed later by their project of creating a "civil
society" and "nation"; 3) the ways in which nationalist mobilizations invited the
emergence of sub-proletarians as a collective political force typically allied – by the
principle of homology – with marginalized elements of the provincial sub-intelli-
gentsia or with maverick defectors banished from the ruling elite for their
"populistic ambition."

The category of the sub-proletariat, derived from Bourdieu, constitutes his third
major influence on my analysis. This class often appears inchoate and unarticulated,
and thereby seems elusive both empirically and theoretically. Yet it acquired a
centrality in explaining the violent escalations in ethnic conflicts which admittedly
initially caused me bewilderment. How does one operationalize in research
the residual category of "no-longer-peasants" that variously goes by the names of
"Street," "marginals," "subaltern peoples," "crowds," "underclass," "adolescent
gangs," "lumpens," or, very broadly and negatively, "de-ruralized populations"?
Bourdieu's discussion of the Algerian sub-proletariat demonstrated ways of meaningfully incorporating in our analyses this most awkward of all classes – a class that
is increasingly important, both numerically and politically, in the contemporary
world. Bourdieu offered only guidelines for the analysis of sub-proletarians, and
the elaborations presented in this book are of course fully my own responsibility.
They are still tentative and thereby likely to be superceded in the future. Nonetheless
it seemed imperative to focus the analysis on this category of people, whose violent
political acts (typically misconstrued as simply criminal, savage, and atavistic) were
a crucial component everywhere in the post-Soviet ethnic conflicts.[20]

But the category of sub-proletariat (or, for that matter, of national intelligentsia)
still seemed too abstract to explain the actual processes of violent mobilization.
Historically speaking, violence against whole racial and ethnic groups, all the way
up to genocide, was more typically the result of state action, such as in the colonial conquests, or the world wars of the twentieth century; or of catastrophic
socioeconomic distress, as suffered by many once well-established classes of
German society in the sequence that brought Hitler to power; or, finally, as a consequence of a combination of acute distress, a breakdown of central governance,
and opportunistic scheming on the part of the threatened communist *nomenklatura*,
such as Serbia's Slobodan Milošević.[21] Clearly, sub-proletarian action would not have
been able to become a political factor without openings in the structure of political opportunity that were in turn created by the severe crisis of state power. As a
general rule, sub-proletarians gain force where and when the state weakens. This is

why the kind of class analysis developed in this book had to go hand in hand with the analysis of state structures, social movements, and revolutions. The latter, of course, have in recent years been the subject matter of one of the most productive and increasingly sophisticated fields of historical-comparative sociology that was opened in the 1960s–1970s by scholars such as Barrington Moore Jr., Stein Rokkan, Theda Skocpol, and Charles Tilly.[22]

A significant effort was required in order to adapt their theoretical tools developed for the most part in application to the core capitalist states of Western Europe to fit them for analysis of the Soviet and post-Soviet environments, and especially the peripheral Caucasus. In this I was able to rely on the work of scholars who studied the socio-historical aspects of Soviet formation. This rich tradition counts among its pioneering generation names such as Isaac Deutscher, E.H. Carr, Barrington Moore Jr., and Moshe Lewin. It reached maturity in the works of scholars such as Sheila Fitzpatrick, Stephen Cohen, and, especially congenial to my own project, Valerie Bunce, Ronald Grigor Suny, Michael Burawoy, and Iván Szelényi. The successor generation of today is large and diverse, and includes many scholars from the former socialist countries.

The field of post-Soviet area studies is, however, facing dilemmas structurally similar to those of other such domains whose focus is on Africa, Latin America, Arab countries, or South Asia. On the one hand, these domains are institutionally established both in the West and in the countries that now possess their own research potential; the intellectual workforce is substantial, well-trained, and connected through personal and professional networks as well as the Internet; moreover, these domains are endowed with a rich intellectual inheritance from predecessors who pioneered the studies of "developing" world areas in the 1950s–1970s period; and, last but not least, many political barriers to research have fallen or at least weakened. But on the other hand, the field of development studies suffered terribly from the compound effects of the disintegration of developmental ambition – a key part of which was the state commitment to higher education and scholarship – and from the global spread of a market orthodoxy that favors schools of business and administration over traditional university departments, that explicitly makes bureaucratic knowledge (the infamous "policy relevance") a prerequisite for funding, and that propagates anti-historical modes of theorizing derived from neoclassical economics which privilege transaction technologies and formal modeling over any kind of substantive historically-grounded knowledge. In the ideological conjuncture of recent decades the various area studies found themselves embattled and suffered numerous encroachments and defections.[23] The trend is summed up by the hard-nosed dictum "there is no developmental economics, only good and bad economics," where "bad" means anything deviating from the utilitarianist faith in rational market behavior and the "mathematics of general equilibria."[24]

The underlying polemic of this book has sought to resist the onslaught of an ideologically fashionable and, on balance, astonishingly sterile academism and consultancy expertise intent on bulldozing the traditions of developmental area studies along with the social history, political economy, anthropology, and sociology of non-Western countries. On the intellectual plane, effective resistance means advancing substantive alternatives to those now prevalent schemes that, regarding ethnic conflict and state collapse in the world periphery, stress either the games of manipulative "ethnic entrepreneurs" or the failure of peripheral nations to grasp the essentials of market democratization due to their twisted collective memories, endemic corruption, wicked corporatism, religious traditionalism, and other such forms of inherited deviance. On the institutional plane of scholarly production, resistance evidently involves a long positional struggle on many fronts, which we may fight as social scientists ourselves by drawing on our sociological theories of intellectual creativity, movement mobilizing, and contentious politics. Still, the struggle would be futile unless we can produce scholarly work that is not only based on robust theories and enriched with empirical detail, but would furthermore be capable of reaching the educated readership outside the walls of academia. This seems not only possible, but today more possible than ever given that the world has never had as many educated readers, professional scholars, and such a wealth of accumulated knowledge. And the public need for such scholarship explaining the real world has already returned amidst the political upheaval of the last years.

Inevitably, I could not avoid invading the domain of economic operations. What theories could help me forcefully confront the orthodoxy that considers the Soviet-type enterprise merely deviant and the free markets the only healthy norm? Finding tools appropriate to an adequate analysis of the political economy of state socialism and the post-Soviet period indeed proved to be a major problem in the writing of this book. The main reason, besides the lingering ideological mystifications of the Cold War era, was clearly the present-day hegemony of neoclassical economics. This problem had to be dealt with in various ways. At the level of macrohistorical generalization, the concept of the developmental state, originally advanced by Chalmers Johnson, offered at least a first approximation of a meaningful alternative definition. This could then be extended to include the socialist states as representative of the political strategy of catching up with the core Western economies, which in turn meant situating these states in the world-systems analysis of Immanuel Wallerstein and especially Giovanni Arrighi and Bruce Cumings. At the intermediate level of the Soviet economy and its successors, the theories of Vladimir Popov and David Woodruff were a major help. Popov's theory regarding the material life-cycle of command economies, although still needing elaboration, offers us a reasonable chance of explaining how such economies in their initial phases achieved tremendous levels of material output before falling into protracted stagnation. Woodruff's work on the persistence of informal networks of barter exchange during and especially after state socialism highlighted the obscure operations orchestrated by post-communist provincial governors that turned out to be at the heart of oligarchic restorations in the 1990s.

The provincial governors played a key role both in tearing apart the Soviet Union when the preservation of central governance threatened their positions, and later in establishing corrupt bailiwicks and political "machines" in their territorial power bases. Once again, in the hegemonic utilitarianist paradigm these phenomena are either simply ignored, or else explained away, under the various rubrics of deviance, as a result of rent-seeking behaviour, corruption, nepotism, cronyism, the underground economy, or organized crime. Of course, anyone who was able to observe the flow of power through patronage networks in places like Georgia or Azerbaijan may well have wondered why so many Western political scientists, economists, and consultants chose to remain blind to these essential mechanisms in the local exercise of social power, or else attributed them to individual moral failings and "bad old habits" supposedly predating modernity. It was here that the Weberian concept of neopatrimonialism, i.e. the personalistic de facto privatization of public office, offered a meaningful alternative. Ken Jowitt and his students pioneered the concept of neopatrimonial possession and political barter in application to the former Soviet Union. Since analogous patterns of rule have long been studied in relation to the Third World countries – the theoretical lineage goes back to the formulations of Guenther Roth and S.N. Eisenstadt in the 1960s – additional insight could be gained by way of Africanists such as Jean-François Medard and Will Reno. The groundbreaking works of Vadim Volkov and Federico Varese on organized crime in the new Russia also helped to fill in another gap in the picture.

Beyond the operations of bureaucratic patronage there still remained the networks of "good old families," alienated intellectuals, warlords, religious fundamentalists, black marketeers, and the sub-proletarian "informal economies." Empirical observations suggested strongly that the abstract categories of social class and status group acquired their political dynamic predominantly through the activation of social networks which may consist of extended kin, friends, neighbors, colleagues, co-ethnics, co-religionists, acquaintances made through barter, or perhaps through time spent in prison. In the Caucasus, as indeed almost every-where else, people must regularly rely on these kinds of informal networks to obtain promotions, university admissions, access to scarce goods, health care, personal security, escape routes to emigration, business opportunities, or potential spouses. But it is also these ordinary-life networks that are activated in the extraordinary situations of ethnic violence, coups, rebellions, fundamentalist proselytizing, or paramilitary recruitment. To ignore this basic fact amounts to expunging virtually all the human dynamics of daily life from our explanatory schemes while ascribing the dynamics of social action to reified abstractions such as classes, nations, political fronts, or religions.

The standard sociological theories of networks, however, proved of little help because of their tendency to sacrifice historical context and meaning for the sake of economics-like mathematical abstraction. At first mostly by way of a coincidence of titles (the "Whiskey Rebellion" rhymed with my vodka rebellions) I came to appreciate the deeply historical network analysis of the late Roger Gould. Possibly Gould went a bit too far in stressing the network links over the old ideas of class-based politics; nonetheless, despite his cruelly premature death, Gould's contri-bution to historical sociology has been enduring. John Padgett and Christopher Ansell suggested another profitable way of tracing the flow of political power through partially overlapping networks located in a classical patrimonial setting. Their meticulous reconstruction of the "robust action" operating through patronage, marriage alliances, and familial enterprise that brought the Medicis to power in Renaissance Florence, might also find application in many national capitals of our own times. And, last but not least, Richard Lachmann's masterfully crafted study of the routes by which the feudal elite networks of the early modern West resulted in the emergence of "capitalists in spite of themselves" finds a more than superficial reflection in the latest self-transformation of the communist *nomenklatura*.

The concepts of network and social "embeddedness" have recently come into fashion, which brings with it dangers. A good antidote may be found in the warning of Arthur Stinchcombe, that grumpy old fighter for substantive meaning in the methods of social research. Stinchcombe points out that while the rich and varied historical insights of Charles Tilly "virtually always" arise from "some sort of network analysis," they are not of the usual kind because Tilly is interested rather in "what it is that flows over the links between people" and in what historical context this takes place.[25] Perhaps one could similarly describe the network methods of Roger Gould, John Padgett, or Richard Lachmann. But Stinchcombe's characterization, in my opinion, again leads us to the legacy of Pierre Bourdieu. Questions such as "what is it that flows over the links between people?" or, "what is the differential of levels that produces the flow in the first place?" can be addressed by way of notions such as social capital, homology, and individual or group trajectories towards occupying positions in a social field. By contrast, the usual network analysis seems so divorced from reality because it virtually always ignores the differential of power embodied in social position and capital. Power in the forms of material and symbolic goods, personal connections, or special kinds of knowledge, is what flows over the network links. In the real world such flows make domination possible but they can also help to bypass, subvert, and, sometimes, openly resist particular forms of domination.

The concept of a network clearly involves a spatial metaphor. But what is the nature of the space in which the networks are located? Bourdieu's imagery of social field offers one way of bringing into our analyses this spatial dimension, though by way of a pretty abstract, analytical conceptualization. Fernand Braudel offered a more historically concrete approach drawn from geography. Braudel left us his magisterial vision of the modern world-economy as a continuously evolving ecology of human spaces consisting of three "floors": the elementary structures of everyday life, the laterally extended markets, and the upper floor where Braudel located the capitalist and state powers. All three levels, in Braudel's formulation, explicitly comprise a multitude of networks, which he gloriously attempted to map simultaneously. A still more ambitious macroscopic vision was recently outlined in the remarkable father-and-son collaboration of William and John McNeill. Their "human web" is constituted by multiple overlapping networks of exchange that have been evolving throughout the entire duration of human history and across the whole globe.[26]

Can we map civilizations as cultural fields and the diffusion of world religions as the transport of symbolic capital? Possibly. The question here is not whether it is possible to write histories of whole worlds. This will remain a recurrent scholarly ambition. The question rather pertains to how such an ambition might be realized in the next intellectual generation; or how the macroscopic vision of history might relate to theoretical generalizations and, in turn, translate into microscopic studies of specific situations – which will surely remain the daily bread of social research. Specifically, might the world-system or world-historical conceptualizations of social space mesh with the theories of Bourdieu or Tilly? I believe this to be possible because – beneath the differences of focus, terminology, and favored modes of exposition – we find, at the level of epistemology, common concerns with time/space and a view of the world as social environmental topology. But I also believe that such questions cannot be answered solely in an abstract theoretical fashion, since our theoretical propositions must be put to the test of empirical research.

While classes, social networks, the structures of state and political economy, and the dynamics of protest mobilization eventually became the central themes of this book, theories of nationalism and ethnic identity came to be a secondary concern. This shift came as a surprise, particularly since I had previously spent much time following developments in the intellectually vibrant domain that had been launched two decades earlier by such thinkers as Tom Nairn, Ernest Gellner, Eric Hobsbawm, and Benedict Anderson. These intellectual currents explore the general historical conditions for the emergence and spread of nationalism in the modern epoch and focus on the discursive processes involved. (Of course, in contemporary studies of nationalism one also finds the social history of Miroslav Hroch or the institutional sociology of Rogers Brubaker.) But my own sense was that putting nationalism at the center of the investigation was fraught with the danger of reification. The main thing to explain seemed rather to be the unfinished revolution that brought the Soviet Union to an end, sending its fragments along multiple pathways towards very different forms of nationalism corresponding to divergent political patterns and class configurations: Westernizing and market-oriented patterns in the Baltic states, insurgency in Armenia and Chechnya, and conservative power-patriotic reconfiguration in the majority of the other post-Soviet states. My decision may yet prove to be wrong, as over the years, Benedict Anderson has proven me wrong on more than one occasion, but this remains to be seen.

Let me strees that the theory of so-called "ethnic conflicts" formulated in this book centers on class, state, and social networks rather than nationalism or identity. This shift in analytical categorization allowed us to bridge the gaps that separated the liberal Westernizing outcomes of Central European revolutions from the violent debacles in the Balkans and the Caucasus, and from the conservative restorations under the aegis of former *nomenklatura* that in current political discourse go under the ill-defined label of "failed transitions." This formulation was influenced in major ways by the meticulous discussion of modern European states and revolutions as developed in recent decades by the historical sociologists. The extensive knowledge accumulated in the former Soviet area studies also provided much substance. In addition, borrowing from the East Asian context the idea of the developmental state, and from African studies the concept of neopatrimonial rule, enabled me to de-exoticize Soviet and post-Soviet realities and place them in comparative perspective. The sociological notions of Bourdieu introduced into the analysis the dynamics of social classes, status groups, elites, and specific individuals; while the macro-perspective of world-system theory provided the horizon from which to integrate these several theoretical sources. It is from here that the full house of variation, in the expression of Stephen Jay Gould, finds its whole system of relations.

Such is my list of mapping devices, for if we are dealing with networks and spaces then we must make maps. But the list is by no means complete or final; it is rather an invitation to think collectively about the resources available to social analysis today, and what we might do with its various tools. It must be re-stressed that what is at stake here is not only the future of some of the most promising intellectual innovations in social science associated with the area studies of the 1960s and 1970s, and with emblematic names such as Bourdieu, Tilly, and Wallerstein. The program of expanding and synthesizing these innovations also carries the potential of generating serious alternatives to the increasingly metaphysical academic mainstream. Ultimately, the highest stakes involve advancing reasoned alternatives to the reigning political ideology of brutal economization ("structural adjustment") and self-regulating markets.

Predicting the future may be futile. Yet, consciously or not, contemporary generations participate in shaping the future by continuously structuring and readjusting their expectations (a process which often lies at the center of political contention); extending their networks of trust and various impersonal solidarities; creating organizational and cognitive resources that help people to envision the future (such as rational social science); and seeking to lock political and social gains in various institutional forms to ensure that what they consider to be a more desirable future becomes more likely.[27] Of course, there also exist plenty of possibilities of screwing up the future. All humans and human organizations regularly commit mistakes, and one hardly needs to read Charles Tilly to know this is true.[28] But the mistakes are easier to detect and correct if we know our course on the roadmap and if we can develop the habit of regularly casting a critical gaze at ourselves. Then the pathways leading from the past might bring us to a more desirable future. Besides, once these pathways are reasonably charted, we might be better able to see both the dangerous pits and the alternative pathways that may not have been noticed before. This is what Immanuel Wallerstein provocatively calls *utopistics*, by which he means an intellectual enterprise that, unlike the willful speculation that breeds "utopian illusions and therefore, inevitably, disillusionments," engages instead in the "sober, rational, and realistic evaluation of human social systems, the constraints on what they can be, and the zones open to human creativity."[29]

The essential aim of this collective analytical effort should be a big map, extended into the past and thereby useful in understanding the present and in charting possible roads to different futures. It would constitute an atlas of social worlds, hopefully clear in detail and meaningfully coordinated overall – which is not possible without daring to embrace a world-historical breadth.[30]

But maps are not very practical things without a compass. Unlike the planetary magnetic field in physical geography, in the fields of culture, politics or, for that matter, social science, our compasses are constituted by the fundamental choices we make regarding ourselves and our ways of participating in social processes. All socially competent humans carry such compasses, albeit some may parade theirs out of the righteous conviction of possessing the truth and the ambition of converting others to their creed – examples might be forces as different as orthodox Marxists in a previous epoch or, presently, neo-conservative ideologues, market reformers, and the proponents of rational action theories in social science. Others may seek to hide their compass behind the objectivist pretenses of positivism or, seemingly its obverse, the cultural-relativistic thicket of post-modernist discourse. Perhaps the most consequential contribution of Pierre Bourdieu to the practice of social analysis was his elaboration of reflexive sociological techniques that require producers of social knowledge to situate themselves in the social world. Such techniques may allow us to see more clearly how we arrive at choosing our social compasses and what might actually be involved in such choices. Ultimately, in a kind of dialectics whose intellectual lineage reaches back to Hegel, the daring imagination of the young Karl Marx, and the emancipatory ambition of Freud, a theorized and reflexive knowledge of how we make the social choices we do may enable us to become not only more rationally responsible but also perhaps more free.

DEMOCRATIZATION AND DISPOSSESSION

The overall conclusion should now be evident. Globalization was not the direct cause of ethnic violence in the newly emergent post-Soviet peripheries. The common cause was the breakdown of central governance in a very large state that institutionalized nationality in its political structures and operated through informal networks of bureaucratic patronage many of which were predicated on nationality.

But if market globalization was not the initial cause, further down the road it does, in effect, become the major structural condition for the perpetuation of ethnic conflicts. The immediately obvious effect of globalization is to turn the anger of threatened and dispossessed groups away from their increasingly irrelevant national or local governments towards competing groups as well as towards the world's dominant group, construed as "American plutocrats." The latter, due to the enormous social and physical distances separating them from those dispossessed or threatened, assume mythical proportions in the popular imagination. Such distance makes the usual forms of contention impossible. But in September 2001 a daring group of conspirators showed how ideological fantasies can materialize with devastating effects.

The second effect of global market restructuring on the character of peripheral contention is far more consequential. The connection, however, seems less evident because of its deeply structural nature. Additionally, it comes buried under the weight of ideological clichés. I refer to the social and political effects of de-industrialization in the former developmental states that cannot compete on the world market. It was widely assumed that post-communist transitions would result in democratization by liberating latent civil societies and creating new property-owning middle classes. This is one of the central tenets of neoliberalism.[31] Indeed, in past epochs the middle classes − artisans, petty bourgeoisie, entrepreneurial farmers, or autonomous professionals − often were found in the forefront of democratization in Western countries. In the capitalist core, historical conditions favored the existence of large middle classes in the first place. Yet even there, as Tilly can attest with the authority of detailed expertise, the success of democratization alliances often depended on the support of organized proletarians.[32]

In the post-communist peripheral countries the new middle classes turned out to be not as big nor nearly as autonomous. Today many educated and well-placed Muscovites who, on the basis of comfortable wages paid in dollars, claim to be middle class are, in fact, privileged proletarian clerks employed by the banks and firms directly connected to global capitalist flows. But since their wages come from comprador profits and stand far above the low average, the dispositions of this group are very "un-proletarian." Not surprisingly, they feel very ambiguous about democratization in locales where wealth is linked to political patronage and foreign connections, where income disparities are large, and where the presence of under-employed workers and sub-proletarian masses perennially threatens social problems and political unpredictability. The persistent fantasy-ruler of the post-communist middle classes has been Thatcher or even General Pinochet rather than Lincoln. So far, the hegemonic vision of neoliberalism imposes conformity on the peripheral states. The result, however, is only a shallow emulation of electoral procedures and capitalist transaction technologies − as David Woodruff has argued in a truly path-breaking article.[33] Woodruff provides an illuminating discussion of social mechanisms that continuously generate a disjunction in the realms of provincial paternalism between institutional and rhetorical conformity to the mandates of neoliberal ideology and the profoundly different foundations of social power.

This poses the question: what has actually been achieved by the latest worldwide wave of democratization? We need to know what the relationship is (negative, positive, or non-existent?) between the actual structures of domestic politics in various countries and the new geoculture of human rights, and internationally monitored elections, and their effects on the credit ratings of governments. Does the globally-induced spread of democratization further or subvert older structural trends that were engendered by developmentalist proletarianization? Can global democratization eventually put down deeper local roots, and if so, by what social mechanisms? Or will the veneer peel off when the global climate changes, as was in fact the fate of the British-style parliamentarism emulated in many Latin American and southern European countries before 1914? We might also ask whether de-industrialization, and the resulting social marginalization of the populations of so many countries, will make less or more likely a global confrontation between, on the one hand, neo-nativist political forces, who offer the angry masses a retrograde kind of protection against unregulated world markets, and, on the other hand, the globally-connected capitalists and comprador intermediaries who are benefiting from this sort of globalization. And how might the empowered segments of the world's population react against the seething hatred and possible violence of the world's dispossessed segments? In other words, through what processes might the "Clash of Civilizations" actually become a self-fulfilling prophecy?

Clearly, these are not abstract questions. Tilly is deeply troubled by the declining ability of states – and he evidently refers to the strongest core states – to guarantee workers' rights in the face of globalizing capitalism.[34] In his response to Tilly, Wallerstein appears less worried about the future of unionized Western workers, whose children and grandchildren, he predicts, will be a global "middle class – some doing well, but others less well," and thereby more likely to engage in the right-wing politics of racism and anti-immigration protection. Wallerstein concludes on a still more troubling note, predicting a return to the pre-1848 situation when the workers will once again have become the "dangerous classes," but their skin color will have changed and the class struggle will be a race struggle. To this prognosis, I would add that, around the globe, many such workers would be sub-proletarians, with all the expected consequences for their class outlook and habitus. This would surely contribute not only to violence in many different forms, but also encourage the more privileged groups residing in the core countries and the globally-connected peripheral enclaves to erect still harsher protection barriers. This suggests the scenario of a globalized but also internally-walled future world.

But, though we must not forfeit such sobering analyses, we need not end on such a pessimistic note. As a mental experiment, let us indulge for a moment in the intellectuals' favorite game of imagining a better world. If the findings of historical sociologists strongly suggest that, in the modern era, the existence of a large and stable proletariat has been a major condition of democratization, and that this kind of broad social citizenship institutionalized within national states is what historically pacified class conflicts in the West, then our first policy recommendation seems obvious: In order to prevent anomie and violence, including ethnic violence, we must promote a fully advantageous proletarianization, with lengthy formal education leading to jobs, adequate wages and welfare safety nets. A world policy of full employment would then rely on the promotion of rationally directed markets. Markets, or for that matter, bureaucracy, must not be construed in terms of absolute evil or good. They are rather complex social mechanisms that can be used for the benefit of smaller or larger groups in modern society. In the Western experience, the combination of bureaucratic organization and directed markets lifted the core countries from the terrible ruin of world war and depression and promoted three decades of extraordinary beneficial growth after 1945. We need more research on how this recovery was actually accomplished, with a view to drawing lessons for the future. Politically speaking, our slogan might be that of instituting *democratic world markets*, rather than the promotion of markets and formal democratization separately.

This point needs clarification because the abstraction "markets" has, for the long duration of the Cold War, served as a slogan for some ideological currents and as an anti-slogan for others. Karl Polanyi, an increasingly relevant classic thinker, offers a more nuanced perspective on markets. The stress in interpretations of Polanyi's thought has been on his historically detailed and devastating critique of the utilitarianist faith in self-regulating markets. What remains to be recovered theoretically and, possibly, become an agenda for action, is the idea of "fictitious commodities": money, land (i.e. the natural environment), and labor. Polanyi's key argument is that these cannot be treated as regular commodities fully subjected to market forces because money, land, and labor are either not produced or they serve to support the very substance of human society. In particular, a progressive protection of labor (instead of a retrograde paternalism) implies a judicious exemption from full market accountability and therefore a partial or complete de-commodification of those industries that in modern times have replaced traditional communities in the social reproduction of human life itself. I mean industries as fundamentally important as healthcare, education, and the care of the elderly, but perhaps also sports and entertainment (where perhaps the BBC or the amazing American institution of public radio and television could offer examples of non-commodified mass media). A different kind of economics would be needed to posit and seek answers to the questions of how one might rationally organize the supply of money, or environmental protection, or the social reproduction of labor, while at the same time creating genuinely functional market accountability and competitive innovation especially in the manufacturing and service sectors. This kind of substantive economic rationality at least ought to be seriously explored as a possibility.

Let me bring in another kind of "fictitious commodity" that has been traded in many situations, especially in recent years. Namely, political patronage derived from the monopoly of public office. Many post-developmentalist regimes have today emerged in neopatrimonial and downright "sultanistic" configurations under the cynical disguise of corrupt and manipulated democracies – which is evidently the case in many former Soviet republics. Theorists of revolution have determined that this sort of regime is most likely to end up in violent upheaval.[35] Therefore our second policy recommendation would be to complement proletarianization with substantive democratization, rather than a mere emulation of elections for the sake of international observers.

But now we need a dose of sobering reflection. To whom are these demands addressed? What will be the mechanisms of deliberation and implementation? Where would the resources come from? Indeed, are there even enough resources to perform on a global scale the kind of redistribution that once pacified class conflicts in the core countries? If the existing resources prove insufficient, which they probably would, how can we set up mechanisms to generate the beneficial cycle of a truly worldwide economic growth in order to create more resources, as the West achieved after 1945? Moreover, which programs in existing state budgets would have to be cut (presumably, in the first place, military expenditure), and who among the world's privileged groups would have to be additionally taxed in order to provide the seed investments? Whose subsidies and trade protections would have to be scrapped for the sake of rational affirmative action in the world markets to benefit the economic interests of poorer countries?

But let us now consider an even bolder hypothesis derived from the propositions of macrohistorical sociology. The nineteenth-century industrialization in core countries proved conducive to a broadening citizenship primarily because democratic and welfare institutions were invented to provide institutional remedies for the dangerous effects of massive proletarianization (not just the threat of revolution but also such problems as poor people's migration, family demographics, crime, sanitary conditions, and various aspects of social anomie, all of which greatly preoccupied governments and social movements at the time). Globalization today means fundamentally a new phase in the expansion and deepening of capitalism worldwide. The process first took off in the nineteenth century, when it was conducted predominantly in the form of imperialist conquest and colonial modernization. The self-destruction of the Western imperialist powers after 1914, and the success of twentieth-century revolutions, significantly slowed the global expansion of capitalism.[36] Today, as the disintegration of erstwhile revolutionary developmental regimes has cleared the way to another capitalist globalization, the world might indeed come to resemble the pre-1848 West writ global.[37] What is emerging is not a global village – village life with its traditional identities and security is vanishing at record speed. The actual trend seems rather a global spread of de-ruralized slums surrounding gated communities of sheltered prosperity enjoyed by the minority of some 10 to 20 per cent of the world's population. A hugely aggravating factor is that in the peripheral countries state structures have, since the end of developmentalist hopes, been institutionally and morally weakening, and in some instances have disintegrated altogether. Given the existing world demographics, the persistence of ethnocultural social stratification at world level, the highly uneven distribution of industrial bases, and actual de-industrialization in many places, we should not nurture any illusions regarding the sub-proletarian character of the world's emerging poor. The latter are rarely engaged in organized class politics as the nineteenth-century Western workers were, but rather in forms of protest and protection that are classified in today's political discourse as ethnic violence, illicit trafficking, the informal economy, religious fundamentalism, crime, crowd rage, or terrorism. In the coming decades we will no doubt see many different attempts to deal with this rising peripheral disorder. They will be pursued by national governments, capitalist multinational groups, international agencies, transnational social movements, and perhaps other actors whom we can barely imagine today. One way or another, these attempts to regulate the global realm will be moving in the direction of institutionalizing a world political and ideological arena. We might envision these processes as being analogous to the institutionalization of national arenas in the nineteenth-century West, which took place primarily in response to class and nationalist contention. The analogy is arguably imperfect (more research would be necessary to determine just how imperfect), but so far it is the only one available to guide our analysis.

The global arena, now emerging throughout the global space of economic flows, will become the locus of struggles, including the struggle over the ways to contain "ethnic" violence. The first reaction of powerful actors who seek to control global capitalist restructuring can safely be predicted to be reactionary and coercive. We have seen this in many countries already, with electoral triumphs of rightwing forces whose agenda by previous standards seems scandalous; with the enactment of new barriers to immigration; and of course most explicitly with the American "war on terror." Military coercion is often the most economical and ideologically advantageous means in the calculus of power – as was known by the nineteenth-century imperialists and the architects of the Cold War order, and as is evidently realized today in Washington. But, as Napoleon warned long ago, there is a limit to what can be achieved with bayonets. The political forces favoring coercive containment will run into numerous constraints.

The imperial approach of today has revived the age-old choices of empires: slow blockade of the "rogues" versus vigorous military forays; erecting border walls or moving forward bases; sending in spies or merchants and missionaries (i.e. market consultants and non-governmental organizations); cultivating mercenary allies among the new "barbarians," etc. Such tactics, historically brought to perfection by the rulers of Byzantine and Chinese empires, nevertheless offered only an imperfect degree of security, and even that periodically broke down with disastrous consequences. The advantages of modern technology seem to offer a dubious hope because technology always comes with long chains of unintended consequences and uncalculable indirect costs. On balance, it seems highly improbable that contemporary capitalism can thrive by reinventing the defensive mechanisms of agrarian empires. The Israeli security experience, evidently the most advanced of its kind, points to the diminishing returns of capital-intensive warfare and defensive technology.

The result could be, as in the late nineteenth-century West, a growing pressure towards extending economic and political participation to the "dangerous classes." We cannot tell at present whether a global democratization might rely on the patterns of democratization that first emerged in core countries – maybe the forms will be quite novel, or else some new combination of old forms. What is doubtful is that such future democratization will be carried by the framework of national states as was the historical pattern in the West. Generally, we must remain vigilant regarding the dire consequences that followed from the enormous concentration of power structures in the hands of political movements and states that set out to change the world in the twentieth century.[38] Nonetheless a sufficiently utopian ideology may prove necessary in order to foster a Durkheimian sense of moral solidarity among the large impersonal community of all humans. Historically, the ability to produce such solidarity was the major strength of nationalist and socialist movements. Can ideology possibly be at the same time utopian and rationally open to self-criticism as a mechanism for preventing cults and self-serving misappropriations? Can morality have rational bases that extend over historical cultural borders? These are very big questions for social scientists who study ideologies, solidarity-fostering rituals, and broadly discursive practices.

The enterprise of re-writing the world history of the evolution of human societies in the light of recent theoretical formulations may prove to be a highly practical and future-oriented pursuit. Such a history must avoid both the nineteenth-century scheme of a uni-directional evolution ascending in progressive stages (a model which evolutionary biologists as well as anthropologists have criticized with great vigor), and examples of more recent attempts to present world history as a conglomerate of multicultural particularisms. It now seems possible to construct a more adequate model of historical reality by way of a nuanced account of multi-linear evolution spreading through varied human communities located in different environments. But this must not be a sanitized account which shies away from the fundamental fact that only a few centuries ago, i.e. quite recently in world-historical terms, the capitalist mutation on one branch of historical evolution in the West produced the current unprecedented world-system that ended all other evolutions and brought humanity together under an imperialist framework. Yet this does not mean that it will or must remain a world-system of such tremendous inequality, despite the way in which it was created. A different configuration must be possible, perhaps not a uniform and culturally assimilated "world society," but rather a system based on organizational traits such as non-monopolistic markets, rational democratic regulation, and the conscious cultivation of historically created local cultures that connect us with our ancestors and provide individual humanizing aspects within the globally emergent human web.

I hope that this hypothetical prospect looks both sufficiently sweeping and daring to inspire others, and yet reasonable enough to serve as a starting point for further exploration.[39] Moreover, in seeking to pursue such a project we must practice both intellectual responsibility and sociological reflexivity, including being critically reflexive about the role of intellectuals. Pierre Bourdieu kept over his desk a photograph of Musa Shanibov, in his *papaha* hat – perhaps not out of vanity but rather as a reminder, that chances are, we cannot even imagine who might be influenced by our work, or how remote from us they might be.

Table 1. An impressionistic sketch of social structure in the Caucasus, 1950s–2000s.

Class and its relative size	Typical occupations	Principal capital	Career patterns	Range and sources of income, in dollars per year	
				Before 1991*	After 1991
The ruling bureaucrats, (*nomenklatura*) incl. family members, up to 10% of total population.	State and Party top functionaries; industrial managers; generals of police, army, and KGB; university rectors and deans; editors-in-chief. After 1991: industrial managers turned businessmen.	Administrative capital: *nomenklatura* rank, intra-elite patronage, special bureaucratic knowledge.	Upward-mobile or lateral shifts among various bureaucratic appointments. After 1991: privatization of administered assets.	Wages: 3,000–6,000. Official perks: cars with chauffeurs, upscale apartments, special medical and vacation facilities, special stores, cash bonuses. Corruption is uneven by sectors: lowest in heavy industry; highest in consumer commerce.	Wages: 5,000–12,000. Official perks: same. Corruption widespread and massive, intertwined with privatization. Capitalist profits available to majority of the class in various ways, but amounts vary enormously.
The wage-dependent proletarians of different categories, 50%–60% of total population.	Technical cadres (engineers); Intellectual cadres (culture, education); state-employed proto-professionals (medical, jurists, etc.); civil and military personnel; Industrial workers, State farm labor.	Generic occupational capital: work skills credentialed by education and experience; shopfloor solidarity and bargaining power.	Typically, life-long employment of both spouses; after 1991 this pattern is problematic. Today only a few manage to go into private business, and then mostly in petty trade and services.	Stable wages: 1,500–4,000. Workplace benefits: free apartments after 5–15 years of service, the enterprise provided health and sports facilities, opportunities to buy quality goods, cash bonuses. Extra incomes (jobs at home, moonlighting): 600–10,000. Occasional bribes and workplace theft.	Unstable wages averagely 300–1,200 a year. Workplace benefits sharply reduced and uncertain. Other incomes: from petty (side-trades) to substantial (doctors, technical consultants, transborder commerce). Subsistence: newly important for large majorities.
Sub-proletarians, 15% to 50% in different locations (but growing everywhere after 1991).	Subsistence and truck farmers; market vendors; artisans; taxi drivers; day, seasonal, and migrant laborers; black marketeers and criminals.	The marginal social capital: survival skills, kinship and regional solidarity or extra-legal connections.	Choppy life courses, different jobs at irregular intervals. Up to a fifth of males served prison time. Women work at markets, garden plots, or at home.	Wages: 800–2,000 but some migrant workers could get up to 15,000 for a season. A significant reliance on subsistence agriculture. Illegal proceeds (smuggling, theft, gambling, prostitution): no estimate but significant.	Wages (remittances, tips): 200–5,000, all less stable and overall depressed. Subsistence: very important. Charities. Market profits: from miserable to huge (in cross-border trade and illegal activities).

Source: field observations and interviews in the southern regions of Russia and Transcaucasia between 1988 and 2002.
* For simplicity, the Soviet pre-1991 rubles are calculated in dollars at the official exchange rate.

Table 2. Homological correspondences between the class fractions of late Soviet society.

GROUP / ATTRIBUTES	RULING BUREAUCRACY			PROLETARIANIZED CITIZENRY			MARGINALS
	Reform *nomenklatura*	Ordinary *nomenklatura*	Elite dissenters and defectors (e.g. Yeltsin, Dudayev)	State-invested intellectuals and other specialists	Professional and technical specialists, intelligentsia	Workers	Sub-proletariat
Social capital	Ascendant administrative capital ranging from lower to top rank.	Stable administrative capital mostly at medium ranks.	Previously rapidly ascendant administrative capital.	Stable occupational capital linked to administrative patronage.	Higher ascendant occupational capital often opposed to administrative.	Lower and mostly stable occupational capital.	Unstable social capital located outside the state (unofficial skills and connections).
Dispositions and aspirations	Expansive and activist; rapid orderly change towards more rational and vigorous state, economic management.	Reserved and routine; stability of office tenure, patronage and corporativism.	Very ambitious, and rough; individualistic careerism; opportunistic in patronage or ideas.	Dogmatic, suspicious of innovation; group and personal aspirations linked to official institutions and hierarchy.	Frustrated mobility, hopes for rapid and orderly changes in official framework towards initiative, rationalization, self-governance.	Adapted to systemic irrationalities through tacit bargaining on shopfloor; hope to get a better ratio in wages to effort.	Precariously adapted to survival outside the official framework; hope to muddle through or find rich, if risky opportunities.
Political project	Introduction of market and political competition; cooperation with the West.	Minimal and slow changes in domestic and foreign policy.	Rapid, even if disorderly change of status quo in almost any direction, mainly liberal or nationalist.	Hardline defense of existing order, activist conservatism (mostly Stalinist).	Market and political competition; "civil society" and integration into Europe.	Majority is politically undecided, but generally favor orderly change towards better conditions.	No own political project but can mobilize for short and often violent fights against the near, visible targets.
Homologies and Political Alliances	REFORM	PATERNALISM	REFORM!	PATERNALISM	REFORM	REFORM?	
						PATERNALISM	
			Populism		Lower strata populism	Lower strata populism	Populism

Table 3. Soviet *nomenklatura* grouped by the type of assets and their strategies of post-communist transformation into dominant classes.

TERRITORIAL AGENCIES			SECTORAL AGENCIES		
Easiest to separate from the "Center": agencies possess the assets of autonomous and politically legitimate value	Less easy to separate: agency assets are of ambiguous value	Makes no sense to separate: agency assets have little legitimacy or value outside old state	Makes no sense to separate: agency assets have little legitimacy or value outside old state	Less easy to separate: agency assets are of ambiguous value	Easiest to separate from the "Center": agencies possess the assets of autonomous and market-legitimate value
The fifteen Union Republics of the USSR (from Armenia to Estonia to Uzbekistan) that possessed the constitutional right to national secession.	More than twenty subordinate ethnic ASSRs within the Union Republics such as: Abkhazia and South Ossetia in Georgia; Karabagh in Azerbaijan, Tatarstan and Chechnya in Russian Federation (or Serbia's Kosovo).	Ordinary (i.e. predominantly Russian) town, district, and provincial governments.	State coercive apparatus such as the military, police, and the KGB; judiciary; tax, state audit, and licensing agencies.	Majority of manufacturing industries including military-industrial complex; state and collective farms; science and education; health care; social and municipal services.	Industries in the extraction and exports of raw materials (oil, natural gas, aluminum); banking and financial services; mass media (formerly state propaganda); consumer services, retail commerce.
Strategy after breakdown: NATIONAL SEPARATISM ↓		Strategy after breakdown: CENTRALIZING STATISM			Strategy after breakdown: CAPITALIST PRIVATIZATION ↑

Table 4. Shanibov's personal contacts in social movements, 1968–2000.

FIRST PERIOD, 1968–1985 BREZHNEVIST REACTION(*)

Friends and former students, by social group	Reform communism	Liberal dissidence	Nationalist dissidence	Read banned literature	Alternative lifestyle (yoga, mysticism)	Unofficial music (jazz, rock, bards)	Did not participate in anything after 1968
Nomenklatura, 5	4	0	0	4	1	3	1
Intellectual, 22	19	0	0	16	12	22	13
Worker, 3	3	0	0	1	0	2	1
Sub-proletarian, 2	1	0	0	1	2	1	1

SECOND PERIOD, 1985–1989 GORBACHEV'S PERESTROIKA (**)

Old friends, former students, new movement activists	Sobriety movement, 1985	"Informal" youth groups, 1985–1986	Local elections, 1990	Ecology, 1985–1987	Exposing Stalin-era crimes, 1987–1989	Preservation of ethnic cultures, 1986–1988	Economic discussion clubs, 1986–1988	Popular Fronts for Perestroika 1988	Voters for free elections 1989	Independent Trade Unions 1989–1990
Nomenklatura, 7	2	1	0	2	1	4	5	0	0	0
Intellectual, 40–50	1	5	17	11	29	31	34	4	17	3
Worker, 7	2	0	5?	2	7	7	3	1	1	2
Sub-proletarian, 9	0	3	3	5	8	9	0	2	1	0

THIRD PERIOD, 1990–2001, POST-SOVIET TRANSITION

Old friends, new allies, and many new political contacts	Mountain Confederation 1989–1992	Local elections, 1990	Kabardin National Congress, 1992–1995	Revolutionary situation I, Fall 1991	Revolutionary situation II, Fall 1992	War in Abkhazia, Aug. 1992–1994	New Islamism, 1996–2000
Nomenklatura, 15–20	8	0	12	All	All	All helped	0
Entrepreneur, 18–22	4	17	18	All	All	20+ bought supplies, 2 actually fought	3
Intellectuals, over 100	11	40–50	90–100	All	All	35+ students fought, others protested	10–20+?
Worker, 50–70	1	9–12	17–19	All	All	20–25+ fought	10–15+?
Gangster, dozens???	2–3?	5?	20–22?	All	All?	Fought and helped	1–2?
Sub-proletarian, 300?	2	3	100–150	200–300	400–500	Majority of fighters	Unknown

Source: estimates by the participants and local observers. * Individuals could participate simultaneously in multiple categories.
**In 1989–1995 the network expanded beyond the circle of old friends and many numbers become very approximate.

Table 5. Peripheral configurations during and after state socialism: three typical examples.

Ethno-territorial unit	Starting Condition	Sustaining Structures	Breakdown Pattern	Contenders and political goals	Intervening factors	Post-communist outcomes
	1956–1988		1989–1991		1992–present drift	
			Moscow incapacitated by dual government after 1990			
Kabardino-Balkaria ASSR (Autonomous Soviet Socialist Republic) in Russia	Durable and extensive patronage network based on generational and inter-ethnic division of powers ("Lebanese protocol").	Moscow's investments and subsidies. Affirmative action enforced by the local patronage. Potential contenders kept in internal exile.	The Balkar loss in the competitive elections and the revived memories of 1944 deportation lead to *separatist mobilization*; it provokes *Kabardin countermobilization*.	Vertical split along ethnic lines; previously excluded intellectuals and entrepreneurs fighting with the *nomenklatura* to lead mobilizations.	After Yeltsin consolidates his power, Moscow lends coercive, political, and financial resources to local *nomenklatura* in exchange for their allegiance.	*Nomenklatura restoration* with "sultanist" tendencies. Reduced continuation of the old patterns ("*industrial involution*").
Chechnya (Checheno-Ingushetia ASSR before 1991)	De facto exclusion of indigenous peoples from urban industrial spaces by the Russian proletarian and bureaucrat settlers. Majority of Chechens driven into sub-proletarian condition.	Central investments in oil industry. Moscow's toleration of local non-enforcement of affirmative action. Labor migrations externalize the Chechen mobility.	In the aftermath of the August 1991 coup in Moscow, street jubilation escalated into the Chechen ethnic revolution and popular fight for independence.	Previously excluded fractions of low-status intellectuals and criminalized entrepreneurs seek independence from Russia.	The Chechen revolution succeeds before Yeltsin's regime is consolidated. In 1994 Russia invades, provokes popular resistance. Chechen warlords come to rely on hostage-trade, smuggling, and international Islamic aid.	*Perennial war* with terroristic tendencies on both sides. Destruction of state, industry, and urban life.
Abkhazia (ASSR in Georgia before 1991)	Durable and extensive rivalry between the Georgian majority and Abkhaz minority over the semi-official markets of sub-tropical fruits and tourism. Extraordinary prosperity of all groups derived from geographic advantages.	Monopolistic rents from the inter-USSR fruit exports and tourism. The Abkhaz control of affirmative action. Moscow pours large subsidies into the "all-Union resort" thus hoping to control the ethnic competition.	The prospects of an independent Georgia and privatization lead the Abkhazes to defend the Soviet affirmative action, then secede. Clashes escalate into civil war after the armed invasion by Georgian nationalist forces.	Violent separation along ethnic lines. On both sides ethnic intellectuals and entrepreneurs overcome the *nomenklatura* and some become warlords. Weak *nomenklatura* restorations on both sides after the war.	Russia covertly aided the Abkhaz side including the dispatch of the Mountain Confederation fighters. Georgia loses the war, but as the UN member state, it blocks the international recognition of Abkhazia.	"*Frozen*" war under UN mediation. On both sides, very weak sultanist regimes and utterly devastated economies.

Table 6. Historical trajectory of Soviet developmentalism.

PHASE	Coercive developmentalism (Stalin) 1929–1953	Normalization (Khrushchev) 1953–1968	Conservative paternalism (Brezhnevism) 1969–1982	Rationalization (Andropov and Gorbachev) 1982–1989	State breakdown, 1990–1992 (early Yeltsin)	Restoration after 1994 (later Yeltsin and Putin)
Master process	The state terroristic concentration of assets towards the militarized rapid industrialization.	Civilian industrialization, pacification and normalization of all life spheres.	Slowdown of industrial growth, bureaucratic ossification, repressive avoidance of conflict.	Attempts to accelerate economy and regain central governance over the bureaucratic realms.	Planning abandoned for the shock therapy; uncontrolled shrinkage of state; mediation via patronage, corruption, organized crime.	Exchange prevails over production; local barter staves off markets; new dependency on oil exports, foreign debt.
Key social effects	Destruction of all previous classes; creation of *nomenklatura* and new proletariat.	Massive benign proletarianization; spread of higher education. New technocratic *nomenklatura* displace Stalinists, gain life-long tenure.	Bureaucratic rank closure, creation of administrative rents. Proletarianization and all social mobility slows dramatically. New black markets emerge.	Forcible rotation in *nomenklatura* ranks; leading intellectuals gain huge symbolic capitals; popular enthusiasm for politics; legalization of market entrepreneurship.	Elite rivalries over privatizing state assets (sectoral or territorial). Power of industrial managers and workers erodes; intellectuals split, demoralized. Many sub-proletarians enter politics, markets.	Unstable bureaucratic patronage; wealthy commercial, criminal intermediaries; proletarians scramble to preserve their life structures; massive sub-proletarianization of society, culture.
Sources of legitimation	Military victories, new urban life, charismatic state cult of paternalistic great Leader.	Economic expansion, world leadership and peace, science and technology, enthusiasm of young proletarians.	Generous consumer subsidies, superpower might, tacit toleration of corruption and inefficiency in exchange for loyalty.	Reinvigorated governance; end of Cold War; promotion of public debate, freer press, social experimentation.	Neoliberal promise of market miracle, rejection of communist past; competing nationalisms.	Paternalism, new official ideology of ritualized nationalism and capitalism. Weak officialdom, still weaker opposition.
Shape of polity and contention	Inner circle intrigues; isolated revolts in peasant and ethnic communities.	Massive turnover of *nomenklatura*. Young educated proletarians push to expand and institutionalize the polity; romantic social movements.	Repressive rituals instead of politics. Bureaucratic corporativist lobbying. Dissident, intellectual, and youth counter-cultures coalesce in latent against bureaucracy.	Rapid expansion of polity, class-based contention led by specialists and public intellectuals for the institutionalization of civil rights.	Inchoate and violent struggles for assets and patronage among new centers of political power. Intrigues, coups, revolutions, ethnic wars.	Polity shrank to the circle of political insiders and market oligarchs; warlords prevail in the collapsed states. Population is largely demobilized.

Figure 1a. Conservative bureaucratic paternalism: Brezhnevism and oligarchic restorations in the 1990s.

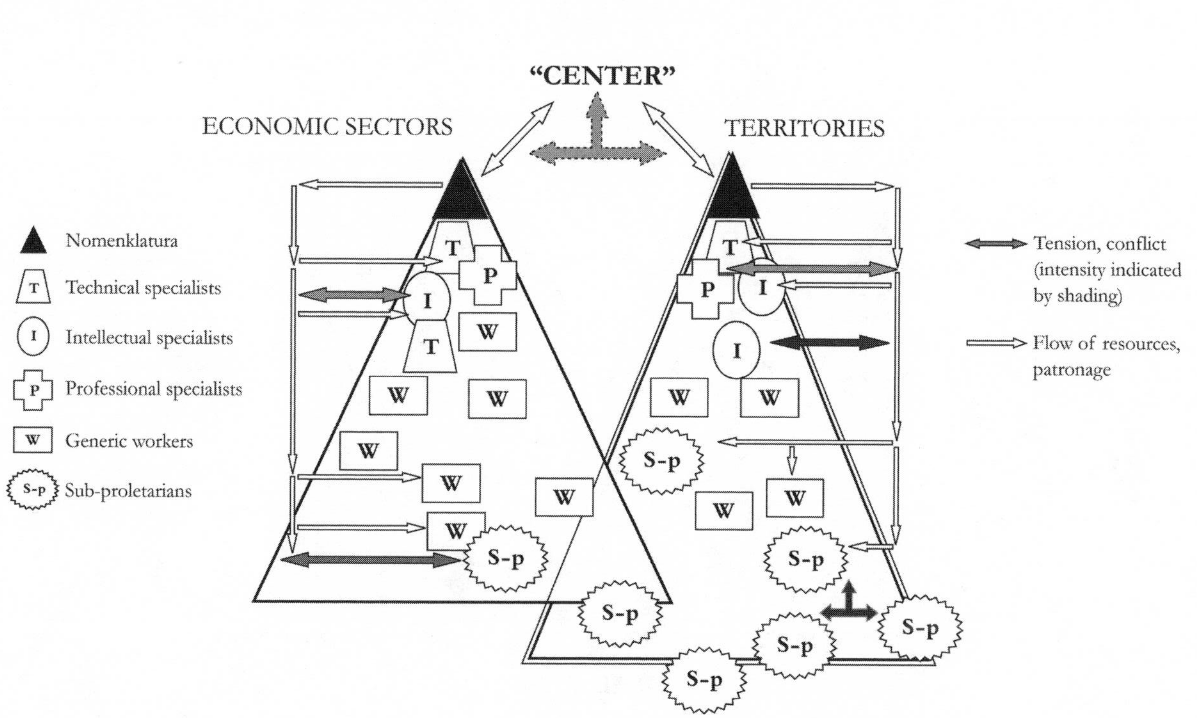

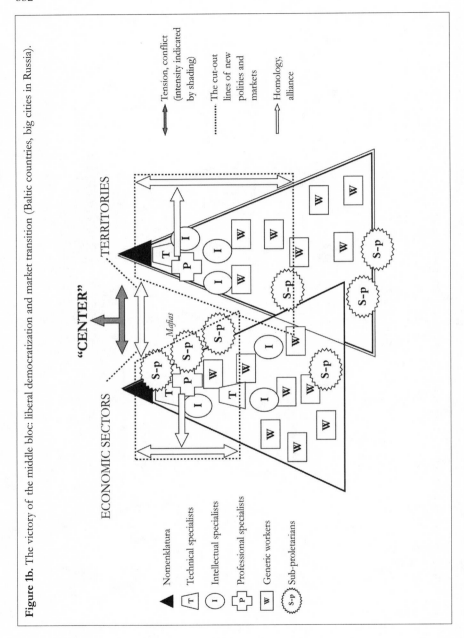

Figure 1b. The victory of the middle bloc: liberal democratization and market transition (Baltic countries, big cities in Russia).

Figure 1c. Elite defections, collapse in the middle, sub-proletarian breakthrough into polity: ethnic conflict.

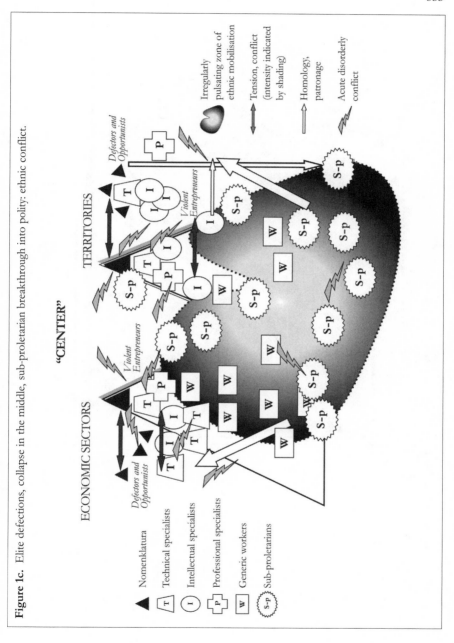

334

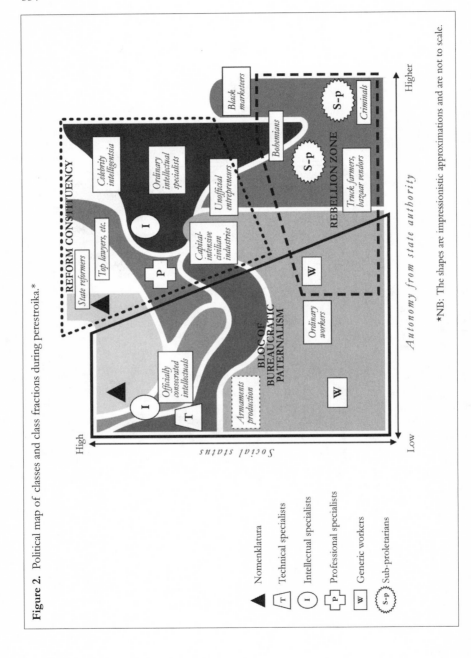

Figure 2. Political map of classes and class fractions during perestroika.*

Social status — High / Low

Autonomy from state authority — Higher

REFORM CONSTITUENCY

State reformers

Top lawyers, etc.

Celebrity intelligentsia

Ordinary intellectual specialists

Black marketers

Unofficial entrepreneurs

Bohemians

Capital-intensive civilian industries

S-p

S-p

Criminals

Truck farmers, bazaar vendors

REBELLION ZONE

W

Ordinary workers

W

Officially consecrated intellectuals

I

P

I

T

Armaments production

BLOC OF BUREAUCRATIC PATERNALISM

*NB: The shapes are impressionistic approximations and are not to scale.

▲ Nomenklatura

T Technical specialists

I Intellectual specialists

P Professional specialists

W Generic workers

S-p Sub-proletarians

NOTES

INTRODUCTION

1 Shamil Basayev, for those who don't know, is the Chechen Islamist warlord who claimed responsibility for organizing the seizure of several hundred hostages at a theater in Moscow in October 2002. A sketch of this character is provided in chapter one. In chapter seven I briefly describe Ruslan Gelayev's opening act when in 1992 he and his detachment captured at gunpoint the police and civilian authorities of a town in southern Russia demanding free passage to Abkhazian territory and ostensibly acting on the orders of Musa Shanib. In 2001–2002 Gelayev gained international notoriety as presumably the Chechen warlord in control of Pankisi gorge, a small enclave in Georgia on the border with Chechnya which American and Russian officials claimed to be an al-Qaeda sanctuary. Despite their well-known animosity towards each other, Basayev and Gelayev remained in the early 2000s Russia's main enemies in Chechnya. In February 2004 the Russian military announced that they had at last killed Gelayev.

2 What I had in mind was the penetrating and humorous article by Michèle Lamont, "How to Become a Dominant French Philosopher: The Case of Jacques Derrida," in *American Journal of Sociology*, 93: 3; (1987): 584–622.

3 Giovanni Arrighi, Terence K. Hopkins, and Immanuel Wallerstein, "1989: The Continuation of 1968," in George Katsiaficas (ed.), *After the Fall: 1989 and the Future of Freedom*, New York: Routledge, 2001.

4   A sharp and intimately knowledgeable exposition is provided by Alexandr Lukin, *The Political Culture of Russian "Democrats,"* Oxford: Oxford University Press, 2000. For a broader theoretical discussion see chapter three, "The Ideology of the Post-Communist Power Elite," in Gil Eyal, Iván Szelényi, and Eleanor Townsley, *Making Capitalism without Capitalists: Class Formation and Elite Struggles in Postcommunist Central Europe*, London: Verso, 1998.

5   Throughout this book direct speech is italicized for the sake of clarity.

6   Stephen Jay Gould, *Full House: The Spread of Excellence from Plato to Darwin*, New York: Harmony Books, 1996.

7   A clarification is in order because social science still suffers from the legacy of 'sociobiology' and particularly its nastiest form, 'social Darwinism.' Gould was himself a forceful and eloquent critic of the attempts to justify social inequalities by a presumably all-determining biological inheritance at the levels of race, sex, or individual genetics (see Gould's *The Mismeasure of Man*, New York: Norton, 1981). If anything, the ideas of Gould, his collaborator Niles Eldredge, and other insurgent evolutionists of the late sixties and seventies powerfully questioned the direct application of Darwinian principles to the analysis of social evolution or social problems. On this, see Randall Collins, "Upheavals in Biological Theory Undermine Sociobiology," *Sociological Theory*, vol. 1 (1983).

8   For one of the most authoritative and sophisticated expressions of this view, see Ian Buruma and Avishai Margalit, "Occidentalism," *New York Review of Books*, January 17, 2002.

9   I thank Randall for sharing his paper with me, reasserting as it did an old principle of mine, formulated in encounters with Soviet officialdom: feel emotional, for it is what makes us human, but do not remain only emotional – treat the experience as a problem of social analysis.

10 For a more detailed discussion, see Georgi Derluguian and Walter Goldfrank, "Repetition, Variation, and Transmutation as Scenarios for the Twenty-First Century," in Georgi Derluguian and Scott L. Greer (eds), *Questioning Geopolitics*, Westport, CT: Praeger, 2000.

11 Karl Polanyi, *The Great Transformation*, Boston: Beacon Press, 1957 (c1944).

12 Michael Burawoy, "The Great Involution: Russia's Response to the Market" (unpublished paper available at Burawoy's web page), University of California at Berkeley, Department of Sociology.

13 Admittedly the balance was not easy to maintain. Here I call as a witness the great storyteller Fazil Iskander, our "Mark Twain of Abkhazia," whose wise

and ironic words I used as the epigraph to this Introduction: indeed, in the Caucasus all good stories tend to branch out. In my case, the justification is that we need to appreciate the richness of empirical patterns and their variation within whole systems of relations.

14 See Randall Collins, *Macrohistory: Essays in Sociology of the Long Run*, Stanford: Stanford University Press, 1999, especially the Introduction.

15 Randall Collins, "The European Sociological Tradition and Twenty-First-Century World Sociology," in Janet L. Abu-Lughod (ed.), *Sociology for the Twenty-First Century*, Chicago: University of Chicago Press, 1999.

1 THE FIELD

1 Special thanks to Peter Katzenstein for suggesting I publish extracts from the field report I compiled.

2 Quoted in Richard Swedberg, *Schumpeter: A Biography*, Princeton: Princeton University Press, 1991, p. 181.

3 Pierre Bourdieu, *The Logic of Practice*, Cambridge: Polity Press, 1990, p. 16, and personal correspondence.

4 Galina Kovalskaya was one of the best Russian reporters and regularly wrote for Russian democratic magazines such as *Itogi* (before the hostile takeover in 2001), and then for *Moskovskie novosti* and *Ezhenedelnyi zhurnal*. In May 2003 she died in a helicopter crash. In English, see Anne Nivat, *Chienne de Guerre: A Woman Reporter Behind the Lines of the War in Chechnya*, New York: Public Affairs, 2001; and Anna Politkovskaya, *A Small Corner of Hell: Dispatches from Chechnya*, Chicago: University of Chicago Press, 2003.

5 Conversation with "Ch.," February 1995.

6 Anthropologists, of course, know this very well. See, for example, Marshall Sahlins, "Cosmologies of Capitalism: The Trans-Pacific Sector of 'The World System,'" in Nicholas B. Dirks, Geoff Eley, and Sherry B. Ortners (eds), *Culture/Power/History*, Princeton: Princeton University Press, 1994.

7 Neal Ascherson masterfully conveys the incredible details and romantic air of those adventures in the geography of rising imperialism in *Black Sea*, London: Jonathan Cape, 1995.

8 A literary investigation into this tradition is provided by Susan Layton, *Russian Literature and Empire: Conquest of the Caucasus from Pushkin to Tolstoy*, New York: Cambridge University Press, 1994.

9 Late in 1994, when the Russian army first began moving into Chechnya, the popular weekly *Argumenty i fakty* (no. 49) commissioned a sociological survey that asked the residents of big Russian towns about the sources of their opinion regarding the Chechens. It turned out that only 7 per cent of the respondents had ever met a Chechen in their life (among whom the majority were left with a positive impression). Nearly 40 per cent relied on television and the newspapers, and just as many named the poems of Lermontov and Tolstoy's novels which are part of school syllabus in Russian classical literature. Since the majority of adult Chechens received the same schooling, they are very keenly aware of their literary image.

10 Randall Collins, "Social Movements and the Focus of Emotional Attention," in Jeff Goodwin, James Jasper, and Francesca Poletta (eds), *Passionate Politics: Emotions and Social Movements*, Chicago: University of Chicago Press, 2001, pp. 27–44.

11 Later I told Khrushchev's son, Sergei, about the square in Chechnya named after his father – which surprised him. Likewise, Gorbachev had only vaguely heard of the Grozny street being renamed. This means that the Chechen nationalists failed to deliver their well-intended message, but it also means that the journalists failed to mention this fact, which did not fit the prevalent descriptions of Chechnya's rebellion against Russia.

12 On Friday February 13, 2004, Zelimkhan Yandarbiyev was blown up in his car as he was leaving the mosque in Qatar where he lived in exile after losing his Taliban hosts in Afghanistan. The Qatari police soon arrested three Russian agents accused of staging the assassination. In response, borderguards seized the Qatari judo wrestlers on their way through Moscow, claiming that these were in fact terrorist associates and would be treated accordingly unless the Qataris release the Russian counter-terrorism "experts" as they have been described.

13 *Ghazawat* is essentially synonymous with *jihad* and means the raiding of infidel lands by the Islamic warriors, or *ghazi*.

14 Georgi Derluguian, "Che Guevaras in Turbans," *New Left Review*, I/237 (September–October 1999).

15 In November 2002 Basayev admitted planning the seizure of the theatre in Moscow, which was intended to repeat the success of his Budyonnovsk operation.

16 For a discussion of Chechen paganism, see Anna Zelkina, *In Quest for God and Freedom: The Sufi Response to the Russian Advance in the North Caucasus*, London: Hurst & Co, 2000.

17 Personal communication of Vahit Akayev, Moscow, June 1999.

18 Personal communication of Lyoma Usmanov, Washington, April 1997.

19 Personal communication of Fiona Hill, Evanston, December 1999.

20 In neighboring Ingushetia the comment on Fiona Hill's story was: *This surely sounds like our Chechen brethren, but we, the Ingushes, favor instead the ideas of another Scotsman, Adam Smith.* The Ingush boasting of capitalist pragmatism, however, came from the top of General Aushev's regime of enlightened military despotism. Its own operations, undoubtedly beneficial to the maintenance of peace in Ingushetia, for no less pragmatic reasons could not fit the Smithian prescriptions. Instead the relative stability in Ingushetia was financed with the proceeds from the extremely shady tax exemptions that Moscow had granted in reward for Ingushetia's loyalty and simply because of the lack of funds in the central budget.

21 Khattab died sometime in spring 2002, either from his old wounds or, as widely speculated in Russian newspapers at the time, from a poisoned letter that was passed to him by a Russian double agent or by the Jordanian intelligence service, which was eliminating its enemies by such medieval methods.

22 The Organization for Security and Cooperation in Europe (OSCE) is the institutional outcome of the 1975 Helsinki accords (the high point of the détente intermission during the Cold War) which were signed by the heads of all thirty-five states then existing in Europe and North America. During the ethnic wars of the nineties the OSCE was revived as the collective diplomatic channel of West European governments.

23 Timothy Earle generously helped me in clarifying the social mechanisms and functions of clans. See Timothy Earle, *How Chiefs Come to Power: The Political Economy in Prehistory*, Stanford: Stanford University Press, 1997. Here, I combine Earle's anthropological insights with Bourdieu's idea of social capital and with concepts drawn from the sociological literature on trust, such as Diego Gambetta (ed), *Trust: Making and Breaking Cooperative Relations*, Oxford: Blackwell, 1988.

24 Though not the observant Carlotta Gall and Thomas de Waal. See p. 366 in their *Chechnya: Calamity in the Caucasus*, New York: NYU Press, 1998.

25 Timur Muzaev, *Chechenskii krizis-99* [The Chechen Crisis-99], Moscow: "Panorama," 1999.

26 This notorious operation and its political fallout are discussed in excellent detail by the journalists Carlotta Gall and Thomas de Waal in *Chechnya: Calamity in the Caucasus*, New York: NYU Press, 1998.

27   On this expedition, which provoked the second Russian invasion of Chechnya, see Georgi Derluguian, "Che Guevaras in Turbans," *New Left Review* I/237 (September–October).

28   Galina Khizriyeva generously shared her extensive knowledge of these trends.

29   Here I am following mostly the discussion of Pierre Bourdieu and Loïc Wacquant, *An Invitation to Reflexive Sociology*, Chicago: University of Chicago Press, 1992.

30   In 2000, shortly after the second invasion of Chechnya, Salman Raduyev was captured by Russian troops, tried, and sentenced to life in prison. The verdict was protested by such figures as Solzhenitsyn, who scandalously demanded the public execution of terrorists, but Russia had pledged before the European Council to abolish the death penalty. Raduyev died in prison late in 2002, officially from the internal bleeding caused by his old wounds and the weakening of his body after fasting during the Muslim month of Ramadan. It was widely speculated, however, that the bleeding was caused by a severe beating.

31   Anna Politkovskaya, *A Small Corner of Hell*, Chicago: University of Chicago Press, 2003.

32   I am quoting from Cynthia Buckley's so far unpublished report on the Russian census of 2002.

33   I.G. Kosikov and L.S. Kosikova, *Severnyi Kavkaz: sotsialno-ekonomicheskii spravochnik* [The Northern Caucasus: A Socioeconomic Handbook], Moscow: Exclusive-Press, 1999, pp. 115–117.

34   The irony of this propagandistic invention did not escape contemporaries, as is shown in the popular joke suggesting that the golden star of the Hero of Socialist Labor also be awarded posthumously to Goshanei's father Prince Temryuk for his historical foresight in joining the future motherland of world socialism some 350 years in advance.

35   On religious fundamentalism as the extension of heterodoxy, see S.N. Eisenstadt, *Fundamentalism, Sectarianism, and Revolution: the Jacobin Dimension of Modernity*, Cambridge: Cambridge University Press, 1999; also see the discussion of heresies in the medieval Christian West by Michael Mann, *The Sources of Social Power. Vol. 1*, Cambridge: Cambridge University Press, 1986.

36   Alena Ledeneva, *Russia's Economy of Favors: Blat, Networking, and Informal Exchange*, Cambridge: Cambridge University Press, 1998.

37   Eric Hobsbawm and Terence Ranger (eds), *The Invention of Tradition*, Cambridge: Cambridge University Press, 1983.

2 COMPLEX TRIANGULATIONS

1 Randall Collins, "The European Sociological Tradition and Twenty-First-Century World Sociology," in Janet L. Abu-Lughod (ed.), *Sociology for the Twenty-First Century*, Chicago: University of Chicago Press, 1999, p. 27.

2 Theda Skocpol was an important early critic of the world-systems perspective; however, Wallerstein did not engage in a counter-argument. On this, see Giovanni Arrighi, "Capitalism and the Modern World-System: Rethinking the Non-Debates of the 1970s," *Review*, XXI, 1, 1998.

3 A good way of overcoming many prejudices and misconceptions regarding these three schools might be to read in conjuncture the three epistemic manifestoes: Immanuel Wallerstein's *Unthinking Social Science* (Cambridge: Polity Press, 1991); Charles Tilly's *Big Structures, Large Processes, Huge Comparisons* (New York: Russell Sage, 1984); and the systematic 'catechism' of Pierre Bourdieu and Loïc Wacquant, *An Invitation to Reflexive Sociology* (Chicago: University of Chicago Press, 1992).

4 Randall Collins, "The Mega-Historians," *Sociological Theory*, vol. 3, no. 1 (Spring 1985), p. 115.

5 Iliya Ilf, *Zapisnye knizhki 1925–1937* [The Notebooks], Moscow: Tekst, 2000, pp. 312–313.

6 See Pierre Bourdieu, *Acts of Resistance: Against the Tyranny of the Market,* New York: The New Press, 1998; and Immanuel Wallerstein et al., *Open the Social Sciences: Report of the Gulbenkian Commission on the Restructuring of the Social Sciences*, Stanford: Stanford University Press, 1996.

7 See Perry Anderson, "The Ends of History," in his collection *A Zone of Contention*, London: Verso, 1992.

8 Randall Collins, *Macrohistory: Essays in the Sociology of the Long Run*, Stanford: Stanford University Press, 1999, especially "Introduction: The Golden Age of Macrohistorical Sociology."

9 In Europe, both in the Western part and in the Soviet bloc, the intellectual trend for questioning authority started perhaps a whole decade earlier, with the turmoil caused by the de-Stalinization of the Marxist Left after 1956. Yet America registered some of the strongest social movements of its age and besides that, the richest country in the world simply concentrated more academic resources and researchers.

10 See Richard Lee, "Structures of Knowledge," in Terence Hopkins, Immanuel Wallerstein et al., *The Age of Transition: Trajectory of the World-System, 1945–2025*,

London: Zed, 1996, pp. 179–206. This volume is now available in a dozen different languages.

11 Immanuel Wallerstein, *Unthinking Social Science: The Limits of Nineteenth-Century Paradigms*, Cambridge: Polity Press, 1991.

12 Pierre Bourdieu, *Distinction: A Social Critique of the Judgement of Taste*, Cambridge, MA: Harvard University Press, 1984, pp. 485–500.

13 Andrew Abbott, *Chaos of Disciplines*, Chicago: University of Chicago Press, 2001.

14 On how this happened, see for instance Yuval Yonay, *The Struggle over the Soul of Economics: Institutionalist and Neoclassical Economists in America Between the Wars*, Princeton: Princeton University Press, 1998.

15 Randall Collins, "Situational Stratification: A Micro–Macro Theory of Inequality," *Sociological Theory* 18 (2000).

16 See Samuel Huntington, *Political Order in Changing Societies*, New Haven: Yale University Press, 1968; and idem, *The Clash of Civilizations*, New York: Norton, 1995.

17 Albert Hirschman, *The Rhetoric of Reaction: Perversity, Futility, Jeopardy*, Cambridge, MA: Belknap Press, 1991.

18 Charles Tilly, "Does Modernization Breed Revolution?" *Comparative Politics* 5 (1973). This article was reproduced in numerous collections, including Charles Tilly, *Roads from Past to Future*, Lanham, MD: Rowman & Littlefield, 1997.

19 Theda Skocpol, *States and Social Revolutions*, Cambridge: Cambridge University Press, 1979.

20 Good summaries are provided by Randall Collins in chapter one, "Maturation of the State-Centered Theory of Revolution and Ideology," in his *Macrohistory*, Stanford: Stanford University Press, 1999; and in Jeff Goodwin's *No Other Way Out: States And Revolutionary Movements, 1945–1991*, Cambridge: Cambridge University Press, 2001.

21 See Theda Skocpol, *Protecting Soldiers and Mothers: The Political Origins of Social Policy in the United States*, Cambridge MA: Belknap Press, 1992; George Steinmetz, *Regulating the Social: The Welfare State and Local Politics in Imperial Germany*, Princeton: Princeton University Press, 1993; and from the "regulation school" perspective, see Bob Jessop's *State Theory: Putting the Capitalist State in its Place*, University Park: Pennsylvania State University Press, 1990; Robert Boyer and Rogers J. Hollingsworth (eds), *Contemporary Capitalism: The Embeddedness of Institutions*, Cambridge: Cambridge University Press, 1997.

22 Michael Mann, *The Sources of Social Power. Vol 2: The Rise of Classes and Nation-States, 1760–1914*, Cambridge: Cambridge University Press, 1993; Dietrich

Rueschemeyer, Evelyn Huber Stephens, and John D. Stephens, *Capitalist Development and Democracy*, Chicago: University of Chicago Press, 1992.

23 The rising internal pressures to dismantle the developmental states are analyzed by Peter Evans, *Embedded Autonomy: States and Industrial Transformation*, Princeton, NJ: Princeton University Press, 1995, especially in chapter 10. Also see Meredith Woo-Cumings (ed.), *The Developmental State*, Ithaca: Cornell University Press; and Milton Esman and Ronald J. Herring (eds), *Carrots, Sticks, and Ethnic Conflict: Rethinking Development Assistance*, Ann Arbor: University of Michigan Press, 2001. The powerful external pressures to dismantle the developmental states are analyzed in a recent article by Giovanni Arrighi, "The African Crisis: World-Systemic and Regional Aspects," *New Left Review* II/15 (May–June 2002).

24 The expression was invented by Benjamin Barber, *Jihad vs. McWorld*, New York: Ballantine Books, 1996. For the sociological analysis of Western middle-class phobias, see Bernard Beck, Scott L. Greer, and Charles Ragin, "Radicalism, Resistance, and Cultural Lags: A Commentary on Benjamin Barber's *Jihad vs. McWorld*," in Georgi Derluguian and Scott L. Greer (eds) *Questioning Geopolitics: Political Projects in a Changing World-System*, Westport, CT: Praeger, 2000, pp. 101–110.

25 Arthur Stinchcombe, "The Preconditions of World Capitalism: Weber Updated," *Journal of Political Philosophy*, vol. 3, no. 4 (December 2003), pp. 411–436.

26 As Charles Tilly knowledgeably asserts in "Globalization Threatens Labor's Rights," *International Labor and Working-Class History* 47 (Spring 1995); and in particular in his sweeping and, if this can be said of social science, poetically beautiful essay "Democracy Is a Lake," in Charles Tilly (ed.), *Roads from Past to Future*, Lanham: Rowman & Littlefield, 1997.

27 Beverly Silver, *Forces of Labour*, Cambridge: Cambridge University Press, 2003.

28 An important exposition of this idea is to be found in Michael Burawoy, *Politics of Production: Factory Regimes Under Capitalism and Socialism*, London: Verso, 1985; and Michael Burawoy and János Lukács, *The Radiant Past: Ideology and Reality in Hungary's Road to Capitalism*, Chicago: University of Chicago Press, 1992.

29 See Charles Tilly, *European Revolutions, 1492–1992*, Oxford: Blackwell, 1993; the most recent reformulation is in Doug McAdam, Sidney Tarrow, and Charles Tilly, *The Dynamics of Contention*, New York: Cambridge University Press, 2001.

30 Arthur Stinchcombe, "Reviews and Two Markets for Sociology Books," *Contemporary Sociology*, vol. 30, no. 1 (January 2001).

31   Pierre Bourdieu, "A Reasoned Utopia and Economic Fatalism," *New Left Review* I/227 (January–February 1998), pp. 125–130.

32   Giovanni Arrighi, in "Globalization and Historical Macrosociology" (in Janet L. Lughod [ed.] *Sociology for the Twenty-First Century*, Chicago: University of Chicago Press, 1999), identifies the blind spots of both schools and proposes the "unthinkings" that each school needs to do. From the standpoint of geopolitical theory, see Randall Collins and David Waller, "Predictions of Geopolitical Theory and the Modern World-System," in Georgi Derluguian and Scott L. Greer (eds), *Questioning Geopolitics: Political Projects in a Changing World-System*, Westport: Praeger, 2000.

33   Giovanni Arrighi, *The Long Twentieth Century*, London: Verso, 1994; Giovanni Arrighi, Beverly Silver, and collaborators, *Chaos and Governance in the Modern World-System*, Minneapolis: University of Minnesota Press, 1999.

34   Gil Eyal, Ivan Szelényi, and Eleanor Townsley, *Making Capitalism without Capitalists: Class Formation and Elite Struggles in Postcommunist Central Europe*, London: Verso, 1998.

35   Over the last decade many political scientists have proposed a variety of formal models comparing the market and democratic transitions across continents (see Adam Przeworski, *Democracy and the Market: Political and Economic Reforms in Eastern Europe and Latin America*, Cambridge: Cambridge University Press, 1991). But these models tend to ignore the historical context in order to present the transitions as calculated games played by the elite actors. For a trenchant methodological critique, see Valerie Bunce, "Comparative Democratization: Big and Bounded Generalizations," *Comparative Political Studies* 33, no. 6–7 (2000); for a world-system reformulation, see Albert Bergesen, "Regime Change in the Semi-Periphery: Democratization in Latin America and the Socialist Bloc," *Sociological Perspectives* 35 (1992).

36   In very different ways this observation was made first by the Russian émigré Nikolai Berdiaev in the thirties, and theorized later in the sixties and seventies by Reinhard Bendix and S.N. Eisenstadt.

37   Michael Mann, *The Sources of Social Power. Vol. 2: The Rise of Classes and Nation-States, 1760–1914*, Cambridge: Cambridge University Press, 1993.

38   Ronald Suny, *The Revenge of the Past*, Stanford, Stanford University Press, 1993.

39   For an inventive meshing of the insights of Karl Marx and Michel Foucault in recovering the "hidden transcripts" in such a high-level power game as the American trade negotiations in the 1990s, see Bruce Cumings, *Parallax Visions: Making Sense of American–East Asian Relations at the End of the Century*, Durham:

Duke University Press, 1999.

40   For a lucid exposition of the concept of "regimes of accumulation" (the most famous of which was named Fordism by the political economists of the "regulation school") see Alan Lipietz, *Mirages and Miracles: The Crises of Global Fordism*, London: Verso, 1987; Bob Jessop, *The Future of the Capitalist State*, Cambridge: Polity, 2002.

41   József Böröcz, "Dual Dependency and Property Vacuum: Social Change on the State Socialist Semiperiphery," *Theory and Society* 21 (1992); and Lawrence P. King, "Making Markets: A Comparative Study of Postcommunist Managerial Strategies in Central Europe," *Theory and Society* 30 (2001).

42   Robert Hislope, "Organized Crime in a Disorganized State," in *Problems of Post-Communism*, vol. 49, issue 3 (May–June 2002).

43   Theodore Gerber and Michael Hout, "More Shock Than Therapy: Market Transition, Employment, and Income in Russia, 1991–1995," *American Journal of Sociology*, vol. 104, no. 1 (July 1998); and Vadim Volkov, *Violent Entrepreneurs: The Use of Force in the Making of Russian Capitalism*, Ithaca: Cornell University Press, 2002.

44   Michael Mann, "Globalization After September 11," *New Left Review* II/12 (November–December 2001).

45   A significant exception, of course, is the synthetic approach that draws on Weber and Bourdieu proposed by Gil Eyal, Iván Szelényi, and Eleanor Townsley, *Making Capitalism without Capitalists: Class Formation and Elite Struggles in Postcommunist Central Europe*, London: Verso, 1998.

46   See the friendly critique and penetrating analysis of Walter Goldfrank, "Paradigm Regained? The Rules of Wallerstein's World-System Method," in the on-line *Journal of World-Systems Research*, VI, 2 (Summer–Fall 2000) at <http://csf.colorado.edu/jwsr>.

47   See Doug McAdam, Sidney Tarrow, and Charles Tilly, *The Dynamics of Contention*, New York: Cambridge University Press, 2001.

48   The intellectual pathways discovered by Erving Goffman and furthered by Randall Collins display many parallels with the themes and concerns of Bourdieu. This must be noted, but here only in passing, because I do not feel qualified to say much more in this regard. This remains a very promising direction for future research. Besides, I stick here with Bourdieu's conceptual apparatus because this book, after all, is about Bourdieu's secret admirer. Goffman and Collins remain less known in Chechnya, although perhaps no longer so in Siberia where a few energetic Russian scholars have been recently

publishing translations of Collins's works.

49   Dorothy E. Smith, "From Women's Standpoint to a Sociology for People," in Janet L. Lughod (ed.) *Sociology for the Twenty-First Century*, Chicago: University of Chicago Press, 1999, pp. 66–67.

50   Arthur Stinchcombe, "Tilly on the Past as a Sequence of Futures," a review essay in the volume edited by Charles Tilly, *Roads from Past to Future*, Lanham: Rowman & Littlefield, 1997, pp. 392 and 397.

51   Pierre Bourdieu and Loïc Wacquant, *An Invitation to Reflexive Sociology*, Chicago: University of Chicago Press, 1992, p. 91.

52   For an example of Wallerstein, elegantly and inventively as ever, playing on the themes more commonly associated with Tilly and Bourdieu, see his "Bourgeois(ie) as Concept and Reality," in *The Essential Wallerstein*, New York: The New Press, 2000.

53   Tilly's recognition of a narrative genre in social science, however, comes conditioned by many warnings, caveats, and clauses, all of which I am ready to accept. Tilly, in his own words, advocates moving towards a "*historicizing causal analysis in an interactionist framework ... informing it with a clearer understanding of culture.*" See Charles Tilly, "Future Social Science," in *Roads from Past to Future*, Lanham, MD: Rowman & Littlefield, 1997, p. 25.

3 THE DYNAMICS OF DE-STALINIZATION

1   Barrington Moore Jr., *Soviet Politics – The Dilemma of Power*, New York: Harper & Row, 1965 (c1950), p. 430.

2   Karl Marx and Friedrich Engels, *The Introduction to The Critique of Hegel's Philosophy of Right*, <http://www.marxists.org/archive/marx/works/1844/df-jahrbucher/law-abs.htm>.

3   A graphic portrayal and some rare statistics regarding the cadres' race for credentials in one of the Caucasus republics are provided by the émigré sociologist Iliya Zemtsov, *Partiia ili mafiia? Azerbaijan: razvorovannaia respublika.* [The Party of the Mafia? Azerbaijan: The Stolen Republic], Paris: Les Éditeurs Réunis, 1976.

4   *Partiynaya organizatsiya K-B ASSR za pyatdesyat let*, Nalchik: Gosknigoizdat, 1967.

5   Furthermore, it finds a resonance in the predictions made at the time by the wise political thinker Isaac Deutscher. See Isaac Deutscher, *Russia: What Next?* Oxford: Oxford University Press, 1953.

6 Amy Knight, *Beria, Stalin's First Lieutenant*, Princeton: Princeton University Press, 1993.

7 An innovative analysis of the Khrushchev-era construction of a new foreign policy around the rhetorics of peaceful coexistence with the West and alliance with Third World progressive forces is provided by Ted Hopf, *Social Construction of International Politics: Identities and Foreign Policies, Moscow, 1955 and 1999*, Ithaca: Cornell University Press, 2002.

8 In 1965 Soviet national income per capita was 53 per cent of the US level, according to Moscow's Goskomstat (GDP, including services, was not computed at that time), whereas in reality Soviet GDP per capita was probably less than 30 per cent of the US level, whereas consumption per capita (i.e. GDP minus investment and defense spending) was probably just 20 per cent. The proverbial "average American" thus was five times richer than an equally statistically fictitious "common Soviet man." Nonetheless, life expectancy in 1966 was 74 years for American and Soviet women and 67 and 66 for men respectively (official Soviet data). See the first chart in: <http://www.rand.org/publications/MR/MR1273/MR1273.ch4.pdf>.
   Actually, with an average life expectancy of 70 years the Soviet citizens were near the top of the list – the highest life expectancy was in the Netherlands at 74 years. Special thanks to Vladimir Popov for leading me to these data.

9 Ronald Grigor Suny, *The Making of the Georgian Nation*, Bloomington: Indiana University Press, 1994.

10 V. S. Lel'chuk, "1959: Rasstrel v Temirtau" ["The Shooting in Temirtau"], in Yuri Afanasiev (ed.), *Sovetskoe obschestvo*, vol. 2, Moscow: RGGU, 1997.

11 Reminiscences of a KGB veteran published in Krasnodar's FSB newsletter, February 2001.

12 Yuri Afanasiev (ed.), *Sovetskoe obschestvo*, vol. 2, Moscow: RGGU, 1997, p. 706.

13 Valery Abramkin and Valentina Chesnokova, *Tyuremnyi mir glazami politzak-lyuchennyh, 1940-e – 1980-e gody* [Prison world through the eyes of political prisoners], Moscow: Muravei, 1998, pp. 7–8. This study is a rare example of historical criminological study of the Soviet period.

14 Ibid., p. 12.

15 Norbert Elias, *The Civilizing Process*, Oxford: Oxford University Press, 1978.

16 Fedor Razzakov, *Bandity vremen sotsializma, 1917–1991* [The Criminals of the Socialist Times], Moscow: EKSMO, 1997, p. 78.

17 Miroslav Hroch, *Social Preconditions of National Revival in Europe*, Cambridge: Cambridge University Press, 1985; Pierre Bourdieu, *The Rules of Art: Genesis*

and Structure of the Literary Field, Cambridge: Polity Press, 1996; Randall Collins, *The Sociology of Philosophies: A Global Theory of Intellectual Change*, Cambridge: Harvard University Press, 1998.

18 Fazil Iskander, *Sandro of Chegem*, New York: Vintage Books, 1983.

19 An early and very perceptive analysis of communist conservatism is Victor Zaslavsky, *The Neo-Stalinist State: Class, Ethnicity, and Consensus in Soviet Society*, Armonk, NY: M.E. Sharpe, 1982.

4 FROM 1968 TO 1989

1 Immanuel Wallerstein, "Bourgeois(ie) as Concept and Reality," in *The Essential Wallerstein*, New York: New Press, 2000.

2 Valerie Bunce, "The Political Economy of Postsocialism," *Slavic Review* 58: 4 (Winter), p. 777.

3 The classic work is János Kornai, *The Economy of Shortage*, Amsterdam: De Gruyter, 1982. But see the sociologically nuanced explanation of information scarcity by Michael Urban, *The Rebirth of Politics in Russia*, Cambridge: Cambridge University Press, 1997.

4 Valerie Bunce, *Subversive Institutions: The Design and the Destruction of Socialism and the State*, New York: Cambridge University Press, 1998.

5 For an empirically detailed analysis of the continuity between 1956, 1968, and 1989 in Poland, see Grzegorz Ekiert, *The State Against Society: Political Crises and Their Aftermath in East-Central Europe*, Princeton: Princeton University Press, 1996; a general theoretical appraisal is Giovanni Arrighi, Terence K. Hopkins, and Immanuel Wallerstein, "1989: The Continuation of 1968," in George Katsiaficas (ed.), *After the Fall: 1989 and the Future of Freedom*, New York: Routledge, 2001.

6 On this count, Yugoslavia remained an eccentric example to its tragic end, although note the smooth post-communist trajectory of Slovenia.

7 Gale Stokes, *The Walls Came Tumbling Down: The Collapse of Communism in Eastern Europe*, New York: Oxford University Press, 1993, pp. 225–228.

8 Donna Bahry, *Outside Moscow: Power, Politics, and Budgetary Policy in the Soviet Republics*, New York: Columbia University Press, 1987; and Michael Urban, *An Algebra of Soviet Power: Elite Circulation in the Belorussian Republic, 1966–86*, New York: Cambridge University Press, 1989.

9 See for the Hungarian example Gil Eyal, Iván Szelényi, and Eleanor Townsley, *Making Capitalism without Capitalists*, London: Verso, 1998; and for Poland,

Maryjane Osa, *Solidarity and Contention: The Networks of Polish Opposition*, Minneapolis: University of Minnesota Press, 2003.

10 Arthur Stinchcombe, "Tilly on the Past as a Sequence of Futures," review essay in Charles Tilly (ed.), *Roads from Past to Future*, Lanham, MD: Rowman & Littlefield, 1997.

11 Valery Abramkin and Valentina Chesnokova, "Introduction," in *Tyuremnyi mir glazami politzaklyuchennyh*, Moscow: "Muravei,"1998, pp. 7–8.

12 See Federico Varese, *The Russian Mafia: Private Protection in a New Market Economy*, Oxford: Oxford University Press, 2001, especially chapters 3 and 7.

13 One of the authors who related this trend to the prediction of Moscow's imminent dilemmas was Valerie Bunce, "The Empire Strikes Back: The Evolution of the Eastern Bloc from a Soviet Asset to a Soviet Liability," *International Organization*, 39 (Winter 1985).

14 The commercialization of warfare was a key capitalist advantage centuries before Keynes, but in the American hegemony the technique reached its highest rationalization, as argues Giovanni Arrighi, *The Long Twentieth Century: Money, Power, and the Making of Our Times*, London: Verso, 1994.

15 Randall Collins, "The Geopolitical Basis of Revolution: The Prediction of the Soviet Collapse," in *Macrohistory*, Stanford: Stanford University Press, 1999.

16 This theory of "perverse" class struggle under state socialism builds on the pioneering formulations of Victor Zaslavsky, *The Neo-Stalinist State*, Armonk, NY: M.E. Sharpe, 1982; Michael Burawoy, *Politics of Production: Factory Regimes under Capitalism and Socialism*, London: Verso, 1985; and Donald Filtzer, *Soviet Workers and De-Stalinization*, Cambridge: Cambridge University Press, 1992.

17 David Woodruff, *Money Unmade: Barter and the Fate of Russian Capitalism*, Ithaca, NY: Cornell University Press, 1999.

18 Manuel Castells and Emma Kiselyova, *The Collapse of Soviet Communism: A View from the Information Society*, Berkeley: University of California, International and Area Studies, 1995.

19 This example is taken from the book that probably remains the best (and best-written) outline of the Soviet economy to date: Nikolai Shmelev and Vladimir Popov, *The Turning Point: Revitalizing the Soviet Economy*, London: I.B. Tauris, 1990.

20 Valerie Bunce, "The Political Economy of the Brezhnev Era: The Rise and Fall of Corporatism," *British Journal of Political Science*, 13 (January 1993), pp. 129–158.

21 In English, see Nikolai Shmelev and Vladimir Popov, *The Turning Point: Revitalizing the Soviet Economy*, London: I.B. Tauris, 1990.

22   Peter Evans, *Embedded Autonomy: States and Industrial Transformation*, Princeton: Princeton University Press, 1995.

23   On the processes and effects of bureaucratic self-encapsulation in the Soviet territorial and sectoral agencies, see Michael Urban and Russell Reed, "Regionalism in a Systems Perspective: Explaining Elite Circulation in a Soviet Republic," *Slavic Review* 48, no. 3 (Fall 1989); Jan Winiecki, *Resistance to Change in the Soviet Economic System: A Property Rights Approach*, London: Routledge, 1991; Peter Rutland, *The Politics of Economic Stagnation in the Soviet Union: The Role of Local Party Organs in Economic Management*, Cambridge: Cambridge University Press, 1993.

24   Theda Skocpol, *States and Social Revolutions*, Cambridge: Cambridge University Press, 1979.

25   Giovanni Arrighi, "The Social and Political Economy of Global Turbulence," *New Left Review* 20 (March–April 2003).

26   Leslie Holmes, *The End of Communist Power: Anti-Corruption Campaigns and Legitimation Crisis*, Oxford: Oxford University Press, 1993.

27   See Isaac Deutscher, *Russia: What Next?* Oxford: Oxford University Press, 1953; Barrington Moore, Jr., *Soviet Politics – The Dilemma of Power*, New York: Harper & Row, 1965 (c1950), pp. 427–430.

28   Yegor K. Ligachev, *Zagadka Gorbacheva* [The Mystery of Gorbachev], Novosibirsk: Interbook, 1992, pp. 20–21.

29   The first to formulate this contradiction intelligently was the dissident author Andrei Amalrik, in *Will the Soviet Union Survive Until 1984?* New York: Harper & Row, 1970.

30   Marc Garcelon, "The Estate Change: The Specialist Rebellion and the Democratic Movement in Moscow, 1989–1991," *Theory and Society* 26 (1997), p. 44.

31   Jeff Goodwin, *No Other Way Out: States And Revolutionary Movements, 1945–1991*, Cambridge: Cambridge University Press 2001, pp. 278–283.

5 SOCIAL STRUCTURE

1   For a recent example of such a controversy see Aage Sørensen, Erik Olin Wright, John Goldthorpe, Dietrich Rueschemeyer and James Mahoney, "Symposium on Class Analysis," *American Journal of Sociology*, vol. 105, no. 6 (2000). A different and promising approach is offered by Randall Collins,

"Situational Stratification: A Micro-macro Theory of Inequality," *Sociological Theory* 18 (2000).

2   Another good example is the collection of essays edited by George Steinmetz, *State/Culture: State-Formation After the Cultural Turn*, Ithaca NY: Cornell University Press, 1999. Also see the wide-ranging discussion in the volume organized by Julia Adams, Elizabeth Clemens, and Ann Shola Orloff, *Remaking Modernity: Politics, History and Sociology*, Durham: Duke University Press, 2004.

3   See Iván Szelényi, "The Intelligentsia in the Class Structure of State-Socialist Societies," in Michael Burawoy and Theda Skocpol (eds), *Marxist Inquiries*, supplement to *American Journal of Sociology*, vol. 88 (1982); George Konrád and Iván Szelényi, *The Intellectuals on the Road to Class Power*, New York: Harcourt Brace Jovanovich, 1979; Gil Eyal, Iván Szelényi, and Eleanor Townsley, *Making Capitalism without Capitalists: Class Formation and Elite Struggles in Postcommunist Central Europe*, London: Verso, 1998.

4   See chapter one, "Classes and Elites in the Changing Structures of Twentieth-century Central European Societies," in Gil Eyal, Iván Szelényi, and Eleanor Townsley, *Making Capitalism without Capitalists: Class Formation and Elite Struggles in Postcommunist Central Europe*, London: Verso, 1998.

5   Giovanni Arrighi, Terence Hopkins, and Immanuel Wallerstein, "Rethinking the Concepts of Class and Status-Group in a World-Systems Perspective," in *Antisystemic Movements*, London: Verso, 1989, pp. 3–28.

6   An insightful discussion is provided by Michèle Lamont and Annette Lareau, "Social Capital: Allusions, Gaps and Glissandos in Recent Theoretical Developments," *Sociological Theory*, vol. 6 (Fall 1988), pp. 153–168. Also see the authoritative exposition of Alejandro Portes, "'Social Capital' Its Origins and Applications in Modern Sociology," *Annual Review of Sociology* 24 (1998), pp. 1–24. A necessary cautionary note is Stephen Samuel Smith and Jessica Kulynych, "It May Be Social, but Why Is It Capital?" *Politics and Society*, vol. 30, no. 1, pp. 149–186.

7   Wallerstein spontaneously offered this explanation during a conversation in response to my question (11 November 1994). He admitted to little intellectual difference with Bourdieu on this issue. On a less serious note, Wallerstein added: *One thing is how they speak in Paris, and another is how we do things in New York – pragmatically.*

8   Stephen Hanson, *Time and Revolution: Marxism and the Design of Soviet Institutions*, Chapel Hill: University of North Carolina Press, 1997, p. 19.

9   Alan Lipietz, *Mirages and Miracles: The Crises of Global Fordism*, London: Verso, 1987.

10 See the classic work by Moshe Lewin, *The Gorbachev Phenomenon: A Historical Interpretation*, Berkeley: University of California Press, 1988; and the wide-ranging collection edited by William Rosenberg and Lewis H. Siegelbaum, *Social Dimensions of Soviet Industrialization*, Bloomington: Indiana University Press, 1993.

11 George Steinmetz, *Regulating the Social: The Welfare State and Local Politics in Imperial Germany*, Princeton: Princeton University Press, 1993; Michael Mann, *The Sources of Social Power, Vol 2: The Rise of Classes and Nation-States, 1760–1914*, Cambridge: Cambridge University Press, 1993.

12 Vladimir Popov generously shared his as yet unpublished data. Also see Vladimir Popov and Nikolai Shmelev, *The Turning Point: Revitalizing the Soviet Economy*, London: I.B. Tauris, 1990.

13 Just how common this kind of technocratic thinking became in the 1930s–1950s, which extended far beyond socialism, was amply demonstrated by Martha Lampland, "Developing a Rational Economy: The Transition to Stalinism in Hungary," paper presented at the annual meeting of The American Sociological Association in Chicago, 2002.

14 See the authoritative exposition of the concept by Peter Evans, *Embedded Autonomy: States and Industrial Transformation*, Princeton: Princeton University Press, 1995, and the excellent collection edited by Meredith Woo-Cumings, *The Developmental State*, Ithaca: Cornell University Press, 1999.

15 Barrington Moore Jr., *Soviet Politics – The Dilemma of Power*, New York: Harper & Row, 2nd edn, 1965 (c1950).

16 Immanuel Wallerstein, "Marxism, Marxism-Leninism, and the Socialist Experiences in World-System," in *After Liberalism*, New York: New Press, 1995.

17 See Bruce Cumings, "Webs with No Spiders, Spiders with No Webs: The Genealogy of the Developmental State," in Meredith Woo-Cumings (ed.), *The Developmental State*, Ithaca: Cornell University Press, 1999.

18 The Italian and other Mediterranean authoritarianisms of the interwar period are excellently discussed in the volume edited by Giovanni Arrighi, *Semiperipheral Development: The Politics of Southern Europe in the Twentieth Century*, Beverly Hills: Sage Publications, 1985. In addition, I am indebted to Wolfram Latsch for his comments on the Nazi economic policies in occupied Eastern Europe.

19 For an elaboration see Georgi Derluguian, "The Capitalist World-System and Socialism," in Alexander Motyl (ed.), *Encyclopedia of Nationalism, Vol. 1, Fundamental Issues*, New York: Academic Press, 2001.

20 David Lane, *The End of Social Inequality? Class, Status and Power under State Socialism*, London: George Allen & Unwin, 1982.

21 Vadim Radaev and Ovsey Shkaratan, "Etacratism: Power and Property – Evidence from the Soviet Experience," *International Sociology*, vol. 7, no. 3 (September 1992), pp. 301–316.

22 M.S. Voslenskii, *Nomenklatura: the Soviet Ruling Class*, Garden City, NJ: Doubleday, 1984.

23 Chalmers Johnson, *MITI and the Japanese Miracle*, Stanford: Stanford University Press, 1982; Pierre Bourdieu, *The State Nobility: Elite Schools and the Field of Power*, Cambridge: Polity Press, 1996.

24 Valerie Bunce, *Subversive Institutions: The Design and Destruction of Socialism and the State*, New York: Cambridge University Press, 1998.

25 T.H. Rigby, *Political Elites in the USSR: Central Leaders and Local Cadres from Lenin to Gorbachev*, Aldershot: Edward Elgar, 1990.

26 Regarding the differentiation of the *nomenklatura* according to the kind of assets that were administered and the relevant strategies of privatization after 1989, see the pathbreaking study of Steven Solnick, *Stealing the State: Control and Collapse in Soviet Institutions*, Cambridge: Harvard University Press, 1998.

27 Mervyn Matthews, *Privilege in the Soviet Union: A Study of Elite Life-styles under Communism*, London: Allen & Unwin, 1978; Ilya Zemtsov, *The Private Life of the Soviet Elite*, New York: Crane Russak, 1985.

28 For a journalistic exposé of Brezhnev-era bureaucratic corruption, see Arkady Vaksberg, *The Soviet Mafia*, New York: St. Martin's Press, 1991.

29 The data from large surveys of the kind conducted by Iván Szelényi's group in Russia and in Central European countries tend to underestimate the proportion of *nomenklatura* among the new rich because the methodology can capture only the instances of the direct conversion of administrative capital vested in *nomenklatura* rank and office into private economic capital. See the special issue of *Theory and Society* 24 (1995). But in the areas of traditionally entrenched corruption the conversions are often indirect, through family members and clients. Identifying this sort of process requires a profound local knowledge.

30 Victor Zaslavsky, *The Neo-Stalinist State: Class, Ethnicity, and Consensus in Soviet Society*, Armonk, NY: M.E. Sharpe, 1982.

31 See the penetrating sociological studies of Michael Burawoy, *Politics of Production: Factory Regimes under Capitalism and Socialism*, London: Verso, 1985; Michael Burawoy and János Lukács, *The Radiant Past: Ideology and Reality in Hungary's Road to Capitalism*, Chicago: University of Chicago Press, 1992; and the work of historian Donald Filtzer, *Soviet Workers and De-Stalinization: The*

Consolidation of the Modern System of Soviet Production Relations, 1953–1964, Cambridge: Cambridge University Press, 1992.

32   An artful and very observant overview of Soviet "middle-class" culture in the 1960s is provided by Petr Vail and Alexander Genis, *60-e: mir sovetskogo cheloveka* [The 60s: The World of the Soviet Person], Ann Arbor: Ardis, 1988.

33   On this, see the excellent study of different groups in the Soviet industrial proletariat by Stephen Crowley, *Hot Coal, Cold Steel: Russian and Ukrainian Workers from the End of the Soviet Union to Postcommunist Transformation*, Ann Arbor: University of Michigan Press, 1997.

34   James Scott, *Weapons of the Weak: Everyday Forms of Peasant Resistance*, New Haven: Yale University Press, 1985.

35   The best in the field remains Nancy Lubin, *Labor and Nationality in Soviet Central Asia: An Uneasy Compromise*, Princeton: Princeton University Press, 1984.

36   During perestroika, it was revealed that an estimated seven million engineers had concealed their diplomas from personnel departments primarily in order to hold on to the less demanding and better rewarded positions of manual workers (*Sotsialisticheskaia industria*, July 17, 1987).

37   An excellent discussion in this regard is found in Gerald Mars and Yochanan Altman, "The Cultural Bases of Soviet Georgia's Second Economy," *Soviet Studies* XXXV, no. 4 (October 1983), pp. 546–60.

38   The most comprehensive historical account, based on the contemporaneous accounts of nationalist émigrés and Bolsheviks from the 1920s, remains Richard Pipes, *The Formation of the Soviet Union: Communism and Nationalism, 1917–1923*, Cambridge, MA: Harvard University Press, 1954. In 1918 several radical factions of North Caucasian peasants sided with the Bolsheviks, whose Marxist doctrine, after a fascinating debate, they equated with *jihad*. In 1919, when General Deniken's White volunteers were closing in on Moscow, the Chechen and Ingush ethnic militias struck in the Whites' rear, which quite probably saved the Bolshevik regime.

39   Ronald Grigor Suny, *The Revenge of the Past: Nationalism, Revolution, and the Collapse of the Soviet Union*, Stanford: Stanford University Press, 1993.

40   Terry Martin, *The Affirmative Action Empire: Nations and Nationalism in the Soviet Union*, Ithaca, NY: Cornell University Press, 2001.

41   Similar arguments were advanced by the political scientist Philip G. Roeder, *Red Sunset: The Failure of Soviet Politics*, Princeton: Princeton University Press, 1993; and the sociologist Rogers Brubaker, *Nationalism Reframed: Nationhood and the National Question in the New Europe*, Cambridge: Cambridge University Press, 1996.

42 Zelimkhan Yandarbiyev, chief ideologist of Chechen independence and interim president after Dudayev's death in 1996, fondly recalls in his memoirs his friendship and the passionate conversations he shared with fellow students at the Literary Institute in Moscow during the mid-1980s. Among them were a Ukrainian, a Pole, a Lithuanian, a Georgian, and an ethnic German from the community deported to Kazakhstan. See Zelimkha Iandarbiev [sic], *Chechenia: bitva za svobodu* [Chechenia: The Battle for Freedom], Lvov: Svoboda narodiv, 1996.

43 Pierre Bourdieu, "The Algerian Subproletariat," in I.W. Zartman (ed.), *Man, State, and Society in the Contemporary Maghreb*, London: Pall Mall, 1973, pp. 83–89.

44 See Alejandro Portes and József Böröcz, "The Informal Sector Under Capitalism and State Socialism: a Preliminary Comparison," *Social Justice*, vol. 15, nos 3–4 (1988).

45 Stephen Wegren, "Private Agriculture in the Soviet Union Under Gorbachev," *Soviet Union/Union Sovietique* 16, nos 2–3 (1989), pp. 105–144.

46 Many of these cars would have been stolen in Germany and resold through a chain of Polish and Ukrainian intermediaries. Since the local police now receive the descriptions from Interpol, occasionally they recover such cars. Which stolen cars will be found, however, evidently depends in part on the whims of the police and in part on their calculations regarding whom they should not touch.

47 Vadim Volkov, *Violent Entrepreneurs: The Use of Force in the Making of Russian Capitalism*, Ithaca, NY: Cornell University Press, 2002.

48 A rare look into these operations is provided by S. Yu. Barsukova, "Solidarnost uchastnikov neformalnoi ekonomiki: na primere strategii migrantov i predprinimatelei." ["Solidarity among the participants in the informal economy: the strategies of migrants and entrepreneurs"], *Sotsiologicheskie issledovaniya* 216 (April 2002), pp. 3–11.

49 Pierre Bourdieu, *Distinction: A Social Critique of the Judgement of Taste*, Cambridge, MA: Harvard University Press, 1984.

50 Pierre Bourdieu, *Nachala* [The Russian translation of *Choses Dites*, Paris: Minuit, 1988], Moscow: SocioLogos, 1994, pp. 21–24.

51 Arthur Stinchcombe, "Tilly on the Past as a Sequence of Futures," review essay in Charles Tilly (ed.), *Roads from Past to Future*, Lanham: Rowman & Littlefield, 1997.

52 Charles Tilly, "Parliamentarization of Popular Contention in Great Britain, 1758–1834," in Tilly (ed.), *Roads from Past to Future*, Lanham MD: Rowman & Littlefield, 1997.

53 Albert Hirschman, *Exit, Voice, and Loyalty: Responses to Decline in Firms, Organizations, and States*, Cambridge, MA: Harvard University Press, 1970.

54 The lineage of recent skepticism regarding the natural histories of nations goes back to the famous volume edited by Eric Hobsbawm and Terence Ranger, *The Invention of Tradition*, Cambridge: Cambridge University Press, 1983. Also see the recent collection edited by John A. Hall, *The State of the Nation: Ernest Gellner and the Theory of Nationalism*, Cambridge: Cambridge University Press, 1998. It can serve as a splendid guide to the whole debate on nations and nationalism.

55 Benedict Anderson, *Imagined Communities. Reflections on the Origin and Spread of Nationalism*, London: Verso, 1983.

56 The issues of ethnicity and class re-emerge in various forms in the broadly representative collection edited by George Steinmetz, *State/Culture: State-Formation After the Cultural Turn*, Ithaca NY: Cornell University Press, 1999.

57 McAdam, Tarrow, and Tilly (*Dynamics of Contention*, pp. 228–233) issue the warning that the recent studies of nationalism overbent the stick by concentrating on nationalism as discourse to the neglect of contentious politics and state-building. The resurgence of interest in class formation could eventually help to correct this bias. In any case, the most productive way to move ahead seems to combine what previously were wholly separate intellectual fields.

58 Richard Lachmann, *Capitalists in Spite of Themselves: Elite Conflict and Economic Transitions in Early Modern Europe*, New York: Oxford University Press, 2000.

59 Julia Adams, "Materialists in Spite of Ourselves?" *The Newsletter of the Comparative and Historical Sociology Section of the American Sociological Association*, vol. 15, no. 1 (Spring 2003), <http://www.cla.sc.edu/socy/faculty/deflem/comphist/ chs03Spr.html>.

60 One of the best analytical models on this subject is offered by Michael Urban, *The Rebirth of Politics in Russia*, Cambridge: Cambridge University Press, 1997.

61 Charles Tilly, "The Invisible Elbow," in *Roads from Past to Future*, Lanham, Maryland: Rowman & Littlefield, 1997.

62 Most forcefully this route of overcoming the antinomy between agency and structure is presented in Immanuel Wallerstein's *Utopistics*, New York: The New Press, 1998.

6 THE NATIONALIZATION OF PROVINCIAL REVOLUTIONS

1   Amidst the dazzling diversity of nearly fifty autochthonous ethnicities, the Caucasus exhibits a remarkable unity of traditional socioanthropological patterns. See the authoritative summary by three world-renowned anthropologists: Malkhaz A. Abdushelishvili, Sergei A. Arutyunov, and Boris A. Kaloyev, *Narody Kavkaza: antropologia, lingvistika, hozyaistvo* [The Peoples of the Caucasus: Anthropology, Linguistics, Traditional Economy], Moscow: Institut antropologii i etnologii RAN, 1994.

2   Mark Beissinger suggested this mental experiment.

3   A leading exponent of the thesis of an Islamic threat to the Soviet Union was the French Academician Hélène Carrère d'Encausse. It might be instructive to re-read today her bestseller, *Decline of an Empire: The Soviet Socialist Republics in Revolt*, New York: Newsweek Books, 1979. An astute dissection of this sort of analysis was performed by Muriel Atkin, "The Islamic Revolution that Overthrew the Soviet State?" in Nikki Keddie (ed.), *Debating Revolutions*, New York: NYU Press, 1995, pp. 296–313.

4   To the credit of the *Far Eastern Economic Review*, when the Western media were still celebrating the springtime of nations, this journal in 1992 ran the cover story under the blunt title "Dumping Central Asia" in an article that had been written in large part by the Pakistani journalist Ahmed Rashid.

5   As with all such violent episodes, a reasonably detailed and conclusive investigation cannot be the responsibility of scholars. What I am suggesting here and elsewhere regarding the circumstances and causes of pogroms and other violent forms of conflict should be treated as sociological reconstructions based on a theoretical understanding of plausible hypotheses that tie in with the empirical evidence available. How to gather such facts is a separate methodological problem. I am afraid that fieldwork, or whatever approximates to fieldwork, will always be necessary. The local people often know what is really going on (especially if they are involved in it directly), although this knowledge is usually unanalyzed, or buried in the ethnic stereotypes and political rhetoric borrowed from current propaganda.

6   Nancy Lubin, *Labor and Nationality in Soviet Central Asia*, Princeton: Princeton University Press, 1984.

7   Leslie Holmes, *The End of Communist Power: Anti-Corruption Campaigns and Legitimation Crisis*, Oxford: Oxford University Press, 1993.

8   "Myatezh? Kto ili chto stoit za sobytiyami v Ferganskoi doline" ["Mutiny?

Who or What Stands Behind the Events in Fergana Valley"], *Komsomolskaia pravda*, July 7, 1989; Vladimir Gribanov, "Zhit v Tashkente" ["To Live in Tashkent"], *Stolitsa*, no. 19, 1994; "Propavshee zoloto" ["The Missing Gold"], *Nezavisimaya gazeta*, February 23, 1993.

9   Gorbachev's appointee in Uzbekistan, Rafik Nishanov, moved to Moscow to become the Speaker of the newly elected Soviet of the Nationalities, the USSR's equivalent of a senate. Such moves from governorships in troubled republics to senatorial positions in Moscow became familiar in 1989–1990, and were repeated, for instance, in Checheno-Ingushetia and Kabardino-Balkaria by the locally isolated governors.

10   Vladimir Popov, "Shock Therapy Versus Gradualism: The End of the Debate," *Comparative Economic Studies*, vol. 42, no. 1 (2000), pp. 1–57.

11   Alexander J. Motyl, *The Turn to the Right: The Ideological Origins and Development of Ukrainian Nationalism, 1919–1929*, New York: Columbia University Press, 1980; Anatol Lieven, *The Baltic Revolution: Estonia, Latvia, Lithuania and the Path to Independence*, New Haven: Yale University Press, 1994.

12   I am particularly grateful to the Yerevan sociologist Ruben Karapetyan for his discussion of Armenian elite formation in Soviet times.

13   Marc Garcelon, "The Estate Change: The Specialist Rebellion and the Democratic Movement in Moscow, 1989–1991," *Theory and Society* 26 (1997), p. 51.

14   Olga Kryshtanovskaya and Yuri Khutoryansky, "Elita i vozrast: put naverh" ["Elite and age: the road upward"], *Sotsiologicheskie issledovania*, no. 4, 2002.

15   This strategy was co-invented by the ethnic Russian *nomenklatura* as well. In the Krasnodar and Stavropol regions, also situated in the North Caucasus, the ultra-conservative regional party leaders sponsored first the creation of a "Russian Communist Party" and later the overtly chauvinistic Cossack revival that, fortunately, remained only half-successful. See Anatol Lieven, *Chechnya, the Tombstone of Russian Power*, New Haven: Yale University Press, 1998, especially chapter 6, pointedly called "Failure of the Serbian Option"; and Georgi Derluguian, "The Russian Neo-Cossacks: Militant Provincials in the Geoculture of Clashing Civilizations," in John Guidry, Michael Kennedy, and Mayer Zald (eds), *Globalizations and Social Movements*, Ann Arbor: University of Michigan Press, 2000.

16   Kristina Juraité, *Environmental Consciousness and Mass Communication*, doctoral thesis, Kaunas: Vytautas Magnus University, 2002.

17   Zviad Gamsakhurdia was the son of the famous writer and Stalin laureate Konstantine Gamsakhurdia. Zviad's initiation into contention was in the

bloody 1956 clashes defending Stalin's statue against Soviet troops in Tbilisi – for Stalin was, after all, also a Georgian. Together with Kostava, Zviad Gamsakhurdia was jailed in 1979 for inciting student protests over the issues of the official status of the Georgian language and the allocation of university positions according to Soviet nationality principles, which were further related by Georgian nationalists to the issue of control over autonomous Abkhazia. In the KGB prison, Zviad Gamsakhurdia rapidly recanted and made a televised apology, after which he was released. Kostava remained unrepentant and imprisoned. His steadfastness during his incarceration made Kostava the likeliest leader of Georgian radical nationalism, but soon after his release from prison he died in a car crash. By default, Zviad Gamsakhurdia became the leader of the radicals. The death of Kostava remains shrouded in speculation regarding whether the accident was staged by the KGB, which implies perhaps that Zviad was an agent provocateur. Contrary to many such conspiracy theories, the compromised leader's collaboration with the secret police did not seem to matter once revolutionary mobilization had propelled him into power.

18 Kamil Azamatov et al., *Cherekskaia tragedia* [The Tragedy in Cherek], Nalchik: Elbrus, 1994.

19 The North Caucasus proved to be the Russian Empire's longest and costliest conquest. The extraordinary resistance of Daghestanis, Chechens, and Circassian peoples (today the Kabardins, Cherkesses, Adygheis and Abkhazes) to the imperial conquest was made possible by the concatenation of a number of factors: the mountain terrain often described by Russian conquerors as a natural fortress, the warrior traditions of local peoples, the ample availability of firearms imported from Turkey or produced locally by native cottage industry, and finally the pan-tribal Islamic ideology of *ghazawat* (jihad, the Holy War) propagated from Daghestan by the charismatic preacher and very capable statebuilder Imam Shamil. The Caucasus War, which consisted mostly of the highlanders' lightning raids and Russian punitive expeditions into the mountains, lasted more than forty years, until the honorable surrender of Imam Shamil in 1859 and the final destruction of Circassian mountain strongholds in 1864. This defeat and the conditions imposed by the Russian command forced into a hectic exodus perhaps half a million native North Caucasians, the majority of whom belonged to various Circassian tribes. Many refugees died en route, others settled down in Ottoman lands such as Syria and Anatolia, where there exist today sizable communities of the descendants of Circassian and Chechen

refugees called in Islamic tradition the *muhajeers*. Were it not for this massive forced migration, claim today's North Caucasian authors, their nations wouldn't be as small. On the Caucasus War, see Moshe Gammer, *Muslim Resistance to the Tsar: Shamil and the Conquest of Chechnia and Daghestan*, London: F. Cass, 1994. A major source on the Islamic peasant war in the North Caucasus is Nikolai Ilyich Pokrovsky, *Kavkazskaia voina i Imamat Shamilya* [The Caucasus War and Shamil's Imamate], Moscow: POSSPEN. Pokrovsky wrote his book in 1934 but it was published only in 2000 by his son. Despite Pokrovsky's thoroughly Marxist approach, Soviet academic publishers felt too unnerved by the topic.

20 Mark Beissinger, *Nationalist Mobilization and the Collapse of the Soviet State*, New York: Cambridge University Press, 2002.

21 Telegram from the Revkom (revolutionary committee) of Soviet Azerbaijan to the Revkom of Soviet Armenia, 30 November 1920, in *Karabahskii vopros, v dokumentah i faktah* [The Karabagh Question in Documents and Facts], Stepanakert: Artsakh, 1989, p. 43.

22 Grigory Platonovich Lezhava is a Georgian refugee from Abkhazia who was given a temporary position at the Institute of Ethnology and Anthropology in Moscow. I am very grateful to Dr. Lezhava for sharing his findings and hope that his age and difficult circumstances will not be an obstacle to his publishing them.

23 To appreciate how incredibly fluid the situation was, consider these facts. In 1921 the insurgent Turkish government in Angora (Ankara) was the only external ally of Soviet Russia against the Entente Powers. Therefore the question of Adjaria, formerly an Ottoman territory acquired by the Russian Empire only in 1878, caused considerable uneasiness. Batumi was connected to the oilfields of Baku by one of the earliest pipelines in the world. Ironically from today's viewpoint, the country later called Saudi Arabia used to get its kerosene from Baku via Batumi. Underscoring the value of Batumi's port, during 1917–1921 it was claimed by Turkey, by Russia (both Denikin's Whites and the Bolsheviks), by the independent Georgia on the grounds that the Adjarians were linguistically Georgian, by Azerbaijan because the Adjarians were also Muslims, by Armenia simply because it needed access to the sea, and by the British occupation forces that intended to make Batumi a *porto fanco*. The Adjarians themselves were torn between their progressive national intelligentsia, who advocated a confederation with Georgia, and the traditionalists, who longed for the restoration of the Ottoman Sultan's rule. See Firuz Kazemzadeh, *The Struggle for Transcaucasia, 1917–1921*, New York: Philosophical Library, 1951.

24 Ronald Grigor Suny, *Looking toward Ararat: Armenia in Modern History*, Bloomington: Indiana University Press, 1993.

25 A typical anecdote from the period claims that in the 1920s Turkey protested to the USSR that one of its republics, namely Armenia, displayed Mount Ararat on its coat of arms, despite the fact that Ararat was not in Armenia's possession. The USSR People's Commissar for Foreign Affairs, Litvinov, diplomatically pointed out to his counterpart that Turkey itself was displaying the crescent moon on its flag, despite the fact that the moon was not in Turkish possession. The anecdote, almost certainly apocryphal, illustrates the Armenian attitude to Russia's protection even more than its hostile attitude towards Turkey.

26 See Levon Abrahamian and A.A. Borodatova, "Avgust 1991: prazdnik, ne uspevshii razvernutsya" ["August 1991: The Festivity That Did Not Have Time to Unfold"], *Etnograficheskoe obozrenie*, no. 3, 1992, pp. 47–57.

27 A meticulous reconstruction of these events is provided by Thomas De Waal, *Black Garden: Armenia and Azerbaijan Through Peace and War*, New York: NYU Press, 2003.

28 At first, Kocharyan impolitely refused his foreign policy advisor who, feeling terribly impressed by my coming from America, volunteered herself as an intermediary (this hospitable woman had only recently been a teacher of German). I didn't consider Kocharyan's refusal a pity – encounters with officials usually force you to listen to statements rehearsed for journalists. The Karabagh leader himself sent for me when he learned that I had also been to Abkhazia and Chechnya – he avidly wanted insider information about these comparable conflicts. Excusing himself, Kocharyan offered his devastating critique of applied social science: *I am visited by hordes of scholars from all those Harvard-marvard Oxford-shmoksford foreign universities, who come to teach me about conflict resolution, minority rights, and such like. In very learned language they tell me everything that I already know. But they don't know themselves what I don't know but want to know.* Compared with the rest of the Karabagh officials, Kocharyan cut an impressive figure, albeit with a distinctly Machiavellian air. In 1998 Robert Kocharyan became President of Armenia as a result of what was essentially a coup conducted by the veterans of the Karabagh War. A year later several popular politicians and rivals to Kocharyan, including the former guerrilla commander and Armenia's Premier Vazgen Sarkissian, were gunned down during a parliamentary session. The perpetrators, a bohemian journalist and several of his friends, were caught on the spot but the question of whether the gunmen acted on their own remained a matter of hotly contentious speculation.

29 Heydar Aliyev is a former KGB general, was Azerbaijan's First Secretary in 1969–1983, a member of Politburo until 1987, and is a politician of legendary cunning. During the confused coup in 1993, Aliyev jumped at the opportunity this offered and triumphantly returned to power as President of independent Azerbaijan. For more on these events, see the first-person account of Thomas Goltz, *Azerbaijan Diary*, Armonk, NY: M.E. Sharpe, 1998.

30 At least, this is how Gorbachev's aides explained their dilemmas when speaking to me at the Gorbachev Foundation in Moscow in 1994 and again in 1999.

31 The rituals of interethnic trade and statutory kinship were extensively documented by anthropologists who worked in the area in the early twentieth century, such as Stepan Lisitsian, *Armyane Nagornogo Karabaha* [The Armenians of Mountainous Karabagh], Yerevan: Izdatelstvo erevanskogo universiteta, 1992.

32 Emotions remain an awkward consideration in the predominantly structural analyses of mass mobilization. But see the recent collection *Passionate Politics: Emotions and Social Movements*, Chicago: University of Chicago Press, 2001, edited by Jeff Goodwin, James Jasper, and Francesca Polletta.

33 Personal communication, for which I am very grateful to Levon Abrahamian.

34 Rajab Mamedov, Mais Nazarli, and Shahin Mustafayev were of particular help to me in piecing together the picture of events in Baku that, as an Armenian, I could not study on location. The best published account to date is in Russian: Dmitry E. Furman (ed.), *Azerbaidzhan i Rossiia: obschestva i gosudarstva* [Azerbaijan and Russia: Societies and States], Moscow: Letnii sad, 2001.

35 On these cultural struggles, see Tadeusz Swietochowski, *Russian Azerbaijan, 1905–1920: The Shaping of National Identity in a Muslim Community*, New York: Cambridge University Press, 1985.

36 I am grateful to Vardan Hovhannisian, an independent documentary cinematographer from Yerevan, for the use of his video archive.

37 See the discussion of the "opuskanie" (gang rape) ritual in the Introduction to Valery Abramkin and Valentina Chesnokova, *Tyuremnyi mir glazami politzak-lyuchennyh*, Moscow: "Muravei," 1998.

38 A very popular conspiracy theory blames the secret directive of Zbigniew Brzezinski which allegedly instructed the CIA to start the Armenian–Azeri quarrel with a pogrom, with the aim of destroying the USSR. It is part of local culture that people passionately insist that they, of course, know what there is in the secret directives of the White House. Brzezinski became a celebrity owing to his demonization in Soviet propaganda in the late 1970s.

39 See Edward H. Judge, *Easter in Kishinev: Anatomy of a Pogrom*, New York: New York University Press, 1992.

40 Before 1917 nearly 7 per cent of Georgians possessed titles of nobility, compared to 3 per cent among the Russians. The record was set by the Polish subjects of the Russian empire, among whom nearly 10 per cent claimed to belong to the traditional *szlachta* (see L. Ishkhanian, *Sotsialno-istoricheskie korni gruzino-armyanskoi draki* [The Sociohistorical Roots of the Georgian–Armenian Quarrel], Tiflis, n/p, 1918). These are exceedingly high proportions of ennoblement in comparison to the coercive-agrarian states of the West, where the proportion of nobility stood much lower, normally at around 1 per cent – for how many gentlemen could really help to support an agrarian population? Hypothetically, the strong influence of petty noble dispositions on the formation of its modern intelligentsia makes Georgia comparable to Poland and Hungary, the other Soviet bloc countries where the intelligentsia-inspired political contention during socialism reached exceptional peaks.

41 Ghia Nodia, Ketevan Rostiashvili, Gia Tarkhan-Mouravi, Murat Chavleishvili, Zurik Margania, Irina Mamasahlisi-Kuznetsova, Mzia and Alexander Gochua, and several anonymous interviewees shared their impressions regarding the social character of the activists at the Zviadist rallies. Their accounts are consistent and verifiable through other sources. However, to my knowledge, no systematic sociological research on this issue exists.

42 Liubov Kurtynova-Derluguian, *Tsar's Abolitionists: The Russian Suppression of the Slave Trade in the Caucasus, 1801–1864*, PhD dissertation, Binghamton University, Department of History, 1995.

43 Another Caucasian joke exaggerates the situation only slightly. A young woman explains her reason for wanting a divorce: *He's a damn liar! When he was courting me, it was flowers, restaurants, and taxis, and he told me that he was a bartender. When we got married, it was a room in the factory dormitory and a monthly salary of ninety rubles. He turned out to be an engineer!*

44 Gerald Mars and Yochanan Altman, "The Cultural Bases of Soviet Georgia's Second Economy," *Soviet Studies* XXXV, no. 4 (October 1983), pp. 546–560.

45 In 1989 a group of Georgian intellectuals, including a couple of economists, explained to me that Georgia would be immensely better off if its wines and mineral water were sold at world market prices, earning hard currency directly for their republic. When I cautiously suggested that although Georgian wines could be of celestial quality, they would face serious competition from the established French brands, the response was suddenly icy: *You are full of the imperial mentality.*

46   Commentators who suggest that Gorbachev was simply naïve regarding national
sentiments and Caucasus realities fail to explain how this could be possible.
Gorbachev was a native of the North Caucasus and formerly the First Secretary
of the Stavropol region, which included the Karachai-Circassian Autonomous
Province and bordered on Daghestan, Chechnya, and Kabardino-Balkaria. Also,
Gorbachev's close associate during perestroika was Eduard Shevardnadze, an
experienced Georgian, who in 1979 gave sanction to the arrest of Gamsakhurdia
and Kostava. If in dealing with the nationalist uprisings during perestroika
Gorbachev and Shevardnadze favored evasiveness over action, they must have
considered this course absolutely unavoidable. A detailed reconstruction of their
political constraints and internal reasoning must be left to historians.

47   See Michael Urban, *The Rebirth of Politics in Russia*, Cambridge: Cambridge
University Press, 1997.

48   A typical joke of the period illustrates the situation when Moscow becomes
the center of public attention and at the same time is perceived as the source
of all problems – which suggests political separation as an omni-solution.
The nightly news program Vremya – broadcast from Moscow over all the
twelve times zones of the USSR (watching it was a nightly social ritual) –
ends with the forecast that promises bad weather in Georgia. *"Damn Moscow!
Just look what they are doing to us,"* exclaims a Georgian viewer.

49   See Sidney Tarrow, *Power in Movement: Social Movements, Collective Action, and
Politics*, New York: Cambridge University Press, 1994, p. 143.

50   An excellent study of such politically relevant networks in Poland is Maryjane
Osa, *Solidarity and Contention: The Networks of Polish Opposition*, Minneapolis:
University of Minnesota Press, 2003.

51   A good account of how this happened was written by the Soviet economist
who soon afterwards became the Minister of Foreign Trade in the Russian
cabinet of neoliberal shock-therapy, and who later became an oligarchic
financier. See Petr Aven, "Economic Policy and the Reform of Mikhail
Gorbachev: A Short History," in Merton J. Peck and Thomas J. Richardson
(eds), *What Is to be Done? Proposals for the Soviet Transition to the Market*,
New Haven: Yale University Press, 1991.

52   See the remarkable article based on field research in Buriatia and Tuva by
Caroline Humphrey, "'Icebergs,' Barter, and the Mafia in Provincial Russia,"
Anthropology Today, vol. 7, no. 2 (April 1991).

53   An even stronger example of the same kind was Checheno-Ingushetia, where
during 1988–1990 the ecologists and intelligentsia democrats, united in the local

Popular Front for Perestroika, dominated the oppositional field and thus kept the aspiring nationalists on the margins. See Timur Muzaev and Zurab Todua, *Novaia Checheno-Ingushetiia* [The New Checheno-Ingushetia], Moscow: "Panorama," 1992.

54 Miroslav Hroch, *Social Preconditions of National Revival in Europe*, Cambridge: Cambridge University Press, 1985.

55 Incidentally, a leading local Islamist was previously a secular environmentalist and still earlier one of Shanibov's student activists.

56 Elena Bitova, Aslan Borov, and Kasbolat Dzamikhov, *Sovremennaia Kabardino-Balkaria: problemy obschestvennoi dinamiki, nauki i obrazovania* [Contemporary Kabardino-Balkaria: Problems of Social Dynamics, Science and Education], Nalchik: El-Fa, 1996, pp. 12–16.

57 Elena Bitova, *Sotsialnaia istoria Balkarii XIX veka* [The Social History of Balkaria in the Nineteenth Century], Nalchik: Elbrus, 1997.

58 According to a widespread rumor, Moscow offered the prospective president of separatist Balkaria, General Suffian Beppayev, a choice between a prison cell and a comfortable, but inconspicuous office in the government of united Kabardino-Balkaria. In the last years of the Soviet Union, General Beppayev served at the Transcaucasian Regional Military Command in Tbilisi, where allegedly he had amassed a personal fortune by selling arms to various ethnic militias. The rumor could be malicious; there is no way of knowing.

7 THE SCRAMBLE FOR SOVIET SPOILS

1 Arthur Stinchcombe, "Tilly on the Past as a Sequence of Futures," review essay in Charles Tilly (ed.), *Roads from Past to Future*, Lanham, Maryland: Rowman & Littlefield, 1997.

2 Fernand Braudel, *Afterthoughts on Material Civilization and Capitalism*, Baltimore: Johns Hopkins University Press, 1986.

3 See Giovanni Arrighi, Terence K. Hopkins, and Immanuel Wallerstein, "1989: The Continuation of 1968," in George Katsiaficas (ed.), *After the Fall*, New York: Routledge, 2001.

4 The mechanisms and current effects of renewed semi-peripherality in Central Europe are best described by Lawrence King, "Making Markets: A Comparative Study of Postcommunist Managerial Strategies in Central Europe," *Theory and Society* 30 (2001).

5   Alain Lipietz, *Mirages and Miracles: The Crises of Global Fordism.* London: Verso, 1987.

6   On Soviet bureaucratic isomorphism, see Victor Zaslavsky, *The Neo-Stalinist State*, Armonk, NY: M.E. Sharpe, 1982.

7   Michael Mann, *The Sources of Social Power, Vol. 2: The Rise of Classes and Nation-States, 1760–1914*, Cambridge: Cambridge University Press, 1993; and Joel Migdal, *Strong Societies and Weak States: State-Society Relations and State Capabilities in the Third World*, Princeton: Princeton University Press, 1988.

8   A founding piece in the neopatrimonialist characterization of the patterns of rule in the contemporary post-colonial periphery was by Max Weber's prominent interpreter Guenther Roth, in "Personal Rulership, Patrimonialism, and Empirebuilding in the New States," *World Politics*, vol. 20, no. 2 (1968), pp. 194–206. Further theoretical and empirical implications were explored by S.N. Eisenstadt, *Traditional Patrimonialism and Modern Neopatrimonialism*, London: Sage, 1973; and Jean-François Medard, "The Underdeveloped State in Tropical Africa: Political Clientelism or Neopatrimonialism," in Christopher Clapham (ed.), *Private Patronage and Public Power*, New York: St. Martin's Press, 1982, pp. 162–192. Regarding neopatrimonial patterns in the Soviet party/state, see Ken Jowitt, *New World Disorder: The Leninist Extinction*, Berkeley: University of California Press, 1992. A lucid and erudite outline of the concept of neopatrimonialism as it applies to the post-communist Ukraine is Oleksandr Fisun, "Politiko-rezhimnaia trans-formatsia Ukrainy: dilemmy neopatrimonialnogo razvitia" [The Political-Regime Transformation in the Ukraine: Dilemmas of Neopatrimonial Development], *Stylos*, Kyïv, 2002, pp. 4–14.

9   Aníbal Quijano, *La economía popular y sus caminos en America Latina*, Lima: Mosca Azul Editores, 1998.

10 See chapter 10 in Eric Hobsbawm's *The Age of Extremes, 1914–1991*, New York: Vintage, 1994; and the exchanges between Charles Tilly, Immanuel Wallerstein, Eric Hobsbawm, Aristide Zolberg, and Lourdes Benería in *International Labor and Working-Class History* 47 (Spring 1995).

11 Hendrik Spruyt, "The Origins, Development, and Possible Decline of the Modern State," *Annual Review of Political Science* 5 (2002).

12 William Reno, *Warlord Politics and African States*, Boulder, CO: Lynne Rienner Publishers, 1998.

13 Good overviews of the new theories of the state are provided by Hendrik Spruyt, "The Origins, Development, and Possible Decline of the Modern State," *Annual Review of Political Science*, vol. 5 (2002), and Randall Collins,

"Maturation of the State-Centered Theory of Revolution and Ideology," in his *Macrohistory*, Stanford: Stanford University Press, 1999.

14 Charles Tilly points to the difference between the manner in which Western states and the contemporary peripheral states developed in his conclusion to *Coercion, Capital, and European States, AD 990–1992*, Oxford: Blackwell, 1992.

15 Giuseppe di Lampedusa, *The Leopard*, New York: The Limited Editions Club, 1988.

16 On the comparison between the patterns of post-communist collapse in Serbia and Russia, see Valerie Bunce, *Subversive Institutions*, New York: Cambridge University Press, 1998; Veljko Vujacic, "Historical Legacies, Nationalist Mobilization, and Political Outcomes in Russia and Serbia," *Theory and Society* 25 (1996); and Anatol Lieven, *Chechnya: The Tombstone of Russian Power*, New Haven: Yale University Press, 1998, chapters 6 and 7.

17 *Moskovskii komsomolets*, April 17, 1993.

18 The tireless archival researcher Grigory Lezhava found in Moscow's secret police files a school notebook which contained a moving manuscript written by Memed Abashidze in prison while awaiting execution. Addressing himself to Stalin (whom he had known since before the revolution, because Stalin's career as an agitator started in Batumi's port), Abashidze passionately explained that he had long accepted the Bolshevik regime, even if he did not subscribe to its methods, because his own dream was of a secular, modern, educated, and industrialized Adjaria, which would belong to a world federation of socialist nationalities.

19 For more, see Georgi Derluguian, "Why Adjaria Is Not Like Bosnia: Historical Determinants, Human Agency, and Contingency in the Chaotic Transition," in George Katsiaficas (ed.), *After the Fall: 1989 and the Future of Freedom*, New York: Routledge, 2001.

20 Analytically, South Ossetia is very similar to Abkhazia and we omit this case.

21 Iván Szelényi, with Robert Manchin et al., *Socialist Entrepreneurs: Embourgeoisement in Rural Hungary*, Madison: University of Wisconsin Press, 1988.

22 See Fazil Iskander's hilarious and charming short story about how uncle Sandro was looking for an intermediary, preferably a prince in the old tradition, to make a traffic policeman rescind his speeding ticket. Fazil Iskander, *Sandro of Chegem*, New York: Vintage Books, 1983.

23 Miroslav Hroch, *Social Preconditions of National Revival in Europe*, Cambridge: Cambridge University Press, 1985.

24   Grigory P. Lezhava, *Mezhdu Gruziei i Rossiei: istoricheskie korni i sovremennye faktory abkhazo-gruzinskogo konflikta* [Between Georgia and Russia: the historical roots and contemporary factors of the Abkhaz–Georgian conflict], Moscow: Institut etnologii i antropologii RAN, 1997.

25   On the construction of "national mainlands" see Rogers Brubaker, *Nationalism Reframed: Nationhood and the National Question in the New Europe*, Cambridge: Cambridge University Press, 1996.

26   This explanation was advanced by Dmitry Furman, *Chechnia i Rossiia: obschestva i gosudarstva* [Chechnya and Russia: Societies and States], Moscow: Polinform-Talburi, 1999.

27   In various forms, organized crime was an important social reality in the Caucasus throughout the Soviet period and its role vastly increased in the last years of communist rule. There is, however, virtually no relevant research on the topic. Regarding post-communist Russia, see the excellent recent work of Federico Varese, *The Russian Mafia. Private Protection in a New Market Economy*, Oxford: Oxford University Press, 2001; and Vadim Volkov, *Violent Entrepreneurs: The Use of Force in the Making of Russian Capitalism*, Ithaca, NY: Cornell University Press, 2002.

28   Arguably many of the rallies, boycotts, hunger strikes, riots, and pogroms had some shadowy sponsors, but their backstage manipulation is overrated by pervasive local conspiracy theories. Errors of communication, estimation, and execution seem no less common in the secretive arena of the Mafia than in the post-Soviet nationalist rebellions. See Diego Gambetta, *The Sicilian Mafia*, Cambridge: Harvard University Press. 1995.

29   Yakov Gordin, *Kavkaz: zemlya i krov'* [The Caucasus: Land and Blood], St. Petersburg: "Zvezda," 2000, p. 121. Also see the young Leo Tolstoy's stories "Cutting Wood," "The Raid," and "Prisoner of the Caucasus" reproduced in many of his collections (such as *How Much Land Does a Man Need, and Other Stories*, London: Penguin Classics, 1993) and the short novel *Haji Murat* that reflects Tolstoy's transition from the Russian patriotism of the early years when he had served as a volunteer artillery officer in the Caucasus to the pacifism of his later life.

30   Anatol Lieven, *Chechnya: The Tombstone of Russian Power*, New Haven: Yale University Press, 1998, pp. 322–323.

31   Guzhin, G.S. and N.V. Chugunova, *Selskaia mestnost Checheno-Ingushetii i yeyo problemy* [The Countryside of Checheno-Ingushetia and its Problems], Grozny: Checheno-ingushskoe knizhnoe izdatelstvo, 1988.

32 There are plenty of heroic but overall quite credible stories about a meager handful of Chechens brazenly intimidating or even attacking headlong much larger Russian gangs. The pre-rational calculation of these stories is to induce the impression that the Chechens involved are absolutely fearless, madly violent or perhaps supported by an entire clan of unknown size. This typical Caucasian bravado and bluff actually can work, especially in poorly-defined, chance confrontations. At the same time, the Chechen gangsters are often described as very loyal to their allies and clients, which they proclaim the "law of the mountains." But a reputation for reliability, of course, can be as advantageous in the world of the mafia as it is in banking.

33 Zelimkhan Yandarbiyev, *V preddverii nezavisimosti* [On the Eve of Independence], Grozny: "Ichkeria," 1994, pp. 41–51.

34 Ernest Gellner, *Nations and Nationalism*, Oxford: Blackwell, 1983.

35 Dudayev's former advisor describes how he rushed to prevent the general from declaring the nationalization of Chechnya's oil industry and explained that, in the spirit of the times, they must rather privatize the oil industry and attract Western investors to Chechnya. See Taimaz Abubakarov, *Rezhim Dzhokhara Dudaeva: pravda i vymysel: zapiski dudaevskogo ministra ekonomiki i finansov*, [The Regime of Djohar Dudayev: Truth and Fiction: The Notes of Dudayev's Minister of Economy and Finance], Moscow: INSAN, 1998.

36 Timur Muzaev and Zurab Todua, *Novaia Checheno-Ingushetiia* [The New Checheno-Ingushetia], Moscow: "Panorama," 1992.

37 A detailed, sober, and sophisticated scholarly analysis of the conflicting territorial claims and the associated political imagery is provided by Artur Tsutsiyev, *Osetino-ingushskii konflikt (1992 – …?) ego predystoria i factory razvitiya* [The Ossetin-Ingush conflict, 1992 – …? antecedents and developmental factors], Moscow: ROSSPEN, 1998.

38 Cristopher Panico, *Conflicts in the Caucasus: Russia's War in Chechnya*, Conflict Studies 281, Washington: Research Institute for the Study of Conflict and Terrorism, 1995, p. 7.

39 Carlotta Gall and Thomas de Waal, *Chechnya: Calamity in the Caucasus*. New York: NYU Press, 1998.

40 This controversial issue is soberly analyzed by the Russian activists of the human rights society "Memorial," Oleg Orlov and Alexander Cherkasov, *Rossia – Chechnya: tsep' oshibok i prestuplenii* [Russia – Chechnya: The Chain of Blunders and Crimes], Moscow: Zvenia, 1998; also see Dmitry Furman (ed.), *Chechnia i Rossiia: obschestva i gosudarstva* [Chechnya and Russia: Societies and States],

Moscow: Polinform-Talburi, 1999.

41 Arthur Stinchcombe, "Ending Revolutions and Building New Governments," *Annual Review of Political Science* 2 (1999), p. 49.

42 Anna Politkovskaya, *A Small Corner of Hell: Reports from Chechnya*, Chicago: University of Chicago Press, 2003.

43 Arthur Stinchcombe, "Ending Revolutions and Building New Governments," *Annual Review of Political Science* 2 (1999), p. 70.

44 Will Reno, *Warlord Politics and African States*, Boulder: Lynne Rienner, 1998.

45 For a meticulous and clear-headed summary, see Matthew Evangelista, *The Chechen Wars*, Washington DC: The Brookings Institution, 2002.

46 The general census conducted in Russia in Fall 2002 gave a totally improbable number of over one million people living in Chechnya. The number was so patently fantastic that the authorities in Moscow had to open an investigation (its results are yet not published). Two hypotheses were circulated at the time: the pro-Russian Chechen authorities thoughtlessly inflated the number in order to get more social payments from Moscow, which is the main source of embezzlement, or to saturate the electoral registers with "dead souls" for purposes of electoral fraud.

47 For more details, see Georgi Derluguian, "Che Guevaras in Turbans," *New Left Review* I/237 (September–October 1999), pp. 3–27.

48 Alexei Malashenko, *Islamskie orientiry Severnogo Kavkaza* [The Islamic Coordinates of the North Caucasus], Moscow: Fond Carnegie, 1999.

49 Fieldwork in Chechnya is practically impossible these days: dozens of people continue to disappear each month. I rely on conversations with refugees and people who have recently visited Chechnya in various capacities. In English, see the book by the Russian investigative journalist Anna Politkovskaya, *A Small Corner of Hell: Reports from Chechnya*, Chicago: University of Chicago Press, 2003.

50 See the overview in Anna Matveeva and Duncan Hiscock (eds), *The Caucasus: Armed and Divided. (Small arms and light weapons proliferation and humanitarian consequences in the Caucasus)*, London: Safeworld Report, April 2003.

51 Louis Snyder, *Macro-Nationalisms: A History of the Pan-Movements*, Westport: Greenwood Press, 1984.

52 Yusup Soslambekov was a young sub-proletarian who had not had a university education and had spent several years in prison. He was, however, a capable autodidact and, by all accounts, a very impressive speaker, especially at the rallies. In Chechnya, Soslambekov was considered a serious rival to General Dudayev, which eventually led to their quarreling. Before the first Chechen

war, Soslambekov left for self-imposed exile in Moscow, where he was mysteriously assassinated in 2001.

53 Incidentally, on the Georgian side a small contingent of Ukrainian nationalists also fought, seeing this as their own opportunity to fight "Russian imperialism."

54 Probably the best account of early Islam is provided by Oleg G. Bolshakov, *Istoria khalifata* [A History of the Caliphate], Vol. 1,. Moscow: Nauka, 2000.

55 Interview with Ardzinba, *Nezavisimaya gazeta*, N 212, 1993.

56 Gil Eyal, Iván Szelényi, and Eleanor Townsley, *Making Capitalism without Capitalists*, London: Verso, 1998.

57 Vladimir Popov, "Shock Therapy Versus Gradualism: The End of the Debate," *Comparative Economic Studies*, vol. 42, no. 1 (2000) pp. 1–57.

58 In 2001 it was disbanded by Putin in a move apparently designed to replace the decentralized paternalistic authoritarianism with a centralized one.

59 This discussion follows the groundbreaking analyses of David Woodruff, *Money Unmade: Barter and the Fate of Russian Capitalism*, Ithaca, NY: Cornell University Press, 1999; and Lawrence P. King, "Making Markets: A Comparative Study of Postcommunist Managerial Strategies in Central Europe," *Theory and Society* 30 (2001).

60 Valerie Bunce, "The Political Economy of Postsocialism," *Slavic Review* 58: 4 (Winter 1999).

61 Vadim Volkov, *Violent Entrepreneurs: The Use of Force in the Making of Russian Capitalism*, Ithaca: Cornell University Press, 2002.

62 For a detailed discussion of post-Soviet enterprise dependency, see Stephen Crowley, *Hot Coal, Cold Steel: Russian and Ukrainian Workers from the End of the Soviet Union to Postcommunist Transformation*, Ann Arbor: University of Michigan Press, 1997; and A.M. Nikulin, "Kubanskiy kolkhoz – v holding ili as'endu?" ["The Kolkhoz of the Kuban region: into a Holding or a Hacienda?"], *Sotsiologicheskie issledovania*, no. 1 (213), January 2002, pp. 41–52.

63 On the factory as the key site of the Soviet civilizing process, see Stephen Kotkin, *Magnetic Mountain: Stalinism as a Civilization*, Berkeley: University of California Press, 1995.

64 Rostislav Kapelyushnikov, "Nenuzhnyi spasatelnyi krug" [The Redundant Safety Net], *Ekspert* N 22 (June 16) 2003, pp. 64–66.

65 Dmitry Furman generously shared his data. For the published version, see Dmitry Furman and Kimmo Kaariainen, *Starye tserkvi, novye veruyuschie: religia v massovom soznanii postsovetskoi Rossii*. [Old Churches, New Believers. Religion in the Mass consciousness of Post-Soviet Russia], Moscow: Letniy sad, 2000.

Also see the data regularly published in *Monitoring obschestvennogo mneniya* [The Public Opinion Monitor], Moscow: WCIOM.

66 Michael Burawoy, *The Great Involution: Russia's Response to the Market*, unpublished paper, 1999.

67 See Jeff Goodwin, *No Other Way Out: States And Revolutionary Movements, 1945–1991*, Cambridge: Cambridge University Press, 2001, Chapter 9.

68 Will Reno, *Warlord Politics*, 1998.

THEORETICAL REPRISE

1   See Giovanni Arrighi, *The Long Twentieth Century: Money, Power, and the Origins of Our Times*, London: Verso, 1994; Michael Mann, *The Sources of Social Power. Vol. 2: The Rise of Classes and Nation-States, 1760–1914*, Cambridge: Cambridge University Press, 1993; and also Mann's update "Globalization and September 11," *New Left Review* II/12, (November–December 2001).

2   Prominent authors from across the political spectrum – such as Samuel Huntington in his *Clash of Civilizations* (New York: Norton, 1995); Joseph Stiglitz in the "Foreword" to the new edition of Karl Polanyi's classic *The Great Transformation* (Boston: Beacon Press, 2001); or David Harvey in *New Imperialism* (Oxford: Oxford University Press, 2003) – make direct cautionary references to the fall of Pax Britannica when they approach the contemporary dilemmas of Pax Americana. The similarities indeed look evocative and, possibly, might prove informative. Yet we must resist the temptation of tearing the writings of Polanyi or Lenin into darkly foreboding quotations. A serious comparative analysis of the two periods of globalization must account in a theoretically structured fashion both for the cyclical repetition and the no less significant variation, as Beverly Silver and Giovanni Arrighi forcefully argue in "Polanyi's 'Double Movement': The *Belle Époques* of British and U.S. Hegemony Compared," *Politics and Society*, vol. 31, no. 2, June 2003.

3   A magisterial global summary is Eric Hobsbawm, *The Age of Extremes: A History of the World, 1914–1991*, New York: Vintage, 1994. The policies and institutions of world capitalist recovery under US hegemony are analyzed by Giovanni Arrighi, *The Long Twentieth Century*, London: Verso, 1994 and Beverly Silver, *Forces of Labor: Worker's Movements and Globalization since 1870*, Cambridge: Cambridge University Press, 2003.

4   Geoffrey Barraclough, *An Introduction to Contemporary History*, London: Pelican Books, 1967, pp. 153–154.

5   Immanuel Wallerstein, "The French Revolution as a World-Historical Event," in his *Unthinking Social Science*, Cambridge: Polity Press, 1991.

6   The best historical overview to date remains L.S. Stavrianos, *The Global Rift: The Third World Comes of Age*, New York: William Morrow, 1981.

7   A sociologically sophisticated analysis of Moscow's embrace of Third World developmentalism can be found in Ted Hopf, *Social Construction of International Politics: Identities and Foreign Policies, Moscow, 1955 and 1999*, Ithaca: Cornell University Press, 2002.

8   Eric Hobsbawm, *The Age of Extremes*, New York: Vintage Books, p. 288.

9   Recent and very innovative expositions of the origins of the Soviet state in the structural crisis of the tsarist regime and the ensuing civil war are found in: Andrea Graziosi, *A New, Peculiar State: Exploration in Soviet history, 1917–1937*, Westport, CT: Praeger, 2000; and Peter Holquist, *Making War, Forging Revolution: Russia's Continuum of Crisis, 1914–1921*, Cambridge, MA: Harvard University Press, 2002.

10 Immanuel Wallerstein, "Social Science and the Communist Interlude," in *The Essential Wallerstein*, New York: New Press, 2000.

11 A good example of cruder Bolshevik cadres recruited *en masse* during the civil war might be Nikita Khrushchev himself. See the recent biography of this wonderfully contradictory personality by William Taubman, *Khrushchev: The Man and His Era*, New York: W.W. Norton, 2003.

12 Bruce Cumings, "Webs with No Spiders, Spiders with No Webs: The Genealogy of the Developmental State," in Meredith Woo-Cumings (ed.), *The Developmental State*, Ithaca: Cornell University Press, 1999.

13 For a promising approach to explaining how the revolutionary state found itself re-ordering the most basic structures of social reproduction, rituals and perceptions, see Oleg Kharkhordin, *The Collective and the Individual in Russia: A Study of Practices*, Berkeley: University of California Press, 1999.

14 Charles Tilly, "Democracy Is a Lake," *Roads from Past to Future*, Lanham, MD: Rowman & Littlefield, 1997, p. 199.

15 Perry Anderson, *Lineages of the Absolutist State*, London: New Left Books, 1974, p. 11, italics in the original.

16 Doug McAdam, Sidney Tarrow, and Charles Tilly in their recent analysis of Spain's transition to democracy make clear the crucial role of European inte-

gration which allowed Spain to avoid the resumption of civil war after the death of Franco; see *Dynamics of Contention* (Cambridge: Cambridge University Press, 2001). But it does not take a stretch of imagination to see how Spain could have disintegrated along ethnic-territorial lines – similarly to the USSR, Czechoslovakia, and Yugoslavia – had the European prospect proved too distant or restrictive.

17 The highly indicative irony is that this ruler was Eduard Shevardnadze – the man who had been morphing in the succession of different epochs from a rising Stalinist cadre into a police general with the reputation of being a corruption-buster, then himself an inevitably corrupt First Secretary of Soviet Georgia before becoming a leading perestroika-era reformer, and, finally, the consolidator of a neopatrimonial restoration in a Georgia devastated by post-Soviet civil wars. On a cynical note, one might observe that Shevardnadze indeed always knew the rules of the game. But let us try to imagine a different outcome: what a splendid senior social democrat Shevardnadze could have made had perestroika succeeded.

18 On East Asian "tigers" and "dragons," see Meredith Woo-Cumings (ed.), *The Developmental State*, Ithaca: Cornell University Press, 1999; and Giovanni Arrighi, Takeshi Hamashita, and Mark Selden (eds), *The Resurgence of East Asia: 500, 150 and 50 Year Perspectives*, New York: Routledge, 2003.

19 Charles Tilly made this remark regarding the legacy of Bourdieu at the annual session of the American Sociological Association in Atlanta, August 2003.

20 This realization was reinforced by the acute analysis of Carl-Ulrich Schierup, "Quasi-proletarians and a Patriarchal Bureaucracy: Aspects of Yugoslavia's Re-peripheralization," *Soviet Studies*, vol. 44, no. 1 (1992).

21 If we are ever to embark seriously on constructing a grander theory of ethnic violence, let me mention the following diverse formulations that could provide the robust starting bases: Michael Mann, *The Sources of Social Power. Vol. 2: The Rise of Classes and Nation-States, 1760–1914*, especially chapters 20 and 21 (Cambridge: Cambridge University Press, 1993); Randall Collins, "German-Bashing and the Theory of Democratic Modernization" (in *Macrohistory*, Stanford: Stanford University Press 1999); George Steinmetz, "'The Devil's Handwriting': Precolonial Discourse, Ethnographic Acuity, and Cross-Identification in German Colonialism" (*Comparative Studies in Society and History*, 45:1, 2003); and Immanuel Wallerstein, "Racism: Our Albatross" (in his *The Decline of American Power*, New York: New Press, 2003).

22 For an up-to-date summary of developments in the field, see Jeff Goodwin,

No Other Way Out: States And Revolutionary Movements, 1945–1991, Cambridge: Cambridge University Press, 2001.

23 The latest developments associated with the American war on terror may make things even worse as the promise of increased funding, especially for the study of Islamic regions, comes in a political package of the variety to which American academia once, during the war in Vietnam, developed an impressive immunity; in more recent years this immunity seems to have eroded substantially.

24 This prescient characterization of academic economics belongs, again, to Randall Collins, "The European Sociological Tradition and Twenty-First-Century World Sociology," in Janet L. Lughod (ed.), *Sociology for the Twenty-First Century*, Chicago: University of Chicago Press, 1999, p. 27.

25 Arthur Stinchcombe, "Tilly on the Past as a Sequence of Futures," in Charles Tilly, *Roads from Past to Future*, Lanham: Rowman & Littlefield, 1997, p. 392. For additional force, Stinchcombe's arguments might be combined with Giovanni Arrighi's "Braudel, Capitalism and the New Economic Sociology," *Review*, XXIV, 1 (2001).

26 William McNeill and John Robert McNeill, *The Human Web: A Bird's Eye View of World History*, New York: W.W. Norton & Company, 2003. For an appreciation of William McNeill's place in the writing of world history, see Randall Collins, "The Mega-Historians," *Sociological Theory*, vol. 3, no. 1 (Spring 1985).

27 If here I sound like I am paraphrasing Arthur Stinchcombe, then I am. I would not dare to write such an ambitious paragraph unless after re-reading Stinchcombe's caustic little essay "On Softheadedness on the Future," *Ethics* 93 (October 1982).

28 And still, regarding human mistakes and the shaping of historical patterns, one must read Charles Tilly, "Invisible Elbow," in *Roads from Past to Future*, Lanham, MD: Rowman & Littlefield, 1997.

29 Immanuel Wallerstein, *Utopistics: Historical Choices for the Twenty-first Century*, New York: The New Press, 1998, pp. 1–2.

30 For a lucid and very promising methodological discussion of how we could apply the world-system perspective in empirical research, see Philip McMichael, "Incorporating Comparison within a World-Historical Perspective," *American Sociological Review* 55: 3 (1990).

31 A lucid and forceful discussion of neoliberalism as the project of "combining greater freedom with great control and governability" in the world is found in chapter 3 of Gil Eyal, Iván Szelényi, and Eleanor Townsley, *Making Capitalism*

without Capitalists: Class Formation and Elite Struggles in Postcommunist Central Europe, London: Verso, 1998.

32   Charles Tilly, "Democracy is a Lake," in *Roads from Past to Future*, Lanham, MD: Rowman & Littlefield, 1997, pp. 210–211.

33   David Woodruff, "Rules for Followers: Institutional Theory and the New Politics of Economic Backwardness in Russia," *Politics and Society* 28:4 (December 2001).

34   See Charles Tilly, "Globalization Threatens Labor's Rights," *International Labor and Working-Class History* 47 (Spring 1995), and the responses by Immanuel Wallerstein, Eric Hobsbawm, Aristide Zolberg, and Lourdes Beneria.

35   Jeff Goodwin, *No Other Way Out: States And Revolutionary Movements, 1945–1991*, Cambridge: Cambridge University Press, 2001.

36   Arthur Stinchcombe, "The Preconditions of World Capitalism: Weber Updated," *Journal of Political Philosophy*, vol. 3, no. 4 (December 2003).

37   See the theoretical convergence on this point of Randall Collins, "The European Sociological Tradition and Twenty-First-Century World Sociology," (in Janet L. Lughod (ed.), *Sociology for the Twenty-First Century*, Chicago: University of Chicago Press 1999) and Immanuel Wallerstein, "Marxism, Marxism-Leninism, and the Socialist Experiences in World-System," in *After Liberalism*, New York: New Press, 1995.

38   James C. Scott, *Seeing Like a State: How Certain Schemes to Improve the Human Condition Have Failed*, New Haven: Yale University Press, 1998.

39   Pierre Bourdieu, "A Reasoned Utopia and Economic Fatalism," *New Left Review* I/227 (January–February 1998); and Immanuel Wallerstein, *Utopistics: Historical Choices for the Twenty-first Century*, New York: The New Press, 1998.

Bibliography

Abramkin, Valery and Valentina Chesnokova. 1998. *Tyuremnyi mir glazami politzak-lyuchennyh, 1940-e–1980-e gody* [The prison world through the eyes of political prisoners], Moscow: "Muravei."

Abubakarov, Taimaz. 1998. *Rezhim Dzhokhara Dudaeva: pravda i vymysel: zapiski dudaevskogo ministra ekonomiki i finansov* [The Regime of Djohar Dudayev: Truth and Fiction: The Notes of Dudayev's Minister of Economy and Finance], Moscow: INSAN.

Adams, Julia. 2003. "Materialists in Spite of Ourselves?" (Comments on Richard Lachmann's *Capitalists in Spite of Themselves*), *The newsletter of the Comparative and Historical Sociology Section of the American Sociological Association*, vol. 15, no. 1 (Spring 2003), http://www.cla.sc.edu/socy/faculty/deflem/comphist/chs03Spr.html.

Adams, Julia, Elizabeth Clemens, and Ann Shola Orloff (eds) 2004. *Remaking Modernity: Politics, History and Sociology*, Durham: Duke University Press.

Abrahamian, Levon, and A.A. Borodatova. 1992. "Avgust 1991: prazdnik, ne uspevshii razvernutsya" [August 1991: The Festival That Failed to Emerge], *Etnograficheskoe obozrenie*, n. 3, pp. 47–57.

Aglarov, M.A. 1988. *Selskaia obshchina v Nagornom Daghestane, XVII–nachalo XIX vv.* [Rural Community in the Mountainous Daghestan in the 17th–Early 19th Centuries], Moscow: Nauka.

Amalrik, Andrei. 1970. *Will the Soviet Union Survive Until 1984?* New York: Harper & Row.

Anderson, Perry. 2000 (c1974). *Lineages of the Absolutist State*, London: Verso.
— 1992. *A Zone of Contention*, London: Verso.
Arrighi, Giovanni. 1994. *The Long Twentieth Century: Money, Power, and the Making of Our Times*, London: Verso.
— 1999. "Globalization and Historical Macrosociology," in Janet L. Lughod (ed.), *Sociology for the Twenty-First Century*, Chicago: University of Chicago Press, pp. 117–133.
— 2001. "Braudel, Capitalism and the New Economic Sociology," *Review*, XXIV, 1, pp. 107–123.
— 2003. "The Social and Political Economy of Global Turbulence," *New Left Review* 20 (March–April), pp. 5–71.
Arrighi, Giovanni, Terence K. Hopkins, and Immanuel Wallerstein. 1989. "Rethinking the Concepts of Class and Status-Group in a World-Systems Perspective," in *Antisystemic Movements*, London: Verso, pp. 3–28.
— 2001. "1989: The Continuation of 1968," in George Katsiaficas (ed.), *After the Fall: 1989 and the Future of Freedom*, New York: Routledge, pp. 35–51. (Originally presented at the XIth International Colloquium on the World-Economy, Starnberg, Germany, June 28–39, 1991.)
Arrighi, Giovanni, and Beverly Silver et al. 1999. *Chaos and Governance in the Modern World-System*, Minneapolis: University of Minnesota Press.
Arrighi, Giovanni, Takeshi Hamashita, Mark Selden et al. 2003. *The Resurgence of East Asia: 500, 150 and 50 Year Perspectives*, New York: Routledge.
Ascherson, Neal. 1995. *Black Sea*, London: Jonathan Cape.
Atkin, Muriel. 1995. "The Islamic Revolution that Overthrew the Soviet State?" in Nikki Keddie (ed.), *Debating Revolutions*, New York: NYU Press, pp. 296–313.
Aven, Petr O. 1991. "Economic Policy and the Reform of Mikhail Gorbachev: A Short History," in Merton J. Peck and Thomas J. Richardson (eds), *What Is to be Done? Proposals for the Soviet Transition to the Market*, New Haven: Yale University Press, pp. 179–206.
Bahry, Donna. 1987. *Outside Moscow: Power, Politics, and Budgetary Policy in the Soviet Republics*, New York: Columbia University Press.
Barber, Benjamin. 1996. *Jihad vs. McWorld*, New York: Ballantine Books.
Baron, Samuel H. 2001. *Bloody Saturday in the Soviet Union: Novocherkassk, 1962*, Stanford: Stanford University Press.
Barraclough, Geoffrey. 1967. *An Introduction to Contemporary History*, London: Pelican Books.

Barsukova, S. Yu. 2002. "Solidarnost uchastnikov neformalnoi ekonomiki: na primere strategii migrantov i predprinimatelei" [Solidarity Among the Participants in Informal Economy: the Examples of Migrants and Entrepreneurs], *Sotsiologicheskie issledovaniya* N 4 (216), pp. 3–11.

Beck, Bernard, Scott L. Greer, and Charles Ragin. 2000. "Radicalism, Resistance, and Cultural Lags: A Commentary on Benjamin Barber's *Jihad vs. McWorld*," in Georgi Derluguian and Scott L. Greer (eds), *Questioning Geopolitics: Political Projects in a Changing World-System*, Westport, CT: Praeger, pp. 101–110.

Beissinger, Mark. 2002. *Nationalist Mobilization and the Collapse of the Soviet State*, New York: Cambridge University Press.

Berdahl, Daphne, Matti Bunzl, and Martha Lampland (eds). 2000. *Altering States: Ethnographies of Transition in Eastern Europe and the Former Soviet Union*, Ann Arbor: University of Michigan Press.

Berdiaev, Nikolai. 1937. *The Origin of Russian Communism*, London: G. Bles.

Bergesen, Albert. 1992. "Regime Change in the Semi-Periphery: Democratization in Latin America and the Socialist Bloc," *Sociological Perspectives* 35, pp. 405–413.

Bgazhnokov, Barasbi. 1999. *Adygskaia etika* [The Adyghe Ethics], Nalchik: El-Fa.

Bitova, Elena, Aslan Borov and Kasbolat Dzamikhov. 1996. *Sovremennaia Kabardino-Balkaria: problemy obschestvennoi dinamiki, nauki i obrazovania* [The Contemporary Kabardino-Balkaria: Problems of Social Dynamics, Science and Education], Nalchik: El-Fa.

Böröcz, József. 1992. "Dual Dependency and Property Vacuum: Social Change on the State Socialist Semiperiphery," *Theory and Society* 21, pp. 77–104.

Bourdieu, Pierre. 1973. "The Algerian Subproletariate," in I.W. Zartman (ed.), *Man, State, and Society in the Contemporary Maghreb*, London: Pall Mall, pp. 83–89.

—— 1984. *Distinction. A Social Critique of the Judgement of Taste*, Cambridge, MA: Harvard University Press.

—— 1988. *Homo Academicus*, Cambridge: Polity Press.

—— 1990. *The Logic of Practice*, Cambridge: Polity Press.

—— 1994. *Nachala* [The Russian translation of *Choses Dites*, Paris: Minuit, 1988], Moscow: SocioLogos.

—— 1996. *The State Nobility: Elite Schools and the Field of Power*, Cambridge: Polity Press.

—— 1998. "A Reasoned Utopia and Economic Fatalism," *New Left Review* I/227 (January–February), pp. 125–130.

— and Loïc J.D. Wacquant. 1992. *An Invitation to Reflexive Sociology*, Chicago: University of Chicago Press.

Braudel, Fernand. 1986. *Afterthoughts on Material Civilization and Capitalism*, Baltimore: Johns Hopkins University Press.

Brubaker, Rogers. 1996. *Nationalism Reframed: Nationhood and the National Question in the New Europe*, Cambridge: Cambridge University Press.

Bruszt, László and David Stark. 1998. *Postsocialist Pathways: Transforming Politics and Property in East Central Europe*, Cambridge: Cambridge University Press.

Bunce, Valerie. 1985. "The Empire Strikes Back: The Evolution of the Eastern Bloc from a Soviet Asset to a Soviet Liability," *International Organization*, 39 (Winter), pp. 1–46.

— 1993. "The Political Economy of Brezhnev Era: The Rise and Fall of Corporatism," *British Journal of Political Science*, 13 (January), pp. 129–158.

— 1998. *Subversive Institutions: The Design and the Destruction of Socialism and the State*, New York: Cambridge University Press.

— 2000. "Quand le lieu compte spécificités des passés autoritaires et réformes économiques dans les transitions à la démocratie," *Revue Française de Science Politique*, vol. 50, no. 4–5 (Août–Octobre), pp. 633–656.

Burawoy, Michael. 1985. *Politics of Production: Factory Regimes under Capitalism and Socialism*, London: Verso.

— 1999. "The Great Involution: Russia's Response to the Market," unpublished paper, at http://sociology.berkeley.edu/faculty/burawoy/

Burawoy, Michael, and János Lukács. 1992. *The Radiant Past: Ideology and Reality in Hungary's Road to Capitalism*, Chicago: University of Chicago Press.

Burawoy, Michael, and Katherine Verdery (eds). 1999. *Uncertain Transitions: Ethnographies of Change in the Postsocialist World*, Lanham MD: Rowman & Littlefield.

Burawoy, Michael, et al. 2000. *Global Ethnography: Forces, Connections, and Imaginations in a Postmodern World*, Berkeley: University of California Press.

Castells, Manuel and Emma Kiselyova. 1995. *The Collapse of Soviet Communism: A View from the Information Society*, Berkeley: University of California, International and Area Studies.

Collins, Randall. 1983. "Upheavals in Biological Theory Undermine Sociobiology," *Sociological Theory*, vol. 1, pp. 306–318.

— 1985. "The Mega-Historians," *Sociological Theory*, vol. 3, no. 1 (Spring), pp. 114–122.

— 1998. *The Sociology of Philosophies: A Global Theory of Intellectual Change*, Cambridge, MA: Belknap Press of Harvard University Press.

— 1999. *Macrohistory: Essays in Sociology of the Long Run*, Stanford, CA: Stanford University Press.

— 1999. "The European Sociological Tradition and Twenty-First-Century World Sociology," in Janet L. Lughod (ed.), *Sociology for the Twenty-First Century*, Chicago: University of Chicago Press, pp. 26–42.

Collins, Randall, and David Waller. 2000. "Predictions of Geopolitical Theory and the Modern World-System," in Georgi Derluguian and Scott L. Greer (eds) *Questioning Geopolitics: Political Projects in a Changing World-System*, Westport, CT: Praeger, pp. 51–66.

Cornia, Giovanni Andrea and Vladimir Popov. 2002. *Transitions and Institutions: the Experience of Gradual and Late Reformers*, Helsinki: World Institute for Development Economic Research (UNU/WIDER).

Crowley, Stephen. 1997. *Hot Coal, Cold Steel: Russian and Ukrainian Workers from the End of the Soviet Union to Postcommunist Transformation*, Ann Arbor: University of Michigan Press.

Cumings, Bruce. 1999. "Webs with No Spiders, Spiders with No Webs: The Genealogy of the Developmental State," in Meredith Woo-Cumings (ed.), *The Developmental State*, Ithaca: Cornell University Press, pp. 61–92.

— 2000. "Mr. X or Doctrine X? A Modest Proposal for Thinking About the New Geopolitics," in Georgi Derluguian and Scott L. Greer (eds), *Questioning Geopolitics: Political Projects in a Changing World-System*, Westport, CT: Praeger, pp. 85–100.

Derluguian, Georgi. 1999. "Che Guevaras in Turbans," *New Left Review* I/237 (September–October), pp. 3–27.

— 2000. "The Neo-Cossacks: Militant Provincials in the Geoculture of Clashing Civilizations," in John Guidry, Michael D. Kennedy, and Mayer N. Zald (eds), *Globalizations and Social Movements*, Ann Arbor: University of Michigan Press, pp. 288–314.

— 2001. "The Capitalist World-System and Socialism," in Alexander J. Motyl (ed.), *Encyclopedia of Nationalism. Vol. 1. Fundamental Issues*, New York: Academic Press, pp. 55–80.

— 2001. "Why Adjaria Is Not Like Bosnia: Historical Determinants, Human Agency, and Contingency in the Chaotic Transition," in George Katsiaficas (ed.), *After the Fall: 1989 and the Future of Freedom*, New York: Routledge, pp. 103–124.

Deutscher, Isaac. 1953. *Russia: What Next?* Oxford: Oxford University Press.

De Waal. Thomas. 2003. *Black Garden: Armenia and Azerbaijan Through Peace and War*, New York: NYU Press.

Duskin, J. Eric. 2001. *Stalinist Reconstruction and the Confirmation of New Elite, 1945–1953*, New York: Palgrave.

Dzuyev, G.K. 1997. *Krovavoe leto 1928-go* [The Bloody Summer of 1928], Nalchik: Elbrus.

Eisenstadt, S.N. 1973. *Traditional Patrimonialism and Modern Neopatrimonialism*, London: Sage.

— 1999. *Fundamentalism, Sectarianism, and Revolution: The Jacobin Dimension of Modernity*, Cambridge: Cambridge University Press.

Elias, Norbert. 1978. *The Civilizing Process*, Oxford: Oxford University Press.

Ekiert, Grzegorz. 1996. *The State Against Society: Political Crises and Their Aftermath in East-Central Europe*, Princeton: Princeton University Press.

Emirbayer, Mustafa, and Jeff Goodwin. 1996. "Symbols, Positions, Objects: Towards a New Theory of Revolutions and Collective Action," *History and Theory* 38, pp. 358–374.

Evangelista, Matthew. 2002. *The Chechen Wars: Will Russia Go the Way of the Soviet Union?* Washington DC: The Brookings Institution.

Evans, Peter. 1995. *Embedded Autonomy: States & Industrial Transformation*, Princeton, NJ: Princeton University Press.

Evtuhov, Catherine, and Stephen Kotkin (eds). 2003. *The Cultural Gradient: The Transmission of Ideas in Europe, 1789–1991*, Lanham, Maryland: Rowman & Littlefield.

Eyal, Gil, Iván Szelényi, and Eleanor Townsley. 1998. *Making Capitalism without Capitalists: Class Formation and Elite Struggles in Postcommunist Central Europe*, London: Verso.

Filtzer, Donald. 1992. *Soviet Workers and De-Stalinization: The Consolidation of the Modern System of Soviet Production Relations, 1953–1964*, Cambridge: Cambridge University Press.

Fisun, Oleksandr. 2002. "Politiko-rezhimnaia transformatsia Ukrainy: dilemmy neopatrimonialnogo razvitia" [The Political-Regime Transformation in Ukraine: Dilemmas of Neopatrimonial Development], *Stylos* (Kyïv), pp. 4–14.

Fitzpatrick, Sheila. 1982. *The Russian Revolution, 1917–1932*, Oxford: Oxford University Press.

Foran, John. 1995. "Revolutionizing Theory/Theorizing Revolutions: State, Culture, and Society in Recent Works on Revolution," in Nikki R. Keddie (ed.), *Debating Revolutions*, New York: New York University Press, pp. 112–135.

Friedrich, Paul. 2003. "Tolstoy and the Chechens: Problems in literary Anthropology," *Russian History/Histoire Russe*, 30, nos. 1–2, pp. 113–43.

Furman, Dmitry E. (ed.). 1999. *Chechnia i Rossiia: obschestva i gosudarstva* [Chechnya and Russia: Societies and States], Moscow: Polinform-Talburi.

— 2001. *Azerbaidzhan i Rossiia: obschestva i gosudarstva* [Azerbaijan and Russia: Societies and States], Moscow: Letnii sad.

Gakayev, Djabrail. 1997. *Ocherki politicheskoi istorii Chechni* [Sketches of the Political History of Chechnya], Moscow: Izdatelstvo ChKTs.

Gall, Carlotta, and Thomas de Waal. 1998. *Chechnya: Calamity in the Caucasus*, New York: NYU Press.

Galtz, Naomi Roslyn. 2003. "The Strength of Small Freedoms: A Response to Ionin, by way of Stories Told at the Dacha," in Daniel Bertaux, Anna Rotkrich, Paul Thompson (eds), *Living Through Soviet Russia*, New York: Routledge, pp. 176–194.

Gambetta, Diego. 1993. *The Sicilian Mafia: The Business of Private Protection*, Cambridge, MA: Harvard University Press.

Gammer, Moshe. 1994. *Muslim Resistance to the Tsar: Shamil and the Conquest of Chechnia and Daghestan*, London: F. Cass.

Garcelon, Marc. 1997. "The Estate Change: The Specialist Rebellion and the Democratic Movement in Moscow, 1989–1991," *Theory and Society* 26, pp. 39–85.

Gerber, Theodore P., and Michael Hout. 1998. "More Shock Than Therapy: market Transition, Employment, and Income in Russia, 1991–1995," *American Journal of Sociology*, vol. 104, no. 1 (July), pp. 1–50.

Glenny, Misha. 1999. *The Balkans, 1804–1999: Nationalism, War, and the Great Powers*, London: Granta.

Goldfrank, Walter, and Georgi Derluguian. 2000. "Repetition, Variation, and Transmutation as Scenarios for the Twenty-First Century," in Georgi Derluguian and Scott L. Greer (eds), *Questioning Geopolitics: Political Projects in a Changing World-System*. Westport, CT: Praeger, pp. 1–12.

Goldstone, Jack. 1991. *Revolution and Rebellion in the Early Modern World*, Berkeley: University of California Press.

Goltz, Thomas. 1998. *Azerbaijan Diary: A Rogue Reporter's Adventures in an Oil-rich, War-torn, Post-Soviet Republic*, Armonk, NY: M.E. Sharpe.

— 2003. *Chechnya Diary: A War Correspondent's Story*, New York: St.Martin's Press.

Goodwin, Jeff. 2001. *No Other Way Out: States And Revolutionary Movements, 1945–1991*, Cambridge: Cambridge University Press.

Goodwin, Jeff, James M. Jasper, and Francesca Polletta (eds). 2001. *Passionate Politics: Emotions and Social Movements*, Chicago: University of Chicago Press.

Gould, Roger V. 1995. *Insurgent Identities: Class, Community, and Protest in Paris from 1848 to the Commune*, Chicago: University of Chicago Press.

— 1996. "Patron-Client Ties, State Centralization, and the Whiskey Rebellion," *American Journal of Sociology*, vol. 102, no. 2, pp. 400–429.

Gould, Stephen Jay. 1981. *The Mismeasure of Man*, New York: Norton.

— 1996. *Full House: The Spread of Excellence from Plato to Darwin*, New York: Three Rivers Press.

Graziosi, Andrea. 2000. *A New, Peculiar State: Explorations in Soviet History, 1917–1937*, Westport, CT: Praeger.

Grushin, Boris A. 2001. *Chetyre zhizni Rossii v zerkale oprosov obshchestvennogo mnenia: Zhizn 1-a Epokha Khrushcheva* [The Four Lives of Russia in the Mirror of Public Opinion Polls: The First Life, the Epoch of Khrushchev], Moscow: Traditsia.

Guzhin, G.S. and N.V. Chugunova. 1988. *Selskaia mestnost Checheno-Ingushetii i yeyo problemy* [The Countryside of Checheno-Ingushetia and its Problems], Grozny: Checheno-ingushskoe knizhnoe izdatelstvo.

Hanson, Stephen. 1997. *Time and Revolution: Marxism and the Design of Soviet Institutions*, Chapel Hill: University of North Carolina Press.

Hirschman, Albert. 1970. *Exit, Voice, and Loyalty: Responses to Decline in Firms, Organizations, and States*, Cambridge, MA: Harvard University Press.

— 1991. *The Rhetoric of Reaction: Perversity, Futility, Jeopardy*, Cambridge, MA: Belknap Press.

Hislope, Robert. 2002. "Organized Crime in a Disorganized State," in *Problems of Post-Communism*. (May–June) vol. 49, issue 3.

Hobsbawm, Eric. 1994. *The Age of Extremes: A History of the World, 1914–1991*, New York: Vintage.

Hobsbawm, Eric, and Terence Ranger (eds). 1983. *The Invention of Tradition*, Cambridge: Cambridge University Press.

Hoffman, David E. 2002. *The Oligarchs: Wealth and Power in the New Russia.* New York: Public Affairs.

Holmes, Leslie. 1993. *The End of Communist Power: Anti-Corruption Campaigns and Legitimation Crisis*, Oxford: Oxford University Press.

Holquist, Peter. 2002. *Making War, Forging Revolution: Russia's Continuum Crisis 1914–1921*, Cambidge, MA: Harvard University Press.

Hopf, Ted. 2002. *Social Construction of International Politics: Identities & Foreign Policies, Moscow, 1955 and 1999*, Ithaca: Cornell University Press.

— Forthcoming. "Identities, Institutions, and Interests in Moscow's Foreign Policy, 1945–2000," *Cambridge History of Modern Russia*, Vol. 3, Cambridge:

Cambridge University Press.

Hopkins, Terence, Immanuel Wallerstein, et al. 1996. *The Age of Transition: Trajectories of the World-System, 1945–2025*, London: Zed.

Hroch, Miroslav. 1985. *Social Preconditions of National Revival in Europe*, Cambridge: Cambridge University Press.

Humphrey, Caroline. 1991. "'Icebergs', Barter, and the Mafia in Provincial Russia," *Anthropology Today*, vol. 7, no. 2 (April).

Huntington, Samuel. 1968. *Political Order in Changing Societies*, New Haven: Yale University Press.

— 1995. *The Clash of Civilizations*, New York: Norton.

Iandarbiev, Zelimkha (i.e. Zelimkhan Yandarbiyev). 1996. *Chechenia: bitva za svobodu* [Chechenia: The Battle for Freedom], Lvov: "Svoboda narodiv."

Ishkhanian, L. 1918. *Sotsialno-istoricheskie korni gruzino-armyanskoi draki* [The Socio-historical Roots of Georgian-Armenian Quarrel], Tiflis: n/p.

Iskander, Fazil. 1983. *Sandro of Chegem*, New York: Vintage Books.

Jaimoukha, Amjad. 2001. *The Circassians: A Handbook*, New York: Palgrave.

Jessop, Bob. 2002. *The Future of the Capitalist State*, Cambridge: Polity Press.

Johnson, Chalmers. 1999. "The Developmental State: Odyssey of a Concept," in Meredith Woo-Cumings (ed.), *The Developmental State*, Ithaca: Cornell University Press, pp. 32–60.

Jowitt, Ken. 1992. *New World Disorder: The Leninist Extinction*, Berkeley: University of California Press.

Judge, Edward H. 1992. *Easter in Kishinev: Anatomy of a Pogrom*, New York: New York University Press.

Juraité, Kristina. 2002. *Environmental Consciousness and Mass Communication*, Doctoral thesis, Kaunas: Vytautas Magnus University.

Kazemzadeh, Firuz. 1951. *The Struggle for Transcaucasia, 1917–1921*, New York: Philosophical Library.

Kennedy, Michael D. 1991. *Professionals, Power, and Solidarity in Poland: A Critical Sociology of Soviet-type Society*, Cambridge: Cambridge University Press.

Kharkhordin, Oleg. 1999. *The Collective and the Individual in Russia: A Study of Practices*, Berkeley: University of California Press.

Khodarkovsky, Michael. 2002. *Russia's Steppe Frontier: The Making of a Colonial Empire, 1500–1800*, Bloomington: Indiana University Press.

King, Lawrence P. 2001. "Making Markets: A Comparative Study of Postcommunist Managerial Strategies in Central Europe," *Theory and Society* 30, pp. 493–538.

Knight, Amy. 1993. *Beria, Stalin's First Lieutenant*, Princeton: Princeton University Press.

Konrád, George, and Iván Szelényi. 1979. *The Intellectuals on the Road to Class Power*, New York: Harcourt Brace Jovanovich.

Kornai, János. 1982. *The Economy of Shortage*, 2 vols, Amsterdam: De Gruyter.

Kosikov I.G. and L.S. Kosikova. 1999. *Severnyi Kavkaz: sotsialno-ekonomicheskii spravochnik* [The Northern Caucasus: A Socio-economic Handbook], Moscow: Exclusive-Press.

Kotkin, Stephen. 1995. *Magnetic Mountain: Stalinism as a Civilization*, Berkeley: University of California Press.

Kotkin, Stephen. 2001. *Armageddon Averted: The Soviet Collapse, 1970–2000*, Oxford: Oxford University Press.

Kozlov, Vladimir A. 2002. *Mass Uprisings in the USSR: Protest and rebellion in the Post-Stalin Years*, translated and edited by Elaine McClarnand MacKinnon, Armonk, NY: M.E. Sharpe.

Kryshtanovskaya, O.V. 2002. "Transformatsia biznes-elity Rossii: 1998–2002" [The Transformation of Russia's Business Elite, 1998–2002], *Sotsiologicheskie issledovania*, N 8 (218), pp. 17–29.

Kryshtanovskaya, O.V., and Yu.V. Khutoryansky. 2002. "Elita i vozrast: put naverh" [Elite and Age: the Road Upward], *Sotsiologicheskie issledovania*, N 4 (214), pp. 49–60.

Kulavig, Erik. 2002. *Dissent in the Years of Khrushchev: Nine Stories about Disobedient Russians*, Basingstoke: Palgrave.

Kurtynova-Derluguian, Liubov. 1995. *Tsar's Abolitionists. The Russian Suppression of Slave Trade in the Caucasus, 1801–1864*, Ph.D. dissertation, Binghamton University, Department of History.

Lachmann Richard. 2000. *Capitalists in Spite of Themselves: Elite Conflict and Economic Transitions in Early Modern Europe*, New York: Oxford University Press.

Lane, David. 1982. *The End of Social Inequality? Class, Status and Power under State Socialism*, London: George Allen & Unwin.

Lamont, Michèle, 1987. "How to Become a Dominant French Philosopher: The Case of Jacques Derrida," *American Journal of Sociology* 93 (3): 584–622.

Lamont, Michèle, and Annette Lareau. 1988. "Social Capital: Allusions, Gaps and Glissandos in Recent Theoretical Developments," *Sociological Theory*, vol. 6 (Fall), pp. 153–168.

Lampland, Martha. 2002. *Developing a Rational Economy: The Transition to Stalinism in Hungary*, paper presented at the annual meeting of ASA in Chicago.

Lapidus, Gail Warshofsky. 1978. *Women in Soviet Society: Equality, Development, and Social Change*, Berkeley: University of California Press.

Latham, Robert. 1997. *The Liberal Moment: Modernity, Security, and the Making of Postwar International Order*, New York: Columbia University Press.

Layton, Susan. 1994. *Russian Literature and Empire: Conquest of the Caucasus from Pushkin to Tolstoy*, New York: Cambridge University Press.

Ledeneva, Alena. 1998. *Russia's Economy of Favors: Blat, Networking, and Informal Exchange*, Cambridge: Cambridge University Press.

Lel'chuk, V.S. 1997. "1959: Rasstrel v Temirtau" [The Shooting in Temirtau], in Yuri Afanasiev (ed.), *Sovetskoe obschestvo,* Tom 2, Moscow: RGGU.

Lewin, Moshe. 1988. *The Gorbachev Phenomenon: A Historical Interpretation*, Berkeley: University of California Press.

— 1991. *Stalinism and the Seeds of Soviet Reform: The Debates of the 1960s*, London: Pluto Press.

Lezhava, Grigory P. 1997. *Mezhdu Gruziei i Rossiei: istoricheskie korni i sovremennye faktory abkhazo-gruzinskogo konflikta* [Between Georgia and Russia: the Historical Roots and Contemporary Factors of Abkhaz–Georgian Conflict], Moscow: Institut etnologii i antropologii RAN.

Lieberson, Stanley, and Freda B. Lynn. 2002. "Barking Up the Wrong Branch: Scientific Alternatives to the Current Model of Sociological Science," *Annual Review of Sociology* 28, pp. 1–19.

Lieven, Anatol. 1994. *The Baltic Revolution: Estonia, Latvia, Lithuania and the Path to Independence*, New Haven: Yale University Press.

— 1998. *Chechnya: The Tombstone of Russian Power*, New Haven, CT: Yale University Press.

Ligachev, Yegor K. 1992. *Zagadka Gorbacheva* [The Mystery of Gorbachev], Novosibirsk: Interbook.

Linz, Juan J. and Alfred Stepan. 1996. *Problems of Democratic Transition and Consolidation: Southern Europe, South America, and Post-Communist Europe*, Baltimore: Johns Hopkins University Press.

Lipietz, Alan. 1987. *Mirages and Miracles: The Crises of Global Fordism*, London: Verso.

Lisitsian, Stepan. 1990. *Armyane Nagornogo Karabaha* [The Armenians of Mountainous Karabagh], Yerevan.

Lubin, Nancy. 1984. *Labor and Nationality in Soviet Central Asia: An Uneasy Compromise*, Princeton: Princeton University Press.

Lukin, Alexandr. 2000. *The Political Culture of Russian "Democrats,"* Oxford: Oxford University Press.

Mann, Michael. 1986. *The Sources of Social Power. Vol. 1: A History of Power from the Beginning to A.D. 1760*, Cambridge: Cambridge University Press.
— 1993. *The Sources of Social Power. Vol. 2: The Rise of Classes and Nation-States, 1760–1914*, Cambridge: Cambridge University Press.
— 2001. "Globalization and September 11," *New Left Review* II/12 (November–December), pp. 51–72.

Markoff, John. 1996. *The Abolition of Feudalism: Peasants, Lords, and Legislators in the French Revolution*, Pennsylvania State University Press.

Mars, Gerald and Yochanan Altman. 1983. "The Cultural Bases of Soviet Georgia's Second Economy," *Soviet Studies* XXXV, no. 4 (October), pp. 546–60.

Martin, Terry. 2001. *The Affirmative Action Empire. Nations and Nationalism in the Soviet Union*, Ithaca, NY: Cornell University Press.

Matveeva, Anna and Duncan Hiscock (eds). 2003. *The Caucasus: Armed and Divided. (Small arms and light weapons proliferation and humanitarian consequences in the Caucasus)*, London: Safeworld Report.

McAdam, Doug, Sidney Tarrow, and Charles Tilly. 2001. *Dynamics of Contention*, Cambridge: Cambridge University Press.

McMichael, Philip. 1990. "Incorporating Comparison within a World-Historical Perspective," *American Sociological Review* 55 (3), pp. 385–397.

McNeill, William H., and John Robert McNeill. 2003. *The Human Web: A Bird's eye View of World History*, New York: W.W. Norton & Company.

Medard, Jean-François. 1982. "The Underdeveloped State in Tropical Africa: Political Clientelism or Neopatrimonialism," in Christopher Clapham (ed.), *Private Patronage and Public Power*, New York: St. Martin's Press, pp. 162–192.

Migdal, Joel S. 1988. *Strong Societies and Weak States: State-Society Relations and State Capabilities in the Third World*, Princeton: Princeton University Press.

Moore, Barrington Jr. 1965 (c1950). *Soviet Politics – The Dilemma of Power*, New York: Harper & Row. 2nd ed.

Muzaev, Timur. 1999. *Chechenskii krizis-99* [The Chechen Crisis-99], Moscow: "Panorama."

Muzaev, Timur, and Zurab Todua. 1992. *Novaia Checheno-Ingushetiia* [The New Checheno-Ingushetia], Moscow: "Panorama."

Nikulin, A.M. 2002. "Kubanskiy kolkhoz – v holding ili as'endu?" [The Kolkhoz of Kuban Region: into a Holding or a Hacienda?], *Sotsiologicheskie issledovania*, N 1 (213), pp. 41–52.

Nivat, Anne. 2001. *Chienne de Guerre: A Woman Reporter Behind the Lines of the War in Chechnya,* New York: Public Affairs.

Nodia, Ghia. 2002. *Conflict and Regional Security in the Caucasus*, paper presented at the Yale Center for the Study of Globalization, 22 September.

Nove, Alec. 1977. *The Soviet Economic System*, London: Allen & Unwin.

Orlov, Oleg and Alexander Cherkasov. 1998. *Rossia – Chechnya: tsep' oshibok i prestuplenii* [Russia – Chechnya: The Chain of Blunders and Crimes], Moscow: Zvenia.

Osa, Maryjane. 2003. *Solidarity and Contention: The Networks of Polish Opposition*, Minneapolis: University of Minnesota Press.

Padgett, John F., and Christopher K. Ansell. 1993. "Robust Action and the Rise of the Medici, 1400–1434," *American Journal of Sociology*, vol. 38, no. 6 (May), pp. 1259–1319.

Panico, Christopher. 1995. *Conflicts in the Caucasus: Russia's War in Chechnya*, Conflict Studies 281, Washington: Research Institute for the Study of Conflict and Terrorism.

Pipes, Richard. 1954. *The Formation of the Soviet Union: Communism and Nationalism, 1917–1923*, Cambridge, MA: Harvard University Press.

Pokrovsky, Nikolai Ilich. 2000. *Kavkazskaia voina i Imamat Shamilya* [The Caucasus War and Shamil's Imamate], Moscow: POSSPEN.

Polanyi, Karl. 2001 (c1944). *The Great Transformation*, Boston: Beacon Press, 2nd ed.

Politkovskaya, Anna. 2003. *A Small Corner of Hell: Reports from Chechnya*, with an Introduction by Georgi Derluguian, Chicago: University of Chicago Press.

Portes, Alejandro. 1998. "'Social Capital' Its Origins and Applications in Modern Sociology," *Annual Review of Sociology* 24, pp. 1–24.

Portes, Alejandro, and József Böröcz. 1988. "The Informal Sector Under Capitalism and State Socialism: a Preliminary Comparison," *Social Justice*, vol. 15, nos 3–4.

Popov, Vladimir. 2000. "Shock Therapy Versus Gradualism: The End of the Debate," *Comparative Economic Studies*, vol. 42, no. 1, pp. 1–57.

Popov, Vladimir, and Nikolai Shmelev. 1990. *The Turning Point: Revitalizing the Soviet Economy*, London: I.B. Tauris.

Prigogine, Ilya, in collaboration with Isabelle Stengers. 1997. *The End of Certainty: Time, Chaos, and the New Laws of Nature*, New York: Free Press.

Przeworski, Adam. 1991. *Democracy and the Market: Political and Economic Reforms in Eastern Europe and Latin America*, Cambridge: Cambridge University Press.

Quijano, Aníbal. 1998. *La economía popular y sus caminos en America Latina*, Lima: Mosca Azul Editores.

Radaev, Vadim and Ovsey Shkaratan. 1992. "Etacratism: Power and Property –

Evidence from the Soviet Experience," *International Sociology*, vol. 7, no. 3 (September), pp. 301–316.

Razzakov, Fedor. 1997. *Bandity vremen sotsializma, 1917–1991* [The Criminals of the Socialist Times], Moscow: EKSMO.

Reno, William. 1998. *Warlord Politics and African States*, Boulder, Colo.: Lynne Rienner Publishers.

Riazantsev, S.V. 2002. "Demograficheskaya situatsia na Severnom Kavkaze" [The Demographic Situation in the North Caucasus], *Sotsiologicheskie issledovania*, N 1 (213), pp. 77–87.

Rigby, T.H. 1990. *Political Elites in the USSR: Central Leaders and Local Cadres from Lenin to Gorbachev*, Aldershot: Edward Elgar.

Roeder, Philip. 1993. *Red Sunset: The Failure of Soviet Politics*, Princeton: Princeton University Press.

Rokkan, Stein. 1999. *State Formation, Nation-Building, and Mass Politics in Europe: The Theory of Stein Rokkan Based on His Collected Works,* (edited by Peter Flora with Stein Kuhnle and Derek Urwin), Oxford: Oxford University Press.

Rosenberg, William, and Lewis H. Siegelbaum (eds). 1993. *Social Dimensions of Soviet Industrialization*, Bloomington: Indiana University Press.

Roth, Guenther. 1968. "Personal Rulership, Patrimonialism, and Empire-building in the New States," *World Politics*, vol. 20, no. 2., pp. 194–206.

Rueschemeyer, Dietrich, Evelyn H. Stephens, and John D. Stephens. 1992. *Capitalist Development and Democracy*, Chicago: University of Chicago Press.

Rutland, Peter. 1993. *The Politics of Economic Stagnation in the Soviet Union: The Role of Local Party Organs in Economic Management*, Cambridge: Cambridge University Press.

Sahlins, Marshall. 1994. "Cosmologies of Capitalism: The Trans-Pacific Sector of 'The World System'," in Nicholas B. Dirks, Geoff Eley, and Sherry B. Ortners (eds), *Culture/Power/History*, Princeton: Princeton University Press, pp. 412–455.

Schierup, Carl-Ulrich. 1992. "Quasi-proletarians and a Patriarchal Bureaucracy: Aspects of Yugoslavia's Re-peripheralization," *Soviet Studies*, vol. 44, no. 1, pp. 79–99.

Scott, James C. 1976. *The Moral Economy of the Peasant: Rebellion and Subsistence in Southeast Asia*, New Haven: Yale University Press.

— 1998. *Seeing Like a State: How Certain Schemes to Improve the Human Condition Have Failed*, New Haven: Yale University Press.

Seidman, Gay W. 2000. "Adjusting the Lens: What Do Globalizations, Trans-nationalism, and the Anti-apartheid Movement Mean for Social Movement Theory?" in John Guidry, Michael D. Kennedt, and Mayer N. Zald (eds),

Globalizations and Social Movements, Ann Arbor: University of Michigan Press, pp. 339–357.

Silver, Beverly J. 2003. *Forces of Labor: Worker's Movements and Globalization since 1870*, Cambridge: Cambridge University Press.

Silver, Beverly J., and Giovanni Arrighi. 2003. "Polanyi's 'Double Movement': The *Belle Époques* of British and U.S. Hegemony Compared," *Politics & Society*, vol. 31, no. 2 (June), pp. 325–355.

Skocpol, Theda. 1979. *States and Social Revolutions*, Cambridge: Cambridge University Press.

— 1992. *Protecting Soldiers and Mothers: The Political Origins of Social Policy in the United States*, Cambridge MA: Belknap Press.

Smith, Dorothy E. 1999. "From Women's Standpoint to a Sociology for People," in Janet L. Lughod (ed.), *Sociology for the Twenty-First Century*, Chicago: University of Chicago Press, pp. 65–82.

Smith, Stephen Samuel, and Jessica Kulynych. 2002. "It May be Social, but Why Is It Capital?" *Politics and Society*, vol. 30, no. 1, pp. 149–186.

Snyder, Louis. 1984. *Macro-Nationalisms: A History of the Pan-Movements*, Westport: Greenwood Press.

Sohrabi, Nader. 2002. "Global Waves, Local Actors: What the Young Turks Knew about Other Revolutions and Why It Mattered," *Comparative Studies in Society and History* 44 (1), pp. 45–79.

Solnick, Steven L. 1998. *Stealing the State: Control and Collapse in Soviet Institutions.* Cambridge, MA: Harvard University Press.

Sørensen, Aage, Erik Olin Wright, John Goldthorpe, Dietrich Rueschemeyer and James Mahoney. 2000. "Symposium on Class Analysis," *American Journal of Sociology*, vol. 105, no. 6, pp. 1523–1591.

Spruyt, Hendrik. 2002. "The Origins, Development, and Possible Decline of Modern State," *Annual Review of Political Science*, vol. 5, pp. 127–149.

Stavrianos, Leften S. 1981. *The Global Rift: The Third World Comes of Age*, New York: William Morrow.

Steinmetz, George. 1993. *Regulating the Social: The Welfare State and Local Politics in Imperial Germany*, Princeton: Princeton University Press.

— 1999. (ed.) *State/Culture: State-Formation After the Cultural Turn*, Ithaca NY: Cornell University Press.

— 2003. "'The Devil's Handwriting': Precolonial Discourse, Ethnographic Acuity, and Cross-Identification in German Colonialism," *Comparative Studies in Society and History*, 45:1, pp. 41–95.

Stiglitz, Joseph E. 2001. "Foreword," in Karl Polanyi, *The Great Transformation*, Second edition, Boston: Beacon Press, 2001, pp. vii–xvii.

Stinchcombe, Arthur. 1982. "On Softheadedness on the Future," *Ethics* 93 (October), pp. 114–128.

— 1997. "Tilly on the Past as a Sequence of Futures," review essay in *Roads from Past to Future*, edited by Charles Tilly, Lanham, Maryland: Rowman & Littlefield, pp. 387–409.

— 1999. "Ending Revolutions and Building New Governments," *Annual Review of Political Science* 2, pp. 49–73.

— 2003. "The Preconditions of World Capitalism: Weber Updated," *Journal of Political Philosophy*, vol. 3, no. 4 (December), pp. 411–436.

Suny, Ronald Grigor. 1993a. *Looking toward Ararat: Armenia in Modern History*, Bloomington: Indiana University Press.

— 1993b. *The Revenge of the Past: Nationalism, Revolution, and the Collapse of the Soviet Union*, Stanford: Stanford University Press.

— 1994. *The Making of the Georgian Nation*, 2nd ed., Bloomington: Indiana University Press.

Swedberg, Richard. 1991. *Schumpeter: A Biography*, Princeton: Princeton University Press.

Swietochowski, Tadeusz. 1985. *Russian Azerbaijan, 1905–1920: The Shaping of National Identity in a Muslim Community*, New York: Cambridge University Press.

Szelényi, Iván. 1982. "The Intelligentsia in the Class Structure of State-Socialist Societies," in Michael Burawoy and Theda Skocpol (eds), *Marxist Inquiries*, Supplement to *American Journal of Sociology*, vol. 88, pp. S287–326.

Szelényi, Iván, with Robert Manchin et al. 1988. *Socialist Entrepreneurs: Embourgeoisement in Rural Hungary*, Madison: University of Wisconsin Press.

Szelényi, Iván, and Balazs Szelényi. 1994. "Why Socialism Failed: Toward a Theory of System Breakdown — Causes of Disintegration of East European State Socialism," *Theory and Society* 23, pp. 211–231.

Szelényi, Iván, and Szonja Szelényi. 1995. "Circulation or Reproduction of Elites During the Postcommunist Transition of Eastern Europe: Introduction," *Theory and Society* 24, pp. 615–638.

Tarrow, Sidney. 1994. *Power in Movement: Social Movements, Collective Action, and Politics*, New York: Cambridge University Press.

Taubman, William. 2003. *Khrushchev: The Man and his Era*, New York: W.W. Norton.

Tilly, Charles. 1973. "Does Modernization Breed Revolution?" *Comparative Politics* 5, pp. 425–447. (Reprinted in Charles Tilly (ed.), *Roads from Past to Future*, Lanham, Maryland: Rowman & Littlefield, 1997.)

— 1984. *Big Structures, Large Processes, Huge Comparisons*, New York: Russell Sage Foundation.

— 1992. *Coercion, Capital, and European States, AD 990–1992*, (revised ed.), Oxford: Blackwell.

— 1993. *European Revolutions, 1492–1992*, Oxford: Blackwell.

— 1995. "Globalization Threatens Labor's Rights," *International Labor and Working-Class History* 47 (Spring), pp. 1–23.

— 1997. (ed.) *Roads from Past to Future*, Lanham, Maryland: Rowman & Littlefield.

Tishkov, Valery A. 1997. *Ethnicity, Nationalism and Conflict in and after the Soviet Union: The Mind Aflame*, Thousand Oaks, CA: Sage.

Tocqueville, Alexis de. 1955. *The Old Régime and the French Revolution*, translated by Stuart Gilbert, Garden City, N.Y., Doubleday.

Tsutsiyev, Artur. 1998. *Osetino-ingushskii konflikt (1992–…) ego predystoria i factory razvitiya* [The Ossetino-Ingush Conflict, 1992–…, Antecedents and Developmental Factors], Moscow: ROSSPEN.

Urban, Michael. 1989. *An Algebra of Soviet Power: Elite Circulation in the Belorussian Republic, 1966–86,* New York: Cambridge University Press.

Urban, Michael, with Vyacheslav Igrunov and Sergei Mitrokhin. 1997. *The Rebirth of Politics in Russia*, Cambridge: Cambridge University Press.

Vail, Petr, and Alexander Genis, 1988. *60-e: mir sovetskogo cheloveka* [The '60s: The World of the Soviet Person], Ann Arbor: Ardis.

Varese, Federico. 2001. *The Russian Mafia: Private Protection in a New Market Economy*, Oxford: Oxford University Press.

Volkov, Vadim. 2002. *Violent Entrepreneurs: The Use of Force in the Making of Russian Capitalism*, Ithaca, NY: Cornell University Press.

Voslenskii, M.S. 1984. *Nomenklatura: the Soviet Ruling Class*, Garden City, NJ: Doubleday.

Vujacic, Veljko. 1996. "Historical Legacies, Nationalist Mobilization, and Political Outcomes in Russia and Serbia: A Weberian View," *Theory and Society* 25, pp. 763–801.

Wallerstein, Immanuel. 1991. *Unthinking Social Science: The Limits of Nineteenth-century Paradigms*, Cambridge: Polity Press.

— 1995. "Declining States, Declining Rights?" response to Charles Tilly, *International Labor and Working-Class History* 47 (Spring), pp. 24–27.

— 1998. *Utopistics. Or, Historical Choices for the Twenty-first Century*, New York: The New Press.

— 2000. *The Essential Wallerstein*, New York: The New Press.

— 2003. *The Decline of American Power*, New York: The New Press.

Wegren, Stephen. 1989. "Private Agriculture in the Soviet Union Under Gorbachev," *Soviet Union/Union Sovietique* 16, nos 2–3, pp. 105–144.

Woodruff, David. 1999. *Money Unmade: Barter and the Fate of Russian Capitalism*, Ithaca, NY: Cornell University Press.

— 2000. "Rules for Followers: Institutional Theory and the New Politics of Economic Backwardness in Russia," *Politics & Society* 28:4 (December), pp. 437–482.

Yandarbiyev, Zelimkhan. 1994. *V preddverii nezavisimosti* [On the Eve of Independence], Grozny: "Ichkeria."

Zaslavsky, Victor. 1982. *The Neo-Stalinist State: Class, Ethnicity, and Consensus in Soviet Society*, Armonk, NY: M.E. Sharpe.

Zaslavsky, Victor. 1993. "Success and Collapse: Traditional Soviet Nationality Policy," in Ian Bremmer and Ray Taras (eds), *Nation and Politics in the Soviet Successor States*, Cambridge: Cambridge University Press, pp. 29–42.

Zelkina, Anna. 2000. *In Quest for God and Freedom: The Sufi Response to the Russian Advance in the North Caucasus*, London: Hurst & Co.

Zemtsov, Ilya. 1976. *Partiia ili mafiia? Azerbaijan: razvorovannaia respublika* [The Party of the Mafia? Azerbaijan: The Stolen Republic], Paris: Les Éditeurs Réunis.

Zubkova, Elena. 1998. *Russia After the War: Hopes, Illusions, and Disappointments, 1945–1957*, translated and edited by Hugh Ragsdale, Armonk, NY: M.E. Sharpe.

INDEX